THE ROUGH GUIDE TO

# Film Musicals

www.roughguides.com

## Credits

**The Rough Guide to Film Musicals**

**Editing:** Tracy Hopkins, Sean Mahoney
**Layout:** Diana Jarvis
**Picture research:** Tracy Hopkins, Andrew Lockett
**Proofreading:** Amanda Jones
**Indexing:** Tracy Hopkins
**Production:** Aimee Hampson, Katherine Owers

**Rough Guides Reference**

**Series editor:** Mark Ellingham
**Editors:** Peter Buckley, Duncan Clark, Tracy Hopkins, Sean Mahoney, Matthew Milton, Joe Staines, Ruth Tidball
**Director:** Andrew Lockett

## Publishing Information

This first edition published May 2007 by
Rough Guides Ltd, 80 Strand, London WC2R 0RL
345 Hudson St, 4th Floor, New York 10014, USA
Email: mail@roughguides.com

Distributed by the Penguin Group
Penguin Books Ltd, 80 Strand, London WC2R 0RL
Penguin Putnam, Inc., 375 Hudson Street, NY 10014, USA
Penguin Group (Australia), 250 Camberwell Road, Camberwell, Victoria 3124, Australia
Penguin Books Canada Ltd, 90 Eglinton Avenue East, Toronto, Ontario, Canada M4P 2YE
Penguin Group (New Zealand), 67 Apollo Drive, Mairongi Bay, Auckland 1310, New Zealand

Printed in Italy by LegoPrint S.p.A

Typeset in Helvetica Neue and Bembo to an original design by Henry Iles


336 pages; includes index

A catalogue record for this book is available from the British Library

ISBN 13: 978-1-84353-650-5
ISBN 10: 1-84353-650-1

1 3 5 7 9 8 6 4 2

THE ROUGH GUIDE TO

# Film Musicals

by
David Parkinson

# Contents

# Introduction

**The musical is a foreign place – they do things differently there. On the surface, the American musical appears to be a bright, breezy form of escapist entertainment whose primary purpose is to provide a temporary release from the pressures of everyday reality. But despite being produced within an industrialized studio system, the Hollywood musical had more in common with art-house than commercial cinema.**

The studio musicals made between 1927 and 1957 were promoted as undemanding fantasies featuring household names and melodramatic or comic storylines that were punctuated with song and dance routines designed to send you home humming the showstopper. However, they were actually conceived as something much more intricate and ingenious. They invariably fitted into one of three categories – the backstage, the fairy-tale or the folk musical – and their primary concern was not the chronological progression of the narrative from A to B, but how the oppositional aspects of the pivotal lovers' relationship could be resolved by the musical numbers that established the structure and meaning of the film.

This may seem like a rather complex concept to spring in the introduction to a Rough Guide, but it's the key to gaining a fuller understanding of this much-maligned genre. As you'll see in "Puttin' On The Ritz", there's far more to film musicals than stellar performances, spectacular set pieces and memorable tunes. You don't have to watch musicals with these theories in mind, but you may well appreciate them more if you do.

With the obvious exception of the chapter entitled "A World Of Entertainment", this is a book about the American musical. Other than the fact that they all contain songs, surprisingly few tropes are shared by Hollywood musicals and those produced in other countries. Non-American stars, composers and directors have certainly made significant contributions to the genre, but there are no "foreign" musicals in "The Canon", as the musical does not lend itself to international interpretation as readily as, say, horror or gangster movies.

So, what is a film musical? And what is so distinctive about the Hollywood variety? Predictably, critics have yet to come up with a definition on which they can all agree. They even argue over the genre's genesis. Most would cite *The Jazz Singer* (1927) as the first screen musical. But others would point to the countless sound experiments that were conducted from the 1890s, and which featured the leading operatic and vaudeville stars of the day. Yet others would insist on including so-called silent adaptations of popular stage shows and operas, as they were rarely screened in silence, thanks to the live accompaniment of theatre orchestras, organists and pianists.

However, even if we accept that the musical didn't become an established film genre before the universal conversion to sound, we're still no closer to establishing a definitive formula. At the height of the studio era, any film with three or more songs was considered a musical. Yet the Erich von Stroheim ventriloquism saga, *The Great Gabbo* (1929), is usually disqualified, despite containing eight songs. Similarly, pictures starring the likes of the Marx Brothers, Mae West and Bob Hope were deemed comedies, even though they often fulfilled the song quotient.

The historian Gerald Mast suggested that "a film is a musical if its primary entertainment value and investment lie in the musical numbers themselves". But this contention is challenged by Rick Altman, the doyen of musical studies, who excludes opera and ballet from the genre because they lack a suitable balance between the musical content and the dramatic narrative. He also excludes concert movies and documentaries because they don't possess a narrative from which the music can emanate. Where this leaves features like *The Hollywood Revue Of 1929* (1929) or *Ziegfeld Follies* (1946), which were essentially filmed variety shows devoid of a linking plotline, is anyone's guess. Exploiting this confusion, *The Rough Guide To Film Musicals* includes the odd opera or ballet, as they retain dramatic elements. But it omits documentary and concert movies, as they concern reality (even though that may be a constructed reality), rather than an artifice devised by the filmmaker.

Just as the origin and form of the musical is disputed, so too is its welfare. Some traditionalists aver that the Hollywood musical died in 1957, with Fred Astaire's last star vehicles, *Funny Face* and *Silk Stockings*. Other critics will argue that the genre lingered until *The Sound Of Music* (1965) or *Cabaret* (1972). But while there's no point in denying that the musical is no longer a thriving genre, it's clear that its periodic revivals are becoming increasingly frequent. So long as New York's Broadway and London's West End keep tempting movie producers with potentially profitable projects, like *Dreamgirls* and *Mamma Mia!*, the screen musical will never disappear completely.

With this continual re-development and resurgence, the style of the Hollywood musical has also changed significantly since its heyday. Shifting domestic, civic, socioeconomic and cultural attitudes have all affected the genre, but the most detrimental impact was made by the sexual revolution. In the 1930s and 40s, romance was a crucial part of the movie musical – but sex was not. And neither were the problems of sustaining a relationship beyond the first flush of passion and the happy ending fade out. But by the 1950s and 60s, American cinema had become more self-reflexive in its dismantling of the marriage myth, and the sordid realities that had been so scrupulously omitted from the genre's highly moral escapism came flooding in. Consequently, the musical's trademark innocence and contrivance began to feel twee and were replaced by grittier, less idealized subject matter that was largely devoid of fantasy. But by attempting to integrate realism and the very elements whose exclusion had been key to its success, the Hollywood musical helped destroy itself.

However, the demise of the genre hasn't just come from within. Changing musical tastes have proved equally deleterious, as rock'n'roll, pop, disco and hip-hop refused to fit neatly into Hollywood's conventional musical template. They also fragmented the audience and, with family trips to the cinema to see the latest musical spectacular becoming a thing of the past, the studios failed to capture a new generation of fans. As a result, the musical slipped down the film genre hierarchy until it became a risky curio rather than a box-office staple.

Nevertheless, the genre has continued to defy its critics and refused to go quietly. But then the movie musical has always suffered from some degree of critical snobbery. Broadway scribes have dismissed it as a poor substitute for a live show, while film reviewers have tended to sneer at its middlebrow pretensions. Consequently, only a handful of the films discussed in this volume feature in general histories of the cinema, as populist entertainment isn't always deemed intellectually valid. It's about time, therefore, that this undervalued genre, and the extraordinarily talented people that have worked both behind and in front of the camera to create so many indelible musical memories, are given their proper due.

David Parkinson, 2007

## About the author

David Parkinson is a film critic and historian. He is a Contributing Editor at *Empire* magazine and Associate Editor of *The Radio Times Guide To Films*. In addition to editing *Mornings In The Dark: The Graham Greene Film Reader*, he has also written *A History Of Film*, *The Young Oxford Book Of Cinema* and *Oxford At The Movies*. He is currently working on a study of movie musicals from across the world and an A–Z of songs by The Beatles.

## Acknowledgements

Thanks to Andrew Lockett for commissioning this book and for his patient efforts, along with those of Tracy Hopkins and Sean Mahoney, during its editing. Also to Alex Ballinger, John Naughton, Adam Smith and Justin Hopper for providing sympathetic ears in bleak times. Finally, thanks to Siobhan Lancaster for allowing me to fill the house with books, tapes and discs and for putting up with me in the five years since I damaged my back.

This book is dedicated to Ma, Da, Pig and Snid.

# Setting The Stage:
## the origins

With its revealing costumes and saucy content, *The Black Crook* (1866) was a five-hour extravanganza that launched American musical theatre.

# Setting The Stage:
# the origins

America had been entertained by singing and dancing long before Thomas Edison and other inventors developed the technology to create the first moving pictures and reproduce musical entertainment on screen. The beginnings of the film musical were a long time in the making.

## First Notes

In 1735, fifty years before **Royall Tyler**'s *The Contrast* (1787) became America's first indigenous play, English-language musical theatre was launched in the thirteen colonies with a performance of the pantomime, *The Adventures Of Harlequin And Scaramouche.* Two weeks later, the same venue in Charleston, South Carolina hosted the **ballad opera**, *Flora, Or The Hole In The Wall.* New York, however, had to wait a further fifteen years for its first taste of formal musical entertainment, when a travelling troupe led by Walter Murray and Thomas Kean staged John Gay's *The Beggar's Opera* (1750) at the Nassau Street Theatre.

The majority of these pioneering productions were mounted by itinerant troupes like **Lewis Hallam's American Company**. But the theatre was considered a frivolous diversion during the Revolutionary War, so it wasn't until the 1790s that the first "American" musicals began to appear, although composers like Victor Pelissier (*Edwin And Angelina*, 1791), James Hewitt (*Tammanay*, 1794) and Benjamin Clark (*The Archers*, 1796) were all European immigrants writing in the continental tradition.

In the early nineteenth century, stock companies began taking up residency in the larger towns. Nearly half of their repertoire was musical, with Pelissier and William Dunlap's *The Voice Of Nature* (1803) creating a vogue for **melodramas**, in which the action was punctuated by thirty to forty "melos" or musical cues that served much the same dramatic and psychological purposes as the movie soundtrack does today. Shows often ran between four and five hours and included a ballad or comic opera, a range of musical diversions and a pantomimic afterpiece.

Initially patrons tended to come and go, eat and drink, heckle and participate as they saw fit. But viewing manners became more refined as the entertainments became more rarefied. **Italian opera** was introduced to America by Spanish tenor Manuel Garcia in 1825. Three years later, Madame Celeste Keppler Elliott brought **ballet** to the melodrama with *The Female Spy*, and dance soon became a fixture of musical shows. As theatre-going became a twice-weekly habit, English singers like Elizabeth Austin and Anne and Edward Seguin became the first stars. Their sellout touring renditions of comic operas and translated versions of Mozart and Rossini fostered a classless approach to what would now be considered highbrow art.

In 1821, the first African-American impresario, **William Henry Brown**, was forced to close his New York theatre by envious white rivals, and

## Minstrelsy

The minstrel show was traditionally divided into three distinct sections. The first, the **"walk around"**, comprised the entire cast in blackface and ostentatious costumes forming into the classic minstrel line to perform a selection of songs. This section concluded with a comic dialogue between the Interlocutor and a pair of characters called Mr Tambo and Mr Bones (who were named after their instruments, the tambourine and the spoons). Next came the **"olio"**, a medley of variety acts performed non-blackface in front of a painted backdrop, which was comprised of topical songs and sketches in either Irish, German or African-American dialects. These two opening segments remained largely unchanged for the duration of minstrelsy, but the finale changed significantly after the Civil War. The customary **short comic plays** or **skits** about plantation life were dropped and replaced with parodies of either Shakesepeare or current hit plays. Gradually, the three elements of the minstrel show evolved into the basic components of all American stage entertainment. The minstrel line evolved into what became known as the "coon show" before emerging as revue, the olio developed into vaudeville, and the concluding sketch inspired both burlesque and the musical comedy.

Minstrel shows like this one impossibly glamorized the everyday experience of black Americans.

a century was to pass before black entertainers returned to Broadway. However, slave music proved popular with the antebellum white masses and white performers in **blackface** like Thomas D. Rice and Edwin Christy developed **"Jim Crow"** novelty acts (full of broad comedy, colourful costumes and sentimental songs), which acquired theatrical respectability following the success of the Virginia Minstrels in 1843. Shortly after the Civil War, the first African-American minstrel troupe, the **Georgia Minstrels**, was formed, and was soon imitated by the blackface performers of Charles B. Hicks's company and the Georgia Slave Troupe Minstrels. However, in the 1870s, the Hyers sisters, Anna Madah and Emma Louise, decided to provide an alternative to minstrelsy and fashioned more cultivated **musical dramas** like *Urbana, The African Princess*, *Uncle Tom's Cabin* and the musical comedy *Out Of Bondage*. Sadly, the segregation of both performers and audiences ensured that it would be another twenty years before all-black musicals made any significant progress.

By the 1850s, numerous musical diversions were available to American audiences: pantomime, burletta, extravaganza, spectacle and operetta, as well as high, comic, ballad, light and parlour opera. However, none of these could be described as a musical in the modern sense, and historians continue to squabble about the exact codification of the various hybrids. There's even a dispute about the identity of the first "**musical comedy**", with the 1866 double bill of *The Black Domino* and *Between You, Me And The Post* competing for the distinction with *The Pet Of The Petticoats* (also 1866), *Evangeline* (1874) and *The Gaiety Girl* (1894). What can be said without much fear of contradiction, however, is that the various forms of musical entertainment in America were changing rapidly and decisively in the face of internal competition and external influence.

## New Influences

From the 1840s, **burletta** (a blend of satire and musical interlude) benefited from the introduction of ever more sensational stage gimmickry, which was prompted by the competition between rival actor-managers **William Mitchell** and **John Brougham**. The Revel brothers from France similarly sought to enliven pantomime between 1832 and 1858 through a combination of athletic virtuosity and ingenious stage machinery. They had as much influence on the nascent spectacle and extravaganza as Austrian dancer Fanny Elssler's ballet tours in the 1840s and long-running Broadway productions like Laura Keene's *Seven Sisters* (1860), which included dance, burlesque, lavish costumes and sets, and wondrous transformation scenes.

**Italian opera** exerted a considerable influence on the American arts from the 1850s, with band concerts, theatrical *entr'actes*, dances, balls and the sale of sheet music helping to sustain its popularity. However, an element of elitism eventually crept in as many of opera's biggest stars opted to perform exclusively in New York. Although opera became the preserve of high society, there was still a national outpouring of grief in 1891 following the death of soprano **Emma Abbott**, who had earned the nickname "the people's prima donna" for her translated renditions of the more accessible Italian and German operas. The Civil War period also saw a boom in French *opéra-bouffe*, Viennese operetta and English comic opera, which inspired composer Julius Eichberg to attempt the Offenbachian outing *The Duke Of Alcantara*, which opened to moderate acclaim in Boston in 1862. However, his subsequent works, *A Night In Rome* (1864), *The Two Cadis* and *The Rose Of Tyrol* (both 1865), made markedly less impact.

Maria Bonfanti, an Italian member of the corps de ballet that made *The Black Crook* (1866) one of the first must-see shows to hit New York.

Although these shows had their admirers, nothing really fired the public imagination before **Charles M. Barras** and **Thomas Baker**'s *The Black Crook* (1866), the first uncontested hit of the American musical stage, which opened at William Wheatley's theatre, **Niblo's Garden**, in New York. Based on Carl Maria von Weber's 1821 Faustian opera, *Der Freischütz* (*The Free-Shooter*), it was packed with melodrama, comedy, romance and speciality acts. Boasting unprecedented production values, the show ran for five and a half hours – although the majority of the male audience didn't seem to mind as it included a hundred dancers in black tights from the **Great Parisian Ballet Troupe** (who were co-opted into the show after their venue, the Academy of Music, burnt down). The production cost a staggering $25,000 to mount, but it grossed over $1 million during its initial run and toured endlessly over the next few years, with its appeal being boosted by the protests of the moral majority. The sheer scale of *The Black Crook* meant that few could replicate its success, although many sought to imitate its saucy content.

Written and produced by **Lydia Thompson**, the mythological lampoon *Ixiom* (1868) mixed musical styles with gleeful disregard and challenged the buttoned-down conventions of American society with its revealing costumes. But few of those who gazed upon Thompson's "British blondes" shared her interpretation of female emancipation, and the show was better known for helping **burlesque** earn its bawdy reputation and for ushering in the "girlie show". Producer Michael Leavitt added scantily clad girls to minstrelsy, the Rentz-Santley shows introduced the cancan, and dancer Little Egypt premiered the hootchy-kootchy dance at the 1893 Chicago World's Fair. Shortly afterwards, the Columbia circuit risked **nudity** – first in *tab-*

*leaux vivants* (living pictures) and then in ordinary dance routines – before the striptease was finally incorporated into burlesque in the late 1920s to counteract the allure of the talkies.

The real beneficiary of *The Black Crook* phenomenon, however, was composer-producer **Edward Everett Rice**, who was responsible for eighteen burlesque extravaganzas by the 1890s. The most celebrated of these were *Evangeline* (1874) and *Adonis* (1884), which both toured the States for decades thanks to their blend of burlesque, spectacle, minstrelsy, variety and comic opera, not to mention their lavish costumes, sets and mechanical gimmickry. Less flamboyant, but equally acclaimed were John Denier's **pantomime** *Humpty Dumpty* (1868), starring comedian George L. Fox, and Nate Salisbury's confections *The Brook* (1879) and *Erminie* (1886), the latter of which made a star of actor Francis Wilson.

However, not all nineteenth-century theatregoers desired flesh and fantasy: many were relieved when the *opéra-bouffe* boom (which had been sparked by Jacques Offenbach's *The Good Duchess Of Gerolstein* in 1867) gave way to Gilbert and Sullivan mania. Within a year of its 1878 premiere, ninety different productions of **W.S. Gilbert** and **Arthur Sullivan**'s *H.M.S. Pinafore* were playing across the United States. *The Pirates Of Penzance* (1880) and *Patience* (1881) proved even more popular, as patrician audiences warmed to stories that were more literate and wholesome than their risqué French counterparts. But even more significant for American musical theatre was the fact that the duo's **Savoy operas** placed words and music at the service of narrative and characterization. The wit and dexterity of Gilbert's lyrics were to have a profound influence on the work of Ira Gershwin, Lorenz Hart and Cole Porter.

**Viennese operetta** also began to flourish in this period, following the presentation of five works by Austrian composer **Johann Strauss II** at New York's Casino Theatre from 1875 to 1885. They not only introduced American composers to Hungarian and gyspy melodies, but also to the waltz. Offering an *haute* equivalent to the likes of *The Black Crook* (by wrapping up the sauciness in sophistication), such shows broke with tradition by dispensing with matchmaking parents as prominent characters and replacing them with scheming or mischievous courtiers and servants. These operettas also made the lovers older than the juvenile couples of the established **pastorale style**. This resulted in more intriguing dramas, as the protagonists' emotions lay deeper and took longer to emerge from tales of adulterous couples meeting in secret or diffident sweethearts resisting seduction. Consequently, Strauss not only paved the way for **operettas** like *The Merry Widow*, but also for the chic Jeanette MacDonald and Maurice Chevalier films of the early sound era and the romantic comedies of Fred Astaire and Ginger Rogers.

Eventually, American composers felt sufficiently confident to give operetta a try. The first, **Willard Spencer**'s *The Little Tycoon* (1886), was followed by Reginald De Koven's *Robin Hood* (1891), classical composer George Whitfield Chadwick's *Tabasco* (1894) and "March King" John Philip Sousa's *El Capitan* (1896). But these American originals rarely proved as popular as the English translations of Offenbach and his Viennese contemporaries or the revivals of established works like Michael William Balfe's *The Bohemian Girl* (1843) and Daniel François-Esprit Auber's *Frà diavolo* (1830) (which were both later filmed by Laurel and Hardy).

**Vaudeville** also came into its own in the 1870s. Initially consisting of popular songs and fast-paced comedy, these variety shows were invariably staged in saloons and beer parlours for mainly immigrant audiences. Such lowbrow diversions were essentially for male audiences only, until 1865 when a former Barnum Circus clown took over Volk's Garden in New York's Bowery district and turned it into **Tony Pastor's Opera House**. This celebrated "Temple of Amusement" produced shows that were suitable for polite audiences, and Pastor went on to launch such comic double acts as Harrigan & Hart and Weber & Fields, as well as Broadway icons like Lillian Russell and George M. Cohan.

Tony Pastor also played a key role in theatreland's move uptown to 14th Street, which enabled vaudeville to become a respectable form of family entertainment. Indeed, by 1885, vaudeville had become a national pastime thanks to theatre circuits managed by Benjamin Keith, Edward Albee and F.F. Proctor, which introduced the idea of continuous performance in matinee and evening shows. **Marcus Loew**'s theatre chain further refined the form by showcasing foreign stars, opera singers and legitimate stage actors and, from 1913, its luxuriant Palace Theatre came

## The birth of Broadway

New York has long been home to the American musical. The first theatres appeared on Manhattan's Park Row in the 1810s, but popular musical entertainment was largely confined to inner-city neighbourhoods like **the Bowery**, which offered a mix of minstrelsy, gospel, blues, opera, German beer-hall *lieder*, Irish ballads, sentimental Yiddish ditties and lots of violin, accordion and brass instrumentation (much of it in the Jewish Klezmer style). However, following the success of *The Black Crook* (1866) at Niblo's Garden, on the corner of Broadway and Prince in the smarter part of town, the musical gained a new respectability (which was reinforced by the arrival of French, German and Viennese operetta, as well as English comic opera and music hall).

There were no theatres north of 42nd Street in 1893, and the Tenderloin district that preceded Broadway was more synonymous with stables and brothels than showbiz. By 1901, venues were springing up throughout the district, and advertising executive O.J. Gude dubbed Broadway the **"Great White Way"**, on account of all the electric lights on the theatre billboards and advertising hoardings. Within a year, *The New York Times* publisher Adolph S. Ochs had moved his paper's offices to the area and created **Times Square**. The subway arrived soon afterwards and Broadway rapidly confirmed its status as America's entertainment capital. Theatres, restaurants and nightclubs were in abundance from 39th to 45th Street and, as show business became big business, the area also became home to a growing number of song publishers, booking agents, PR companies and trade suppliers.

The writers and pluggers of American popular music worked for sheet music houses like Harms, Witmark and Remick, whose offices were clustered between West 28th Street and 6th Avenue. The area came to be known as **"Tin Pan Alley"**, after journalist Monroe Rosenfeld compared the sound of its countless tinny pianos to the cacophony in a kitchen.

By 1907, showmen like **Florenz Ziegfeld** and brothers **Lee and J.J. Shubert** had reinvented themselves as Broadway's first impresarios. They made creative, as well as financial, contributions to their shows and, in the process, they changed the very nature of American stage performance. Not content with respectively presiding over the opulent New Amsterdam and Winter Garden theatres, they also became talent spotters and discovered some of the biggest names in Broadway history, including Fanny Brice, Eddie Cantor, Al Jolson and Marilyn Miller.

to exemplify Broadway class.

After leaving Pastor's theatre, Irish performers **Edward "Ned" Harrigan** and **Tony Hart** assembled multi-ethnic ensembles for comic musicals like *The Mulligan Guards Ball* (1879) and *McSorley's Inflation* (1882), which Harrigan scored with his father-in-law, David Braham (with whom he wrote over two hundred songs in twenty years). Harrigan's shows focused on the racial tensions, corruption and gangland violence that was then prevalent in America's inner cities. Their blend of immigrant realism, broad comedy and topical songs delighted audiences who preferred to see enactments of their own everyday experiences rather than irrelevant escapism. If Harrigan and Hart played a crucial role in shaping what was becoming known as musical comedy, then the comic duo of Weber and Fields was key in the development of both the comic burlesque and the revue.

Supposedly the inventors of the custard pie gag, **Joe Weber** and **Lew Fields** were Polish Jews who started out together as boys in blackface. However, by the 1890s, they had become America's biggest "Dutch" comedy act, with a routine based on the disintegration of the neighbourhood, which combined knockabout, parody and ethnic schtick. Speaking in cod-Germanic accents as the recurring characters Mike and Meyer, the tall, thin Fields invariably tried to bully or dupe the shorter, fatter Weber in sketches that anticipated the zaniness of the Marx Brothers, while still highlighting the tough reality of both working-class and immigrant life.

"**Weberfields**" dropped the Dutch elements of their act in 1896, when their Weber and Fields Music Hall began presenting all-star bills in the manner of George Lederer's *The Passing Show*, which had brought revue to Broadway two years earlier. The first act of these **variety shows** usually comprised of musical numbers and comedy routines bound in a notional plot, while dance performances filled the interval. The second act was dominated by a lampoon of a current hit show. Thanks to choreographer **Julian Mitchell**, spoofs like "Cyranose de Bric-a-Brac" and "Alexander's Bagpipe Band" integrated dance into parody's loose comic narratives, while composer **John Stromberg** established the concept of a production having a single musical voice rather than a pick'n'mix of popular Tin Pan Alley tunes. The Weberfields emphasis was always more on spectacle than musical, but their casual linkage of

Joe Weber and Lew Fields refined vaudeville knockabout to lay the foundations of both revue and the musical comedy.

story, song and dance had a profound influence on future producers like Florenz Ziegfeld and book show composers like Jerome Kern.

Weber and Fields split in 1904 (although they frequently reunited over the next thirty years). Fields went on to become a major player on Broadway and was responsible for forty shows from 1904 to 1916 that ranged from vaudeville to musical comedy. He sought to break with the prevailing Anglo-European styles to create a form of uniquely American entertainment, in which songs drove the plot and provided insights into the characters' emotions. When Mitchell left to join Ziegfeld, Fields hired choreographer **Ned Wayburn** (who had invented tap dancing in 1902 and was a pioneer of the chorus line routine). Together they made stars of Marie Dressler, Fay Templeton and Irene Castle. Fields also collaborated with operetta composer Victor Herbert and persuaded the Shubert brothers (who had liberated American theatre from the all-powerful Theatrical Syndicate led by Abraham Erlanger and Marc Klaw) to build the **Winter Garden Theatre** for him in 1911. Yet for all his achievements, Fields's greatest legacy lay in fostering the talents of his librettist sons Herbert and Joseph, and his lyricist daughter Dorothy.

Lew Fields's ambition to combine vaudeville and operetta led to him becoming known as the "King of Musical Comedy". However, the **scored play** had already acquired a new intimacy, courtesy of Charles H. Hoyt and Percy Gaunt's farce, *A Trip To Chinatown* (1890). Along with *The Belle Of New York* (1897) and a trio of London imports – *The Gaiety Girl* (1894), *Floradora* (1900) and *A Chinese Honeymoon* (1902) – this largely forgotten show was to have a profound influence on the direction of the Broadway musical. Indeed, when director James Whale sought a song to sum up the mood of the entire era in his film *Show Boat* (1936, see Canon), he opted for *A Trip To Chinatown*'s biggest hit, "After The Ball".

In the vanguard of this book show revolution was **George M. Cohan**, who started out in his family's vaudeville act, the Four Cohans, before going solo in his twenties, as a librettist, composer, producer and star. His first Broadway hit, *The Governor's Son* (1901), bore the Irish-American influence of Harrigan and Hart with its rhythms of urban life. But three years later, by marrying the narrative coherence of European operetta with the American vernacular, Cohan transformed musical theatre with *Little Johnny Jones* (1904). Considered by many to be the **first authentic American musical**, it introduced the hits "Give My Regards To Broadway" and "Yankee Doodle Boy", which both used parlour-song brio to atone for what they lacked in new-century sophistication. By merging street argot with variety and the musical play, Cohan further developed his "melting pot" concept of entertainment in *45 Minutes From Broadway* and *George Washington Jr.* (both 1906). However, few would argue that such displays of sentimentality and **shameless patriotism** were high art and some have even questioned the extent of the egotistical Cohan's influence on the musical. "The Man Who Owned Broadway" was loathed by his peers, but songs like the wartime anthem "Over There" appealed to audiences of all backgrounds. Cohan – who was immortalized in the 1942 biopic *Yankee Doodle Dandy* (see Canon) – remains the only performer to have a statue on the Great White Way.

If Cohan's contribution is doubted in some quarters, that of the Dublin-born, classically trained composer **Victor Herbert** is not. The melodies in his hits *Babes In Toyland* (1903), *The Red Mill* (1906), *Naughty Marietta* (1910) and *Sweethearts* (1913) had a continental sophistication that changed the status of music in American theatre by making it central to the entertainment. But, more significantly, Herbert insisted on his conceptual shows having a **unified script and score** that militated against the interpolation of songs by other composers. Herbert remained active until 1924, although by then his blend of European refinement and American sentiment had been superseded by the more contemporary works of those he had inspired, including Jerome Kern and Richard Rodgers.

While Cohan and Herbert were pioneering the American musical, Broadway witnessed the arrival of the single most important production of the early 1900s. **Franz Léhar**'s *The Merry Widow* (1907) was a slice of Ruritanian escapism that not only restored the popularity of **Viennese operetta**, but also confirmed the growing divergence between vaudeville and the book show by playing down comedy in favour of romance. *The Merry Widow* also confirmed choreography as a key component of musical theatre and sparked a **dance craze** that opened doors for the likes of Vernon and Irene Castle (who were a huge influence on the young Fred Astaire). Whereas Strauss had made the waltz the big finale, Léhar gave it a romantic function that brought a new sexual intimacy to non-balletic dance. Subsequent shows required greater suggestive physicality, which appalled the prudes as much as it dismayed portly opera singers whose livelihoods were jeopardized by Broadway's new preference for performers who could not only sing, but could also move with athletic grace while remaining in character.

The end, however, was far from nigh for operetta specialists, as Léhar's triumph was succeeded by imports like Leo Fall's *The Dollar Princess* and Oskar Strauss's *The Chocolate Soldier* (both 1909). These were followed by indigenous efforts by the likes of **Rudolf Friml** (*The Firefly*, 1912, *Rose-Marie*, 1924 and *The Vagabond King*, 1925) and **Sigmund Romberg** (*Maytime*, 1917, *Blossom Time*, 1921, *The Student Prince*, 1924, and *The Desert Song*, 1926), who were given an unexpected opportunity to dominate the field after German and Austrian shows fell from favour during World War I.

Operetta reached the peak of its popularity around the same time as the **revue**, the variation on vaudeville that was initially an excuse to peddle female flesh amidst the singers, comics, dancers, jugglers, magicians and other speciality acts on the bill. However, inspired by the Folies Bergère in Paris, Broadway impresario **Florenz Ziegfeld** contrived a revue programme of skits, songs and skin that he called the *Follies*, and which became an almost annual event for the next twenty years. Anticipating the famous **Freed Unit** at MGM in the 1940s, Ziegfeld assembled a peerless backroom team that enabled him not only to glorify the American girl, but also to showcase talents such as W.C. Fields, Bert Williams, Ed Wynn, Will Rogers, Eddie Cantor, Fanny Brice and Ann Pennington and to introduce such standards as "Shine On Harvest Moon", "A Pretty Girl Is Like A Melody" and "By The Light Of The Silvery Moon".

Ziegfeld's success meant that Broadway was soon playing host to an array of imitations: Earl Carroll's *Vanities*, the Shuberts' *Passing Shows*, Irving Berlin's *Music Box Revues* and John Murray Anderson's *Greenwich Village Follies*. But Ziegfeld's only serious competition came from one of his former dancers, **George White**. More urbane and modish than the rarefied *Follies*, White's *Scandals* (1919–39) shamelessly cashed in on the latest dance crazes and hired modern composers like George Gershwin (1920–24).

While audiences were flocking to these ever more lavish and audacious revues, the **musical**

**comedy** was also quietly coming into its own. Some of the impetus again came from London imports, such as *The Pink Lady* (1911) and *Maid Of The Mountains* (1917). But a new generation of American songwriters were about to announce themselves on the Broadway stage, led by **Irving Berlin** and **Jerome Kern**. Berlin (who had made his name with "Alexander's Ragtime Band" in 1911), scored his first full show, *Watch Your Step*, for Vernon and Irene Castle in 1914, the same year that Kern's ballad "They Didn't Believe Me" was interpolated into the West End transfer, *The Girl From Utah*. In 1915, Kern teamed up with librettists Guy Bolton and P.G. Wodehouse on *Very Good Eddie* (1915). The first in a series of small-scale **integrated musical comedies** staged at the Princess Theatre, *Eddie* was followed by *Oh Boy!* (1917) and *Oh, Lady! Lady!* (1918). Kern was then commissioned by Florenz Ziegfeld to score a Cinderella story for **Marilyn Miller**,

## The Great Glorifier

The son of a concert pianist, Chicago-born **Florenz Ziegfeld Jr.** became hooked on show business after seeing Buffalo Bill's Wild West Show. He made his initial impact at the **1893 World's Fair** in Chicago, by exhibiting the strongman Eugene Sandow at the Trocadero nightclub. But his sights were already set on Broadway, and three years later, he hired French actress **Anna Held** for his producing debut, *A Parlor Match*. Held eventually became Ziegfeld's wife and took him to Europe to tutor him in fashion and the arts. She also suggested bringing a Parisian touch to his first **revue**, *Follies Of The Day* (1907), even though its notional theme was Pocahontas. However, the show's combination of song, topical satire and impudent pulchritude proved hugely popular. Over the next few years, Ziegfeld brought a new blend of crowd-pleasing spectacle and aesthetic sophistication to his revues, which bore his own name from 1911.

Ziegfeld spent $13,800 on the inaugural *Follies*. But costs had risen to $150,000 by the time the series reached its peak in 1919 – although the money was quickly recouped, as the $2.50 tickets were the most expensive on Broadway. Much of the budget went on the plush production values, which gave the *Follies* their unrivalled glamour and chic. And much of the credit went to Ziegfeld's backstage crew of director **Julian Mitchell**, choreographer **Ned Wayburn**, songwriters Gene Buck and Harry B. Smith, and costumier Lucille (aka Lady Duff Gordon). However, Ziegfeld was most reliant on art director **Joseph Urban**, to the extent that entire shows were devised around his sets. Urban designed for over sixty Ziegfeld productions and, in the process, transformed the use of theatrical space. In 1915, Urban modified the use of the apron stage, which not only allowed performers to get closer to their audience, but also enabled quick set changes behind the curtain. He also introduced platforms, so the action could be arranged on multiple planes, and made innovative use of lighting and colour to enhance the ambience of the various routines.

Although Ziegfeld's name is synonymous with the revue, he also mounted such epoch-making productions as *Sally* (1920), *Rio Rita* (1926) and *Show Boat* (1927). But he struggled to recover from the Wall Street Crash and his later stage offerings, like *Show Girls* (1929), *Smiles* (1930) and *Hot-Cha!* (1932), proved disappointing. Success proved similarly elusive in Hollywood, although he was lionized by the likes of **Samuel Goldwyn**, with whom he co-produced his only notable picture, the 1930 version of his 1928 stage hit, *Whoopee!*. Ziegfeld was himself twice portrayed on screen by **William Powell** – in the Oscar-winning biopic *The Great Ziegfeld* (1936), and in the Technicolor celestial revue, *Ziegfeld Follies* (1946).

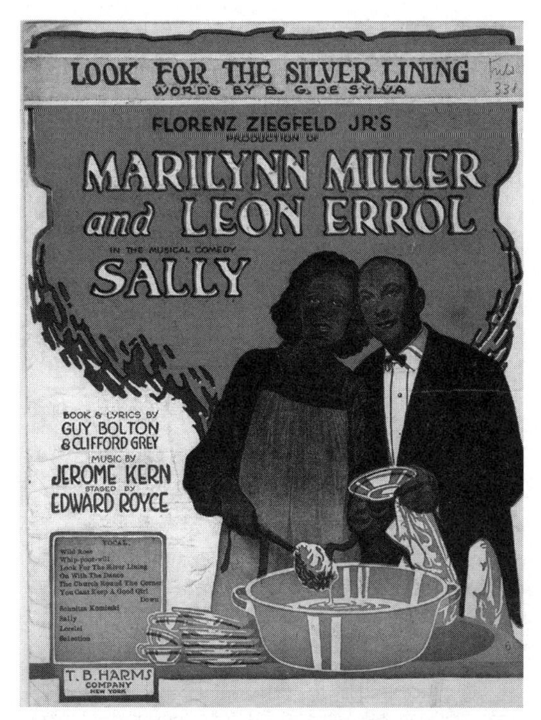


Despite earning $1,000 an hour, Marilyn Miller (she dropped the second "n") failed to repeat her Broadway triumph when she headlined the 1929 screen version of Kern's classic show.

*Sally* (1920) (which contained her signature tune "Look For The Silver Lining"), and the following year he wrote *Sunny* with Otto Harbach and Oscar Hammerstein II.

Among the other newcomers, songwriting duo **Richard Rodgers** and **Lorenz Hart**, and composer Vincent Youmans had respective 1925 hits with *Dearest Enemy* and *No, No Nanette*. Buddy DeSylva enlisted Ray Henderson and Lew Brown for *Good News* (1927), and Cole Porter announced his arrival with *Paris* (1928) and *Fifty Million Frenchmen* (1929), which added extra frisson to the Broadway lyric with "Let's Do It" and "You Do Something To Me" respectively.

There was a great modernity about the musical in the 1920s, with many productions dealing with emancipated women, campus life, sports and popular news stories. A key factor in this fresh approach was the shift from ragtime to jazz syncopation following **George and Ira Gershwin**'s *Lady, Be Good!* (1924) (whose opening coincided with jazz musician Louis Armstrong's first appearance with the Fletcher Henderson Orchestra in Harlem). However, operetta remained inordinately popular, comprising six of the eleven longest-running Broadway shows of the 1920s. Waltz-time tunes still dominated, but the growing influence of **Tin Pan Alley** could be felt as the likes of Rudolf Friml's *The Vagabond King* were adapted for the cinema. Operetta's settings were also acquiring a greater exoticism, with the action of *Rose-Marie* taking place in Canada, *The Desert Song* in North Africa and *The New Moon* (1919) in Louisiana and the Caribbean.

In the 1930s, the musical's emphasis switched to politics and the state of America, although the notoriously strict Production Code clipped Hollywood's claws and few of the more contentious shows made during this period found their way onto the screen. **Swing** also came into play, which further detached the American musical from its European roots. However, it was the Wall Street Crash of 1929 that had the most calamitous effect on operetta, as audiences came to demand lighter, more upbeat entertainment instead of its sentimentality, nostalgia and melodrama. However, operetta retained its provincial audience through stock and amateur productions, and thanks largely to Rodgers and Hammerstein, traces of its pseudo-classical style continued to exist in American musical theatre well into the late 1950s.

Although **book shows** were now firmly the

talk of the town, they were still not considered sacrosanct, and stars frequently interpolated their own theme tunes or other bits of speciality business into the proceedings (often coming out of character to do so). Such showboating can partly be explained by the rise of the gramophone record and the radio, as audiences nationwide were now familiar with Broadway's finest and wanted to see their set pieces for themselves. Among those performers most in demand were Al Jolson and Sophie Tucker.

## New Voices

Debuting on Broadway in *La Belle Paree* (1911), **Al Jolson** became the toast of the Shuberts' Winter Garden Theatre with a trio of hits – *Sinbad* (1920), *Bombo* (1921) and *Big Boy* (1924) – built around his blackface character, Gus. **Sophie Tucker**, who also performed in blackface, was known as the "World-Renowned Coon Shouter" before she began concentrating on ragtime and the blues. Her signature tune, "Some

### Silent musicals

In the early 1910s, **pioneering filmmakers** drew inspiration from literature and the stage for what became known as *films d'art*. They sought to raise the aesthetic quality of motion pictures in a bid to attract a better class of audience. Numerous brief bowdlerizations of famous operas and operettas similarly went before the cameras, even though the actors were restricted to **dumb show** before talking pictures arrived in the late 1920s. With the accompaniment of a single piano or a chamber orchestra, silent musicals proved surprisingly popular and several landmark stage shows were adapted for the screen. In 1915, Walter Morton and Hugh Stanislaus Stange released a film version of *The Chocolate Soldier*, which was followed a year later by Robert G. Vignola's *The Black Crook*.

As the Jazz Age dawned, Broadway hits were being filmed as soon as the rights could be obtained, in order to cash in on their kudos. Moreover, with **feature films** now the norm, movie directors were better equipped to do justice to the source shows – which often ran for up to 150 minutes. In 1919, Albert Capellani adapted the Princess Theatre hit *Oh Boy!* (1919) and its success prompted Maurice Campbell to direct *Oh, Lady, Lady* the following year. The early 1920s also brought a trio of **George M. Cohan** adaptations: *45 Minutes From Broadway* (1920), *Little Johnny Jones* (1923) and *George Washington, Jr.* (1924).

The same period also saw King Baggott direct *The Gaiety Girl* (1924), Robert P. Kerr produce a version of *A Trip To Chinatown* (1926) and Roscoe "Fatty" Arbuckle guide Marion Davies through Victor Herbert's *The Red Mill* (1927). But now, thanks to radio, silent films were also being boosted by the popularity of their **hit theme tunes**. (Dolores Del Rio had the good fortune to star in several of these pre-sold dramas, including *Ramona*, 1928, and *Evangeline*, 1929.)

In the 1920s, audiences were also becoming familiar with seeing their favourite stars dance on screen: Rudolph Valentino tangoed in *The Four Horsemen Of The Apocalypse* (1921), John Gilbert and Mae Murray executed the waltz in *The Merry Widow* (1925) and Clara Bow performed the Charleston in *It* (1927). However, the master of silent musicality was undoubtedly director **Ernst Lubitsch**, who followed the dazzling dance sequence in *So This Is Paris* (1926) with a charming rendition of a Sigmund Romberg operetta, *The Student Prince In Old Heidelberg* (1927). Lubitsch went on to bring his intuitive understanding of both music and cinema to some of the most sparkling film confections of the early sound era.

## The American popular song

The main musical legacy of operetta was the calcification of songwriting in the waltz (3/4) and march (4/4) signatures. But such stately rhythms were out of step with modern American living, and in around 1910, 3/4 and 4/4 time were replaced by the **2/4 tempo** of the classic popular song, which owed its distinctive sound to a blend of black ragtime and blues, Jewish Klezmer and other white ethnic urban beats.

For the next fifty years, the vast majority of hit tunes had an instrumental opening, an almost conversational verse and a refrain or chorus that carried the song's main **musical and emotional message**. Verse structure was fairly informal and could range from 8 to 64 bars, although 16 or 24 were more usual. But the chorus was fixed at 32 bars, which were typically divided into four 8-bar phrases in either an AABA or ABAC form.

In an AABA song, the first 8-bar A section states the main melodic theme, which is then repeated exactly (or with slight variation) in the second. Known as the release or bridge, the B section provides a link between the refrain and the verse, while the final A section repeats or refines the original phrase. Considered the more passionate and energetic style, the AABA format can be heard in such standards as **Irving Berlin**'s "Blue Skies", **Cole Porter**'s "I Get a Kick Out Of You" and **Jerome Kern**'s "The Way You Look Tonight".

The ABAC structure again sees the first A section carrying the refrain (often twice and occasionally with modifications the second time round). However, the B bars introduce a new melody, which is succeeded by the original A section before the C lines divert off into yet another variation. Deemed more balanced and suggestive of elegance and restraint, the ABAC style informed the likes of **George Gershwin**'s "Swanee", **Richard Rodgers**' "Falling In Love With Love" and **Vincent Youmans**' "Tea For Two".

What was most remarkable about both AABA and ABAC songs, however, was their flexibility, because – depending on their time syncopation, orchestration and lyrical content – they could convey a prodigious range of moods and emotions.

Of These Days", was composed by African-American songwriter **Shelton Brooks**, and while Tucker was famed for her brazen material, she kept singing black music into the 1960s as "The Last of the Red Hot Mamas".

Although blackface was considered an acceptable amusement for white audiences and black musical styles were at the core of the American popular song, African-American performers were still very much marginalized and many still had to perform in blackface. The influence of minstrelsy remained strong when the **first black musical**, Sam Lucas and Sam T. Jack's *The Creole Burlesque Co.*, opened in 1893. Shows like John W. Isham's *Octoroons* (1895) sought to dismantle the minstrel structure and move towards variety, but they still retained many black stereotypes – although these were being challenged by the likes of pioneering soprano **Sissieretta Jones**. From 1896, she fronted a troupe called the Black Patti Troubadours and helped wean audiences off minstrelsy with productions like *A Trip To Africa* (1910) and *Lucky Sam From Alabam* (1914). These consisted of a musical farce segment, an **olio** (see box on p.4) and an "operatic kaleidoscope", in which Jones sang arias in the manner of the Italian opera star, Adelina Patti.

With a score wholly composed by black songwriters, **Paul Laurence Dunbar** and **William Marion Cook**'s *Clorindy, Or The Origin Of The Cakewalk* became the first African-American show to reach Broadway in 1898. In the same

# Biopics of the Broadway maestros

### The Great Ziegfeld
**dir Robert Z. Leonard, 1936, 176m, b/w**

William Powell plays the Broadway maestro in MGM's lavish Oscar-winning biopic, which co-stars Luise Rainer as Anna Held and Myrna Loy as his widow, Billie Burke. Cameos by Ziegfeld alumni like Fanny Brice enhance the self-conscious authenticity, but this film is primarily about choreographer Seymour Felix's re-creation of *Follies* set pieces. For the kitsch classical interlude, Irving Berlin's "A Pretty Girl Is Like A Melody", the centrepiece is a giant revolving pillar accommodating umpteen chorines.

### Night And Day
**dir Michael Curtiz, 1946, 128m**

Facts were at a premium in this coy biopic that purportedly chronicled the career of bisexual songwriter Cole Porter. Fred Astaire, Ethel Merman, Jimmy Durante and Danny Kaye rejected the chance to revisit old hits, but Mary Martin rose to the occasion in reprising "My Heart Belongs To Daddy". Cary Grant rarely looks comfortable as the raffish songwriter, especially while crooning awkwardly through "You're The Top" with the ever-dependable Ginny Simms. Porter was less than concerned, however, as 27 of his tunes were showcased and he pocketed $300,000 for the story rights.

### Till The Clouds Roll By
**dir Richard Whorf, 1946, 137m**

Robert Walker was woefully miscast in this Jerome Kern biopic that studs a fantasy with smart performances by June Allyson, Angela Lansbury and Virginia O'Brien. Judy Garland also shows well as Broadway star Marilyn Miller in Vincente Minnelli's interpretations of "Look For The Silver Lining" and "Who?", while Kathryn Grayson, Lena Horne and Tony Martin make solid contributions to a précised *Show Boat*. But Frank Sinatra's dismal reprise of Caleb Peterson's soulful "Ol' Man River" in the finale makes for an excruciating comparison.

### Deep In My Heart
**dir Stanley Donen, 1954, 132m**

If MGM's biopic is to be believed, Sigmund Romberg devoted so much energy to composing his fifty-plus Broadway shows and operettas that he didn't have time for a life. His work is well served here: by Gene Kelly and his brother, Fred, on "I Like To Go Swimmin' With Wimmin", Ann Miller on "It", and Cyd Charisse and James Mitchell on "One Alone". José Ferrer, who stars as Romberg, also sportingly takes on multiple roles in the Catskills holiday resort parody, *Jazz A Doo*.

Dance director Seymour Felix sought to outdo Busby Berkeley in this showstopper from MGM's Oscar-winning biopic, *The Great Ziegfeld*.

year, actor and composer Bob Cole starred alongside Billy Johnson and Sam Lucas in *A Trip To Coontown*, which had a distinctly vaudeville feel and was the first musical written, directed and performed solely by African-Americans. The biggest black stars at this time were **Bert Williams** and **George Walker**, who were first paired in a "dupe and zip" comedy act in 1893. They abandoned blackface when they appeared in Victor Herbert's *The Gold-Bug* (1896), which featured the cakewalk, a strutting dance with African and plantation roots that was much imitated in the early variety era. Williams and Walker became the first black performers to make a recording (for the Victor Talking Machine Company in 1901) and, the following year, they headlined Dunbar and Cook's *In Dahomey*, which was performed before Edward VII at Buckingham Palace. Unfortunately, the show proved a box-office disappointment in the US, as did their next project, *The Southerners* (1904), which was the first racially integrated entertainment to play on Broadway.

Walker and Williams also starred in Cook's *Abyssinia* (1906) and *Bandanna Land* (1908), before Walker was forced to retire due to bad health in 1909. After Walker's death, the development of African-American theatre was further hampered by Williams joining the *Ziegfeld Follies*. There he was given a fool's licence to indulge his socially acute comic genius by being both innocuous and cutting when taunting the white comic Leon Errol in their scenes together. Williams was criticized by other black performers for appearing in minstrel make-up in an otherwise all-white revue, and he was also never fully accepted by white audiences or his *Follies* co-stars.

Some thirty **African-American shows** were staged on Broadway between 1890 and 1915. But racial discrimination became rampant after Bert Williams's death, despite the attempt of **J. Homer Tutt** and **Salem Tutt Whitney**'s *How Newtown Prospered* (1916) to tone down the stereotypes and give black entertainment a greater contemporary relevance. From 1910 to 1917, the Great White Way pretty much lived down to its name, but black performers remained popular with the white audiences who flocked to the **Cotton Club**, Connie's Inn and Small's Paradise in Harlem.

Although the Cotton Club hired white composers like Harold Arlen and Jimmy McHugh, there were plenty of talented black tunesmiths around too, including **Noble Sissle** and **Eubie Blake**, who teamed up as The Dixie Duo. Refusing to wear blackface, they became the first African-American act to perform in tuxedos and enjoyed an unprecedented run of 504 performances with their 1921 hit, *Shuffle Along*. With its smash song, "I'm Just Wild About Harry", the show brought jazz to Broadway and launched the careers of future stars such as Josephine Baker, **Paul Robeson** and Florence Mills. *Shuffle Along* even challenged Broadway's segregation policy by including black musicians in the orchestra (although they were forced to sit separately). However, conservative groups still tried to get the ballad "Love Will Find A Way" cut from the line-up, as it was deemed indecent for white audiences to be subjected to a romance between black characters.

Sissle and Blake were unable to replicate their success with their next two musicals, *Eloise* (1923) and *The Chocolate Dandies* (1925), but *Shuffle Along* helped spark the **Harlem Renaissance** and prompted both Florenz Ziegfeld and George White to mount imitations. Indeed, the latter's *Runnin' Wild* (1923) headlined the original stars of *Shuffle Along*, Flournoy Miller and Aubrey Lyles, and inspired a new dance craze – the Charleston. **Florence**

## Silent scores

Although they're known as silents, the films produced between 1895 and 1927 were rarely screened in silence. The great MGM producer Irving G. Thalberg once said that cinema would never have survived its novelty phase without the **accompaniment** of shrill upright pianos to give the flickering images mood and meaning. Recognizing the importance of music to the reception of their films, distributors began printing cue sheets to provide pianists in movie theatres with tunes that complemented the action. Some venues even splashed out on Allefex machines, which were capable of producing a wide range of **sound effects**.

However, as movie palaces became more opulent, either side of World War I, small ensembles and occasionally full orchestras accompanied the most prestigious pictures. Among the first prominent composers to write for the cinema was **Camille Saint-Saens**, who scored the *film d'art L'Assassinat du Duc de Guise* (*The Assassination Of The Duke Of Guise*) in 1908. In America, **Clarence Lucas** and **Joseph Carl Breil** captivated audiences with "The Perfect Song", the theme to D.W. Griffith's magnum opus, *The Birth Of A Nation* (1915). The song not only went on to sell thousands of sheet copies, but also became the signature tune for both the radio and television versions of the popular comedy series *Amos'n'Andy* (1928–60).

In 1916, **Jerome Kern** composed incidental music for the serial *Gloria's Romance* and Victor Herbert wrote the accompaniment to *The Fall Of A Nation*. **Sigmund Romberg**'s score for Erich von Stroheim's picture *Foolish Wives* (1922) originally ran for 32 reels, or 6 hours and 48 minutes. **Irving Berlin** wrote the theme for the drama, *The New Moon* (1919), which starred Norma Talmadge, while **Ernest R. Ball** created "For The Sake Of Auld Lang" for Harry Beaumont's *Lights Of The Desert* (1922). By the time that **George Gershwin** had a hit with the theme to the 1923 Western *The Sunshine Trail* (with Ira Gershwin producing the lyrics under the pseudonym Arthur Francis), most major film releases received an advance boost from a well-plugged title track. Therefore, American filmgoers were well primed for the musical revolution that followed Warner Bros' release of *The Jazz Singer* (see Canon) in October 1927.

**Mills**, who had started out as an understudy in *Shuffle Along*, became a major star in Lew Leslie's *Plantation Revue*, a Harlem floor show that transferred uptown in 1922. Two years later, she refused overtures from Ziegfeld to headline what he patronizingly termed his "glorification of American High-Brown" and relocated to London for *From Dover To Dixie* (1924). Mills died shortly after her triumphant performances of *Blackbirds* (1927) in London and Paris. However, she was far from the only African-American performer to be denied the opportunity to fulfil her potential in the US. Echoes of the many sad stories could be heard in Jerome Kern and Oscar Hammerstein's *Show Boat* (see Canon). But even this landmark show was to be upstaged as the cultural sensation of 1927 – as motion pictures had begun to talk!

# No Business Like Show Business: the history

The irrepressible Danny Kaye mugs for the camera, alongside Rosemary Clooney and Bing Crosby in *White Christmas* (1954). Kaye was a late replacement for Donald O'Connor, who broke his leg before shooting began.

# No Business Like Show Business: the history

The musical didn't really exist for the first thirty years of cinema history and it's largely been out of favour with mainstream audiences for the last five decades. Yet it remains one of the most beloved movie genres and its 25 golden years continue to epitomize the romance, glamour and escapism of Hollywood entertainment. So, why has the musical endured such mixed fortunes on the road from ragtime to rap?

## You ain't heard nothin' yet

That arch appropriator of other people's ingenuity, **Thomas Edison** first demonstrated moving pictures accompanied by recorded sound at the Chicago World's Fair in 1893. By the spring of 1895, he had manufactured 45 Kinetophone machines, which were fitted with rubber listening tubes connected to a cylindrical phonograph within a Kinetoscope viewer. Although these machines could just about achieve audiovisual congruity, inventors around the world struggled to solve the problems of precise synchronization and amplification, which were to prove key to the advent of **talking pictures**.

In the meantime, primitive sound shorts

remained a popular novelty on nickelodeon and vaudeville bills. Entrepreneur **J.A. Whitman** hired a studio above Daly's Theatre on Broadway in 1908 and began filming stage stars such as Anna Held, Eva Tanguay, Blanche Ring and Stella Mayhew for his Cameraphone. Several other European synchronized systems were also exhibited across the US. Edison returned to the scene with his new **Kinetophone** in March 1913, which used long-playing records to offer what *Kinematograph Weekly* called "the nearest approach to perfection that singing pictures had yet attained". **D.W. Griffith** even had actor Ralph Graves record a song on the Photokinema sound-on-disc system for his 1921 drama, *Dream Street* – although the synchronization was so poor that the sound was dropped within days of the film's premiere.

All of these early systems relied on performers miming to pre-recorded discs, as the limited range of the first microphones meant that they inevitably appeared in shot during live recording. Audibility in larger venues also caused concern to pioneers like inventor **Lee De Forest**, who began screening his amplified **Phonofilms** in March 1923. In all, he produced over a thousand of these comical, topical and musical shorts and gave viewers nationwide their first glimpse of **Broadway titans** such as Eddie Cantor, Sophie Tucker, Harry Richman and George Jessel. Such was the vogue for these early "**soundies**" that, by 1925, some 35 theatres on the East Coast had been fitted with Phonofilm equipment. However, many in Hollywood resisted these systems that relied on sound-on-film processes because of the expense involved in converting studios and cinemas. They were also reluctant to risk losing foreign markets and exposing the limitations of their established stars by jettisoning the universal language of silence. But, by the mid-1920s, several studios were experiencing severe **financial crises** and sound seemed like the easiest way to make a quick buck.

On 6 August 1926, Warner Bros premiered **Alan Crosland**'s swashbuckler *Don Juan*, with a 78 rpm Vitaphone record containing sound effects and an original score by William Axt. The first feature with a wholly **synchronized soundtrack**, it was accompanied by a programme of shorts that included operatic arias by Giovanni Martinelli, Anna Case and Marion Talley, instrumental turns by the New York Philharmonic and soloists Harold Bauer, Efrem Zimbalist and Mischa Elman, and a performance by the Cansino dance troupe, led by Rita Hayworth's father, Eduardo.

Two months later, a second selection of **Vitaphone shorts** preceded the forgotten silent comedy, *The Better 'Ole*. Among the highlights was *Al Jolson In A Plantation Act*, in which Jolson sang "April Showers", "When The Red, Red Robin" and "Rock-a-Bye Your Baby With A Dixie Melody". Within two years, Vitaphone had produced over four hundred shorts. Warner Bros' Vitaphone Varieties and Broadway Brevities were quickly followed by MGM's Movietones and Colortone Revues, Pathé's Melody Comedies, and Paramount's Christie Talking Plays and Screen Songs (which introduced the bouncing ball over on-screen lyrics to encourage audiences to sing along). These soundies attracted such high-calibre stars as Louis Armstrong, Cab Calloway, Ethel Merman and Maurice Chevalier.

However, Vitaphone's sound quality was often poor, and synchronization proved a persistent problem because the wax discs (that were so fragile they had to be replaced after a dozen or so uses) often jumped or stuck. In January 1927, Fox used a series of Movietone shorts accompanying the wartime comedy, *What Price Glory?*, to introduce the alternative **sound-on-film system** that was eventually to become the industry standard. But, for the time being, the future seemed to belong to Vitaphone, as Warner Bros launched the talkie boom on October 6, 1927 with *The Jazz Singer*, starring **Al Jolson**.

## All-singing, all-dancing

Hollywood has always romanticized *The Jazz Singer* (see Canon), with nostalgic movies invariably depicting it as a sensation that transformed cinema overnight. But panic rather than awe was the overriding reaction of the majority of the studio moguls, as they realized that public clamour for **talking pictures** was going to put a considerable strain on their technical and artistic expertise, as well as their bank balances. Many hoped that talkies would be a **passing fad**, but when Jolson's follow-up, *The Singing Fool* (1928), grossed $5.6 million worldwide on a $388,000 budget, the die was cast. Within nine months, three hundred American theatres

Al Jolson sings "Sonny Boy" to 3-year-old Davey Lee in *The Singing Fool* (1928). De Sylva, Brown and Henderson's ballad became the first song to sell one million copies of sheet music.

had acquired sound equipment and, as audiences soared, Hollywood took a gamble on full conversion and gradually abandoned silent production (although, by 1929, only 2,500 of the nation's 16,000 cinemas had been wired for sound).

The transition to sound was fraught with difficulty. Much is usually made of the **technical problems**, which were so gleefully satirized in *Singin' In The Rain* (1952; see Canon). Live recording meant that microphones had to be concealed around the set, but they picked up the noises made by the arc lamps and the camera motors, in addition to the dialogue. To resolve this, the camera was consigned to a booth, known as an "ice box", that so restricted movement that some critics suggested that motion pictures had been reduced to animated radio.

The introduction of blimps to muffle the whirr of the cameras soon restored intra-frame fluidity, but **dubbed soundtracks** increasingly became the norm after playback was used for the first time, during the filming of MGM's *The Broadway Melody* (1929). When producer **Irving G. Thalberg** ordered "The Wedding Of The Painted Doll" number to be restaged, he insisted that they reshot the sequence using the recording from the first take to save time and money. This also solved the problem of achieving a balance between vocals and orchestration, and mixing soon enabled sound technicians to tinker with the timbre of a performer's voice or to replace it with that of a more accomplished singer.

Despite these advances, many **Broadway stars** remained wary of the movies. Some didn't trust the technology to capture the exuberance and spontaneity of their live acts, while others were unwilling to risk their reputations on what might turn out to be a passing phase. Conversely, Hollywood was concerned that the rarefied stage entertainment that delighted New York sophisticates might not appeal to provincial audiences. And the studios were keen to see whether the **silent icons** they already had under contract could handle dialogue or deliver a song. Therefore, the earliest talkies served almost as auditions for stage and screen stars alike, and the musical genre slowly emerged from this process of trial and error. Several big names fell by the wayside, as they either struggled to acclimatize to the unique demands of filming talking pictures or failed to make an impact at the box office.

A number of leading Tin Pan Alley and Broadway **songwriters** also went West, lured by weekly salaries of $250–1,500 and the prospect of increased royalties from sheet music sales (a stage hit could bring in $30,000 over the first three months, but a movie could generate $100,000–150,000). However, many composers and lyricists resented not being treated with the deference to which they were accustomed back East, while others despised Hollywood's cavalier attitude to their stage scores – especially after the studios realized that they could make additional revenue by replacing expensive buy-ins with **original compositions** leased from their own publishing houses. Warner Bros acquired the Whitmark, Remick and Harms music companies, in order to secure access to the works of Victor Herbert, Stephen Roberts, George M. Cohan, and the songwriting team of B.G. "Buddy" De Sylva, Lew Brown and Ray Henderson. MGM followed suit and procured the Robbins Music Corporation, and Paramount set up Famous Music, which took over Spicer and Coslow in 1929.

The technology, the infrastructure and the personnel were now in place, but no one seemed entirely sure what audiences wanted from the new genre. Some producers exploited the novelty of sound by including **songs in non-musicals**, like "Diane" in *Seventh Heaven* (1927) and "Yo Te Amo" in *Wolf Song* (1928). Others bowdlerized Broadway shows, and yet others sought to produce original entertainments, in order to give the musical a more distinctive Hollywood feel. Many mistakes were made in the early 1930s, as filmmakers tried to fathom how musicals worked. Gradually, they came to realize that what succeeded on stage didn't necessarily do so on screen. Without flops like *Howdy Broadway* and *Heads Up* (both 1930), there could never have been a *Top Hat* (1935; see Canon) or a *Cabaret* (1972; see Canon), and the **pioneers** deserve credit for the speed with which they discarded the stagy sentimentality of *The Singing Fool* (1928) and embraced the cinematic sassiness of *42nd Street* (1933; see Canon).

## Backstage on screen

At the outset, producers were anxious that the average viewer would only understand film musicals if they could see on screen the source of any **diegetic music**. Thus, instead of borrowing Broadway's trusted musical comedy formula of having characters burst into song in everyday settings, Hollywood tended to locate its earliest efforts in theatres, studios and nightclubs, in order to afford the cast an excuse to perform. MGM's *The Broadway Melody* (1929) set the **backstage trend**. Billed as the first "All-Talking! All-Singing! All-Dancing!" musical, it cost $280,000 to produce. Yet by the end of the year, it had grossed over $4 million, at a time when the average cinema ticket cost only 35c. With its songs especially composed by **Arthur Freed** and **Nacio Herb Brown** and its Academy Award for best picture, *The Broadway Melody* earned the genre a new respectability and convinced hesitant East Coasters that Hollywood could do justice to musicals after all.

A glut of copycat followed. Of the 22 fully fledged musicals released in the first half of 1929, seventeen were either backstagers or showbiz related: *Close Harmony*, *Broadway Babies* and *Footlights And Fools* were set in theatreland, while *Honky-Tonk*, *Queen Of The Night Clubs* and *Syncopation* were staged in niteries. The most authentic of these pictures was **John Cromwell**

### Diegetic and non-diegetic sound

The fictional world that exists within a film is known as its diegesis. Sounds whose source is shown on screen (or implied to be present) are known as diegetic sounds. These include the voices of the characters, the noises made by props and the music produced by visible instruments and objects like radios and gramophones. Non-diegetic sounds emanate from sources that are neither visible on screen nor implied to exist within the action. The most obvious examples of these are narration and mood music.

However, musicals confuse the issue by having non-diegetic sounds – such as musical introductions played by an orchestra that doesn't exist within the film's world – become diegetic, as they accompany onscreen characters as they sing or dance. To avoid confusing audiences, the producers of the earliest musicals tended to show the source of any music on screen – hence the number of routines staged in theatres and nightclubs. But as viewers became more familiar with the conventions of the genre, non-diegetic orchestrations became the norm, in order to allow characters to sing in everyday situations.

and **A. Edward Sutherland**'s *The Dance Of Life* (1929). A tough drama with songs that was based on the 1927 stage hit, *Burlesque*, it boasted a fine performance by Hal Skelly (who died in a car crash five years later). It was later remade as *Swing High, Swing Low* (1937), starring Carole Lombard and Fred MacMurray, and as *When My Baby Smiles At Me* (1948), starring Betty Grable and Dan Dailey.

However, audiences reared on a diet of glossy fanzines didn't want realism. They flocked to these **"talkie-singie-dancies"** because they gave movie punters a privilege denied to theatre patrons – seeing what went on in the wings. Backstage musicals revealed the stars to be ordinary people, who shared the viewers' own hopes and dreams, as well as entertaining them with memorable tunes and **escapist spectacle**.

The majority of the song'n'dance routines in these early backstagers were shot from a static camera positioned somewhere in the middle of the stalls. But, for *Broadway* (1929), director **Paul Fejos** and cinematographer **Hal Mohr** utilized a $75,000 multi-directional crane to add excitement to a musical number staged by Maurice Kusell and performed by Glenn Tryon. After peering through the curtains at the Paradise Night Club, Mohr's camera rose up to show the chorines performing on stage before gliding off in pursuit, as they sashayed out around the venue. Choreographer **Albertina Rasch** similarly bucked the trend by introducing the top shot (that would later be made famous by Busby Berkeley) in *The Hollywood Revue Of 1929*, in order to show her ballet company forming floral patterns. And director Robert Florey and choreographer Maria Gombarelli did much the same in the **Marx Brothers**' debut, *The Cocoanuts* (1929), in which Florey also presented the girls in negative form and had cinematographer Joseph Ruttenberg film from between their legs using a long lens.

**Technicolor** was also occasionally used to add to a musical's lustre. Among the most eye-catching examples was "I Want To Be Bad" in *Follow Thru* (1930), which saw a lightning bolt turn some angel costumes crimson and Zelma O'Neal materialize out of a demonic conflagration. But most musicals contented themselves with showing celebrities doing what they did best, whether it was Harry Richman singing **Irving Berlin**'s theme tune in the genial club saga *Puttin' On The Ritz* (1930), or **Bill "Bojangles" Robinson** stealing the two-colour finale in *Dixiana* (1930) with some trademark tapping.

Numerous headliners from opera, vaudeville, cabaret, revue and musical comedy – including stage legends Marilyn Miller, Fanny Brice and Ethel Merman (see box opposite) – failed to make the movie grade. Many more were miscast in **mediocre vehicles** that were rushed into production to meet public demand. Some Broadway stars suffered because they had to work in cramped, ill-equipped New York film studios, while others were mishandled by journeyman directors, who saw musicals as just another job rather than something requiring specialist knowledge. **Gertrude Lawrence**'s first picture, *The Battle Of Paris* (1929), was dubbed a "floperetta", despite containing **Cole Porter**'s first film songs, "Here Comes The Band Wagon" and "They All Fall In Love". She, Ruth Etting and Lillian Roth were all better served by their respective biopics – *Star!* (1968), *Love Me Or Leave Me* (1955) and *I'll Cry Tomorrow* (1955) – than by their own pictures.

Even Broadway legend **George M. Cohan** (see p.10) fell flat when he took on the dual role of a bland financier and a spirited medicine show

## Wasted Broadway talents

The talkies came too late for musical comedy star **Marilyn Miller**. She had played the Broadway leads in *Sally* (1920) and *Sunny* (1921) over five hundred times each, but she looked decidedly uncomfortable in the 1929 and 1930 screen versions. The first film was a critical and commercial success, with two-colour Technicolor visuals and a trio of **Jerome Kern** songs adding to its winsome charm. But despite including the sublime "Who?", *Sunny* consigned most of Kern and **Oscar Hammerstein**'s songs to the soundtrack, and afforded Miller few opportunities to demonstrate her trademark tap dancing. She was marginalized even further in *Her Majesty, Love* (1931), her final picture, which is now best known for giving W.C. Fields his talkie debut and including some flashes of Lubitschian polish from director **William Dieterle**.

Warner Bros thought **Fanny Brice** would be the female **Al Jolson**. But although she sold a song with the same skill, her stage persona was more overtly Yiddish and less naturally ebuillent. She also lacked the classical looks required of a **screen siren**, and she seemed uncomfortable in the romantic scenes in *My Man* and *Be Yourself* (both 1930). Essentially the producers couldn't cope with her individuality and her subversive approach to the material, let alone her sheer versatility with both comic and dramatic songs. She was also unsuited to the **heroine template**, so Hollywood decided to ditch her rather than think of new ways to harness the unique talent that had delighted countless theatregoers.

**Ethel Merman**, the first lady of American musical comedy, was equally mismanaged. Few doubted her unconventional gifts, but she didn't conform to Hollywood standards of beauty. Thus, her supporting role opposite vaudeville star **Ed Wynn** in *Follow The Leader* (1930) set a trend that would continue for the rest of her career. She had to content herself with minor movie roles, while smash hits that she had originated on Broadway were awarded to other actresses: *Girl Crazy* (1930) to Kitty Kelly, *Panama Hattie* (1942) to Ann Sothern, *DuBarry Was A Lady* (1943) to Lucille Ball, *Annie Get Your Gun* (1950) to Betty Hutton and *Gypsy* (1962) to Rosalind Russell.

barker in *The Phantom President* (1932). Denied any involvement with the screenplay, Cohan took out his frustrations on songwriters Rodgers and Hart, who had tried to integrate their songs into the scenario. The result was a squib of a satire that paled beside the Gershwins' Washington gem, *Of Thee I Sing*, which had scandalized Broadway the previous year.

The majority of **silent film actresses** who took a stab at musicals similarly failed to impress. Sue Carol gained some admirers following her performances in *The Big Party* and *Check And Double Check* (both 1930), and Dorothy Jordan made three passable musicals with Ramon Novarro in 1930, *Devil-May-Care*, *In Gay Madrid* and *Call Of The Flesh*. More successful, however, were **Bebe Daniels** and **Nancy Carroll**. Having impressed in RKO's *Rio Rita*, Daniels played a pivotal role in MGM's *The Broadway Melody* (both 1929). But she was frustrated in her ambition to do *Carmen* with Josephine Baker, and she fell victim to Hollywood's sudden aversion to song after *Dixiana* (1930) and *Reaching For The Moon* (1931).

Carroll was the first musical star to emerge from within the Hollywood system. Largely singing songs written by **Richard A. Whiting** and **Leo Robin**, she delighted audiences in *Close Harmony*, *Dance Of Life*, *Sweetie* (all 1929), *Honey* and *Follow Thru* (both 1930). However, she was mismanaged by her studio, Paramount, which excelled at continental chic, but was less proficient with all-American spirit, and Carroll's star faded after *Transatlantic Merry-Go-Round* (1934). Nevertheless, the vivacious redhead did leave a musical legacy, as Alice Faye, Betty Grable, Deanna Durbin, Judy Garland, Doris Day, June Allyson and Debbie Reynolds all followed in her **girl-next-door** footsteps.

With 128 features being released between January 1929 and June 1930, the Hollywood musical had finally begun to find its feet. In addition to adapting existing shows, producers were also attempting **screen originals**. They added songs to stories across the generic range, a fair proportion of which were cheaply made musical remakes of misfiring silents. The rule of thumb was that any picture containing three or more songs was classified as a musical. Yet several acclaimed musicals included fewer numbers, while others that contained more – the war drama *Melody Of Life*, the comedy *The Cock-Eyed World* and the Erich von Stroheim ventriloquism chiller *The Great Gabbo* (all 1929) – were curiously disqualified.

For all this **narrative diversity**, little attempt was made to integrate songs or dance routines into the action, whether to advance the plot or to allow an insight into a character's psychology. However, audiences dealing with the ramifications of the **Wall Street Crash** simply wanted diversions from the inexorable realities of the daily grind. And the studios were more than willing to oblige – if only to recover the enormous costs of converting to sound. As late as 1930, 234 different sound systems were still being used in theatres across the States, and it took a conference in Paris to coerce international filmmakers into settling on a universal sound-on-film format.

Through all this, the **backstager** remained the dominant storyline. However, the pursuit of novelty did lead to a brief vogue for **campus musicals**, such as *College Love*, *Sweetie*, *The Forward Pass* (all 1929) and De Sylva, Brown and Henderson's stage transfer, *Good News* (1930). The same team ventured into science fiction with director David Butler for *Just Imagine* (1930) and created one of the worst musicals ever made. But they had previously succeeded in showing how musicals could centre on ordinary people with *Sunny Side Up* (1929), which had grossed $2 million at the box office and demonstrated a new maturity and ingenuity in the staging of song and dance.

Starring "America's Favourite Lovebirds", **Janet Gaynor** and **Charles Farrell**, as a tenement dweller and her wealthy beau, *Sunny Side Up* combined pleasing standards like "If I Had A Talking Picture Of You" and "I'm A Dreamer" with a finale choreographed by **Seymour Felix** that caused a sensation in its day. Now hailed as the "first purely cinematic" production number, "Turn On The Heat" went from monochrome to Multicolor, as 36 chorines shed Eskimo costumes for scanties more suitable for a tropical island, and plunged into the water as the landscape caught fire.

Few producers exhibited similar creativity during this period, preferring instead to invest in **revues** in which the performers simply had to be themselves and do a turn that could be mounted in the traditional vaudeville style or with a little extra cinematic pizzazz. Such **all-star spectacles** were also useful in helping the studios to gauge who could hack it in the new genre. MGM asked its biggest names to attempt something new to surprise the viewers of *The Hollywood Revue Of 1929*. Thus, Marion Davies sang "Tommy Atkins On Parade" between the legs of giant Household Cavalry guardsmen, and Joan Crawford concluded her rendition of "Gotta Feelin' For You" with a charmingly self-conscious Charleston. However, **Laurel and Hardy** stuck to comedy for a magic sketch, and Buster Keaton executed "Dance Of The Sea" dressed as Neptune's daughter. For the much-admired two-colour finale, Cliff "Ukulele" Edwards led the cast in a spirited rendition of "Singin' In The Rain".

The other studios tried to copy MGM's Oscar-nominated formula, but few could match either its line-up or its **kitschy expertise**. Warner Bros failed to corral its superstars for either *On With The Show* or *The Show Of Shows* (both 1929), the latter of which culminated in an interminable showstopper featuring ten separate dance troupes. Fox's *Movietone Follies Of 1929* and *Happy Days* (1930) both got bogged down in their framing stories. *Paramount On Parade* (1930) boasted Maurice Chevalier in three sequences directed by **Ernst Lubitsch**, including the celebrated "Origin Of The Apache", but only Clara Bow's "I'm True To The Navy Now" was of comparable quality.

**Universal**, however, did a much better job with *King Of Jazz* (1930), which opened with a Walter Lantz cartoon. The songs and sketches made use of superimposition, stop-motion, reflections and silhouettes to vary the visuals, which were superbly designed by director **John Murray Anderson**. He also imposed a sense of scale by making the chorus wear giant costumes for "The Bridal Veil" and having John Boles lead five hundred cowboys into the horizon at the climax of "Song Of The Dawn". A young **Bing Crosby** also made an appearance, as one of the Rhythm Boys, for "Mississippi Mud". But the highlight of the revue was the Technicolor debut of George Gershwin's "Rhapsody In Blue", which saw the Paul Whiteman Orchestra rise up from inside a gigantic baby blue grand piano to join an array of blue-costumed chorines and strutting models.

All of these extravaganzas drew heavily on the established Broadway tradition, but Hollywood soon began importing **operettas** to cater for audiences with more refined tastes. The studios were keen to see how their semi-classical scores would go down in the sticks, especially after Universal hurriedly added some musical highlights to its 1929 adaptation of Edna Ferber's novel *Show Boat* (see Canon). The first full screen operetta was Warner dependable Roy Del Ruth's take on *The Desert Song* (1929). It starred **John Boles** as the Pimpernel-like Red Shadow, who periodically broke off from fighting the Arab rebels to give full vent to tunes by Sigmund Romberg and lyricists Otto Harbach and Oscar Hammerstein. The newly formed **RKO studio** rapidly followed suit with *Rio Rita* (1929), which again starred Boles (this time as a Texas Ranger who falls for Bebe Daniels' eponymous heroine while tracking a Mexican bandit).

**George Gershwin**'s Broadway hit, *Song Of The Flame*, was adapted for the screen in 1930 and starred Broadway headliner Alexander Gray, who underwhelmed critics and audiences alike. Lawrence Tibbett similarly struggled to make an impression with *The Rogue Song* (1930) and *The Cuban Love Song* (1931), while Dennis King found himself overshadowed by **Jeanette MacDonald** in the screen remake of Rudolf Friml's operetta, *The Vagabond King* (1930). But not even MacDonald, the Iron Butterfly, could deliver *The Lottery Bride* (1930) from commercial indifference.

Disappointingly few filmmakers at this time had either the tact or the vision to elevate the musical from bibelot to art form. **King Vidor** valiantly attempted to establish an African-American tradition with *Hallelujah!* (1929, see Canon), but the musical's first masters were Ernst Lubitsch and **Rouben Mamoulian**, who capitalized on Paramount's fabled cosmopolitanism. It says much for their dominance in this period that Lubitsch and Mamoulian's collaborations with

Jeanette MacDonald and **Maurice Chevalier** – *The Love Parade* (1929), *Love Me Tonight* (1932) and *The Merry Widow* (1934) – are all featured within this book's Canon of essential film musicals. Mamoulian's *Applause* (1929) and Lubitsch's *Monte Carlo* (1930), *The Smiling Lieutenant* (1931) and *One Hour With You* (1932, co-directed with **George Cukor**) were all superior to their competitors, in terms of their elegance and eloquence and in their use of music as a means of telling the story rather than merely embellishing it.

Such were the deficiencies of most Hollywood musicals that the genre was, by this time, deep in **crisis**. The studios had churned out sixty musicals in 1929 and over eighty in 1930, but only eleven were released in 1931. The public had become so tired of characters warbling in everything from mob movies to Westerns that exhibitors began using the **absence of music** as a selling point. As a result, the majority of the songs were cut from Irving Berlin's *Reaching For The Moon* (1930), Jerome Kern's *Men Of The Sky*, Cole Porter's *Fifty Million Frenchmen*, and De Sylva, Brown and Henderson's *Indiscreet* (all 1931).

With cinema audiences dropping by forty percent in 1930, as the **Depression** began to take hold, Hollywood had no option but to bow to punter pressure and ditch the formulaic plots, forgettable tunes and identikit stars with interchangeable personalities. Around fifty musicals had been announced in the trades for the 1930–31 season, but only a fraction of them were actually produced; *Great Day*, *Hollywood Revue Of 1930*, *Five O'Clock Girl*, *Rosalie*, *Funny Face*, *The Band Wagon* and *Bitter Sweet* were among those to be cancelled. In fact, just 36 musicals were produced between January 1930 and March 1933. The genre seemed to be in danger of becoming defunct, while still in its infancy.

### The Broadway Melody

**dir Harry Beaumont, 1929, 104m, b/w and col**

MGM's first talkie established the musical as a viable Hollywood genre. Its sound quality left much to be desired and the staging was often inert. But the story – of two sisters (Anita Page and Bessie Love) graduating from the small-time vaudeville circuit and falling for the same song-and-dance man (Charles King) – charmed audiences already captivated by Arthur Freed and Nacio Herb Brown's songs "You Were Meant For Me" and "Broadway Melody".

### Applause

**dir Rouben Mamoulian, 1929, 78m b/w**

Helen Morgan excels as self-destructive burlesque star Kitty Darling, whose passion for her two-timing boyfriend (Fuller Mellish Jr.) is matched only by her devotion to her convent-educated daughter, April (Joan Peers). However, it's Mamoulian's masterly use of sound that makes this mawkish melodrama an early musical masterclass.

### One Hour With You

**dir Ernst Lubitsch, George Cukor, 1932, 80m, b/w**

Vamp Genevieve Tobin comes between husband and wife Maurice Chevalier and Jeanette MacDonald in this chic musical remake of Ernst Lubitsch's *The Marriage Circle* (1924). This comedy of manners sparkles with an impudent wit that also informs the polished and effortlessly integrated score by Oscar Straus, Richard A. Whiting and Leo Robin.

# Monochrome magic

## The Berkeley era

The musical was saved by director and choreographer **Busby Berkeley**. He was one of the few survivors of the overkill era, having choreographed a series of outlandish routines for the popular **Eddie Cantor** vehicles that had been munificently produced by Samuel Goldwyn, designed with unsung resplendence by Richard Day and photographed with typical brilliance by Gregg Toland. Berkeley's first number in *Whoopee!* (1930), "Cowboys", was partly sung by 16-year-old Betty Grable and ended with the first of his **trademark top shots**: the camera peered down on the kaleidoscopic patterns created by the chorus girls' hats as they achieved a snake-like movement by ducking their heads in sequence. Headgear also figured prominently in "Stetson", which introduced the **chorine close-up** that later became another Berkeley staple, and "Song Of The Setting Sun', which culminated in a Ziegfeldian tableau that exhibited girls in skimpy Indian costumes and headdresses.

These production numbers were largely irrelevant to the action, but they thrilled Depression-era audiences who eagerly returned for *Palmy Days*, in which the **Goldwyn Girls** used placards to form a train to transport Cantor away at the climax of the hit tune, "My Baby Said Yes, Yes". However, Berkeley's visual ingenuity was beginning to attract critics, the majority of whom despised his brazen **exploitation** of the female form.

In *The Kid From Spain* (1932), the opening segment followed a group of college girls, (including Betty Grable and Paulette Goddard) as they rose from their beds and swam in geometric designs in the dormitory pool. However, the camera then attempted to peek behind the transluscent screens at the **chorines' silhouettes** as they changed out of their wet costumes. Later in the picture, the girls formed a giant tortilla and the head of a bull for Cantor's blackface nightclub number, "What A Perfect Combination". Berkeley reverted to similarly **coy innocence** for "Keep Young And Beautiful" in *Roman Scandals* (1933), but he overstepped the bounds of decency with "No More Love", in which he reduced Civil Rights to abstract shapes in the mud bath sequence and made decoration out of degradation by depicting the flagellation of chorines chained to a giant wedding cake.

Such dubious excesses were largely overlooked after Berkeley's choreography was cited as the prime reason for the critical and commercial success of *42nd Street* (1933, see Canon), which restored the musical's credibility and launched another of its periodic mini-booms. Produced by **Darryl F. Zanuck** for Warner Bros, *42nd Street* was the **ultimate backstager** and it was quickly followed by *Gold Diggers Of 1933* and *Footlight Parade* (both 1933, see Canon), each of which featured three key members of Berkeley's stock company – Joan Blondell, Dick Powell and **Ruby Keeler** (see p.212).

Such was the impact of these three stylish and cynical celebrations of the **gaudy glamour** of show business that the formula was endlessly repeated throughout the 1930s: Warner Bros made four *Gold Diggers* pictures; Paramount, four

"A lot of people used to believe I was crazy," Busby Berkeley once said about routines like the finale in *42nd Street* (1933). "But I can truthfully say one thing: I gave 'em a show!"

*Big Broadcasts*; MGM, three *Broadway Melodies*; and Fox, a pair of *George White's Scandals*. But some in Hollywood found these films faintly ridiculous. The Marx Brothers riotously spoofed Berkeley's style in "The Country's Going To War" number in *Duck Soup* (1933), which saw the wildly dancing ensemble descend into a mêlée devoid of discipline or artistry.

However, not even choreographers of the calibre of **Bobby Connolly**, Seymour Felix, **Dave Gould** and LeRoy Prinz could match Berkeley's ingenuity and audacity. Seemingly every picture he worked on contained a **jaw-dropping showstopper** that exploited the cavernous spaces of the Warner sound stages and finally gave the musical a sense of **cinematic spectacle**. Composer Harry Warren was forced to devise ever longer variations on his themes, as five choruses of "Shuffle Off To Buffalo" in *42nd Street* became eleven reprises of "I Only Have Eyes For You" in *Dames* (1934). Yet the studio was happy to indulge its *wünderkind*, even though routines running up to ten minutes could cost as much as $10,000 per minute to produce.

For "Don't Say Goodnight" in *Wonder Bar* (1934), Berkeley had art director Jack Okey build sixty movable columns and a revolving 27 x 12ft octagonal block of mirrors to give the impression of hundreds of dancers minuetting into infinity, when in reality there were only eight. The Hall of Human Harps, Web of Dreams, and Venus and Her Galley Slave sequences in *Fashions Of 1934* showcased fifty **chorines** in ostrich feathers. In *Dames*, dozens of chorines wearing **Ruby Keeler** masks formed a jigsaw of the actress's face using boards fitted to their backs, and in the titular finale a hundred girls in white blouses and black tights formed a mesmerizing floral mosaic.

These extravagant set pieces soon led to accusations that rather than choreographing light, space and water in an attempt to convey physical harmony, Berkeley's choreography was **dehumanizing women's bodies** for male pleasure, in routines that were so stripped of individuality that they had more in common with the fascist regimentation of the Nuremberg Rallies than musical entertainment. After seeing the "Spin A Little Web Of Dreams" number in *Fashions Of 1934*, one of the chorines' mothers finally snapped and published an article, entitled, "I didn't bring up my daughter to be a human harp". Yet this was nothing compared to the offence caused by "Goin'To Heaven On A Mule" from the **Al Jolson** vehicle, *Wonder Bar*, which featured blackface angels eating pork chops and watermelon.

But while Berkeley was often guilty of these grievous lapses of taste, he was also capable of producing **dark parodies** of the realities of life during the Depression. Audiences gazed upon his kaleidoscopic configurations blithely unaware of the subconscious New Deal messages they were imparting about people playing their small part in the grand design. He also sold **aspiration** to his viewers, although he did warn against the dangers of reaching too far in "Lullaby Of Broadway" in *Gold Diggers Of 1935*.

Berkeley hit his **choreographic peak** with the dazzling and ultimately deeply disturbing parable "Lullaby Of Broadway", which opens with actress **Wini Shaw**'s face a distant white dot on an otherwise black screen. As she sings, her image slowly fills the screen, before it is suddenly flipped on its side and matched with a view of the Manhattan skyline. This shot segues into the main body of the story, as Shaw arrives home at her humble tenement after a hard night's partying. She's soon back out on the tiles again, as she and **Dick Powell** watch Latin dancers Ramon and Rosita before taking to the floor themselves, dancing alongside a hundred other people, whose movements are captured from a dizzying array of angles. Exhilarated and exhausted by the frantic gaiety, Shaw steps out onto a balcony, only to tumble to her death down the side of the skyscraper. The final **montage sequence** scours the city, before the number ends on Shaw's face as it recedes into the distance.

Even by Berkeley's standards, this was a remarkable piece of filmmaking. Yet it still conformed to the tripartite strategy of all his best **Warner Bros** work, as he ensured that each production numbers contained a social, sexual and conceptual element.

### Wonder Bar

**dir Lloyd Bacon, 1934, 84m, b/w**

Warner Bros packed the backstage clichés into this hard-boiled musical melodrama, in which Al Jolson's Parisian nightclub owner competes with band crooner Dick Powell for the affections of cabaret star, Dolores Del Rio. But she only has eyes for her dancing partner Ricardo Cortez, who is being pursued by socialite Kay Francis. Busby Berkeley's tasteless choreography for "Goin' To Heaven On A Mule" proved a career low, but he partially redeemed himself with "Don't Say Goodnight".

### Dames

**dir Ray Enright, 1934, 90m, b/w**

Showgirl Joan Blondell dupes millionaire Guy Kibbee into bankrolling Dick Powell's show in this typical Warner Bros backstager. Busby Berkeley pays eloquent tribute to Ruby Keeler in Harry Warren and Al Dubin's sublime love song "I Only Have Eyes For You", in which the chorines form a giant portrait of the star, and he also slips some trick photography in Blondell's delightful solo, "The Girl At The Ironing Board".

"What do you go for, go see a show for? Tell the truth, you go to see those beautiful dames" from Harry Warren and Al Dubin's title song for *Dames* (1934).

## Fred'n'Ginger

Just as Busby Berkeley's projects revolved around his spectacular showstoppers, the screwball romances of **Fred Astaire** and **Ginger Rogers** were structured around stock set pieces. The duo's set routines and **established formulas** recurred in the majority of the films they made together for RKO between 1933 and 1939.

Recognizing the vulnerability behind her caustic confidence at the start of each picture, Fred invariably fell for Ginger at first sight, only to be spurned because of an unintentional faux pas. In *The Gay Divorcee* (1934), he tore her dress, then crashed into her car; in *Top Hat* (1935, see Canon), his late-night dancing woke her up in her hotel room; in *Roberta* (1935), he threatened to expose her sophisticated socialite as just another small-town girl; in *Swing Time* (1936, see Canon), he nearly had her sacked from a dance studio; in *Shall We Dance* (1937, see Canon), he masqueraded as a pretentious Russian dancer and incurred her wrath; and in *Carefree* (1938), she overheard him calling her a dizzy dame.

After this initial disagreement, they were usually reunited by a coincidence, and when they started to dance together, Ginger began to realize that Fred wasn't such a pest after all. A further spat or a **misunderstanding** inevitably drove them apart once more, with Rogers wrongly thinking that Astaire was her co-respondent in *The Gay Divorcee* and that he was married to her best friend in *Top Hat*. But another dance and a **contrived reconciliation** finally convinced Ginger that while Fred may have been flippant, conceited and cocky, he was also dapper, talented and devoted.

As Fred and Ginger always danced in character and in enclosed spaces that sealed them off from the mundane distractions of the real world, the **integrated duets** in their musicals always revealed the status of their characters' physical and emotional relationship. Moreover, their initial **"challenge" dances** were almost unique because they sprang from animosity, as opposed to amorousness. "I'll Be Hard To Handle" (*Roberta*), "Isn't It A Lovely Day (To Be Caught In The Rain)" (*Top Hat*), "Let Yourself Go", (*Follow The Fleet*, 1936), "They All Laughed" and (*Shall We Dance*) all revolved around competition rather than canoodling.

The second dance frequently reminded Ginger of what she stood to lose if she allowed petty problems to keep them apart. But Fred also had to be more inventive in his approach, and their so-called **"woo to win" numbers** like "Night And Day" (*The Gay Divorce*), "Cheek To Cheek" (*Top Hat*), "Let's Face The Music And Dance" (*Follow The Fleet*), "Waltz In Springtime" (*Swing Time*), and "I Used To Be Colour Blind" (*Carefree*) were always more intense and artistic. But the clincher was often staged on a grander scale and centred on a new **dance craze**: "The Carioca" (*Flying Down To Rio*, 1933), "The Continental" (*The Gay Divorcee*), "The Piccolino" (*Top Hat*), or "The Yam" (*Carefree*). However, "Never Gonna Dance" in *Swing Time* was more of a private duet, in which Fred and Ginger fretted over separation rather than celebrating their new-found passion.

It wasn't just Astaire and Rogers' peerless chemistry that made their musicals so popular. Producer **Pandro S. Berman** surrounded them with experienced *farceurs* such as Edward Everett Horton, Alice Brady, Helen Broderick, Eric Blore and Erik Rhodes, as well as commissioning polished scripts from **Allan Scott** (and a variety of co-writers) and handcrafted scores from composers of the calibre of Jerome Kern, Irving Berlin, Cole Porter and George Gershwin.

Fred Astaire and Ginger Rogers dancing cheek to cheek in one of their more intense and artistic "woo-to-win" numbers in *Top Hat* (1935).

Astaire also relied heavily on his dance team of choreographer **Her es Pan** and rehearsal pianist **Hal Bourne**. Astaire and Pan blocked out the routines, Pan taught them to Rogers, and the duo were then filmed in full-figure by director **Mark Sandrich** and unsung cinematographer David Abel against ethereal Art Deco sets designed by Van Nest Polglase and Carroll Clark.

The majority of their pictures also contained a couple of solo slots for Fred, one at the beginning and one somewhere in the middle. These included, "Needle In A Haystack" (*The Gay Divorcee*), "Top Hat, White Tie And Tails" (*Top Hat*), "I'd Rather Lead A Band" (*Follow The Fleet*), "Bojangles Of Harlem" (*Swing Time*) and "I've Got Beginner's Luck" (*Shall We Dance*). Ginger, on the other hand, had to content herself with just a single **tap solo** for the reprise of "Let Yourself Go" in *Follow The Fleet*, the lead vocal on the cynical duet "A Fine Romance" in *Swing Time*, and the "Yama Yama Man" showcase in *The Story Of Vernon And Irene Castle* (1939).

Such subservience to Astaire renders Rogers' insistence on a break from the act in 1937 entirely understandable. She had been the junior partner ever since Astaire had choreographed "Embraceable You" for her in 1930 for the Gershwins' Broadway hit, *Girl Crazy*, (and they had even briefly dated around that time). Yet she possessed infinitely more screen experience than he when they were first paired in *Flying Down To Rio* in 1933, and she came to resent being regarded as Astaire's shadow.

Astaire himself viewed the **partnership** with some suspicion, as he was keen to establish himself as a solo star after his long stage liaison with his sister, Adele. He was initially dismayed by RKO's decision to reunite him with Rogers after the unexpected success of "The Carioca" and actively lobbied against her casting in *The Gay Divorcee*. But they were each forced to recognize the validity of Katharine Hepburn's contention that "she gives him sex and he gives her class", and they remained box-office favourites for the remainder of the decade.

The couple's **growing disillusionment** with the series coincided with press accusations of self-indulgence following *Shall We Dance*, so they decided to take a break. Rogers went on to prove her comic mettle in *Stage Door* (1937) and *Vicacious Lady* (1938), while Astaire collaborated with Joan Fontaine, **Gracie Allen** and George Burns in 1937 on *A Damsel In Distress* (which boasted such delightful Gershwin songs as "A Foggy Day In London Town", "Nice Work If You Can Get It" and "I Can't Be Bothered Now"). However, the hiatus meant that the balance of the Fred'n'Ginger alliance had shifted when they **reunited** in 1938. *Carefree* had a much-reduced song count to give Ginger the opportunity to demonstrate her new dramatic confidence. Moreover, the narrative formula was changed, so that Ginger's highly strung showgirl pursued Fred's psychiatrist. But the most telling aspect of the picture was the **sense of finality** in the melancholic ballad "Change Partners", which was confirmed by Astaire's death at the end of the biopic, *The Story Of Vernon And Irene Castle*.

Rogers' frustration with Astaire's perfectionism and her increasing unwillingness to fall under his Svengali spell precipitated their split in 1939. But the genre was again in abeyance and, with their grosses falling, RKO could also no longer justify the expense of the pair's pictures. They cheerfully reunited for MGM's *The Barkleys Of Broadway* (1949), after Judy Garland withdrew, but only had two substantial character songs, "You'd Be Hard To Replace", which evoked the good old days, and "A Weekend In The Country", which they shared with **Oscar Levant**. Although Rogers presented Astaire with his Honorary Oscar in 1950, they never performed together in public again.

### Follow The Fleet
**dir Mark Sandrich, 1936, 110m, b/w**

The Harriet Hilliard and Randolph Scott sub-plot proves a dreary distraction from Ginger Rogers' fling with sailor Fred Astaire in RKO's reworking of Hubert Osborne's play *Shore Leave* (1922). "I'm Putting All My Eggs In One Basket" affords the duo their sole comedy routine, but the highlight of Irving Berlin's score is "Let's Face The Music And Dance", a pseudo-balletic duet that ranks among Fred'n'Ginger's most dramatic numbers.

### Carefree
**dir Mark Sandrich, 1938, 80m, b/w**

Fred'n'Ginger were reunited after a fifteen-month hiatus for this musical screwball, in which Ginger's showgirl falls for Fred's psychiatrist. Ginger ably exhibited her gift for comedy, but such was the emphasis on her performance that there was room for only three Irving Berlin duets – "Change Partners", "I Used To Be Colour Blind" and "The Yam" – and Fred's virtuoso golfing speciality, "Since They Turned 'Loch Lomond' Into Swing". The twosome kissed for the first and only time on screen, but signs of estrangement were evident.

## The Depression kicks in

Although the Astaire-Rogers films avoided direct reference to the Depression, their songs' lyrics frequently recognized the audience's concerns and hardships (and not just by way of blasé escapism). The songs often tried to **boost morale** by propounding such sentiments as "Pick Yourself

Up", "Let Yourself Go" and "Let's Face The Music And Dance". **Fred'n'Ginger** may have seemed to exist in a well-heeled world, but the music bound them to reality and they danced as an **antidote to despair**. However, many of their contemporaries sought simply to relieve the gloom by making resolutely **upbeat pictures** that traded shamelessly in sentiment, nostalgia and the feel-good factor. As the Depression bit, unemployment rose from four million in 1930 to eight million in 1931 and fifteen million by 1933, and the studios similarly felt the pinch. RKO lost $5.5 million in 1931 and only MGM turned a profit the following year (of $8 million), while Warner Bros, Paramount and Fox lost $14 million, $16 million and $17 million respectively.

Vaudeville was already going to the wall, due to the combined popularity of radio and the talkies, and the economic slump, and even Hollywood had to try ever harder to entice the 75 percent of Americans still in work to buy tickets. Musicals already contained **universal emotions** that appealed to viewers of all ages, classes and cultures. Moreover, with their modern mythology and formulaic situations, musicals offered audiences the consoling **dependability** of a guaranteed **first-rate show** (without the understudies or off nights that often debilitated stage productions). But now they also began to champion the underprivileged and overlooked. They offered encouragement, while also subtly lowering expectations. Depression musicals were no longer about becoming a star – simply putting on a show was now a triumph of collaboration over circumstance. **Optimistic** and infectious energy was the key to these New Deal pep talks, and this emphasis helps to explain the rise of **child stars** like **Shirley Temple**, Deanna Durbin, Judy Garland and Mickey Rooney, whose innocent disregard for protocol gave them a can-do attitude that inspired viewers to seek their own happy endings.

The studio chiefs may have all agreed on the genre's new purpose, but they had very different approaches to promoting family values, community spirit and the essence of the **American Dream**. Some favoured musicals that were opulent, elitist and conservative. But the majority produced variations on the stock musical types – the personality picture, the ensemble piece and the speciality showcase – that were cheap, fast and fun. And nobody did bright, brisk, brash entertainment better than Fox, having appointed **Darryl F. Zanuck** as head of production on its merger with 20th Century Pictures in 1935. 20th Century-Fox urged folks to smile their way out of the Depression with **democratic musicals** showing ordinary people doing extraordinary things. The studio's stories were usually centred on **family**, struggle and sacrifice, with the odd bit of class conflict and the occasional tragedy thrown in. These difficulties always preceded the inevitable uptempo resolution, which frequently coincided with a major public holiday.

Fox also dabbled in more sophisticated fare, producing pictures like *Folies Bergere* (1935), a literate backstager featuring Maurice Chevalier and plenty of post-Production Code innuendo, and the **Dick Powell** duo of *Thanks A Million* (1935) and *On The Avenue* (1937). *Thanks A Million* borrowed its political satire from the Gershwins' *Let 'Em Eat Cake* (1933), and *On The Avenue* (1937) contained almost as many classic **Irving Berlin** tunes a the studio's *Alexander's Ragtime Band* (1938), which was the first screen musical to realize that the genre chronicled American history. The film, therefore, used songs from 1911 to 1935 to emphasize changing social attitudes and styles, and to show how the European influence had diminished as indigenous songs became syncopated in the jazz clubs, patriotic in the Great War and cultivated in Carnegie Hall.

As the decade progressed, **Fox** began pushing topical sports and campus pictures, like *Pigskin Parade* (1936), which gave **Judy Garland** (on loan from MGM) her feature debut. However, the studio's greatest strength remained its string of female stars: Shirley Temple (see p.230), Alice Faye (see p.200) and Sonja Henie (see p.237).

Similarly, Paramount's biggest draw at this time was **Bing Crosby** (see p.196), who became the most successful crooner in film, radio and recording history. Paramount had benefited from the urbane talents of Lubitsch and Mamoulian in the early sound era, but the easy-going Crosby chimed in with the Depression-era mantra that anything was possible. His future co-star in the *Road To...* series, **Dorothy Lamour**, supplied some wholesome exoticism in *Tropic Holiday* (1938) and *Man About Town* (1939). The latter half of the decade also saw the studio's emphasis begin to shift towards a **zaniness** that suited the likes of Jack Benny (*Artists And Models*, 1937), Bob Hope (*The Big Broadcast Of 1938*), and the duo of George Burns and Gracie Allen (*Honolulu*, 1939). This change also suited directors such as Norman Taurog (*Rhythm On The Range*, 1936), Frank Tuttle (*Waikiki Wedding*, 1937) and Wesley Ruggles (*Sing, You Sinners*, 1938), who all had comedy backgrounds.

The **Marx Brothers** also flourished in this environment, with Groucho delivering such musical gems as "Hooray For Captain Spaulding" in *Animal Crackers* (1930) and "Whatever It Is, I'm Against It" in *Horse Feathers* (1932), while Harpo and Chico had their respective harp and piano solos. Songs were equally plentiful in (albeit peripheral to) the films of **Mae West** and **Marlene Dietrich**. Laced with insinuation, West's numbers like "Easy Rider" (*She Done Him Wrong*, 1933), "That Dallas Man" (*I'm No Angel*, 1933) and "My Old Flame" (*Belle Of The Nineties*, 1934) served the same purpose as Dietrich's "What Am I Bid?" (*Morocco*, 1930), "Hot Voodoo" (*Blonde Venus*, 1932) and "Awake In A Dream" (*Desire*, 1937) in demonstrating the seductive strength and sensuality that snared their men.

Having failed in films like *Coronado* (1934) to turn Betty Burgess and Johnny Downs into its own Ruby Keeler and Dick Powell, **Paramount** concentrated on its successful Big Broadcast series and **campus romps** like *College Humour* (1933), *College Rhythm* (1934), *College Holiday* (1936) and *College Swing* (1938). These were essentially "putting on a show" pictures that also featured dances that the kids could copy on a Saturday night. This **emphasis on youth** was emulated by both Universal and MGM, where **Deanna Durbin** (see p.199) and **Judy Garland** respectively reigned supreme. Universal also released a handful of B-movies showcasing teenagers Gloria Jean (*The Under-Pup*, 1939) and Bobby Breen (*Way Down South*, 1939), but the sublime Durbin was easily the studio's biggest singing star. **Irene Dunne** proved that she could also hold a tune, especially if it was written by **Jerome Kern**, as in *Roberta*, *Sweet Adeline* (both 1935), *Show Boat* (1936; see Canon), *High, Wide And Handsome* (1937; see Canon) and *Joy Of Living* (1938).

After surviving such moderate efforts as *Everybody Sing* and *Listen, Darling* (both 1938), **Judy Garland** found her perfect partner in **Mickey Rooney** (with whom she had first been paired on *Thoroughbreds Don't Cry* in 1937). Rooney's astonishing versatility – as a dancer, singer, musician, impressionist, comic and dramatic actor – helped establish him as America's first teenager in the splendid **Andy Hardy series**. (Garland guest starred as Betsy Booth in three of the sixteen films: *Love Finds Andy Hardy*,

Buddy Ebsen with Judy Garland in *Broadway Melody Of 1938* (1937). He would have been her Tin Man in *The Wizard Of Oz* (1939), but he suffered a near-fatal reaction to the aluminium powder in his make-up.

1938, *Andy Hardy Meets Debutante*, 1940 and *Life Begins For Andy Hardy*, 1941.) But Rooney also gave the ever-insecure Garland the confidence to excel, and the duo's buoyant **barnyard musicals**, *Babes In Arms* (1939), *Strike Up The Band* (1940), *Babes On Broadway* (1941) and *Girl Crazy* (1943), were among MGM's biggest hits of the period.

MGM, who had afforded **Fred Astaire** his screen debut in *Dancing Lady* in 1933, also furnished him with his first post-Ginger outing, *Broadway Melody Of 1940*, in which he was teamed with tap-dancing sensation, **Eleanor Powell**. Shamefully, Powell is now considered as unfashionable as **Jeanette MacDonald**, yet her production numbers (which were choreographed by the likes of Dave Gould and Bobby Connolly) were the only ones to rival Busby Berkeley's in terms of innovation and spectacle.

Having signed to MGM for *The Merry Widow* (1934, see Canon), MacDonald also profited from it's largesse, as it was the only studio that could afford to produce **operettas** with anything approaching stage luxuriance. She was twinned with opera star **Nelson Eddy** for *Naughty Marietta* in 1935 to counter the success of Grace Moore's *One Night Of Love* (1934), and Lily Pons's *I Dream Too Much* (1935). But, while the singing sweethearts' eight films together were regarded as prestige projects, operetta became an increasingly difficult product to peddle. Musicals tastes were changing and America was retreating further into the cultural and diplomatic isolation that resulted in European imports, such as operetta, being branded highbrow.

Furthermore, **American songwriters** were at the peak of their powers between 1935 and 1950, with the established figures being pressed by such newcomers as Hoagy Carmichael, Johnny Mercer, Sammy Cahn, Jule Styne, James Van Heusen and Frank Loesser. More hits came from movie musicals than from Broadway shows between 1929 and 1931, and 1934 and 1948. Although this had much to do with Hollywood's continued practice of replacing stage songs with in-house originals that were plugged remorselessly on the radio and licensed for performance in **dance halls**.

Having jollied America through the Depression, the musical again slipped from favour in the latter third of the 1930s, as the **Production Code** narrowed its horizons, Busby Berkeley left Warner Bros, Fred'n'Ginger grew apart, and the songwriting fraternity mourned the early deaths of **George Gershwin** and **Richard Whiting**. Indeed, only three musicals appeared among the top sixteen grossers of 1938–39 and only three featured in the top twenty the following year. There were still occasional **musical blockbusters**, such as MGM's Oscar-winning biopic, *The Great Ziegfeld* (1936), and films for children like *Snow White And The Seven Dwarfs* (1937, see Canon) and *The Wizard Of Oz* (1939, see Canon), which revived interest in the **integrated score**. However, the public soon came to dance to Hollywood's tune once more, as the country was drawn into another crisis – World War II.

### The Gay Desperado

**dir Rouben Mamoulian, 1936, 85m, b/w**

Lampooning everything from operetta to Warner Bros' gangster flicks and Sergei Eisenstein's Mexican odyssey, this gleeful romp benefited from Mamoulian's typically astute direction, Richard Day's hilarious production design and the spirited playing of Leo Carillo, as the culture-loving Mexican bandit, and Ida Lupino, as his feisty hostage. Shame about Nino Martini's charmless singing, though.

### Broadway Melody Of 1938

**dir Roy Del Ruth, 1937, 110m, b/w**

Eleanor Powell's opera-loving racehorse saves Robert Taylor's show in this amiably derivative Nacio Herb Brown and Arthur Freed backstager. Although Powell dances with typical brio and showbiz landlady Sophie Tucker belts out her signature tune, "One Of These Days", the undoubted highlight is Judy Garland's first appearance in an MGM feature, singing "Dear Mr Gable", Roger Edens' charming take on the sentimental standard, "You Made Me Love You".

### Babes In Arms

**dir Busby Berkeley, 1939, 91m, b/w**

Debuting producer Arthur Freed established the MGM barnyard tradition with this bowdlerization of Rodgers and Hart's 1937 stage hit, which sees Mickey Rooney and Judy Garland putting on a show to help their hard-up vaudevillian families. Freed slipped in four of his own songs, with only the title tune and "Where Or When" surviving from Broadway. The young stars revel in the minstrel interlude and patriotic finale, which contributed towards the versatile Rooney's Oscar nomination.

### Babes On Broadway

**dir Busby Berkeley, 1941, 118m, b/w**

Mickey Rooney and Judy Garland put on a show for some underprivileged kids in this rousing revue, in which Rooney impersonates Carmen Miranda and demonstrates his infectious energy in "Hoe Down", and Garland belts out "Franklin D. Roosevelt Jones". The twosome finally come together for a charming duet of Burton Lane and Ralph Freed's "How About You?" and a unfortunately dated minstrel show finale.

## Swinging for Uncle Sam

Some four hundred musical films were released during **World War II**, reaching a peak of 76 in 1944. They contained around eight hundred songs in total, 46 of which were nominated for Academy Awards (with a record fourteen nominations in 1945 alone). Hollywood churned out these features with factory efficiency, and novelty was soon at a premium. Such was the demand for cheap, cheerful entertainment that the studios began serving up old plots in new settings, with backstagers centring on **troop shows** and campus frolics becoming **boot camp romps**. However, they soon ran out of cash and inspiration, and began adapting lacklustre Broadway shows to maintain production levels.

Promoting **patriotism** and boosting **morale** were the order of the day. Nostalgia became a crucial component of the wartime musical, as cinema sought to remind service personnel of the traditions and values they were fighting for. There was also an emphasis on youth, with **Betty Grable** and **Lena Horne** becoming idealized representations of the girls the GIs had left behind. Yet for all their propagandist intentions, musicals were deemed a drain on human and material resources. In 1942, the War Production Board declared that a maximum of $5,000 could be spent on sets for any one film. It also recommended the curtailment of filmed rehearsals and the implementation of as much one-take shooting as possible. As a result, production numbers were drastically scaled down, and, initially, not even **Busby Berkeley** or Fred Astaire were allowed to experiment.

This placed additional pressure on the **composers**, who were also instructed to score pictures with something to suit every taste. Wartime audiences were treated to everything from ballads, swing, marches, Latin rhythms, folk songs and minstrelsy to big band showstoppers, classical arias, orchestral showcases, instrumental solos and comic digressions. Hollywood had dispensed with the services of the old songwriting guard following the dip in the genre's fortunes in 1937, and a new generation of **lyricists** and composers had to rally to the cause. The likes of Hal Adamson, Ted Koehler, Harry Revel, Ralph Rainger, Jimmy McHugh, Arthur Schwartz, Gene De Paul, Ralph Blane, Hugh Martin, Ray Evans and Jay Livingston all made their mark during the conflict.

However, as in the Great War, the undisputed king of the patriotic song was **Irving Berlin**. His 1938 tune "God Bless America" – which had been dropped from the 1917 show *Yip Yip Yaphank* – became tantamount to a second national anthem, while his own rendition of "Oh, How I Hate To Get Up In The Morning" became the hit of Warner Bros' *This Is The Army* (1943). His other hits included "Any Bonds Today", "I Pay My Income Tax Today", the official Red Cross song, "Angels Of Mercy", and "Freedom Song". The latter featured in *Holiday Inn* (1942) alongside his most famous song, "White Christmas", which became the most requested radio tune of the entire war.

But few of these ditties went down well with **Lyman Bryson**, the Head of the Music Committee of the Office of War Information, who complained that movie songs were doing too little for the **war effort**. He despised "missing you" and "we'll meet again" ballads, for being bad for morale, and felt Home Front numbers like "Co-Operate With Your Air Raid Warden" from *Priorities On Parade* and "He Loved Me Till The All-Clear Came" from *Star Spangled Rhythm* (both 1942) placed too much emphasis on reluctant sacrifice and not enough on enthusiasm for the fight. He even castigated **Oscar Hammerstein** for the defeatism of "The Last Time I Saw Paris" in *Lady Be Good* (1941) and insisted that it should have been entitled "The Next Time I See Paris".

Bryson preferred efforts like "Der Fuehrer's Face" from the 1943 Donald Duck cartoon of the same name. He wanted freedom songs and blatant pieces of flagwaving **jingoism** similar to the anthems that Propaganda Minister Joseph Goebbels had commissioned in Germany. Therefore, in 1943, the **Music War Committee** (an independent group of Broadway and Hollywood songwriters) called on their colleagues to write songs addressing the current situation, and not World War I, and urged them to replace the one- and two-steps that had seen action back then with swing and the foxtrot. The result was the ensemble asserting "It's A Swelluva Life In The Army" in *Hey, Rookie* (1944) and Ethel Merman urging the troops to start thinking about "Marching Through Berlin" in *Stage Door Canteen* (1943). On a more abstract level, **Harold Arlen** came up with "Ac-cent-tchu-ate The Positive" for a blackfaced Bing Crosby in *Here Come The Waves*, and **Jerome Kern** and **Ira Gershwin** had Gene Kelly, Rita Hayworth and Phil Silvers proclaim "Make Way For Tomorrow" in *Cover Girl* (both 1944).

Nevertheless, the primary problem with composing for wartime musicals remained; films took so long to produce and the state of battle changed so rapidly that topical references could easily seem stale or in bad taste by the time the film was released. As a consequence, the majority of numbers were presented in **performance settings** that made them easier to remove if circumstance required.

Hollywood had, however, begun planning for America's involvement in the war long before Pearl Harbor. The studios had started making what *Variety* called **"preparedness pictures"** in 1939, when screenwriter Ben Hecht introduced the themes of ethnic and religious tolerance into *Let Freedom Ring*, in which Nelson Eddy sang paeans to democracy and the American Way. Service comedies began appearing in 1941, with Jack Oakie, Jimmy Durante, and Bud Abbott and Lou Costello respectively signing up for *Navy Blues*, *You're In The Army Now* and *Buck Privates*, the latter of which featured the Andrews Sisters singing the jaunty "Boogie Woogie Bugle Boy".

A number of other musicals reflected the **"gathering clouds" mentality** of the period, with broken marriages featuring in *Lady Be Good*, *Ziegfeld Girl* (both 1941) and *Orchestra Wives* (1942), while poverty, adultery, murder and petty gangsterdom dominated Anatole Litvak's *Blues In The Night* (1941). Yet Litvak's film was also about **communal action** in true Warner Bros Depression style, as it suggested that any breaches in the united front would not only prevent the show from going ahead, but would also lead to death and destruction at the hands of fifth columnists.

These fears of having to fight an enemy on the doorstep prompted the State Department to inaugurate a **Good Neighbour Policy** towards Central and South America in a bid to prevent its governments from allying with the Axis powers. Hollywood realized that Latin audiences could replace their lost markets in occupied Europe and, therefore, responded with alacrity to requests for pictures that emphasized Pan-American unity and the regard with which the US viewed the nations that had given the world the mambo, tango, conga, rhumba, salsa and samba.

Occasional musicals had already been set south of the border, including Thornton Freeland's *Flying Down To Rio* (1933) and Rouben Mamoulian's *The*

*Gay Desperado* (1936). But Hollywood had rather neglected **Latin America** since the Mexican government had complained about Hispanic stereotyping in the 1920s. This time around, even though they dispatched researchers to verify local customs and vogues, the studios still managed to alienate Spanish and Portuguese speakers alike by blithely implying that there was little difference between the states and their cultures. Consequently, the Argentinians resented **Carmen Miranda**, who was raised in Rio, being cast as a national archetype, and the Brazilians were so embarrassed by "The Lady With The Tutti Frutti Hat" in Busby Berkeley's *The Gang's All Here* (1943) that the number was excised by the censors. Moreover, the majority of these pictures were dubbed by New Yorkers whose accents were almost unintelligble in Cuba, Peru and Chile.

RKO's *They Met In Argentina* (1941) was a negligible affair, but at least it attempted to establish a vague **North–South kinship** – unlike Fox's Alice Faye and Betty Grable offerings *Down Argentine Way* (1940), *That Night In Rio* and *Weekend In Havana* (both 1941), which essentially exploited local rhythms and colour. Such was the studio's insensible attitude to Good Neighbour musicals that it shoehorned Carmen Miranda into pictures with little or no Latin relevance, such as *Springtime In The Rockies* (1942), *Greenwich Village* and *Something For The Boys* (both 1944). Disney was no less patronizing in *Saludos Amigos* (1943) and *The Three Caballeros* (1945), which featured a cocky Amazonian parrot named José Carioca. Even **Fred Astaire** was coaxed into paying his Latin dues, starring opposite **Rita Hayworth** in *You Were Never Lovelier* (1942) – which reworked Argentinian Francisco Múgica's musical, *Los Martes orquídeas* (*On Tuesday's Orchids*, 1941) – and opposite **Lucille Bremer** in *Yolanda And The Thief* (1945, see Canon).

When they weren't insinuating that Brazilians and Hispanics danced at the drop of a sombrero, the studios were busy confounding the old **Latin lover caricature** by having clean-cut Yankees such as Richard Carlson, John Payne and Philip Terry win the romantic battle in *Too Many Girls* (1940), *Coney Island* and *Pan Americana* (both 1943). But at least Cesar Romero and Desi Arnaz were allowed to pursue the leading lady – African-American stars were usually barred from even sharing the same frame with them.

Hollywood seemingly saw no irony in encouraging black GIs to do their bit for racial democracy, while **segregating black actors**. Bing Crosby and African-American actress Louise Beavers were kept in separate rooms for "Abraham" in *Holiday Inn* and the Golden Gate Quartet's "The General Jumped At Dawn" was cut from the Deep South print of *Hollywood Canteen* (1944). While the studios were consciously wooing their Latin neighbours and chastizing the Nazis for their anti-Semitism, no one batted an eyelid at the ghettoizing of such talented black performers as Buck and Bubbles, Maxine Sullivan, **Ella Fitzgerald**, Count Basie, **Dorothy Dandridge**, Duke Ellington, **Louis Armstrong**, Nat King Cole and the Nicholas Brothers.

**Lena Horne** was similarly marginalized in the likes of *I Dood It* (1943) and *Swing Fever* (1944), although she also headlined the **all-black musicals** *Cabin In The Sky* and *Stormy Weather* (both 1943). Such duplicity epitomized the "separate but equal" doctrine that blighted so-called liberal thinking in America well into the 1960s. MGM's glossy *Cabin In The Sky*, was a significant improvement on the likes of Warner Bros' *The Green Pastures* (1936). Yet it still brimmed with condescending **stereotypes**, spiritual platitudes and a simplistic sense of romanticized communalism. Fox's offering, *Stormy Weather*, was equally impolitic. Resembling other wartime wallows in its nostalgia, it was packed with hits from black shows dating back to the 1920s, but they didn't really reflect the contemporary African-American experience – and the climactic concert sequence cringingly reinforced the **black rhythm myth**.

There was rarely anything subtle about 20th Century-Fox's musicals in this period. **Alice Faye** soldiered on in the likes of *The Great American Broadcast* (1941) and *Hello Frisco, Hello* (1943). But she had already been eclipsed by the studio's new blonde bombshell, **Betty Grable**, who tended to sock over her numbers, whether she was appearing in contemporary entertainments such as *Moon Over Miami*, *A Yank In The RAF* (both 1941) and *Song Of The Islands* (1942) or costume pictures like *Tin Pan Alley* (1940), *Coney Island* and *Sweet Rosie O'Grady* (both 1943).

Hollywood harked back to the good old days in several other wartime musicals, including *For Me And My Gal* (1942), *Minstrel Man* and *Show Business* (both 1944). This vogue for the past could also be seen in the proliferation of **biopics**, of Stephen Foster (*Swanee River*, 1939), George M. Cohan (*Yankee Doodle Dandy*, 1942, see Canon), Ernest R. Ball (*Irish Eyes Are Smiling*, 1944), George Gershwin (*Rhapsody In Blue*, 1945) and Cole Porter (*Night And Day*, 1946). Furthermore, lots of old **Broadway shows** were revived and revved up, including *Irene* (1940), *No, No Nanette, Sunny* (both 1941), *Panama Hattie* (1942), *Girl Crazy*, *Let's Face It*, *DuBarry Was A Lady* and *Best Foot Forward* (all 1943), while the **Frank Sinatra** vehicle, *Step Lively* (1944), was adapted from the 1938 Marx Brothers comedy, *Room Service*.

George Murphy, Judy Garland and a debuting Gene Kelly do their bit in the flagwaving musical *For Me And My Gal* (1942).

Even **operetta** did its stuff for the war effort, with **Nelson Eddy** starring in *The Chocolate*

*Soldier* (1941), Kathryn Grayson supporting Abbott and Costello in *Rio Rita* (1942) and Dennis Morgan using music to keep the Riff rebels on side in *The Desert Song* (1944). **Jeanette MacDonald** made similarly ingenious use of her voice in *Cairo* (1942), in which her perfect high C exposed a secret hideout and Nazi plans for a robot bomber. Several **classical musicians** also volunteered their services, including Jascha Heifetz (*They Shall Have Music*, 1939), Leopold Stokowski (*Fantasia*, 1940) and José Iturbi, whose appearances in *Music For Millions* and *Two Girls And A Sailor* (both 1944) were overshadowed by his collaboration with **Judy Garland** on "The Joint Is Really Jumpin' Down At Carnegie Hall" in *Thousands Cheer* (1943).

Bandleaders were also keen to be seen stepping up to the plate. Over thirty **bandstand pictures** were made during the war, featuring the likes of Benny Goodman, Xavier Cugat, Bob Crosby, Harry James and Glenn Miller (who stole both *Sun Valley Serenade*, 1941, and *Orchestra Wives*, 1942). The **Dorsey brothers**, Jimmy and Tommy, were also much in demand, especially as one of Tommy's vocalists in *Las Vegas Nights* (1941) and *Ship Ahoy* (1942) was **Frank Sinatra**. However, the most genial frontman was **Kay Kyser**, who made eight films between 1939 and 1944, with Ginny Simms singing a host of hits in such pleasingly offbeat outings as *That's Right, You're Wrong* (1939), *You'll Find Out* (1940) and *Around The World* (1943).

Virtually the entire genre devoted itself to winning the war. Purely **escapist fare** was still being produced, most notably the marvellous *Road To…* movies starring Bing Crosby, **Bob Hope** and **Dorothy Lamour**: *Singapore* (1940), *Zanzibar* (1941), *Morocco* (1942), *Utopia* (1945), *Rio* (1947), *Bali* (1952) and *Hong Kong* (1962). But everyone else seemed to be in uniform, whether it was Fred Astaire in *You'll Never Get Rich* (1941) and *The Sky's The Limit* (1943), **Gene Kelly** in *Thousands Cheer* and *Anchors Aweigh* (1945), Danny Kaye and Dinah Shore in *Up In Arms* (1944), or Joan Leslie in *This Is The Army* and *Here Come The Waves*. Even the vital work of the munitions factories was acknowledged in *Rosie The Riveter* (1944), *Melody Parade* (1943) and *Star Spangled Rhythm* (1942), in the latter of which **Betty Hutton** declared "I'm Doing It For The Defence", while Marjorie Reynolds, Betty Rhodes and Dona Drake went "On The Swing Shift".

*Star Spangled Rhythm* was one of several **all-star spectacles** produced by the studios to show that even Hollywood's biggest names were actively backing Uncle Sam. Numerous celebrities supported the United Services Organization (**USO**) by performing in boot camps at home, as well as on the "foxhole circuit" overseas, to entertain the troops. Among the many were Bob Hope, Judy Garland, Betty Grable, Al Jolson, Lena Horne and Marlene Dietrich.

Those who stayed behind were also eager to chip in. Paramount's *Star Spangled Rhythm* and *The Fleet's In* (both 1942) launched the trend for **patriotic revues**, and Warner Bros quickly followed suit with *Thank Your Lucky Stars* (1943), which featured **Errol Flynn** singing "That's What They Jolly Well Get" and Bette Davis delighting audiences with the Oscar-nominated "They're Either Too Young Or Too Old". Six bands and fifty stars shared the bill in United Artists' *Stage Door Canteen* (1943), while **Bette Davis** resurfaced in *Hollywood Canteen* (1944), in which singing cowboy **Roy Rogers** introduced "Don't Fence Me In". *This Is the Army, Thousands Cheer* (both 1943), *Hey, Rookie, Two Girls And A Sailor, Follow The Boys, Here Come The Waves* (all 1944) and *Duffy's Tavern* (1945) also exploited the **vaudeville** format. As did *Four Jills And A Jeep* (1944), which related the real-life, frontline adventures of stars Kay Francis, Carole Landis, Martha Raye and Mitzi Mayfair – although fellow USO veterans disapproved of them courting publicity from what was supposed to be a selfless exercise.

Surprisingly, little musical fuss was made of the victors' homecoming. **Frank Sinatra** played a returning GI opposite **Kathryn Grayson** in *It Happened In Brooklyn* (1947). But while *Tars And Spars* (1946), *On The Town* (1949, see Canon), *At War With The Army*, *The West Point Story* (both 1950), *G.I. Jane* (1951) and *Three Sailors And A Girl* (1953) all centred around men in uniform, few followed *It's Always Fair Weather* (1955) in exploring the problems of **reintegration**. Hollywood's true attitude to all those flagwavers was rather betrayed by "South America, Take It Away" in *Call Me Mister* (1951), in which Betty Grable's character complains about getting backache from all that Good Neighbour dancing.

A **new generation of stars** had emerged during the war years. Betty Hutton, June Allyson, Ann Miller, Esther Williams, Vera-Ellen, Cyd Charisse, June Haver, June Havoc, Jane Powell, Betty Garrett, Ann Blyth and Jeanne Crain all seemed to exude cheerfulness, kindness and approachability. Futhermore, **Donald O'Connor**, Danny Kaye, Frank Sinatra and Gene Kelly had exhibited a versatility that suggested the genre was in good hands, as it rose to the challenge thrown down by Rodgers and Hammerstein's 1943 landmark Broadway show, *Oklahoma!*.

### Tin Pan Alley
**dir Walter Lang, 1940, 94m, b/w**

Although Alfred Newman's score won an Oscar and Leon Shamroy's photography is superb, the highlight of this nostalgic flagwaver is Seymour Felix's staging of "The Sheik Of Araby" as a saucy vehicle for Alice Faye, Betty Grable and Billy Gilbert – although the Breen Office censors insisted on trimming some of the scantily clad antics. Fox crammed in the period hits, as the singing Blane sisters (Faye and Grable) love and lose songwriters John Payne and Jack Oakie before reuniting during the Great War.

### For Me And My Gal
**dir Busby Berkeley, 1942, 104m, b/w**

Bobby Connolly played to the 30-year-old Gene Kelly's exuberant strengths in choreographing his screen debut. Twenty-one days of retakes were required to remove the *Pal Joey*-esque cynicism and guarantee a morale-boosting hit, in which Kelly's ambitious hoofer comes between vaudevillians Judy Garland and George Murphy, and has to prove himself in the trenches before making it big on Broadway.

### The Sky's The Limit
**dir Edward H. Griffith, 1943, 89m, b/w**

Fred Astaire escaped the white tie and tails for this unlikely tale of a Flying Tiger who falls in love with photographer Joan Leslie while AWOL from a wartime glory tour. He dances divinely to such Harold Arlen and Johnny Mercer numbers as "One For My Baby (And One More For The Road)" and "My Shining Hour", but his snake dance with Robert Ryan is best forgotten.

### Thousands Cheer
**dir George Sidney, 1943, 126m**

MGM roll-called the stars for this flagwaver, which fashions a romance between private Gene Kelly and colonel's daughter Kathryn Grayson as the preamble to a revue finale. The highlights are Lena Horne's "Honeysuckle Rose" and Judy Garland's "The Joint Is Really Jumpin' Down At Carnegie Hall". Eleanor Powell also contributes a typically electrifying tap routine, but the most imaginative choreography can be found in Kelly's "Mop Dance", which established his genius for performing with idiosyncratic props.

### This Is The Army
**dir Michael Curtiz, 1943, 121m**

Disney produced the five most successful musicals of the 1940s, but this brazenly patriotic adaptation of Irving

Berlin's 1942 show came in sixth (although its profits went to the war effort). George Murphy and Ronald Reagan play the father and son who pen patriotic productions in each of the World Wars, but the plotline was almost an irrelevance beside the mass-ranked production numbers and solo slots like Berlin's "Oh, How I Hate To Get Up In The Morning" and Kate Smith's "God Bless America".

### Hollywood Canteen
**dir Delmer Daves, 1944, 124m, b/w**

Warner Bros corralled their A-listers for another bout of morale boosting in this hugely successful revue, built around the fuss made of the Canteen nightclub's millionth visitor, Robert Hutton, and his crush on actress Joan Leslie. The musical highlight is Roy Rogers' performance of Cole Porter's "Don't Fence Me In", but the Oscar nomination went to M.K. Jerome and Ted Koehler's "Sweet Dreams Sweetheart", sung by Kitty Carlisle.

### Where Do We Go From Here?
**dir Gregory Ratoff, 1945, 77m**

An undervalued Kurt Weill and Ira Gershwin score sustains this innovative recruiting picture, in which rejected enlistee Fred MacMurray has his wishes granted by bungling genie Gene Sheldon. He travels back in time to assist Washington at Valley Forge, Columbus en route to the New World (cue the jovially operatic "The Nina, The Pinta And The Santa Maria") and the Dutch in the purchase of Manhattan from the Hackensack Indians, while Joan Leslie and June Haver compete for his affections.

# The Golden Age of MGM

## The Freed Unit

While Hollywood was doing its bit for the war effort, Broadway was revolutionizing the musical. With *Oklahoma!* (1943) and *Carousel* (1945), composer **Richard Rodgers** and lyricist **Oscar Hammerstein** replaced the musical comedy with the musical drama. They also integrated the songs into the action, so that they commented upon the storyline or revealed something about a character's psyche. They also incorporated "dream ballets" into both musicals, which brought a new **artistic intensity** to a genre that had always prioritized escapist entertainment.

Hollywood was suitably impressed. **Ernst Lubitsch** and **Rouben Mamoulian** had attempted something similar with *The Love Parade* (1929, see Canon) and *Love Me Tonight* (1932, see Canon). But these pioneering pictures had rather got lost in the heady chaos that surrounded the coming of sound and the new formulae that concentrated on showcase and spectacle. However, by the mid-1940s, one producer at **MGM** was convinced that the genre's future lay in unashamedly artistic combinations of music and movement, colour and chic, star performance and emotional authenticity. He was **Arthur Freed**, and he was to dominate the screen musical for the next decade.

Arthur Freed's great gift lay in recognizing talent and affording those blessed with it the freedom and the means to attain their vision. He gathered around him a cabal of skilled professionals, who became known as the **Freed Unit**. They included high-calibre performers such as **Fred**

**Astaire**, Judy Garland, **Gene Kelly**, Cyd Charisse, Frank Sinatra and Leslie Caron. Among the directors were Busby Berkeley, Rouben Mamoulian, Vincente Minnelli, **Stanley Donen** and Charles Walters, while choreographers included Robert Alton and Nick Castle, as well as Astaire and **Hermes Pan**, Kelly and Donen, and their selfless assistants, Carol Haney and Jeanne Coyne.

MGM's principal art director **Cedric Gibbons** frequently collaborated with Broadway innovators like Lemuel Ayers, Preston Ames and Jack Martin Smith on Freed pictures. Their **sets** were invariably decorated by Edwin B. Willis, while the **costumes** were designed by Irene, Adrian, Irene Sharaff and Walter Plunkett. Then there were the many **unsung perfectionists**, such as hair stylist Sidney Guilaroff, make-up artist William Tuttle, sound recording director Douglas Shearer, editors Albert Akst and Adrienne Fazan, cinematographers Harry Stradling, Ray June, Charles Rosher, Harold Rosson and George Folsey, and special effects guru, Warren Newcombe. The **maestros**

Serafin (Gene Kelly) the troubadour hypnotizes Caribbean dreamer Manuela (Judy Garland) and unleashes her passion for the buccaneering Macoco in *The Pirate* (1948).

behind the magnificent music included Andre Previn, George Stoll, Adolph Deutsch, George Bassman, Conrad Salinger, Johnny Green, Saul Chaplin and Lennie Hayton, while overseeing every last detail was Freed's loyal lieutenant, **Roger Edens**.

Having served as Ethel Merman's arranger and accompanist, Edens joined MGM in 1934. Fresh from adapting the Arthur Freed and Nacio Herb Brown numbers for *Broadway Melody Of 1936*, he came to the attention of studio chief **Louis B. Mayer** by coaching Judy Garland through a performance of "You Made Me Love You" for Clark Gable's birthday party (the routine eventually found its way into *Broadway Melody Of 1938* as "Dear Mr Gable"). Edens received the first of his eight Oscar nominations for best score for Freed's solo producing debut, *Babes In Arms* (1939), and thereafter became a key figure in the Unit's success, whether supervising the staging and recording of numbers with Kay Thompson or Lela Simone, or writing them in collaboration with Hugh Martin, James Monaco or **Betty Comden** and **Adolph Green**.

Comden and Green were vital members of the Freed Unit, as in addition to songs, they also produced the screenplays for *Good News* (1947), *On The Town* (1949, see Canon), *The Barkleys Of Broadway* (1949), *Singin' In The Rain* (1952, see Canon), *The Band Wagon* (1953, see Canon), *It's*

## Top-grossing MGM musicals

This chart of the fifty highest grossing MGM musicals makes for revealing reading – if only because it confirms that while **Arthur Freed** (AF) may have cornered the market in prestige, the pictures churned out by second-string producers **Joe Pasternak** (JP) and **Jack Cummings** (JC) were often more popular with the public. Indeed, it's fascinating to note how poorly many of the critically acclaimed **Freed Unit** films performed in comparison with the more populist hits.

Of the studio heavyweights, **Gene Kelly** figures in twelve titles, but was the principal star in only five. Half of **Judy Garland**'s eight entries were guest slots, while **Fred Astaire** could muster only two starring vehicles among his tally of five outings. Intriguingly, MGM's runaway box-office champion was **Esther Williams**. She starred in twelve of the top fifty features, which amassed a staggering $38,100,000. However, if you add in her archive clips in the two *That's Entertainment!* compilations, she contributes (albeit in small part) to another $22,100,000. The "Million Dollar Mermaid" may not have been the studio's most gifted star, but she was clearly its most aptly named.

**1** *That's Entertainment!* (1974) $19,100,000

**2** *Victor/Victoria* (1982) $10,500,000

**3** *The Unsinkable Molly Brown* (1964) $7,700,500

**4** *Gigi* (1958; AF) $7,300,000

**5** *I'll Cry Tomorrow* (1955) $6,500,000

**6** *High Society* (1956) $6,500,000

**7** *Meet Me In St Louis* (1944; AF) $5,200,000

**8** *Show Boat* (1951; AF) $5,200,000

**9** *Seven Brides For Seven Brothers* (1954; JC) $5,000,000

**10** *The Wonderful World Of The Brothers Grimm* (1962) $4,800,000

**11** *Till The Clouds Roll By* (1946; AF) $4,700,000

**12** *Anchors Aweigh* (1945; JP) $4,600,000

**13** *The Great Caruso* (1951; JP) $4,500,000

**14** *An American In Paris* (1951; AF) $4,500,000

**15** *Thrill Of A Romance* (1945; JP) $4,400,000

**16** *Easter Parade* (1948; AF) $4,200,000

*Always Fair Weather* (1955) and the Unit's last musical, *Bells Are Ringing* (1960). Screenwriter and lyricist **Alan Jay Lerner** also chipped in with the scripts for *An American In Paris* (1951, see Canon), *Royal Wedding* (1951), *Brigadoon* (1954) and *Gigi* (1958, see Canon).

But it didn't matter which combination of talent Freed assembled. His musicals always bore a **touch of class** that has ensured their longevity, whether they were original items like *Meet Me In St Louis* (1944, see Canon) *Ziegfeld Follies* (1945), *Yolanda And The Thief* (1945, see Canon), *The Pirate*, *Easter Parade* (both 1948, see Canon), *Take Me Out To The Ball Game* (1949), *Pagan Love Song* (1950), *Invitation To The Dance* (1956) and *Silk Stockings* (1957, see Canon) or **Broadway adaptations** such as *Annie Get Your Gun* (1950, see Canon), *Show Boat* (1951), *The Belle Of New York* (1952) and *Kismet* (1955).

Although Freed became the critics' darling for bringing a new depth and refinement to the musical, his pictures weren't always appreciated by the average American. As the list of top-grossing MGM musicals (see box below) reveals, producers **Joe Pasternak** and Jack Cummings were every bit as prolific and often more profitable than Freed, despite managing less presigious units at MGM.

The Hungarian-born Pasternak had cut his teeth as an assistant director at Paramount in

**17** *Annie Get Your Gun* (1950; AF) $4,200,000
**18** *Easy To Wed* (1946; JC) $4,100,000
**19** *The Harvey Girls* (1946; AF) $4,100,000
**20** *Love Me Or Leave Me* (1955; JP) $4,100,000
**21** *San Francisco* (1936) $3,800,000
**22** *Holiday In Mexico* (1946; JP) $3,700,000
**23** *A Date With Judy* (1948; JP) $3,700,000
**24** *The Singing Nun* (1966) $3,700,000
**25** *Ziegfeld Follies* (1946; AF) $3,600,000
**26** *Two Sisters From Boston* (1946; JP) $3,600,000
**27** *This Time For Keeps* (1947; JP) $3,600,000
**28** *Singin' In The Rain* (1952; AF) $3,600,000
**29** *Thousands Cheer* (1943; JP) $3,500,000
**30** *Bathing Beauty* (1944; JC) $3,500,000
**31** *Two Girls And A Sailor* (1944; JP) $3,500,000
**32** *Fiesta* (1947; JC) $3,500,000
**33** *Words And Music* (1948; AF) $3,500,000
**34** *Deep In My Heart* (1954) $3,500,000
**35** *Neptune's Daughter* (1949; JC) $3,450,000
**36** *Maytime* (1937) $3,400,000
**37** *Take Me Out To The Ball Game* (1949; AF) $3,400,000
**38** *In The Good Old Summertime* (1949; JP) $3,400,000
**39** *On An Island With You* (1948; JP) $3,200,000
**40** *The Barkleys Of Broadway* (1948; AF) $3,200,000
**41** *The Broadway Melody* (1929) $3,000,000
**42** *The Great Ziegfeld* (1936) $3,000,000
**43** *Sweethearts* (1938) $3,000,000
**44** *Girl Crazy* (1943; AF) $3,000,000
**45** *That's Entertainment, Part 2* (1976) $3,000,000
**46** *On The Town* (1949; AF) $2,900,000
**47** *Three Little Words* (1950; JC) $2,800,000
**48** *Million Dollar Mermaid* (1952) $2,750,000
**49** *Les Girls* (1957) $2,750,000
**50** *The Duchess Of Idaho* (1950; JP) $2,600,000

the 1920s. His crowning achievement as a producer was the salvation of Universal Studios in conjunction with Deanna Durbin a decade later, although some also credit him with the discovery of **Judy Garland**. He worked with Garland three times after joining MGM as a producer in 1942, on *Presenting Lily Mars* (1943), *In The Good Old Summertime* (1949) and *Summer Stock* (1950). (The latter turned out to be her last picture for the studio, as drug and mental health problems began to take hold.)

Pasternak was also responsible for teaming Gene Kelly with the cartoon character Jerry Mouse in *Anchors Aweigh* (1945), for popularizing light opera with Mario Lanza, and for turning **Esther Williams** (see p.231) into the most successful speciality act in Hollywood history. He also kept such dependables as Cyd Charisse, June Allyson, Ann Miller, Debbie Reynolds, Virginia O'Brien, Van Johnson and Gloria DeHaven gainfully employed between Freed assignments.

The nephew of Louis B. Mayer, **Jack Cummings** rose through the studio ranks, before moving into feature-length musicals with **Eleanor Powell** vehicles such as *Born To Dance* (1936), *Honolulu* (1939), *Ship Ahoy* (1942) and *I Dood It* (1943). He also worked frequently with Esther Williams, as well as such full-throated singers as Jane Powell, Kathryn Grayson and Howard Keel. In addition to remaking his father-in-law Jerome Kern's *Roberta* as *Lovely To Look At* (1952), Cummings also sponsored the works of **less-vaunted directors**, such as George Sidney's *Kiss Me Kate*, (1953, see Canon), Stanley Donen's *Seven Brides For Seven Brothers* (1954, see Canon) and Walter Lang's *Can-Can* (1960). He was one of the few veterans of the Golden Age to survive into the rock era, co-producing **Elvis Presley**'s *Viva Las Vegas* (1964) with director George Sidney.

### The Barkleys Of Broadway
**dir Charles Walters, 1949, 109m**

Judy Garland's indisposition resulted in Fred Astaire and Ginger Rogers reuniting for their sole colour outing, as a dance team parted by her thesping ambitions. They reprised "They Can't Take That Away From Me" and further evoked the olden days with "You'd Be Hard To Replace". But the majority of Harry Warren and Ira Gershwin's numbers occurred within show contexts, and Hermes Pan and Robert Alton's choreography lacked the intimacy of previous pairings. It's still irresistible, especially when a solo Astaire dances with six disembodied pairs of feet to "Shoes With Wings On".

### Show Boat
**dir George Sidney, 1951, 107m**

Arthur Freed tinkered with the text and overdid the grandeur on this remake of Jerome Kern and Oscar Hammerstein's timeless masterpiece. Nonetheless, Kathryn Grayson and Howard Keel sound as good as Charles Rosher's photography and Jack Martin Smith's artwork look. Ava Gardner and William Warfield are moving as Julie and Joe, while Marge and Gower Champion provide some pep, with thanks to Robert Alton's choreography.

### It's Always Fair Weather
**dir Gene Kelly, Stanley Donen, 1955, 102m**

Originally planned as a sequel to *On The Town* (1949, see Canon) this sour insight into the musical in crisis and the self-doubt gripping Cold War America shocked critics and audiences with its cynicism. Yet it's strongly played by Gene Kelly, Dan Dailey and Michael Kidd – as the reuniting army buddies who settle their differences while stymieing some prizefight crooks – and their split-screen and bin-lid stomp routines are splendid. As is Kelly's rollerskating set piece to "I Like Myself". But their thunder is stolen by Cyd Charisse on the vibrant "Baby, You Knock Me Out" and Dolores Gray on the deliciously dismissive "Thanks A Lot, But No Thanks".

## In the shadow of MGM

Faced with such a torrent of excellence from MGM in the **post-war period**, the rest of Hollywood was left with little option but to imitate as budgets would allow. Having splashed his cash on Eddie Cantor in the early 1930s, independent producer **Samuel Goldwyn** was similarly prepared to invest heavily to ensure the success of his latest protégé, all-round entertainer **Danny Kaye**. But, like Cantor, Kaye was more at home before a live audience than a movie camera. A veteran of the so-called borscht circuit of the resorts in the Catskill Mountains, Kaye toured more in hope than expectation in the 1930s.But his fortunes changed after he married songwriter **Sylvia Fine** and he was soon appearing in Broadway shows like *Lady In The Dark* (1940) and *Let's Face It* (1941). In addition to plotting her husband's career (Kaye once admitted to being "a wife-made man"), Fine also developed his genius for tongue-twisting lyrics in the hundred or more songs she produced for him during their forty-year partnership.

Having debuted on screen in *Up In Arms* (1944), Kaye forged a popular partnership with actress **Virginia Mayo** in *Wonder Man* (1945), *The Kid From Brooklyn* (1946), *The Secret Life Of Walter Mitty* (1947) and *A Song Is Born* (1948). But while his cabaret tours continued to draw bumper crowds on both sides of the Atlantic, Kaye's musical comedies like *The Inspector General* (1949), *On The Riviera* (1951), *Knock On Wood* (1954) and *The Court Jester* (1956) captured only a fraction of his genial versatility. Today, his best-loved offerings are *Hans Christian Andersen* (1952) and *White Christmas* (1954), in which he co-starred with **Bing Crosby**, who had rather lost his musical way in the years after the war.

Crosby was still one of America's most popular singing stars, but he was keen to demonstrate his versatility after winning an Oscar for *Going My Way* (1944). He continued to make musicals into the 1960s. But with **Paramount** being unable to match MGM's budgets, outings like

All-round entertainer Danny Kaye (centre) starred with Rosemary Clooney and Bing Crosby in *White Christmas* (1954), one of his best-loved film musicals.

*The Emperor Waltz* (1948), *A Connecticut Yankee In King Arthur's Court* (1949), *Mr Music* (1950), the Frank Capra duo of *Riding High* (1950) and *Here Comes The Groom* (1951), and the remake of *Anything Goes* (1956) proved amiable, but unremarkable entertainment. But Crosby's best 1950s project was *High Society* (1956, see Canon), in which he was teamed with **Frank Sinatra**, who succeeded him as the "King of Croon". However, Sinatra was keen to shake his image as a **bobbysoxer icon** and to prove his worth as a dramatic actor. Consequently, his appearances in musicals like *Guys And Dolls* (1955, see Canon) and *Pal Joey* (1957) became increasingly rare as he sought to extend his range.

Like Sinatra, **Rita Hayworth** was keen to tackle weightier material than musicals. However, **Columbia** chief **Harry Cohn** was determined to present his biggest star as an all-rounder. Thus, while he was happy for her to attempt challenging non-musicals like *Gilda* (1946) – in which she lip-synched provocatively to Anita Ellis's rendition of "Put The Blame On Mame" – he also insisted that she headlined such mediocre musicals as *Tonight And Every Night* (1946) and *Down To Earth* (1947). Hayworth reluctantly went along with Cohn's plans, but at MGM, **Judy Garland** kicked once too often against the studio's strict system and they terminated her contract in 1950. **Warner Bros** offered Garland an opportunity to rebuild her reputation in *A Star Is Born* (1954, see Canon), only to discard her despite her poignant performance and Oscar nomination, and her screen career collapsed.

Instead, Warner Bros decided to concentrate its efforts on rising star **Doris Day** (see p.197), who had followed her debut in *Romance On The High Seas* (1948) with girl-next-door outings opposite Dennis Morgan, Jack Carson and **Gordon MacRae**. In the early 1950s, she was teamed with more musical partners, like Ray Bolger in *April In Paris* (1952), **Howard Keel** in *Calamity Jane* (1953) and Frank Sinatra in *Young At Heart* (1954). But, by the time she made *The Pajama Game* (1957, see Canon), Day had begun to take non-musical roles and was soon ensconced in the **Ross Hunter sex comedies** for which she is now best known.

Paramount and 20th Century-Fox also put their faith in **new blonde stars**. But while the vivacious **Betty Hutton** (see p.243) could never be accused of selling audiences short in her pictures for Paramount, she failed to win their hearts. She split from the studio after it refused to allow her choreographer husband, Charles Curran, to direct her films and wound up working as a cook in a Rhode Island rectory before suffering a nervous breakdown. Fox similarly pinned their hopes on **Marilyn Monroe**, who was equally fragile, but she was also more successfully manipulative. She soon graduated from musicals like *Gentlemen Prefer Blondes* (1953) and *There's No Business Like Show Business* (1954) to more momentous melodramas, although she also sang memorably in *Some Like It Hot* (1958) and *Let's Make Love* (1960). Similarly, Fox were unsure how best to exploit vaudeville star **June Havoc** (the sister of Gypsy Rose Lee, whose career was celebrated in 1962's *Gypsy*). Therefore, she only made occasional musicals, like the costume picture *When My Baby Smiles At Me* (1948).

This adaptation of the much-filmed play, *Burlesque*, also starred **Betty Grable**, who remained Fox's most bankable musical star for a decade after the war. She exuded energy and geniality, whether headlining contemporary items like *Billy Rose's Diamond Horseshoe* (1945), *My Blue Heaven* (1950) and *Meet Me After The Show* (1951) or period pieces like *Mother Wore Tights* (1947), *Wabash Avenue* (1950) and *The Farmer Takes A*

*Wife* (1953). She teamed up with another blonde, **June Haver**, in *The Dolly Sisters* (1945). Haver, who was being groomed as Grable's successor, sparkled briefly in such shameless exercises in **feel-good nostalgia** as *I Wonder Who's Kissing Her Now?* (1947), *Oh, You Beautiful Doll*, the Marilyn Miller biopic *Look For The Silver Lining*, (both 1949) and *The Daughter Of Rosie O'Grady* (1950), but she never matched Grable's popularity. Haver quit the movies in 1953 to enter a convent, but emerged seven and a half months later and married Fred MacMurray, her co-star in the undervalued *Where Do We Go From Here?* (1945).

Fox's fondness for **Americana** chimed in with the post-war populace's need to hark back to a more innocent and reassuring age – one without concentration camps, Communists and atom bombs. But while MGM produced such tasteful evocations of the past as the **Judy Garland vehicles** *Meet Me In St Louis*, *The Harvey Girls* (1946) and *In The Good Old Summertime* (1949), as well as the undervalued *Summer Holiday* (1948, see Canon), Fox responded with a series of more typically brash **Jeanne Crain** outings, including Rodgers and Hammerstein's sole screen original, *State Fair*, plus *Centennial Summer*, *Margie* (all 1946) and *You Were Meant For Me* (1948).

By the early 1950s, with the increasingly suburbanized population preferring to stay at home in front of the television or pursue other leisure activities, Hollywood had to devise new ways to lure **audiences** into cinemas. Therefore, the studios filmed a growing number of musicals in widescreen, colour and stereo. Yet screen soundtracks remained resolutely rooted in the past, because few studios retained in-house songwriters. It was cheaper either to adapt or remake **pre-sold hits** from stage or screen – most notably Rodgers and Hammerstein's *Oklahoma!* (1955, see Canon), *Carousel*, *The King And I* (both 1956, see Canon) and *South Pacific* (1957, see Canon) – or to make **biopics** of popular performers and songwriters whose back catalogues were handled by the studios' own publishing houses.

Facts were often an irrelevance in these fanciful biographies. For example, Evelyn Keyes and Barbara Hale played entirely fictitious wives in *The Jolson Story* (1946) and *Jolson Sings Again* (1949), and the sexual preferences of **Cole Porter** and **Lorenz Hart** were glossed over in *Night And Day* (1946) and *Words And Music* (1948). If a composer's life lacked the lustre of his songbook, the factual elements were played down in favour of an all-star revue, as was the case with MGM's tributes to Jerome Kern (*Till The Clouds Roll By*, 1946) and Sigmund Romberg (*Deep In My Heart*, 1954).

In some instances, the songs were better known than the individual composers, as with the profiles of Bert Kalmer and Harry Ruby (*Three Little Words*, 1950), Gus Kahn (*I'll See You In My Dreams*, 1951) and De Sylva, Brown and Henderson (*The Best Things In Life Are Free*, 1956). With the notable exception of *The Glenn Miller Story* (1954), the same was true of the **biopics of instrumentalists** like Red Nichols (*The Five Pennies*, 1959). But some of the more celebrated performers were better served, with Esther Williams gliding through Annette Kellerman's rise from swimming champion to showbiz icon in *Million Dollar Mermaid* (1952), **Eleanor Parker** exuding graceful courage as polio-afflicted diva Marjorie Lawrence in *Interrupted Melody* and **Bob Hope** revelling in the role of vaudevillian Eddie Foy in *The Seven Little Foys* (both 1955).

However, audiences eventually began to tire of the sound of scraped barrels. The memory lane musical had been inspired by the need to avoid taking box-office risks, as the studios reorganized themselves after the Supreme Court's 1948 decision to strip them of their theatre chains, and thus end the policy of block-booking that had ensured that every picture produced in Hollywood was guaranteed screen time. The inauguration of the so-called **Paramount Decrees** also coincided with changes in viewing habits and the shattering of the musical consensus by the arrival of **rock'n'roll**.

The concept of **family entertainment** had begun to fragment by the mid-1950s. Consequently, musicals like *Nancy Goes To Rio, Two Weeks Without Love* (both 1950), *I Love Melvin* (1953), *Red Garters* (1954), *Happy Go Lovely, Let's Be Happy, The Girl Most Likely* (all 1957) and *Say One For Me* (1959), which were as twee as their titles suggested, failed to appeal to either teenagers or their parents. Brassy and classy offerings similarly struggled to find audiences, with *Call Me Madam* (1953), *Damn Yankees* (1958) and *L'il Abner* (1959) making as little box-office headway as *Carmen Jones* (1954) and *Porgy And Bess* (1959).

Moreover, the genre's biggest names had begun to seek fresh challenges, and Gene Kelly (*Les Girls*), Fred Astaire (*Funny Face*, see Canon) and Frank Sinatra (*The Joker Is Wild*) all made what amounted to their **musical swan songs** in 1957. The Freed Unit enjoyed a final salvo the following year, with *Gigi* (see Canon) converting all nine of its Oscar nominations. But, by then, MGM's biggest musical star was a former truck driver from Tupelo, Mississippi, who, in 1953, had told the engineer at Sun Records in Memphis, as he paid $5 to record a two-sided disc for his mother's birthday, "I don't sing like nobody".

### State Fair
**dir Walter Lang, 1945, 100m**

Rodgers and Hammerstein produced their only original screen score for this musicalization of the 1933 Will Rogers vehicle of the same name. Leon Shamroy's gleaming photography enhances the feel-good Americana of this tale of a homely family's sojourn to Iowa. The soundtrack boasts the Oscar-winning "It Might As Well Be Spring" (on which Jeanne Crain was dubbed by Louanne Hogan), as well as such rousing ensemble numbers as "Our State Fair" and "All I Owe Ioway".

### Words And Music
**dir Norman Taurog, 1948, 119m**

Although few analogies could be drawn between this biographical fantasy starring Tom Drake and Mickey Rooney and the real lives of songwriters Richard Rodgers and Lorenz Hart, MGM staged the duo's greatest hits with customary panache. Gene Kelly and Vera-Ellen's enactment of "Slaughter On Tenth Avenue" is masterly, while Lena Horne and June Allyson excel on "The Lady Is A Tramp" and "Thou Swell", respectively. Rooney also shows well in "Manhattan" and in his reunion with Judy Garland, "I Wish I Were In Love Again".

### Carmen Jones
**dir Otto Preminger, 1954, 105m**

It's customary to decry Fox's screen adaptation of Oscar Hammerstein's 1943 reworking of Georges Bizet's opera, as four of the principals (Dorothy Dandridge, Harry Belafonte, Joe Adams and Diahann Carroll) all had their singing voices dubbed. Yet this remains an exhilarating experience, with the score throbbing with emotion and life – none more so than when Pearl Bailey lets rip on "Beat Out Dat Rhythm On A Drum".

### There's No Business Like Show Business
**dir Walter Lang, 1954, 117m**

Ethel Merman, Dan Dailey, Donald O'Connor, Mitzi Gaynor and a cringingly miscast Johnnie Ray make up the Irish vaudeville family, The Five Donahues, in Fox's typically brash dip into the Irving Berlin songbook. But Marilyn Monroe's showgirl hogs the limelight with Jack Cole's "Heat Wave" and "After You Get It You Don't Want It", before the ensemble reunites for Robert Alton's multi-accented trot through the title track.

**White Christmas**
**dir Michael Curtiz, 1954, 120m**

Bing Crosby and Danny Kaye were teamed in this sentimental variation on *Holiday Inn* (1942), in which two war veterans stage a benefit for their old general. The stars dress in drag to lampoon Rosemary Clooney and Vera-Ellen in "Sisters", but the score isn't Irving Berlin's most distinguished and Robert Alton's staging of the dance numbers is pretty lame. Nevertheless, *White Christmas* remains the fifth highest-grossing musical of all time.

## Don't knock the rock

Contrary to popular belief, **Elvis Presley** (see p.224) was not the first rocker to make movies. A major influence on several rock pioneers, **Louis Jordan** had headlined a trio of musical B-movies for Paramount in the late 1940s – *Beware* (1946), *Reet, Petite And Gone* (1947) and *Look Out Sister* (1948). But Hollywood first got an inkling of the musical revolution about to break when teenagers flocked to the uncompromising high school drama *Blackboard Jungle* (1955) in order to see **Bill Haley and His Comets** perform "Rock Around The Clock".

Haley became a fixture in the early **rock musicals**, many of which were little more than revues, as the studios again embarked on a process of trial and error to identify the next big thing. Another frequent figure in these flagrant attempts to get down with the kids was **Alan Freed**, a DJ who promoted rock almost as tirelessly as he publicized himself (before his career was wrecked by the "Payola Scandal" of 1959). Freed acted as compere in pictures with such calculating titles as *Rock Around The Clock, Don't Knock The Rock, Rock, Rock, Rock* (all 1956), *Mr Rock And Roll* (1957) and *Go, Johnny, Go!* (1959), which were designed to put a new spin on the "putting on a show" format. However, it was Bill Haley, Chuck Berry, Frankie Lymon, Jerry Lee Lewis, Little Richard, Fats Domino, Ritchie Valens, Eddie Cochran, Gene Vincent and The Platters that the 1950s **American youth** wanted to see – hence, Fox packing seventeen songs into the 99 minutes of *The Girl Can't Help It* (1956).

**MGM** also reacted with surprising alacrity to the new trend and snapped up **Elvis** for his debut, *Love Me Tender* (1956), even though several studio veterans were uncertain how pelvic thrusts equated with MGM's traditional family values. However, just as it had tamed the Marx Brothers and Busby Berkeley, the studio proceeded to turn the surly rebel into a **matinee entertainer**, a process made all the easier by his induction into the US Army in 1958. Few of Elvis's contemporaries were prepared to commit to Hollywood's restrictive contracts and lengthy shooting schedules when they could be recording, touring or promoting their records on radio and television. Moreover, with celebrity becoming increasingly transient, executives were wary of signing talents who might turn out to be **one-hit wonders**, who would already be has-beens by the time their movies were released.

Yet such was the Elvis phenomenon that the other studios soon began searching for their own teen idols. Latterday crooner **Pat Boone** was presented as a clean-cut all-American boy in *Bernardine*, *April Love* (both 1957) and *All Hands On Deck* (1961). But his film fortunes quickly waned, despite starring alongside fellow chart-topper **Booby Darin** in *State Fair* (1962). Having appeared with Boone in *Mardi Gras*, **Tommy Sands** played a teen idol in *Sing, Boy, Sing* (both 1958), but his career similarly faltered after he was miscast in Disney's lacklustre live-action adaption of Victor Herbert's operetta, *Babes In Toyland* (1961).

Sparks flew between Elvis Presley and Ann-Margret, and *Viva Las Vegas* (1964) became The King's biggest box-office hit.

**Louis Prima** was better suited to voicing King Louis in Disney's animated classic *The Jungle Book* (1967), which easily outshone his teen-oriented efforts like *Senior Prom*, *Hey Boy! Hey Girl!* (both 1959) and *Twist All Night* (1961). Monroe-wannabe **Mamie Van Doren**'s brush with rock proved equally brief. Having started out in such minor mainstream musicals as *Ain't Misbehavin'* and *The Second Greatest Sex* (both 1955), she headlined *Untamed Youth* (1957) and *Girls Town* (1959), which cashed in on rock's **non-conformist attitude**, before drifitng out of the genre.

Confrontation and the counterculture were key themes of many rock musicals as they were squarely aimed at **teenage audiences**. *Shake,*

*Rattle And Rock* (1956) tackled hostile adults, *Because They're Young* (1960) dealt with school life, *Juke Box Rhythm* (1959) concentrated on love across the tracks, and *Rock, Pretty Baby* (1956) and *The Big Beat* (1957) were all about selling the new sound. Some rock pictures, like *The Hot Rod Gang* (1958) and *The Ghost Of Dragstrip Hollow* (1959), were spin-offs of *The Wild One* (1954) and *Rebel Without A Cause* (1955), and catered mainly for the thriving **drive-in** trade. But the majority were simply musical showcases, whether it was for rock'n'roll in *Carnival Rock* and *Jamboree* (both 1957), rockabilly in *Rock, Baby, Rock It*, 1957), rhythm'n'blues in *Rockin' The Blues* (1957) and calypso in *Bop Girl Goes Calypso* and *Calypso Heat Wave* (both 1957).

Producer **Sam Katzman** even tried to repackage Cuban rhythms in *Cha-Cha-Cha Boom* (1956). A veteran of B-musicals, such as *Junior Prom* (1946) starring Freddie Stewart, Katzman saw the musical as just another exploitation genre and cast **Chubby Checker** in *Twist Around The Clock* (1961) and *Don't Knock The Twist* (1962) and Connie Francis in *Looking For Love* (1964) and *When The Boys Meet The Girls* (1965). Katzman finally hit paydirt with the Elvis vehicles, *Kissin' Cousins* (1964) and *Harum Scarum* (1965). However, his best picture of this period was the Hank Williams biopic, *Your Cheatin' Heart* (1964), starring George Hamilton.

### The Girl Can't Help It
**dir Frank Tashlin, 1957, 99m**

Something of a cult favourite, this reworking of *Born Yesterday* (1950) sees press agent Tom Ewell trying to make a star out of gangster Edmond O'Brien's buxom, blonde moll, Jayne Mansfield. However, the film's true value lies in the performances of such rock icons as Fats Domino ("Blue Monday"), Gene Vincent ("Be Bop A Lula") and Little Richard, who belts out "She's Got It" and "Ready Teddy", as well as the title track.

# The musical in decline

## The sounds of the sixties

Considering the problems it faced with declining audiences, spiralling costs, diminishing talent pools and growing competition, the movie musical began the 1960s on a rapturous note. *West Side Story* (1961, see Canon) became the most Oscar-decorated entry in the genre's history, with ten awards. Then, following the critical and commercial success of *Mary Poppins* and *My Fair Lady* (both 1964. see Canon), **Robert Wise**'s adaptation of Rodgers and Hammerstein's final show, *The Sound Of Music* (1965, see Canon), became the musical's biggest ever **box-office hit**.

Yet, by 1970, the musical had become a cinematic backwater. In just 33 years, it had gone from being the bedrock of Hollywood entertainment to a **cultural irrelevance**. Broadway was also in crisis. But the occasional stage show still turned a handsome profit, and the studios doggedly continued to search for their own elusive, lucrative blockbusters. Amazingly, some forty years later, executives, artists, critics and audiences alike retain faith in a form that is too sporadic to count as a genre any longer, yet which can still generate more indulgent press speculation than almost any other.

Back in the musical's heyday, George Gershwin noted that "we are living in an age of staccato, not legato". However, it was only in the 1960s that the screen musical began to reflect the rhythms of **urban life** that made rural nostalgia feel wincingly twee. Moreover, people were simply too wrapped up in their increasingly insular and fast-paced lives to sit back and enjoy ballads and ballets. They were also no longer listening to the same music, as **rock** had divided the audience into young and old (and it's been further fragmenting ever since). The Western similarly fell out of favour in the same period, as it also represented a past detached from the American present, in which trust and optimism had been replaced by **cynicism and fear**. Consequently, the genres together became Hollywood's equivalent of *cinéma du papa*.

The sale of Hollywood's back catalogue to **television** stalled the musical's demise, as a new generation unfamiliar with the Berkeley and Astaire **monochrome classics** learned to love them on the small screen. Their stock situations, sentimental and contrived storylines, and caricatured figures now acquired a kitsch value, while the innocence and subtlety of musical courtship contrasted with the permissiveness that ultimately forced the collapse of the Production Code in 1968. Even the bland sanguinity of the **easy listening melodies** and the chic innuendo of the lyrics had a charm that stood in contrast to the explicit words of lust and protest found in most modern pop songs.

However, Hollywood missed its chance to re-establish the genre because it alienated an amenable public with a string of indifferent offerings, whose mediocrity was further exposed by comparison with the oldies available for free at home. Conscious of the expense of mounting musicals and keen to avoid undue risk, the studios plumped for **Broadway transfers** like *Flower Drum Song* (1961), *The Music Man*, *Billy Rose's Jumbo* (both 1962), *The Unsinkable Molly Brown* (1964), *A Funny Thing Happened On The Way To The Forum*, *How To Succeed In Business Without Really Trying* (both 1966) and *Finian's Rainbow* (1968). But these reworked stage musicals were largely as devoid of inspiration as the rare originals *Robin And The Seven Hoods* (1964) and *Thoroughly Modern Millie* (1967).

Even **Gene Kelly** failed to recapture the old magic with his version of Jerry Herman's *Hello, Dolly!* (1969), which suffered from stolid staging and the miscasting of **Barbra Streisand** (who had won an Oscar the previous year for her debut in the Fanny Brice saga, *Funny Girl*). Conversely, the filmic flamboyance of director-choreographer **Bob Fosse** swamped Shirley MacLaine's best efforts in *Sweet Charity* (1969), while **Julie Andrews**' bubble was burst by the dismal showing of the Gertrude Lawrence biopic, *Star!* (1968), which refused to shine even after Fox cut the songs and running time and reissued it as *They Were The Happy Days*.

Indeed, the bigger the production, the more disastrously it seemed to perform at the box office. *Doctor Dolittle* (1967), for example, lost so much money that it nearly bankrupted 20th Century-Fox. Yet the success of Lionel Bart's Dickens adaptation, *Oliver!* (1968), persuaded MGM to attempt another **British period piece**, *Goodbye, Mr Chips* (1969) – but it proved a calamity. As did *Camelot* (1967) and *Paint Your Wagon* (1969), which were scored by Alan Jay Lerner and Frederick Loewe on the back of their triumphs with *Gigi* and *My Fair Lady*.

Hollywood had simply lost the knack of making musicals. Such was their expense that they were now treated as **prestige projects** and entrusted to dependable directors. But these journeymen often had little experience of the genre and could no longer rely on the specialist units of yore, as they had been disbanded during the **cutbacks** of the mid-1950s. There was also an acute shortage of genuine **musical icons**, and pivotal roles often had to be conferred upon bankable stars who could neither sing nor dance. But, most significantly, Hollywood was reluctant to depart from the stylistic template established by Fox's **Rodgers and Hammerstein** films. Consequently, the musical was saddled with colourful, widescreen, stereophonic spectacle at a time when cinema worldwide was embracing the **self-reflexive intimacy** of the *nouvelle vague*. Musicals also remained rooted in the outmoded American Dream, and fell out of step with a popular culture that was being shaped by the Civil Rights movement, feminism, the 1960s spate of political assassinations and the war in Vietnam. The optimistic, heart-warming genre that had once helped the nation through some of its darkest days could no longer unify or console and, as a result, the musical seemed on the **verge of extinction**.

### A Funny Thing Happened On The Way To The Forum
**dir Richard Lester, 1966, 99m**

The spirited work of an excellent ensemble is enervated by Richard Lester's fidgety direction in this still enjoyable adaptation of Stephen Sondheim's 1964 show, which was inspired by the writings of Plautus. Re-creating his Broadway role as a freedom-seeking slave, Zero Mostel gets things off to a stirring start with "Comedy Tonight". But, as so much of the original score was dropped, only the scurrilously bawdy "Everybody Ought To Have A Maid" remains to amuse.

### Doctor Dolittle
**dir Richard Fleischer, 1967, 152m**

There were small pleasures to be had in Leslie Bricusse's musicalization of Hugh Lofting's popular novels about a man who could speak 498 animal languages. Unfortunately, there weren't enough of them to prevent Fox from losing a bundle on its $18 million investment. However, with an amiable performance from Rex Harrison and some ingenious special effects enlivening songs like the Oscar-winning "Talk To The Animals", this is infinitely preferable to the ghastly non-singing bowdlerizations from 1998 and 2001, starring Eddie Murphy.

### Paint Your Wagon
**dir Joshua Logan, 1969, 166m**

It remains a mystery why Joshua Logan kept being offered musicals like Paramount's prestigious adaptation of Lerner and Loewe's 1951 tale of the California gold rush. As usual, he imposes a funereal pace on proceedings and encumbers the production numbers with bloated significance. However, there's something likeable about Lee Marvin and Clint Eastwood's valiant efforts to play against type and respectively stay in tune on "Wand'rin' Star" and "I Talk To The Trees".

## Beach parties and rock operas

By the mid-1960s, the rock musical had been overtaken by less threatening **pop outings**, which invariably centred on decorous kids having innocent fun. The epitome of these hearty romps were the **beach movies** produced by American International Pictures (**AIP**). Directed by William Asher and starring teen idols **Frankie Avalon** and **Annette Funicello**, *Beach Party* (1963), *Muscle Beach Party*, *Bikini Beach*, *Pajama Party* (all 1964), *Beach Blanket Bingo* (1965) and *How To Stuff A Wild Bikini* (1966) inspired countless imitations. Director Maury Dexter followed the formula to the letter in *Surf Party*, *The Young Swingers* (both 1963) and *Wild On The Beach* (1965), as did Lennie Weinrib with *Beach Ball* (1965), *Wild Wild Winter* and *Out Of Sight* (both 1966).

Don Taylor proved marginally more inventive with *Ride The Wild Surf* (1964), while **The Beach Boys** made a guest apperance in *The Girls On The Beach* (1965). A jot of variation was provided by both *The Horror Of Beach Party* (1963) and *The Ghost In The Invisible Bikini* (1966), and the off-piste pair, *Ski Party* and *Winter A Go-Go* (both 1965). However, **British imports** like *A Hard Day's Night* (1964) soon exposed the sanitized banality of pop pics like *Catalina Caper* and *The Cool Ones* (both 1967).

The first Broadway musical to include rock songs, *Bye Bye Birdie* (1960), was filmed by **George Sidney** in 1963. It had a decent score and the sound idea of lampooning Elvis, celebrity, adolescence, small-town insularity and the power of television. But what could have been a cherishable **snapshot of American youth** at the junction between bobbysoxers and beatniks, rebellious rockers and counterculture hippies, missed its target. However, it showed there were those on the Hollywood margins who were pre-

Bubblegum rock goes psychedelic: Monkees Peter Tork and Davy Jones chill out in *Head* (1968), which was co-scripted by Jack Nicholson.

pared to take the musical in **new directions**.

Unfortunately, too many departures turned into dead ends, and *Get Yourself A College Girl* (1964), *Blast-Off Girls* (1967), *Blonde On A Bum Trip* (1968) and *Good Times* (1967) are now little more than **curios**. However, all of these films are superior to the execrable *Wild Guitar, Eegah!* (both 1962) and *The Nasty Rabbit* (1964), which were scripted for singer-songwriter **Arch Hall, Jr.** by his dad, under the pseudonym Nicholas Merriwether. Their one-time cohort, Ray Dennis Steckler, directed *Rat Pfink A Boo-Boo* (1965), about a rock star who doubles as a superhero, while **Richard Dreyfuss** fronted a group called The Green Onion in the bubblegum musical, *Hello Down There* (1969), which was set in an underwater nightclub.

Despite these idiosyncratic anomolies, the 1960s did see some laudable **innovation**. Paul Simon and Art Garfunkel introduced the notion of the **meta-musical** with their soundtrack for *The Graduate* (1967), while screenwriter Jack Nicholson and director Bob Rafelson invented the **anti-musical** with *Head* (1968), a psychedelic collage that astutely used America's most artificial pop group, **The Monkees**, to deconstruct its most conservative genre.

The 1960s also saw the emergence of what became known as the **rock opera**. However, the screen adaptations of such **Broadway landmarks** as *Hair*, *Godspell* and *Jesus Christ Superstar* weren't released until the 1970s, by which time the style had become passé. In the meantime, Hollywood tried to produce its own rock operas. But titles like the "first electric Western", *Zachariah* (1971), and *Catch My Soul* (1974), Jack Good's musicalization of *Othello*, misfired as spectacularly as **Brian De Palma**'s Faustian folly, *Phantom Of The Paradise* (1974) and The Bee Gees atrocity *Sgt Pepper's Lonely Hearts Club Band* (1978).

## Beach Blanket Bingo

**dir William Asher, 1965, 98m**

Despite its proasic soundtrack, this is the pick of AIP's seaside frolics, in which Annette Funicello sulks because Frankie Avalon goes off to rescue pop starlet Linda Evans from a biker gang, Buster Keaton executes a few expert pratfalls as a lecherous beachcomber and Harvey Lembeck gets sawn in half by Timothy Carey's buzzsaw.

## Head

**dir Bob Rafelson, 1968, 86m**

Having drowned their bubblegum alter egos The Monkees during "The Porpoise Song", Mickey Dolenz, Davy Jones, Peter Tork and Michael Nesmith embark on a series of trippy encounters with guest stars Victor Mature, Frank Zappa and Annette Funicello. But the music's a sideshow, and time hasn't always been kind to Jack Nicholson's psychedelic script.

## Jesus Christ Superstar

**dir Norman Jewison, 1973, 103m**

Released on screen the same year as David Schwartz's *Godspell*, this reworking of Tim Rice and Andrew Lloyd Webber's rock opera was saddled with a fussy "putting on a show" conceit by Norman Jewison and Melvyn Bragg that wasted the Holy Land settings. However, thanks to André Previn's gutsy orchestration, Ted Neeley sounds fine as Jesus, although he lacks the charisma to compete with Carl Anderson's angry Judas and isn't a patch on Ian Gillan, who took the title role on the original 1968 concept album.

## Hair

**dir Milos Forman, 1979, 121m**

Czech Iconoclast Milos Forman injected new subversive life into James Rado and Gerome Ragni's counterculture musical, which had scandalized theatregoers in 1968 with its anti-Vietnam stance and shameless nudity. Some of the quirkier camera tricks and cornier staging ideas feel forced, but John Savage's Central Park sojourn with hippies Treat Williams and Beverly D'Angelo was galvanized by Twyla Tharp's choreography on "Aquarius" and "Good Morning Starshine", while the boot camp routine, "Black Boys/White Boys", packs a provocative punch. Less an exercise in nostalgia than the dissection of a myth.

## Stayin' alive

The situation scarcely improved in the **1970s**, despite the boost provided by a plethora of rock, pop and disco outings of wildly varying quality. Although languishing in the doldrums, the genre retained a certain cachet, especially with producers inspired by the success of such celebrations of the **rock era** as George Lucas's period meta-musical, *American Graffiti* (1973), and the TV sitcom, *Happy Days* (1974–84). Hoping to cash in on the box-office popularity of *Grease* (1978, see Canon), legendary indie producer **Roger Corman** released *Rock'n'Roll High School* (1979), a typical piece of low-budget exploitation that combined the spirit of **teen rebellion movies** with punk and featured a standout soundtrack by The Ramones. The **nostalgia wave** also instigated countless documentaries, and a series of musical **biopics**: *The Buddy Holly Story* (1978); *This Is Elvis* (1981); *American Hot Wax* (1978), which paid homage to radio DJ Alan Freed; *La Bamba* (1987), which traced the life and early death of Ritchie Valens; and *Great Balls Of Fire* (1989), about rock'n'roller Jerry Lee Lewis.

However, most of Hollywood had gone **disco** in the late 1970s, in the wake of *Saturday Night Fever* (1977), which followed the meta-musical

### Cult musicals

A clutch of the countless **B-musicals** churned out by the major and minor studios alike in the 1930s and 40s have acquired cult status among musical aficionados, including the zany comic rollicks of the **Ritz Brothers** (*Straight, Place And Show*, 1938, and *Never A Dull Moment*, 1943) and the **Three Stooges** (*Rockin' In the Rockies*, 1945, and *Swing Parade Of 1946*). But an embarrassment of camp and kitsch are now required to earn a musical its cult kudos. Consider, for example, **Mark Haggard** and **Bruce Kimmel**'s *The First Nudie Musical* (1976), which brought *42nd Street* (1933, see Canon) into the soft-core era with its plot about a novice director being hired to make a porn flick to save a bankrupt studio. Cindy Williams gives a standout performance as the studio's pragmatic secretary, while songs with titles like "Dancing Dildos" and "Let Them Eat Cake (But Let Me Eat You)" speak for themselves.

The humour is even more idiosyncratic in **Richard Elfman**'s 1980 offering, *Forbidden Zone*. Set in a kingdom ruled by King Fausto (Hervé Villechaize) and his statuesque queen (Susan Tyrell) and populated by a frog butler, a human chandelier, a chicken boy and a jazz-loving Satan, the anti-story was inspired by a **Mystic Knights of the Oingo Boingo** stage show and scored by future Hollywood stalwart, **Danny Elfman**. The influence of the Three Stooges, Federico Fellini and animators Max and Dave Fleischer is evident throughout *Forbidden Zone*. However, for true **cartoon cultishness**, nothing can top **Bill Plympton**'s *The Tune* (1992). Best known for a hilarious head-bashing sequence that was also released as the short, *Push Comes To Shove*, this tale of a songwriter who finds inspiration for a much-needed hit in the village of Flooby Nooby is packed with splendidly off-kilter **Maureen McElheron** ditties like "Isn't It Good Again" and "Lovesick Hotel".

However, the derivative is often more cult-worthy than the original, as in *Reefer Madness: The Movie Musical* (2005). In adapting Kevin Murphy and Dan Studney's off-Broadway curio, director **Andy Fickman** invoked the spirit of *The Rocky Horror Picture Show* (1975, see Canon) to lampoon Louis Gasnier's infamous 1936 anti-dope shocker, *Reefer Madness*. Christian Campbell's hallucinatory reveries are frequently over-cooked, but Jesus Christ's cabaret cameo and **Alan Cumming**'s shamelessly hammy turn as a lecturer warning against the evils of gigglesticks are irresistible.

approach by having **John Travolta** and Karen Lynn Gorney dance to songs on the soundtrack rather than numbers they performed themselves. Travolta reprised the role of Brooklyn disco king Tony Manero in **Sylvester Stallone**'s undistinguished sequel, *Staying Alive* (1983). But even that was infinitely preferable to the competition, which included *Thank God, It's Friday* (1978), *Can't Stop The Music* (1980), *Breakin'* and *Breakin' 2: Electric Boogaloo* (both 1984). Few of these films followed the lead of *The Wiz* (1978) or *Fame* (1980) in using song or dance diegetically, but they continued the vogue for **dance pictures** that reached its 1980s apogee with *Flashdance* (1983), *Footloose* (1984) and *Dirty Dancing* (1987), which were more dramas with musical interludes than genuine genre entries.

By the mid-**1980s**, the **non-traditional musical** had fragmented into isolated efforts designed to pander to widely diverging tastes. Sporadic attempts to push the parameters had been made since the 1970s, including such postmodern outings as Frank Zappa's *200 Motels* (1971) and Robert Altman's *Nashville* (1975, see Canon). They were followed by offbeat **cult items** like **Richard O'Brien**'s *The Rocky Horror Picture Show* (1975, see Canon) and *Shock Treatment* (1981), inspired parodies like **Christopher Guest**'s *This Is Spinal Tap* (1984) and occasional oddities, like *Sextette* (1978), in which Mae West teamed up with Ringo Starr, Alice Cooper and Keith Moon.

### Saturday Night Fever
**dir John Badham, 1977, 119m**

This isn't strictly a musical, but an urban drama with disco interludes. Nevertheless, the story of a blue collar Brooklynite who lives for his Saturday escapism transformed John Travolta into an overnight superstar, while The Bee Gees' bestselling soundtrack and Lester Wilson's choreography launched as many parodies as wannabe imitations.

### The Buddy Holly Story
**dir Steve Rash, 1978, 113m**

The Oscar-nominated Gary Busey excels as the eponymous hero in this laudable, if occasionally factually inaccurate, biopic, which traces the career of the geek from Lubbock, Texas who became a rock superstar before tragically dying in a plane crash. Singing live, Busey captures Holly's unique style and infectious stage presence and this, above all, helped Joe Renzetti's adapted score to scoop its well-deserved Oscar.

### Fame
**dir Alan Parker, 1980, 134m**

Caught between romance and realism, this fragmentary film chronicles four years in the lives of eight socially and ethnically stereotyped wannabes at the New York High School for the Performing Arts. It proved extremely popular and spawned a TV series, featuring several members of the cast, but neither Michael Gore's Oscar-winning score nor Louis Falco's choreography are particularly noteworthy. Athough the rhythmic spontaneity of "Hot Lunch Jam" was better integrated into the narrative than the vivacious, but far-fetched, street celebration to the title tune.

### Footloose
**dir Herbert Ross, 1984, 107m**

The folk musical gets an MTV makeover in this amiable, but always arch teen pic. Unusually earning two best song Oscar nominations, for the vibrant title track and "Let's Hear It For The Boy", *Footloose* benefits from the Andy Hardy-esque Kevin Bacon's can-do defiance of preacher John Lithgow's dancing ban. But the small-town aura and lazy story resolution would have felt old hat forty years earlier.

### Dirty Dancing
**dir Emile Ardolino, 1987, 97m**

The spirit of Ginger Rogers' *Having Wonderful Time* (1938) and Gene Kelly's *Marjorie Morningstar* (1957) irradiate this crowd-pleasing wallow in faux nostalgia. Neither the score nor the choreography owe a jot to the styles of 1963, but the Catskills summer romance between respectable daddy's girl Jennifer Grey and bad-boy hotel hoofer Patrick Swayze struck a chord with audiences, and this remains a baffling feel-good favourite.

## Taking a cue from Broadway

Although the genre had diversified in the 1970s and 80s, Hollywood kept faith with the traditional musical – with mixed results. Despite its occasional descent into pompous lethargy, **Norman Jewison**'s 1971 version of the stage hit, *Fiddler On The Roof*, had sufficent rousing moments to earn its eight Oscar nominations. However, other orthodox outings, like *Man Of La Mancha*, *1776* (both 1972), *Lost Horizon* (1973), *The Little Prince* and *Mame* (both 1974), were buried beneath critical scorn and audience apathy. Their faults were only exacerbated by the release of **MGM's greatest clips** packages, *That's Entertainment!* (1974, 1976 and 1994) and *That's Dancing* (1985), which revealed just how far the musical had fallen from grace.

Inspired by the **concept musicals** that were then the rage on Broadway, **Bob Fosse** scored with *Cabaret* (1972, see Canon) and *All That Jazz* (1979). But even stage hits were now regarded with suspicion by studio executives, who despised highbrow pretentions that couldn't easily be dumbed down for a **blockbuster generation** addled by sci-fi and special effects. It was hard enough selling the increasingly alien concept of characters bursting into song in everyday situations, let alone the Brechtian strategy of music being used to counterpoint and comment upon the action. **Hal Prince** tried to seduce cinemagoers with *A Little Night Music* (1978), but its commerical failure kept other landmark **Stephen Sondheim** shows, like *Company* (1970), *Follies* (1971) and *Sunday In The Park With George* (1984), off the screen.

A handful of 1970s pictures attempted to bring a new **realism** to the genre by brandishing the seedier side of showbiz. **Diana Ross** and **Bette Midler** both deserved their Oscar nominations for *Lady Sings The Blues* (1972) and *The Rose* (1979), which were based on the troubled lives of Billie Holiday and Janis Joplin, respectively. However, **Robert De Niro** and **Liza Minnelli** were overlooked for their doughty performances as a saxophonist and a singer who each put egotistical ambition above passion in **Martin Scorsese**'s *New York, New York* (1977), which laudably sought to demythologize the musical with an uncom-

Bette Midler lets rip Joplin-style in *The Rose* (1979), which lifts the lid on the substance-fuelled reality of the rock business.

promising homage to a bygone age.

Although a revitalized **Broadway** could boast such visionaries as Hal Prince, George Abbott and Michael Bennett, Hollywood continued to allocate musicals to directors whose talents lay elsewhere. **Richard Attenborough** had made a decent fist of the **British musical satire** *Oh! What A Lovely War* in 1969. But he was commonly acknowledged to be an eccentric choice to direct **Michael Bennett**'s *A Chorus Line* (1985) after its record-breaking stage run, nine Tonys and Pulitzer Prize. Once again, Attenborough did a creditable job, but little of the electricity and ingenuity that had captivated Broadway audiences survived. Consequently, Hollywood had missed another opportunity to reconnect with a public that was already well-disposed towards **dance movies** since *Fame*, *Footloose* and *Flashdance*.

In fact, the studios no longer seemed to know what their patrons wanted. If surefire **Broadway smashes** weren't to their taste, what chance did *The Best Little Whorehouse In Texas*, *Annie* (both 1982) and other such lesser lights have? Original offerings like **Gene Kelly's comeback**, *Xanadu* (1980), and the **Francis Ford Coppola** pair of *One From The Heart* (1982) and *The Cotton Club* (1984), proved no more alluring, despite **Gregory Hines**' dazzling dancing display in the latter. Unfortunately, Hines had no better fortune with *White Nights* (1985) or *Tap* (1989), and his acclaimed stage shows, *Eubie* (1978), *Sentimental Ladies* (1981) and *Jelly's Last Jam* (1992), were ignored by cinema altogether.

## Fiddler On The Roof

**dir Norman Jewison, 1971, 181m**

Star Zero Mostel had set Jerry Bock and Sheldon Harnick's show on its way to becoming the fifth longest-running musical in Broadway history. But Norman Jewison preferred to cast Chaim Topol (the star of the West End version) as the Ukrainian shtetl (or Jewish village) milkman who relocates to the US in the early 1900s. Jewison then set about Topol's performance in the cutting room, reducing it to a musical collage that was bereft of genuine emotional power. Thus, the soul of the piece was lost, along with the Chagall-inspired art that director-choreographer Jerome Robbins had imparted on the stage original.

## New York, New York

**dir Martin Scorsese, 1977, 164m**

Inspired by Raoul Walsh's *The Man I Love* (1946), Martin Scorsese's homage to 1940s musicals stumbles over the anachronistic Cassavetes-style improvs, which kill the mood rather than generate the desired behind-the-scenes showbiz grit. However, Robert De Niro and Liza Minnelli are courageously unsympathetic, as a big-band saxophonist who wants to play bebop and his vocalist lover. Minnelli lets rip on John Kander and Fred Ebb's title track, and there's enough in Boris Leven's designs and Ralph Burns's orchestrations to suggest that this much-recut misfire could have been a pastiche masterpiece.

## The Rose

**dir Mark Rydell, 1979, 134m**

An Oscar-nominated Bette Midler lets it all hang out in this grungy rock saga, which was based on the rock'n'roll lifestyle and subsequent burnout of 1960s icons like Janis Joplin. There's a lurid fascination in watching Midler's character spiral out of control, as she seizes on drugs, booze and her manager Alan Bates to help her cope with the pressures of success. But when she performs, most notably during the Greenwich Village cabaret sequence, she sets the screen alight.

## A Chorus Line

**dir Richard Attenborough, 1985, 113m**

Michael Bennett's Broadway landmark deserved better than this, but he declined the invitation to direct. Richard Attenborough's interpretation was occasionally as leaden as Jeffrey Hornaday's choreography, but this film isn't quite the calamity that many detractors claim. The plot of the original show was changed somewhat, as flashbacks were added to explore director Michael Douglas's romance with auditioning dancer, Alyson Reed, but the songs, including "I Can Do It", "Let Me Dance For You" and "What I Did For Love", still capture a credible backstage essence.

# The show must go on

## Any dream will do

Increasingly desperate to revive some of that old musical magic, Hollywood turned to **remakes** (*The Jazz Singer*, 1980), comedy hybrids (*The Blues Brothers*, 1980),TV adaptations (*Pennies From Heaven*, 1981), reworkings of foreign imports (*Victor/Victoria*, 1982), sequels (*Grease 2*, 1982), revivals (*The Pirates Of Penzance*, 1983) and musicalizations of old movies (*Little Shop Of Horrors*, 1986). However, the only reliable musical sources of profit in the 1980s and 90s were **Disney animations** and the **Jim Henson** puppet delights *The Muppet Movie* (1979), *The Great Muppet Caper*

### Musicals for children

As so many Hollywood musicals were aimed at the entire family, the studios rarely catered specifically for children. Consequently, **child star vehicles** featuring Shirley Temple, Deanna Durbin, Mickey Rooney, Judy Garland and B-movie stalwarts Peggy Ryan and Donald O'Connor tended to stick to trusted generic storylines. Even after **Walt Disney** (see p.198) began producing animated features for younger viewers with *Snow White And The Seven Dwarfs* (1927, see Canon), kid-friendly outings like *The Wizard Of Oz* (1939, see Canon) remained sporadic.

However, as more grown-ups came to prefer a night at home in front of the television, Hollywood had to find a new audience. Teenagers could be satiated with **rock movies**, but their younger siblings proved more problematic. Disney again led the way with *Mary Poppins* (1964, see Canon), *Bedknobs And Broomsticks* (1971) and *Pete's Dragon* (1977), which all combined animation and **live-action**. But imitations like *Chitty Chitty Bang Bang* (1968) and *Willy Wonka And The Chocolate Factory* (1971) were never quite as successful, and later efforts like *Annie* (1982) and *Newsies* (1992) flopped alarmingly.

Invariably more inventive and more attuned to young imaginations, **animated musicals** have often fared much better than their live-action counterparts. There are currently 45 features in the official canon of Disney animated classics – nearly all of them have contained songs. The likes of *Pinocchio* (1940), *Dumbo* (1941) and *Bambi* (1942) **integrated musical numbers** into the narrative in a way that traditional musicals didn't manage until the late 1940s. And *Cinderella* (1950), *Alice In Wonderland* (1951), *Peter Pan* (1953) and *Lady And The Tramp* (1955) all produced songs that became **kiddie favourites**.

The standard of songwriting and storytelling at Disney dipped after *The Jungle Book* (1967) and *The Aristocats* (1970), and it wasn't until the 1990s that composer **Alan Menken** revived the studio's fortunes with *The Little Mermaid* (1989), *Beauty And The Beast* (1991) and *Aladdin* (1992). Disney then turned to **pop stars** Elton John, Phil Collins and Sting for more contemporary scores for *The Lion King* (1994, see Canon), *Tarzan* (1999) and *The Emperor's New Groove* (2000) respectively, but *Pocahontas* (1995), *The Hunchback Of Notre Dame* (1996), *Hercules* (1997) and *Mulan* (1998) opted for the more traditional show tune approach.

Although Disney has long been the foremost producer of animated musicals, other filmmakers have also made an impact. Disney émigré, **Don Bluth**, directed a string of hits, including the creature features *All Dogs Go To Heaven* (1989), *Rock-a-Doodle* (1992) and *Thumbelina*

(1981), *The Muppets Take Manhattan* (1984) and *The Muppet Christmas Carol* (1993), as well as his darker fantasy, *Labyrinth* (1986), which starred **David Bowie** as the scheming Goblin King.

by the early 1990s, the best song category at the oscars was dominated by disney's favourite composer, **Alan Menken**. But even the acclaim for the studio's pioneering **animated features** *The Little Mermaid* (1989), *Beauty And The Beast* (1991) and *Aladdin* (1992) couldn't prevent Menken's live-action period piece, *Newsies* (1992), from performing badly. Other screen originals, like *For The Boys* (1991), starring Bette Midler as a USO entertainer, and *Swing Kids* (1993), about the Nazi persecution of three German kids who love American music, similarly disappointed at the box office. Cartoons seemed to be the musical's last refuge, especially after *The Lion King* (1994, see Canon) followed *Beauty And The Beast* to Broadway in 1997.

Despite the prominence of animation, the **indie musical** was acquiring a cult entourage

(1994), while his **Steven Spielberg**-produced migrant mouse saga, *An American Tail* (1986), spawned a non-Bluth sequel, *An American Tail: Fievel Goes West* (1991).

Featuring six songs by Randy Newman and with **Gene Kelly** as its mentor, **Mark Dindal**'s *Cats Don't Dance* (1997) was a charming throwback to Hollywood's backstage heyday. It tells the story of a feline song-and-dance wannabe named Danny who falls foul of Mammoth Pictures' spoilt tot star, Darla Dimple. Conflict and conquest were also key themes in *Happy Feet* (2006), in which a **tap-dancing emperor penguin** called Mumbles is banished from his community for his inability to sing. Directed by **George Miller** (of *Babe* fame), this Oscar winner is as much an eco-parable as a musical, but it is infinitely superior to its green predecessor, *Once Upon A Forest* (1993), and its CGI production numbers have an irresistible Berkeleyesque extravagance.

One-time Disney animator **Tim Burton**, however, has recognized that kids don't just respond to cute. In addition to darkly revisiting **Roald Dahl** in the live-action *Charlie And The Chocolate Factory* (2005), he also produced **Henry Selick**'s stop-motion puppet pic, *The Nightmare Before Christmas* (1993), and reunited with composer **Danny Elfman** for the equally macabre *Corpse Bride* (2005). With **Johnny Depp** voicing the timid pianist who is lured into the underworld by Helena Bonham Carter's lovestruck cadaver, *Corpse Bride* is a touchingly ghoulish concoction, whose highlight is a dance number led by a skeleton named Bonejangles.

### Beauty And The Beast
**dir Gary Trousdale, Kirk Wise, 1991, 85m**

A pioneering blend of hand-drawn graphics and computer wizardry, this was the first animation to be nominated for a best picture Oscar. Borrowing charmingly from Jean Cocteau's *La belle et la bête* (1948), the visuals in this Disneyfication of Madam leprince de Beaumont's enchanting fairy tale are complemented by the accomplished score by Alan Menken and Howard Ashman, which had the usual distinction of landing three best song nominations, for "Belle", "Be Our Guest" and the award-winning title number.

### The Nightmare Before Christmas
**dir Henry Selick, 1993, 75m**

Based on a Tim Burton story, this deliciously dark stop-motion puppet picture has a sentimental side, as Jack Skellington, the Pumpkin King of Halloweentown, discovers that it's best to be yourself after his bid to replace Santa backfires. The inspired visuals and Danny Elfman songs such as "What's This?" and "Kidnap The Sandy Claws" reinforce this enchanting film's gleefully innocent miscreancy.

during this period. Following on from *The First Nudie Musical* (1976) were **John Waters**' trash triumphs, *Hairspray* (1988) and *Cry-Baby* (1990), and **Christopher Guest** built on the success of *This Is Spinal Tap* (1984) with the spoofs *Waiting For Guffman* (1997) and *A Mighty Wind* (2003). *Camp* (2003) and *Reefer Madness: The Movie Musical* (2005) were idiosyncratic, while the Trey Parker and Matt Stone duo of *Cannibal: The Musical* (1996) and *South Park: Bigger, Longer & Uncut* (1999) brought a new edge to the genre in the **MTV era**.

However, the majority of American musicals still sought to sustain trusted tropes. *You Light Up My Life* (1977), *Ladies And Gentlemen, The Fabulous Stains* (1982), *Light Of Day* (1987) and *Hedwig And The Angry Inch* (2001) revised the **backstager**, while *FM* (1978) reinvented the revue. Period evocations like *Eddie And The Cruisers* (1983), *The Five Heartbeats* (1991), *That Thing You Do*, *Grace Of My Heart* (both 1996), *Velvet Goldmine* (1998) and *Almost Famous* (2000) wallowed in **nostalgia**. So did the **biopics** of singers Loretta Lynn (*Coal Miner's Daughter*, 1980), Patsy Cline (*Sweet Dreams*, 1985), Jim Morrison (*The Doors*, 1991), Tina Turner (*What's Love Got To Do With It?*, 1993), Bobby Darin (*Beyond The Sea*, 2004) and Johnny Cash (*Walk The Line*, 2005).

A number of singers and musicians continued striving to make it in music movies, with **Bob Dylan** (*Renaldo And Clara*, 1978, and *Hearts Of Fire*, 1987) and Paul Simon (*One Trick Pony*, 1980) numbering among the earliest casualties. **Prince** briefly carved a niche for himself with *Purple Rain* (1984) and *Under The Cherry Moon* (1986), but his *Sign O' The Times* (1987) and *Graffiti Bridge* (1990) were less accomplished – although they all easily surpassed Michael Jackson's *Moonwalker* (1988). Recent efforts like *Glitter* and *Rock Star* (both 2001) were equally inept and suggested that the **rock'n'pop musical** had finally burned itself out. But Eminem's *8 Mile* (2002) and 50 Cent's *Get Rich Or Die Tryin'* (2005) suggested that the **hip-hop movie** could become the next big thing. Musical tastes continue to change quickly, and Hollywood's failure to keep pace with transient trends has been one of the key factors in the demise of the mainstream genre.

### The Muppet Movie
**dir James Frawley, 1979, 94m**

Puppeteer Jim Henson tells the story of how the wondrous menagerie he assembled for *Sesame Street* and *The Muppet Show* first came together in this sublime pastiche of the musical biopic. From the moment Kermit the Frog sings Paul Williams's "Rainbow Connection" in the swamp, this is impossible to resist, despite the surfeit of self-conscious guest stars, including Orson Welles, Steve Martin, Bob Hope and Mel Brooks.

### Little Shop Of Horrors
**dir Frank Oz, 1986, 88m**

Frank Oz applied lessons learnt from *The Muppet Show* in directing this cartoonish adaptation of Howard Ashman and Alan Menken's off-Broadway musical. The show was based on Roger Corman's darkly comic 1961 B-movie about a geeky shop assistant who has to kill in order to feed his carnivorous plant, Audrey II. The cast enters into the spirit with laudable gusto, with Steve Martin and Bill Murray revelling in their excruciating set piece and Four Tops singer Levi Stubbs providing excellent vocals for Audrey II on "Mean Green Mother From Outer Space" and "Feed Me".

### Velvet Goldmine
**dir Todd Haynes, 1998, 123m**

A glam rock *Citizen Kane* inspired by the lives of Oscar Wilde and David Bowie, this film knowingly captures the dismal desperation of the 1970s, with its spangly costumes, musical mediocrity, teasing pan-sexuality and private pain. The performances are suitably camp, but the music lacks the precision of the best period pastiches. Consequently, this is never as transgressive as Haynes's *Superstar: The Karen Carpenter Story* (1987), which he made with Barbie dolls.

### South Park: Bigger, Longer & Uncut
**dir Trey Parker, 1999, 81m**

Having shown a scathingly satirical knowledge of the genre in *Cannibal: The Musical* (1993), Trey Parker and co-creator Matt Stone indulged themselves to the full in this spin-off from their cult TV series, which pitched Stan, Kyle, Kenny and Cartman against Saddam Hussein. The score caused an uproar with its gleefully scatological ditties "Kyle's Mom's A Bitch", "Uncle Fucka" and the Oscar-nominated "Blame Canada", but it's also wildly funny, with "I Can Change" niftily parodying *Fiddler On The Roof* (1971).

### 8 Mile
**dir Curtis Hanson, 2002, 110m**

Show people have always been considered trash by the Establishment, and this finely observed *film à clef* takes the sub-genre into the trailer park era. Kim Basinger is suitably dishevelled as the mom who can barely keep her family together, but white rapper Eminem dominates proceedings, with his surprising domestic vulnerability and the angry eloquence that enables him to win rap duels and fight for a record deal.

## You still ain't heard nothin' yet

As the musical entered its eighth decade, Hollywood continued trying to **revive** what had once been its most glamorous genre. Even stars and directors with no experience in musicals took their turn, but few were as successful as **Woody Allen**'s *Everyone Says I Love You* (1997). Undeterred by the ignominious failures of Peter Bogdanovich's *At Long Last Love* (1975), in which the cast recorded the **Cole Porter** songs live, and James L. Brooks's *I'll Do Anything* (1994), which had all but one of its tunes removed after ruinous test screenings, Allen had his ensemble of **inexperienced singers** perform their own songs in this consistently entertaining and occasionally exquisite delight. The Coen brothers, Australian director **Baz Luhrmann** and John Turturro subsequently adopted this **karaoke** tactic for *O Brother, Where Art Thou?* (2000), *Moulin Rouge!* (2001, see p.274) and *Romance & Cigarettes* (2005).

**Traditional musicals** remained the Hollywood Grail, despite Michael Ritchie's 1995 adaptation of the Broadway stalwart, *The Fantasticks*, being shelved for five years before its limited release. Renewed flurries of hopeful activity followed the Oscar successes of the **stage adaptations** *Evita* (1996, see Canon) and *Chicago* (2002, see Canon). But pre-solds like *The Singing Detective* (2003), which was based on the Dennis Potter TV series of the same name, the Cole Porter biopic, *De-Lovely* (2004), and the Broadway transfers *The Phantom Of The Opera* (2004), *The Producers* and *Rent* (both 2005) failed to make much impression on critics and audiences alike. Even less propitious were *From Justin To Kelly* (2003), which starred Justin Guarini and Kelly Clarkson from the TV talent show, *American Idol*, and *Idlewild* (2006), which teamed OutKast colleagues Big Boi and André 3000 as Prohibtion-era musicians falling foul of the mob.

Ironically, this latest period of Hollywood indolence has coincided with a resurgence on **Broadway** that has seen imports, revivals, adaptations and originals all thrive. Hollywood seems to have been intimidated by the challenge of adapting such innovative and eye-catching entertainments as **Andrew Lloyd Webber**'s *Cats* (1981) and *Starlight Express* (1984) and **Claude-Michel Schönberg** and **Alain Boublil**'s *Les Miserables* (1980) and *Miss Saigon* (1989). But *Chicago* (1975) and *Dreamgirls* (1981) took 17 and 25 years respestively to be translated to the screen. So the fact that Meryl Streep has agreed to headline a film version of *Mamma Mia!* only eight years

James Thunder Early (Eddie Murphy) charms Lorell (Anika Noni Rose), Deena (Beyoncé Knowles) and Effie (Jennifer Hudson) into becoming his Dreamettes in the Motown-inspired *Dreamgirls* (2006).

after its first stage bow has to be a good sign that Hollywood hasn't finished with the musical just yet. Indeed, Universal Studios was a major investor in **Stephen Schwartz**'s Broadway production *Wicked* (2003), a prequel to *The Wizard Of Oz* (1939, see Canon) that was crammed with the kind off special effects more commonly associated with the screen than the stage. So perhaps Hollywood is becoming proactive in the genre once more.

Cinema has been going strong since 1895, but musicals have only been central to its success for a third of that time. In fact, they disappeared almost as quickly as the silents they replaced. In an industry more concerned with bottom lines than chorus lines, the musical doesn't seem to have much of a future. But few genres can boast such a **glorious past** and, while rumours abound of possible remakes of films like *Bye, Bye Birdie*, *Jesus Christ Superstar* and *Carmen* and Broadway hits like *Pippin* (1972) and *Spamalot* (2005) continue to tantalize movie producers, the musical may never have to face that **final curtain**.

### Everyone Says I Love You
**dir Woody Allen, 1997, 101m**

The master of the meta-musical finally succumbed to letting his protagonists sing in this engaging romantic comedy that owed much to the Dennis Potter sing-along style. The cast warble gamely in voices that essentially belong in the shower (only Drew Barrymore reneged), but this amateurism only adds to the charm of a pleasingly entangled tale, whose highlight is Woody Allen and Goldie Hawn's lighter-than-air duet to "I'm Through With Love" on the banks of the moonlit Seine.

### O Brother, Where Art Thou?
**dir Joel Coen, 2000, 102m**

Homer's *Odyssey* and Preston Sturges' *Sullivan's Travels* (1941) meet head on in this Mississippi picaresque. George Clooney, John Turturro and Tim Blake Nelson's flight from a chain gang is accompanied by a sparkling score that pays its dues to bluegrass, folk, gospel and the blues, as well as such Depression-era gems as Harry McClintock's "Big Rock Candy Mountain".

### The Producers
**dir Susan Stroman, 2005, 134m**

Eschewing the customary Hollywood tendency to overblow a musical in translating it to the screen, this long-awaited take on Mel Brooks's Broadway sensation was so faithful to the original that even the scenes shot around New York felt stagebound. Moreover, in re-living their stage triumphs, Nathan Lane and Matthew Broderick pitch their performances to the upper balcony and fritter away much of the story's desperate pathos and brash satire. The songs are fun, but "Springtime For Hitler" was much funnier in Brooks's original 1968 movie.

### Dreamgirls
**dir Bill Condon, 2006, 130m**

Inspired by the career of Diana Ross and The Supremes, Michael Bennett's 1981 Broadway hit was long touted for the screen. Its astute blend of performance and character songs brings intensity and intimacy to the storyline, as starmaker Jamie Foxx transforms Beyoncé Knowles, Jennifer Hudson and Anika Noni Rose from Eddie Murphy's backing singers to 1960s soul celebrities. The debuting Hudson (a finalist on the *American Idol* TV show) won an Oscar for her powerhouse rendition of "And I Am Telling You I'm Not Going" and "I Am Changing", but Murphy steals the show, with his flirtatious quipping being tempered by his devastating delivery of the protest song, "Patience".

Opposite: King Vidor directed Judy Garland's rendition of "Over The Rainbow" after Victor Fleming left *The Wizard Of Oz* to take over *Gone With The Wind* (both 1939). However, MGM nearly cut the Oscar-winning song because some of the studio executives felt it slowed down the story.

# **The Canon:** 50 essential film musicals

# The Top Ten

## 1 Singin' In The Rain
1952; see p.157

Perennially selected as the best musical of all time, this memoir of the early days of the talkies epitomizes MGM's perfectionist approach to the genre and its unique ability to blend art and entertainment.

## 2 Top Hat
1935; see p.173

An exercise in timeless elegance, Fred'n'Ginger's fourth picture remains their best. It showcases not only their peerless chemistry on the dance floor, but also their underrated gift for screwball comedy.

## 3 Love Me Tonight
1932; see p.122

Rarely has a single film contained such wit, sophistication, romance and musical ingenuity. Rodgers and Hart's integrated score is enchanting and Mamoulian's direction is as masterly as the comic byplay between Parisian tailor Maurice Chevalier and princess Jeanette MacDonald.

## 4 Meet Me In St Louis
1944; see p.128

The most influential movie musical ever, this brought to Hollywood the fresh approach to integrating and staging songs that *Oklahoma!* had introduced on Broadway. It also captures Judy Garland at her most radiant and relaxed.

## 5 Cabaret
1972; see p.83

Revelling in Kander and Ebb's cynical score, Liza Minnelli brilliantly leads a fine ensemble in this prime example of how a hit stage show can be reinvented for the screen. Its eight Oscars suggest a team effort, but the key creator of this vision of a world on the brink was director Bob Fosse.

## 6 The Wizard Of Oz
1939; see p.178

Studded with unforgettable tunes and cherishable performances, this is the most magical musical ever made. Its Technicolor artifice only improves with age, and Judy Garland's "Over The Rainbow" remains the most movingly delivered song in the genre's history.

## 7 Gold Diggers Of 1933
1933; see p.102

Busby Berkeley gives a masterclass in geometric choreography in this ultimate backstager, and proves in the "Remember My Forgotten Man" finale that musicals have the power to be much more than escapist entertainment.

## 8 My Fair Lady
1964; see p.132

Beating Rodgers and Hammerstein at their own game and proving that there was still room for the integrated book musical in the swinging sixties, Lerner and Loewe brought a satirical edge to the genre just when it was in danger of being subsumed by folksy sentiment.

## 9 A Star Is Born
1954; see p.167

There's genuine pain inJudy Garland's terrifyingly honest performance, which is the most powerful ever given in a film musical. This sour riposte to *Singin' In The Rain*'s Tinseltown optimism heralded the end of an era.

## 10 Nashville
1975; see p.135

Robert Altman's uncompromising revisionist assault on the conventions of the musical is scurrilously funny. But it's also desperately sad. It proclaims not only the demise of the genre, but also of the nation that had inspired it.

# The Canon: 50 essential film musicals

## An American In Paris

***dir*** **Vincente Minnelli, 1951, 115m**

***cast*** **Gene Kelly, Leslie Caron, Oscar Levant, George Guétary, Nina Foch** ***cin*** **Alfred Gilks, John Alton** ***m*** **George Gershwin, Ira Gershwin**

---

Intent on proving that film was not merely escapist entertainment, but was legitimately the "seventh art", **Gene Kelly** and **Vincente Minnelli** fused music, design and performance in *An American In Paris* to fashion the story of a GI bent on becoming an artist into a cinematic tone poem.

MGM producer **Arthur Freed** secured **Ira Gershwin**'s permission to create a musical from his brother George's 1928 composition, *An American In Paris*, in 1949, during one of their regular games of pool. Lyricist **Alan Jay Lerner** was hired to write a scenario that could accommodate highlights from the Gershwin songbook at key dramatic and psychological points in the narrative. However, the

Gene Kelly and Leslie Caron in the "An American In Paris" ballet, a masterly amalgam of music and movement, art and artifice, which transformed screen dance.

music also had to reinforce the picture's bid for universal appeal by combining Americans and Europeans, the young and the old, the concert hall and the music hall, friendship and romance, the populist and the highbrow.

Sally Forrest, Cyd Charisse and Odile Versois were all considered for the role of leading lady Lise Bouvier. However, Kelly had seen **Leslie Caron** dancing on stage when she was just 15 years old and was convinced that she had the necessary gamine quality and balletic technique to play the war orphan who steals the heart of his character, Jerry Mulligan, a genial émigré who comes to terms with himself and his talent through her love. Carl Brisson and Maurice Chevalier were mooted for the role of vaudeville star Henri Baurel, but the part eventually went to **Georges Guetary** (who was renowned as the French Fred Astaire) after Chevalier refused to lose the girl.

*An American In Paris* was conceived as a film of set pieces, with each flowing from the storyline but remaining entirely individual. Kelly's rendition of "I Got Rhythm" with a group of street kids, for example, contrasts charmingly with his exhilarating duets with Guetary ("'S Wonderful") and **Oscar Levant** ("By Strauss") and his serenading of Caron with "Our Love Is Here To Stay". The showstoppers are even more ingenious. A grand Folies-Bergère staircase with illuminated steps was created for Guetary's "I'll Build A Stairway To Paradise", while deft process photography was used to enable the six facets of Lise Bouvier's personality to appear simultaneously during "Embraceable You" and to allow Levant to play the entire orchestra and the audience on the third movement of Gershwin's *Concerto In F*.

However, nothing matches the scope, refinement and sheer audacity of the "An American In Paris" ballet, which lasts an unprecedented 16 minutes and 37 seconds, and took a month to shoot. Meticulously designed by **Irene Sharaff** and **Preston Ames** and photographed by **John Alton** with a smoky quality that enhances the pastoral shades, the ballet is a Hollywood tribute to the spirit that inspired both the Impressionists' art and Gershwin's music. Each of the locations evokes the style of a specific painter: Place de la Concorde, Dufy; Madeleine flower market, Renoir; a street carnival, Utrillo; Jardin des Plantes, Rousseau; Place de l'Opéra, Van Gogh; Montmatre, Toulouse-Lautrec. Moving through these Parisian locations, Kelly switches brilliantly between classical and modern ballet, Cohanesque hoofing, tap, jitterbugging and athletic exuberance to counterpoint the character of the visuals and create "a synthesis of old forms and new rhythms".

While this Technicolor extravaganza grossed in excess of $8 million on a $2,723,903 budget, some critics complained about its lack of humour and surfeit of sophistication. Yet Minnelli and Kelly had set out to make a serious musical, and they certainly impressed their peers, who rewarded them with six Oscars, including the award for best picture. Moreover, Kelly received an honorary award "in appreciation of his versatility as an actor, singer, director and dancer, and specifically for his brilliant achievements in the art of choreography on film". *An American In Paris* saw the MGM musical finally become an art form. But, within a decade, it was to become an anachronism.

# Annie Get Your Gun

## *dir* George Sidney, 1950, 107m

*cast* **Betty Hutton, Howard Keel, Louis Calhern, Edward Arnold, Keenan Wynn** *cin* **Charles Rosher** *m* **Irving Berlin**

The capriciousness of the movie business is effectively summed up by the contrasting fates of MGM's *Annie Get Your Gun* and Warner Bros' *Calamity Jane* (1953). Fictionalizing the feats of nineteenth-century sharp-shooters Phoebe Anne Oakley Moses and Martha

## Calamity Jane

Warner Bros produced this rousing slice of entertainment in 1953 to compensate **Doris Day** for missing out on the lead role in *Annie Get Your Gun*. The studio even borrowed **Howard Keel** from MGM to be her co-star and had **Sammy Fain** and **Paul Francis Webster** write "I Can Do Without You" as a challenge song riposte to **Irving Berlin**'s magnificent "Anything You Can Do". But while there was plenty of vim in "The Deadwood Stage" and "Just Blew In From The Windy City", the remaining songs couldn't compete with the gems from Berlin's score. "Secret Love" was a worthy Oscar winner and it afforded Day her third million-selling single, but it was the only true standout in a picture that exposed the actress's shortcomings as an all-rounder as often as it showcased her melodic sweetness.

Jane Burke respectively, they each featured an anachronistically vivacious blonde in the title role, had **Howard Keel** as the leading man and romanticized the harsh realities of life in the Wild West. Yet Warner Bros' highly derivative screen original is much more fondly remembered than MGM's adaptation of **Irving Berlin**'s Broadway hit – even though the latter boasts an infinitely superior score, a stronger supporting ensemble and considerably more wit and charm.

The received wisdom is that **Betty Hutton** hammed her way through Annie Oakley's love-hate relationship with Frank Butler, while **Doris Day** exhibited adorable élan in portraying Calamity's determination to prise Wild Bill Hickok away from chanteuse Katie Brown. In fact, Day is every bit as guilty of gnawing the scenery as Hutton – but she hadn't committed the cardinal sin of replacing **Judy Garland**.

*Annie Get Your Gun*'s successful Broadway run had persuaded MGM to spend a record $650,000 to acquire it as Garland's next big showcase. But her addictions and mental problems had left the 26-year-old in no fit state to tackle her first radical departure from the patented Garland persona. The film's musical director **Roger Edens** first noticed that Garland was struggling to connect with the material when she came to record her nine songs, but it was the stress of working with the aggressive **Busby Berkeley** that prompted her breakdown. Berkeley was eventually dismissed, and Garland rallied briefly under the more solicitous direction of **Charles Walters**. However, she knew she was wrong for the role and, after enduring six days of filming for "I'm An Indian, Too", she was fired for her unprofessional attitude.

Producer **Arthur Freed** initially considered Betty Garrett as Garland's replacement, as she possessed something of the gusto that Ethel Merman had brought to the 1946 stage production. But he finally opted to borrow Hutton from Paramount, even though many MGM insiders were sceptical about her (especially as Doris Day, Judy Canova, June Allyson and Ginger Rogers all supposedly coveted the part). On-set morale was morbidly low. Not only had Walters been callously replaced by **George Sidney**, but Walter Plunkett's costumes had been discarded and **Sidney Sheldon**'s script had been revised to accommodate new comic routines that Hutton had insisted upon to replace Robert Alton's more complex dance numbers. The entire score also had been recast in Hutton's range. Yet

Sidney and Hutton approached their tasks with vigour, because they felt they had something to prove, and Keel (who had avoided much of the chaos by breaking his ankle falling from his horse on the second day of filming) was keen to make a good impression in his first Hollywood musical. All three threw themselves into the project. Hutton burst through the screen during the showstoppers "You Can't Get A Man With A Gun", "Doin' What Comes Natur'lly" and "I'm An Indian Too", and more than held her own against Keel on "Anything You Can Do" and the anthemic "There's No Business Like Show Business".

Costing $3,768,785, *Annie Get Your Gun* grossed more than $8,000,000, and proved to be one of the Freed Unit's most profitabe pictures. It also earned Edens and **Adolph Deutsch** Academy Awards for their score. Audiences warmed to Hutton's courageously exhilarating efforts, although the critics detected a desperation in her performance that was exacerbated by Keel's stiffness. This unfairly disparaged gem not only remained true to its source, but also added plenty of cinematic spectacle, particularly in the rousing finale, and its reappraisal is long overdue.

# The Band Wagon

## *dir* Vincente Minnelli, 1953, 111m

*cast* **Fred Astaire, Cyd Charisse, Oscar Levant, Jack Buchanan, Nanette Fabray, James Mitchell, Robert Gist**
*cin* **Harry Jackson** *m* **Arthur Schwartz, Howard Dietz**

*The Band Wagon* has much in common with *Singin' In The Rain* (1952). Each film showcases a catalogue of popular standards, and each features a song-and-dance man who not only emerges from a potential career crisis with his reputation enhanced, but also finds love with his leading lady. But whereas **Gene Kelly**'s confident classic was an optimistic paean to talking pictures, **Fred Astaire**'s underrated homage to the stage was shrouded in a pessimism that implied that the days of old-time show business were numbered.

One reason for this shift in tone was the imposition of draconian economies on producer Arthur Freed and the **Freed Unit** by the new MGM regime. With costs rising, audiences falling and tastes changing, the studio could no longer afford to bankroll musicals studded with spectacular set pieces – even though Freed was the only consistently profitable producer on the Culver City lot. The end-of-an-era malaise was intensified by the fact that Astaire's contract was about to lapse; *The Band Wagon* was to be his valedictory swan song.

This sense of finality inspired **Betty Comden** and **Adolph Green** to lace their screenplay with biographical details and satirical allusions, much as they had done in *The Barkleys Of Broadway* (1949), which also examined the clash between art and entertainment. Thus, the character of Tony Hunter is Astaire himself, while Lily and Lester Marton (**Nanette Fabray** and **Oscar Levant**) are based on the screenwriters. Despite these ready sources, the script took some contriving because **Arthur Schwartz** and **Howard Dietz** had previously written most of their songs for revues. So, while their compositions were supremely sentimental summations of yesteryear, they were less useful in developing character or plot.

Five songs were retained from the original 1931 Broadway musical (which also starred Astaire), and eight more were imported from other Schwartz-Dietz shows and given narrative functions. For example, "By Myself" and "A Shine On Your Shoes" were used to establish Tony's mindset as he returns washed-up from Hollywood, while "Dancing In The Dark" suggests his growing affection for ballerina Gabrielle Gerard (**Cyd Charisse**), after their initial antipathy at rehearsals.

The majority of the showstoppers were held back for the grand finale, which **Vincente Minnelli** staged with typical ingenuity. Obviously theatrical settings became irresistibly cinematic thanks to his intuitive use of light, colour, space and design. In "New Sun In The Sky", the moving camera gloriously frames Charisse against a blaze of red and gold swirls, while subtle specks of light were used to embellish Fabray's rendition of "Louisiana Hayride". The distortion of perspective that allows Astaire, Fabray and **Jack Buchanan** (as pompous actor-manager Jeffrey Cordova) to play babies in "Triplets" is equally dextrous, while Astaire and Buchanan's pairing on "I Guess I'll Have To Change My Plan" genially evolves into the soft-shoe equivalent of Charlie Chaplin and Buster Keaton's nostalgic masterclass in *Limelight* (1952).

Minnelli surpassed himself with the "Girl Hunt" ballet. Devised by **Alan Jay Lerner** as a Mickey Spillane parody and choreographed by **Michael Kidd**, this pulp reverie recalled Astaire's persona in *Yolanda And The Thief* (1945) and became his favourite routine. Its *noir*-ish atmosphere also reflected the picture's recurring references to Germanic culture (particularly Freud, operetta and Expressionism). This mix of highbrow and lowbrow culture is crucial to the dualism at *The Band Wagon*'s core. By championing tradition and collaboration over modernity and megalomania, the film laid itself open to accusations of anti-elitism: Cordova's latterday *Faust* is exposed as pretentious tosh, while Hunter's triumph proves that nothing can beat good old-fashioned entertainment.

Even though Comden and Green gently lampooned Minnelli's stylistic preoccupations and **Rodgers and Hammerstein**'s predilection for social message, the picture's rousing climax epitomizes the lyrics of "That's Entertainment" by demonstrating that whether it's old or new, classical or popular, every form of art and performance is valid, providing it pleases the public. Moreover, it confirms that class never goes out of style and that, as Cordova suggests, there's "no difference between the magic rhythms of Bill Shakespeare's immortal verse and the magic rhythms of Bill Robinson's immortal feet".

*The Band Wagon*'s intelligent intimacy and thematic and emotional richness failed to lure lapsed patrons away from their new television sets or to impress young cinemagoers eager for widescreen extravaganza. Although a critical triumph, the film had only moderate box-office success, and it convinced Hollywood that the musical's future lay primarily in transferring proven hits from Broadway.

# Cabaret

## *dir* Bob Fosse, 1972, 128m

**_cast_ Liza Minnelli, Michael York, Helmut Griem, Joel Grey, Fritz Wepper, Marisa Berenson _cin_ Geoffrey Unsworth _m_ John Kander, Fred Ebb**

---

*Cabaret* had a convoluted ancestry. **Christopher Isherwood**'s 1937 vingette, "Sally Bowles", had been reworked as both a play and a film called *I Am A Camera* in the 1950s, before Broadway director **Hal Prince** turned the story of a young cabaret singer living in Berlin in

## *Cabaret* on Broadway

Producer and director **Hal Prince** first conceived the idea of a musical version of *I Am A Camera* in the early 1960s, and hired songwriters **John Kander** and **Fred Ebb** to mould the contentious material into shape. They had just collaborated with **Liza Minnelli** on *Flora, The Red Menace* (1965) and wrote the score with her in mind. But she was overlooked when casting time came.

Renamed *Cabaret*, the Broadway production opened in 1966, bearing the musical influence of *The Threepenny Opera* and the visual style of German Expressionists George Grosz and Otto Dix. It ran for 1,165 performances and won eight Tony Awards (a tally that **Bob Fosse**'s movie equalled at the Oscars in 1973).

the 1930s into a musical in 1966. However, **Bob Fosse**'s feature was anything but a typical Hollywoodization of the stage show.

Scriptwriter **Jay Presson Allen** returned to the source, restoring the gay themes that had been deleted from the play and stage show. Her film script refocused attention on the amorous adventures of a naive British writer (**Michael York**), who shares the beds of both a bisexual Prussian nobleman (**Helmut Griem**) and an American chanteuse (**Liza Minnelli**) eking out a living in a seedy nightclub. Consequently, the sub-plot centring on a Berlin landlady and her greengrocer lover was dropped and replaced by one involving a Jewish heiress and a gold-digger. However, the emcee at the Kit Kat Klub (**Joel Grey**) retained his role as a cynical commentator of his patrons indulging in "divine decadence" to escape from the realities of the Weimar Republic's decline.

Most significantly, Allen cut the libretto's story songs. This gave director **Bob Fosse** the opportunity to rid the movie of the "removed reality" it had inherited from the stage. Fosse felt that modern audiences would reject the sight of ordinary people suddenly breaking into song in everyday situations. Therefore, with the notable exception of the chilling "Make Way For Tomorrow", performance was restricted to the tiny nightclub stage, which reinforced the claustrophobic feel of an increasingly fascistic society closing in on its victims.

In many ways, this revisionist approach makes the film less of a musical than the stage show. Fosse was keen to break with the integrated tradition that had held sway since *Oklahoma!* However, he also cuts away from the Kit Kat Klub to allow the song and dance routines to assume a metaphorical significance. A Bavarian slap dance is juxtaposed with the club proprietor's savage back-alley beating, while a high-kicking chorus line is contrasted with goose-stepping Brown Shirts.

Similarly, the songs reflect life in the outside world. By limiting their lyrical insights to the cabaret cast, Fosse makes it clear that the hedonist punters hiding in this hermetic cocoon have chosen not to see what is happening in the wider world. "Wilkommen" represents the club's cosmopolitan clientele, but also anticipates the future hostilities between Britain, France and Germany. "Two Ladies" parodies the Nazi view of homosexuality, while "If You Could See Her" echoes the propagandist depiction of the Jews. "The Money Song" alludes to both the power and corruption of capitalism and the impact of the Depression that prefaced Hitler's dictatorship, while "Don't Tell Mama" contrasts the Weimar Republic's *laissez-faire* attitude with the coming authoritarianism of the Third Reich.

Having been sung so many times outside of its narrative context, "Cabaret" has become something of a kitsch classic. But it's actually the sardonic affirmation of a woman who has elected to discard her lover, abort his baby and remain in a country that's descending into tyranny because in this sad, twisted environment she's a star – and that's her sole concern. Sally Bowles is an anti-heroine, not a *42nd Street* (1933) ingenue with music in her soul. And the song is less a showbiz anthem than a sour celebration of selfishness.

Oblivious to the sinister posters behind them, Liza Minnelli and Michael York revel in a moment away from the "divine decadence" of the Kit Kat Klub.

By having Sally embody the tension between social individualism and political inertia, *Cabaret* champions the right to be different, while also warning against the dangers of the marginalized and the complacent renouncing their responsibilities. Moreover, by confounding the backstage musical formula – by parting the lovers and having the show be anything but a success – the film reveals itself to be a study of obsessions and fears, not hopes and dreams. By opting for introspection rather than escapism *Cabaret* hauls the sub-genre into the real world that it tried so hard to avoid back in the 1930s.

# Carousel

## *dir* Henry King, 1956, 128m

**_cast_ Gordon MacRae, Shirley Jones, Cameron Mitchell, Barbara Ruick, John Dehner _cin_ Charles G. Clarke _m_ Richard Rodgers, Oscar Hammerstein II**

Opening on Broadway in April 1945, *Carousel* was the most underrated of **Richard Rodgers** and **Oscar Hammerstein**'s major musicals. Introducing a trenchant realism and a working-class sensibility, it confirmed all of *Oklahoma!*'s innovations – long musical sequences, dream ballets, reprises and "almost" love songs – and refined them by binding them more tightly into the narrative. *Carousel* was, as Alan Jay Lerner recognized, a "modern operetta", whose dramatic use of melody, lyric and choreography established a new form of "musical play". But more than just altering stage conceptions of musical drama, it also validated the emphasis on greater thematic depth. As Stephen Sondheim later suggested, "*Oklahoma!* is about a picnic; *Carousel* is about life and death."

Unfortunately, 20th Century-Fox's screen version failed to do the show full justice – a dereliction that was made all the more frustrating by the fact that, in the same year, the studio did such a solid job of filming another Rodgers and Hammerstein classic, *The King And I* (1956). The decision to open the action with Billy Bigelow polishing stars and wishing that he could atone for his deficiencies as a husband and father was a major miscalculation. However, the real reason for the movie misfiring was the inadequacy of some of the key personnel.

Although he was a competent director of Americana, **Henry King** had no talent for musicals, and the studio undermined his cause by replacing much of Agnes De Mille's stage choreography with vibrant, but gauche widescreen extravaganzas designed by **Rod Alexander**. Producer **Henry Ephron** also failed to land the dream pairing of Frank Sinatra and Judy Garland. So when his second choice, Gene Kelly, refused to have his singing dubbed, Ephron was left with little option but to reunite *Oklahoma!* (1955) co-stars **Gordon MacRae** and **Shirley Jones**. However, MacRae lacked the actorly instinct to convey the complexity of his character or to interact convincingly with the mix of stylized sets and authentic locations.

Despite its cinematic shortcomings, *Carousel* remains a compositional masterpiece. The score was not only crucial in giving everyday characters a way of expressing emotions they couldn't convey by mere speech, it also set new parameters for musical sophistication. Songs ranged from the melodious "If I Loved You" to the exuberant "June Is Bustin' Out All Over" and the inspirational "You'll Never Walk Alone", which became a 1963 hit for Gerry and the Pacemakers and a football terrace anthem. Most audacious of all was the eight-minute, near-operatic "Soliloquy", which broke with the customary AABA song structure to explore the workshy Bigelow's determination to provide for his trusting wife, Julie, and their unborn child.

*Carousel* is primarily a love story. But it's also about the social hierarchy of 1870s New England, with Billy being a descendant of Hammerstein's wanderlust characters from *Show Boat*, *High, Wide And Handsome* and *Oklahoma!* Indeed, Billy and Jigger's attempted robbery of Mr Bascombe's cotton mill could be seen as a romantic rebellion against an exploitative hypocrite, who uses his wealth to impose his moral code upon the community. Librettist and lyricist Hammerstein clearly sides with Billy and Julie's bid to snatch happiness and suggests that their comic counterparts, Enoch Snow and Carrie Pipperidge, are not quaintly bashful, but are Bascombes in the making, underpinning their relationship with prudish materialism, rather than love.

Although he advocates that life should be lived spontaneously and passionately, Hammerstein upholds the force of the law and prevents the reckless Billy from dying heroically for a noble cause – as so many Americans were doing at the time of the 1945 stage original. In post-war America, the story seemed to promise the nation's bereaved that even though their loved ones were gone, their spirits lived on. However, by 1956, such sentiments seemed maudlin and trite to the rock generation, and the movie reportedly lost $2 million (even though the soundtrack spent 56 weeks on the American album chart). The filmic flaws certainly had a detrimental effect, but there were moments of exhilaration, tragedy and pathos in *Carousel* and it's about time this ambitious and musically glorious fantasy was given its artistic due.

# Chicago

## *dir* Rob Marshall, 2002, 113m

**_cast_ Renée Zellwegger, Catherine Zeta-Jones, Richard Gere, Queen Latifah, John C. Reilly, Lucy Liu, _cin_ Dion Beebe _m_ John Kander, Fred Ebb**

*Chicago* encapsulates the sheer unpredictability of the musical business. **Bob Fosse**'s 1975 stage original perished in the shadow of Michael Bennett's *A Chorus Line*, with mixed reviews preceding a sound thrashing at the Tony Awards, where *Chicago* failed to convert any of its nominations, while Bennett's show landed nine. However, the 1985 film of *A Chorus Line* proved to be a commercial and critical calamity, whereas *Chicago* was given a new lease of life when its record-breaking Broadway revival persuaded Miramax to greenlight **Rob Marshall's** screen adaptation, which went on to land six Oscars and gross over $300 million from a $45 million budget.

This study of celebrity and the public's complicity in its bestowal started as a 1926 stage drama. Playwright **Maurine Dallas Watkins** based the action on her *Chicago Tribune* coverage of the jazz slayings committed by cabaret singer Belva Gaertner and the Windy City's "prettiest prisoner", Beulah Annan, who was acquitted of shooting her lover in the back thanks to a media frenzy and the artful pleading of her attorney. After becoming a Christian, Watkins came to despise the film versions, *Chicago* (1927) and *Roxie Hart* (1942), because of their glamorization of tawdry events, and she frustrated any bids to musicalize the play. After her death in 1969, Fosse and his *Cabaret* collaborators, **John Kander** and **Fred Ebb**, reworked the story as a three-ring circus, to expose how America's principal insitutions had been reduced to cheap entertainments. But such variety schtick led to accusations of excessive cynicism and theatrical decadence and much of it was stripped away by **Walter Bobbie** for his leaner, meaner, sexier 1996 revival.

Thanks to the infamous O.J. Simpson trial, *Chicago* was no longer a satire, but a documentary. The base spirit and sardonic wit that had riled Americans shamed by Watergate and capitulation in Vietnam now chimed in with the public appetite for celebrity scandal, which was shamelessly encouraged by the gutter press. And it was this sensationalism that inspired Marshall's 2002 movie.

Marshall and screenwriter **Bill Condon** had to rethink the libretto to accommodate the MTV generation's scepticism about characters bursting into song in supposedly everyday situations. Their solution came from Lars von Trier's *Dancer In The Dark* (2000), which had presented the musical routines as interior monologues. Therefore, Marshall and Condon set the numbers in Roxie Hart's imagination, in order to exploit her celebrity-fixated conviction that her life was one big song and dance. Marshall further borrowed von Trier's tactic of using random sounds to motivate the escapist shifts – although he also devised some neat visual cues of his own and made shrewd use of symbolism to heighten the corniness of the starstruck contexts.

Marshall had to drop six songs to make the new structure work. Although stage favourites like "Class" were lost, he atoned by mounting bravura renditions of "All That Jazz", "We Reached For The Gun" and "Razzle Dazzle", while "All He Cares About" and "Funny Honey" neatly allude to the *Ziegfeld Follies* and *Show Boat*. **Queen Latifah**, as the sassy prison warden, socks it to "When You're Good To Mama" and **Catherine Zeta-Jones** makes temptress Velma sensually sympathetic. But **Renée Zellwegger** struggles to convey Roxie's growing cunning and **Richard Gere**'s courtroom tap dance lacks pizzazz. However, the most disconcerting element of the film is **Martin Walsh**'s whiplash editing, which constantly disrupts the performances in order to give the visuals an anachronistically modern attention-deficient snap.

With its CGI-enhanced 1920s street scenes evoking the paintings of Reginald Marsh and the photography of Brassaï, *Chicago* was sold as a biting allegory on millennial morality. However, it's

## *Chicago*: the musical no one wanted to make

*Chicago* took a quarter of a century to reach the screen. Liza Minnelli was linked with an adaptation in the mid-1970s, and **Bob Fosse** was planning talks with Madonna when he died in 1987. Another version that never materialized boasted Goldie Hawn and Madonna as Roxie and Velma. **Nicholas Hytner** agreed to direct in 1998, but departed amid speculation that Charlize Theron and Nicole Kidman were set for the female leads, while John Travolta, Kevin Kline and Rupert Everett were competing for the role of Billy Flynn.

A further round of rumours followed **Rob Marshall**'s appointment as director. Catherine Zeta-Jones was always his first choice for Velma, but Gwyneth Paltrow, Cameron Diaz, Toni Collette, Milla Jovovich, Marisa Tomei and Angelina Jolie were all considered before **Renée Zellwegger** was selected for Roxie, despite her admission that she didn't understand the film's shifts between stylized reality and fantastical escapism. Hugh Jackman, John Cusack and Kevin Spacey were also mooted before **Richard Gere** was cast as Billy.

intriguing to note that this self-proclaimed champion of the musical eschewed all mention of song and dance in its trailer. The genre was still clearly considered a risky curio rather than the box-office banker it had once been.

# Easter Parade

## *dir* Charles Walters, 1948, 103m

**_cast_ Judy Garland, Fred Astaire, Ann Miller, Peter Lawford _cin_ Harry Stradling _m_ Irving Berlin**

According to the cynics, *Easter Parade*'s pre-production was more interesting than the picture itself. Set in 1912, it follows the fortunes of a vaudevillian who vows to turn a bar-room chorine into a star after he's dumped by his Broadway-bound dance partner. Although it may not be the **Freed Unit**'s most sophisticated offering, this is certainly their most polished piece of escapist entertainment and it's doubtful whether **Vincente Minnelli** could have done a better job than **Charles Walters** had he not been forced to quit after five days, on the advice of his troubled wife **Judy Garland**'s psychiatrist.

Garland was to star in this MGM project alongside Gene Kelly, but he fractured his ankle playing touch football (although he told the studio that the accident happened during rehearsals) and had to be replaced. Producer **Arthur Freed** briefly considered casting Gene Nelson, before persuading 48-year-old **Fred Astaire** to come out of retirement. Having been reassured that filming couldn't be delayed and that Kelly would be incapacitated for several months, Astaire signed up for his fifth collaboration with composer **Irving Berlin**. Their last film together had been Paramount's *Blue Skies* (1946), the success of which had persuaded Freed to offer Berlin an unprecedented $500,000 fee and a percentage of the profits in return for access to his songbook.

While associate producer **Roger Edens** selected the standards, Berlin produced a raft of new tunes, including "It Only Happens When I Dance With You", "A Fella With An Umbrella" and "Steppin' Out With My Baby". However, "I Love You, You Love Him" and "Mister Monotony" were cut from the final print, and

Freed took exception to the proposed speciality number "Let's Take An Old-Fashioned Walk" – but Berlin replaced it with "A Couple Of Swells" within the hour.

Berlin was also invited to share his early showbiz memories with screenwriters **Frances Goodrich** and **Albert Hackett**. But Walters (who was directing only his second feature film) disliked the script's overreliance on the Pygmalion myth and persuaded Freed to hire **Sidney Sheldon** to tone down its misanthropy. Ultimately, the storyline bore echoes of *For Me And My Gal* (1942), but admirably captured the backstage mood and accommodated Berlin's numbers with seamless ease.

Despite the fact that she had to leave filming to rejoin Minnelli seventeen times for retakes on *The Pirate*, (1948), Garland revelled in this project. She made a delightful job of solos such as "Better Luck Next Time" and of the oldies "I Love A Piano", "Snooky Ookums" and "When That Midnight Choo-Choo Leaves For Alabam" in the marvellous vaudeville montage sequence with Astaire. He also excelled in his duets with both Garland and **Ann Miller**, while his speciality solos, "Drum Crazy" and "Steppin' Out With My Baby", showed no signs of his thirteen-month absence from the screen. Indeed, in the latter routine (which paid homage to *Top Hat*, 1935, and *Carefree*, 1938) he danced a pseudo-ballet, a sultry blues and a zesty jitterbug with three different female partners before launching into a tap solo that culminated in a slo-mo sequence that took four weeks to edit. Yet, for once, Astaire was upstaged: Miller's explosive rendition of "Shaking The Blues Away" demonstrated exactly why MGM had recruited her to replace Eleanor Powell as the studio's resident tap dancer.

Fred Astaire sits this one out in his only screen teaming with Judy Garland.

*Easter Parade* cost an estimated $2,500,000 and grossed $6,800,000, and earned Edens and conductor **Johnny Green** Academy Awards for the best scoring of a musical picture. But most significantly, it relaunced Fred Astaire's career and established the character – the teacher-initiator who falls for his protégée – that he would go on to play in *The Barkleys Of Broadway* (1949), *Daddy Long Legs* (1955), *Funny Face* and *Silk Stockings* (both 1957).

# Evita

### *dir* Alan Parker, 1996, 88m

***cast*** **Madonna, Antonio Banderas, Jonathan Pryce, Jimmy Nail, Victoria Sus, Julian Littman** ***cin*** **Darius Khondji** ***m*** **Andrew Lloyd Webber, Tim Rice**

Strictly speaking, *Evita* shouldn't really be included in a book about musicals. According to the theorists, musicals are stories with songs, rather than sung stories. But while previous drafts of the screenplay contained passages of dialogue, director and screenwriter **Alan Parker** honoured **Tim Rice** and **Andrew Lloyd Webber**'s original intentions and produced an opera that owed as much to their 1976 concept album as the various stage shows that followed it.

Rice conceived the original project after a visit to Argentina in 1974 and based his lyrics on Mary Main's biography, *Evita: The Woman With The Whip* (1952), which has since been challenged for its shaky facts and propagandist slant. Lloyd Webber concurred in this depiction of Eva Perón, dubbing her "easily the most unpleasant character about whom I have written, except perhaps Perón himself". However, Alan Parker sought more balance in his 1996 movie, casting Evita somewhere between the saint claimed by the Perónistas and the demon whore of her enemies.

Although Parker was the first to be offered the movie, he initially declined, as he didn't want to do another musical after *Fame* (1980). So began a fifteen-year cycle of rumour, lobbying and cancellation that saw Ken Russell, Herbert Ross, Alan J. Pakula, Hector Babenco, Franco Zeffirelli, Francis Ford Coppola, Richard Attenborough, Michael Cimino, Glenn Gordon Caron and Oliver Stone all being linked with the project. Parker finally came back on board more than a decade later, and **Madonna** – who eventually won the role of Evita thanks to a frank letter and a powerhouse video – **Antonio Banderas** and **Jonathan Pryce** were cast in the principal roles.

It's now impossible to imagine anyone other than Madonna playing Evita. In addition to the pronounced physical resemblance, Madonna's controversial career has provoked equally polarized reactions. And without her kudos, Parker would never have been allowed to use the Casa Rosada (the presidential palace) in Buenos Aires to shoot the "Don't Cry For Me Argentina" balcony sequence that provides the film's emotional core. Moreover, Madonna's rendition of "You Must Love Me" – in which Evita pleads for reassurance that she means more to Perón than the adoration of the masses – helped Rice and Lloyd Webber land their Oscars for best song (although Madonna herself was shamefully snubbed for best actress).

Parker reportedly made 146 changes to the score and lyrics, most notably switching "Another Suitcase In Another Hall" from Perón's mistress to Evita, and restoring "The Lady's Got Potential" from the original album. However, he retained Rice's insight and wit in creating a sort of self-reflexive musical variation of *Citizen Kane*, in which Che Guevara goes in search of the reasons why Evita's good intentions were corrupted by celebrity, piety and autocratic arrogance, and discovers that her Rosebud was the humiliation of being excluded from her father's funeral by his bourgeois family.

The reviews were mixed, with some criticizing Parker for his impartial stance. But such ambiguity only enhances the film's intellectual and musical appeal. The melodrama of Evita's life is played out against a setting that consciously evokes the grandiose theatricality of fascist Europe. Thus, the shifts between heightened reality and gritty naturalism were perfectly pitched, most

## Casting Evita

Over the years, numerous actresses were slated to play Evita on screen, including:

Elaine Paige, Liza Minnelli, Meryl Streep, Michelle Pfeiffer, Charo, Patti Lupone, Raquel Welch, Ann-Margret, Barbra Streisand, Bette Midler, Diane Keaton, Kim Wilde, Pia Zadora, Olivia Newton-John, Cyndi Lauper, Gloria Estefan, Mariah Carey, Maria Conchita Alonso and Glenn Close.

Wearing outfits inspired by Eva Péron's own wardrobe, Madonna broke the record Elizabeth Taylor set in *Cleopatra* (1963) for the most costume changes in a single movie.

notably during editor **Gerry Hambling**'s exemplary montages for "A New Argentina", "The Rainbow Tour" and "And The Money Kept Rolling In (And Out)", which gave the action impetus without distracting from the sociopolitical cut and thrust of the lyrics.

Much was made of the fact that Madonna wore a record 85 costumes and sported 39 hats, 45 pairs of shoes, 56 pairs of earrings and 42 hairstyles. However, such statistics only reinforced the picture's thesis on fame and the public's willingness to believe that an icon is as honest and philanthropic as they are charismatic and photogenic. This approach to the cult of personality and the relationship between rulers and the ruled brought a new thematic maturity to the musical that challenged its former escapist rationale. Sadly, the genre failed to follow *Evita*'s lead over the ensuing decade and, consequently, it remained something of a cultural irrelevance.

# 42nd Street

## *dir* Lloyd Bacon, 1933, 89m, b/w

**_cast_ Warner Baxter, Bebe Daniels, Ruby Keeler, Dick Powell _cin_ Sol Polito _m_ Harry Warren, Al Dubin**

The musical was considered box-office poison in the 1930s when Warner Bros production chief **Darryl F. Zanuck** embarked on *42nd Street*. According to legend, he prepared two scripts and showed the Warner execs the one without songs, while **Busby Berkeley** was secretly installed in the Vitagraph Studio on Sunset Boulevard to supervise the musical numbers. After everything was finally merged in the cutting room, **Harry Warner** conceded it was "the greatest picture [Zanuck had] sent over in five years".

Although based on a novel by **Bradford Ropes**, the story of an understudy becoming an eleventh-hour star was an old chestnut, which Warner Bros had already exploited for the first all-colour sound feature, *On With The Show* (1929). *42nd Street* is essentially a film about getting a job and making money in tough times, but it reeks of seedy authenticity. Sugar daddy Abner Dillon (**Guy Kibbee**) bankrolls producer Julian Marsh's (**Warner Baxter**) Broadway swan song, *Pretty Lady*, in order to ogle the chorines, as well as to keep his chanteuse mistress (**Bebe Daniels**) happy. Similarly, the chorus boys and stage-door Johnnies are on the make with showgirls like Anytime Annie (**Ginger Rogers**), who wears a monocle and carries a Pekingese with stellar affectation.

However, the movie is also a political parable. It showed 1930s Americans how they could extricate themselves from the Depression by uniting behind a strong leader and pulling for a common cause. It was no coincidence that the cast was invited to President Roosevelt's inauguration. This was a New Deal musical, whose famous line, "You've got to go on and you've got to give, and give and give… You're going out a youngster, but you've got to come back a star!", chimed in with FDR's panacea for the nation's malaise.

A realist picture, *42nd Street* does not sanitize the sweat and toil of rehearsals or the stark fact that a flop would mean hardship for everyone, from the chorines to the sparks. The backstage milieu is populated with hardened professionals, made cynical by the ruthless business of transient fame, envy and treachery. Yet the success of the show is linked directly to the romantic fate of innocent juveniles Peggy Sawyer (**Ruby Keeler**) and Billy Lawler (**Dick Powell**) – a convention that would continue throughout the genre's heyday.

Berkeley's dance routines were New Deal models in themselves. He kept dozens of girls gainfully employed for weeks as he worked his magic on the **Al Dubin** and **Harry Warren** numbers "Shuffle Off To Buffalo", "Young And Healthy" and "42nd Street". The dance numbers also provided the structural tension, as there is no polished perfection in the dramatic sequences, it is only in the glorious finale.

While it seemed to hint at a happy ending, the final shot of Baxter looking exhausted as the theatre empties reiterates the idea that while it may be entertainment and escapism for some, for others showbiz is about enthusiasm, energy and effort. That elusive success is down to the unpredictable reaction of the critics and punters, as much as the quality of the show. Indeed, no guarantees are given that Peggy will sustain her instant celebrity, and it is even implied that she won't truly make it until she became a movie star. Such uncompromising honesty appealed to contemporary audiences, and the musical was relaunched when this $379,000 risk became the year's third-biggest grosser ($2.5 million). No wonder Warner Bros billed it as "The Entertainment Miracle of 1933".

One engineer said the "By A Waterfall" set looked like the engine room of an ocean liner.

# Footlight Parade

## *dir* Lloyd Bacon, 1933, 104m, b/w

*cast* James Cagney, Joan Blondell, Ruby Keeler, Dick Powell *cin* George Barnes *m* Harry Warren, Al Dubin

Keen to exploit the success of *42nd Street* and *Gold Diggers Of 1933* before the rest of Hollywood realized that the screen musical had been revived, Warner Bros found inspiration for its 1933 masterpiece on its own doorstep. The Sunset Boulevard firm of Fanchon and Marco was famed for the vaudeville shows and ciné-variety "prologues" it created, and choreographer **Busby Berkeley** empathized with their constant quest for audiovisual novelty.

The idea for the picture came as Berkeley was leaving the *Gold Diggers* premiere. When the theatre owner asked how he could possibly top "Shadow Waltz" and "Remember My Forgotten Man", Berkeley described the scenario for "By A Waterfall" (much to the mortification of **Jack Warner**, who considered the obviously expensive routine to be a grandstanding folly). Yet, within weeks, one hundred chorines were cavorting around a 80ft x 40ft pool that was fitted not only with glass corridors that enabled Berkeley to shoot underwater, but also with a pumping mechanism that kept 20,000 gallons of water per minute cascading through the various pools, streams, fountains and sprays within the remarkable set.

Despite this aquatic opulence, *Footlight Parade* painted a far from flattering picture of show business. **James Cagney**'s producer is too obsessed with work to save his failing marriage, the impresarios played by **Guy Kibbee** and **Arthur Hohl** are spineless charlatans who keep a double set of books to cream off illicit cash, and **Hugh Herbert**'s moral guardian proves to be every bit as corruptible as the mole who is stealing ideas to sell to rival companies. The coming of talking pictures also reveals the ruthlessness of an industry fixated on the latest fad, as perfectly proficient artistes are tossed onto the scrapheap because their faces no longer fit. *Footlight Parade* was one of the few contemporary pictures to explore the impact of the movie musical upon its stage counterpart, although Berkeley's routines left viewers in little doubt where his sympathies lay.

This is very much a self-reflexive musical, in which the live musical prologues both balance the film programmes they precede and represent the diegetic musical content leavening *Footlight Parade*'s backstage drama. However, the contrast between stage and screen is never quite as simple as Cagney's amusing use of an animated flip book to demonstrate the flexibility of the moving image.

Berkeley's routines were exemplars in the use of form and space to create spectacle. But, while he may have sought to employ physical features to produce abstract patterns that equated to the elusive rhythms and melodies of the score, he was often guilty of suppressing the individual within the grander design. Therefore, a musical wet dream like "By A Waterfall" not only objectified women's bodies, but also dehumanized them. No wonder it was such a favourite of Adolf Hitler.

Politically, *Footlight Parade* couldn't have been more patriotic. Although he was modelled on stage producer **Chester Hale**, Cagney's character also had a touch of President Roosevelt about him. He leads by example, and creates order out of chaos during the "Shanghai Lil" finale, which climaxes with a display of jingoism – comprising the Stars and Stripes, an American eagle and FDR's portrait – that rivalled anything concocted by **George M. Cohan**, who was the byword for patriotic excess. However, for all its politicking pizzazz, *Footlight Parade* proved to be the last Warner Bros musical in which social commitment mattered as much as entertainment.

# Funny Face

## *dir* Stanley Donen, 1957, 103m

**_cast_ Fred Astaire, Audrey Hepburn, Kay Thompson, Michel Auclair, Suzy Parker, Robert Flemyng _cin_ Ray June _m_ George Gershwin, Ira Gershwin**

Considering the influence it exerted on auteur cinema, *Funny Face* is a remarkable example of Hollywood collaboration. In the mid-1950s, MGM persuaded Warner Bros to part with the rights to **George and Ira Gershwin**'s 1927 musical, *Funny Face*, to bolster **Leonard Gershe**'s screenplay about a photographer and his model.

## Farcical *Funny Face*

As well as its echoes of *An American In Paris* and *Singin' In The Rain*, this picture is studded with parodies, with Empathicalism joshing Existentialism, "Bonjour, Paris!" lampooning Cinerama travelogues and "Basal Metabolism" poking fun at both *danse modèrne* and Gene Kelly's dream ballet in *An American In Paris*. Stanley Donen even utilized the poor Parisian weather to comment on the artificial perfection of industrial filmmaking.

However, Paramount refused to loan out **Fred Astaire**'s preferred co-star, **Audrey Hepburn**. So, in a unique gesture of munificence, MGM gave the project to Paramount, together with the expertise of director **Stanley Donen**, producer **Roger Edens** and several key members of the **Freed Unit**. Paramount stalwarts **Hal Pereira** and **George W. Davis** designed the picture, but this undervalued delight still drips with MGM chic and copious references to the studio's finest hours.

The film is essentially a reworking of *An American In Paris* (1951), with the Gershwin score providing the constant and the contrasts coming between Astaire and Gene Kelly, photography and painting, real locations and sound stages, and Donen and Vincente Minnelli. There are also echoes of *Singin' In The Rain* (1952): **Kay Thompson**'s magazine editor recalls Millard Mitchell's studio chief, Astaire coaxes his models like a silent film director, and the model played by **Dovima** is reminiscent of Jean Hagen's superficial actress, who loves the glamour and prestige of her trade, but hasn't the soul to participate fully in its creativity. Consequently, she's replaced by Hepburn's fresh-faced gamine, who shares Debbie Reynolds's passion, independence and eagerness for new experiences.

However, as with *The Band Wagon* (1953), *Funny Face* is also a recapitulation of Astaire's career that allows for plenty of self-reflexive analysis. The "Funny Face" sequence, for example, comments on his passage from RKO monochrome to VistaVision Technicolor, while also exploring the very process of creating pictures and star myths – Astaire photographs, develops, projects and prints Hepburn's portrait before comparing the image with the reality (which is itself merely an illusion on a cinema screen).

This emphasis on modernity and technology, while also referencing and reverencing an accepted iconography, recurs during the "Bonjour, Paris!" sequence and the photo shoot around the City of Light. The latter not only showcases the moving image's unique ability to capture a time, a place and a personality in a manner that's both kinetic and artistic, but also celebrates film techniques from the city symphonies of the silent montage era to the full-colour, widescreen, stereophonic present. Moreover, it also anticipates the *nouvelle vague*'s forthcoming strategies to break with the narrative linearity of commercial cinema.

Donen's use of style is exceedingly ambitious throughout *Funny Face*, from the opening emphasis on pink, through the darkroom dance illuminated by a single red bulb to the use of soft focus, split-screens, freeze frame, negative footage, monochrome and colours that dance as vibrantly as Astaire. By dressing bookstore clerk-turned-model Jo Stockton (Hepburn) in beatnik black, Donen alludes to the European arthouse pictures that were becoming increasingly trendy in American cities, and thus provides a cultural counterpoint to the Hollywood blockbuster and the lie that books alone can provide intellectual sustenance. This equation of fashion with film also makes her claim that cinema and photography represent "a chichi and unrealistic approach to economics" all the more bitingly satirical.

*Funny Face* is, however, occasionally guilty of inverted snobbery. **Michel Auclair**'s philosopher is concerned with ideas not images, and is exposed as pretentious and fraudulent, and Hepburn comes to learn more about Empathicalism from Astaire, as he understands everything about her mind, body and spirit. Indeed, having proved he's mentally attuned to her during "Let's Kiss And Make Up", he offers physical proof of their compatibility during the exquisite "He Loves And She Loves" sequence in the Chantilly churchyard.

Somewhat going over the heads of contemporary American audiences, *Funny Face* lost money on its $4 million budget – but its cinematic inspiration has since proved priceless.

Stanley Donen used Fred Astaire's perfect picture of Audrey Hepburn to satirize the modernism that was in the process of consigning the musical to movie history.

# Gigi

## *dir* Vincente Minnelli, 1958, 116m

**cast Leslie Caron, Maurice Chevalier, Louis Jourdan, Hermione Gingold, Eva Gabor *cin* Joseph Ruttenberg, Ray June *m* Frederick Loewe, Alan Jay Lerner**

**Arthur Freed** and **Maurice Chevalier** were pivotal figures in the birth of the movie musical, so it is apt that they were both involved in the film that proved to be the Golden Age's last hurrah. Returning to Hollywood for the first time in twenty years, Chevalier stole *Gigi* by crooning insouciantly through songs like "Thank Heaven For Little Girls" and "I'm Glad I'm Not Young Any More", which traded mischievously on his image and earned him a special Oscar. While Freed, who seemed to realize that he was presiding over a swan song, meekly allowed screenwriter and lyricist **Alan Jay Lerner** to call the shots during the film's fractious post-production.

The project had stuttered through its protracted development, with the Breen Office censors taking a dim view of both Jacqueline Audry's 1948 screen version and Anita Loos's 1951 stage adaptation of Colette's saucy source novella. Moreover, composer **Frederick Loewe** didn't initially share Lerner's enthusiasm for making a musical out of the story of a trainee *fin-de-siècle* courtesan who snags herself a rich husband – and neither did Audrey Hepburn nor Dirk Bogarde, who refused the leads. This enabled Freed to cast **Leslie Caron** as Gigi (a role she had already played on the London stage) opposite **Louis Jourdan** as Gaston, under director **Vincente Minnelli**.

As with *An American In Paris* (1951), Minnelli drew inspiration from the art world – this time from Seurat, Boudin, Renoir and Manet, as well as the caricaturist Sem – and his vision was refined by the exquisite taste of production designer, **Cecil Beaton**. Minnelli also insisted on shooting in authentic Parisian locations. But 24 days into filming, he was $500,000 over budget and MGM ordered the unit home; the picture was completed in 35 days at Culver City and Venice Beach. However, an uncredited **Charles Walters** was still required to shoot a further eleven days of retakes and new footage to appease Lerner, who was appalled by editor **Margaret Booth**'s charmless preview cut.

It was at this stage, that *Gigi* finally became what historian Gerald Mast called "the best Broadway musical ever written directly for the screen". Lerner and Loewe were men of the theatre and under their influence the picture came closer than ever to resembling their 1956 stage smash, *My Fair Lady*. No wonder Bosley Crowther of the *New York Times* suggested that they "may want to sue themselves" for plagiarism – especially as the song "Say A Prayer for Me Tonight" had originally been written for *My Fair Lady*'s Eliza Doolittle.

However, despite its self-conscious theatricality, *Gigi* exemplifies the screen musical's dependence on structural duality (see p.249). It's a mood piece that emphasizes character and period trappings over the intricacies of the traditional linear narrative. The narrative arc matters less than the twinning of ideas, attitudes and actions. Thus, from the opening sequences, the script divides the Parisian world into male and female domains, and surrounds Gaston and Gigi with parallel people, props and proceedings that, while gender specific, eventually show them to be eminently compatible.

The couple realize that they are part of a cycle of attraction, passion and companionship that has been played out for generations when they are reminded of their social and sexual responsibilities by his uncle and her grandmother, who genially satirize their own love affair in the duet "I Remember It Well". However, Gaston and Gigi's significant age gap is still a problem. It's only when another series of parallels is initiated that they draw closer together, as she grows up and ceases to be an excited teenager and his bored roué relishes the chance to recapture his lost youth. Thus, the marriage of these seemingly diametrically opposed personalities typifies the musical's generic approach to romance and continues the chain initially forged in Chevalier's teamings with Jeanette MacDonald.

After winning nine Oscars and the first Grammy ever awarded to a soundtrack, Freed's penultimate musical went on to make more than $13 million on its $3 million budget. But despite being his most profitable film, *Gigi* confirmed the supremacy of the song show over the dance musical and signalled the shift of musical power back to Broadway. Stage-to-screen transfers were to become the norm, and the days of the prestigious Hollywood musical original were over.

# Gold Diggers Of 1933

## *dir* Mervyn LeRoy, 1933, 94m, b/w

*cast* **Warren William, Joan Blondell, Ruby Keeler, Dick Powell** *cin* **Sol Polito** *m* **Harry Warren, Al Dubin**

Warner Bros began shooting *Gold Diggers Of 1933* soon after the first preview screening of *42nd Street* (1933), knowing it would be a hit. In the absence of pioneering musical producer Darryl F. Zanuck, **Robert Lord** was chosen as producer, having previously worked on the script of the Technicolor musical *Gold Diggers Of Broadway* (1929), a reworking of **Avery Hopwood**'s 1919 play, *The Gold Digger*. However, the screenplay owed more to the Warner Bros house style than Hopwood's backstage comedy. The dialogue fizzed with the authentic argot of a gangster or problem picture, while **Mervyn LeRoy**'s direction was as brisk and uncompromising as that of his social drama *I Am A Fugitive From A Chain Gang* (1932).

After LeRoy managed to land the opening number, "We're In The Money", for his then-girlfriend **Ginger Rogers** (who even sang one verse in Pig Latin), he left the staging of the song and dance routines to **Busby Berkeley**. To retain complete control over the look of each set piece, Berkeley choreographed the musical numbers in the camera and only left the editor with sufficent footage to realize his precise designs. Whereas in *42nd Street* the songs had become increasingly untheatrical, this time Berkeley aimed for cinematic spectacle from the start. He delighted in creating fantasy spaces that could only exist on celluloid, although he retained his habit of opening and closing numbers within the confines of a proscenium.

Berkeley referenced the irresistible delights of the screen during "Pettin' In The Park" by silhouetting disrobing chorines against transluscent screens. Taking the number a step further, he even had a naughty infant (played by midget **Billy Barty**) leer at the girls before handing Brad Roberts (**Dick Powell**) a tin opener to strip Polly Parker (**Ruby Keeler**) out of her metallic bathing suit. Although this cheeky routine was designed to outshine Florenz Ziegfeld in its "glorification of the American girl", the "Shadow Waltz" made more subtle use of the famous Berkeley top shot to capture the shapes formed by sixty dancers in white dresses carrying neon-lit violins. The routine was made all the more remarkable by the fact that it was partly shot during an earthquake.

*Gold Diggers Of 1933* paid less heed to the Depression than either *42nd Street* or *Footlight Parade* (1933). It lacks a strong central character with a single creative vision, and instead focuses on the professional and personal tribulations of a trio of showgirls who find love while mounting their own musical production against the odds. The picture's highlight is undoubtedly the finale, which reinforces its social message, but both the bookends pack a political punch. Ginger Rogers and her attendant chorus wear costumes bedecked with coins for the opening number, "We're In The Money", which generates ironic cash flow imagery before their dress rehearsal is curtailed by bailiffs intent on closing the debt-ridden show. Keen to avoid resorting to the sidewalks, the showgirls eagerly sign up to a young songwriter's new project. But such allusions to unemployment, penury and destitution are largely suppressed by the comic gold-digging until the film's social conscience is finally reawoken by the sobering finale, "Remember My Forgotten Man".

Designed to spur the White House into paying America's World War I veterans the $1000 bonus they were promised in 1925, this stark Expressionist statement was delivered with gutsy power by singers **Joan Blondell** and **Etta Moten** and remains one of the genre's most provocative achievements. It provided a unique spin on the traditional happy ending and gave audiences plenty to think about as they left the theatre and re-entered the austere reality of America in the 1930s.

# Grease

### *dir* Randal Kleiser, 1978, 110m

**_cast_ John Travolta, Olivia Newton-John, Stockard Channing, Jeff Conaway, Didi Conn, Eve Arden, Sid Caesar _cin_ Bill Butler _m_ Jim Jacobs, Warren Casey**

---

*Grease* was the first hit Broadway musical to be composed entirely on a guitar. It was conceived by unemployed actor **Jim Jacobs** and

At 29 and 24 years old, Olivia Newton-John and John Travolta made unconvincing teenagers, but *Grease* was still briefly the third highest grossing film of all time.

bra salesman **Warren Casey** at a party, and opened with an amateur cast at the Kingston Mines Theatre, a former Chicago tram shed, in February 1971. Originally intended to run for just two weekends, the musical was picked up by New York producers **Kenneth Waissmann** and **Maxine Fox** and premiered at the off-Broadway Eden Theatre the following year. The reviews were lukewarm, but word of mouth ensured *Grease*'s success. It was nominated for seven Tony Awards, ran for 3,388 performances and, in 1979, became the longest-running show in Broadway history.

**Ralph Bakshi** was the first to secure the film rights. But when his proposed animated version fell through, **Allan Carr** bought the show in 1976. Carr, who produced and co-wrote the screen adaptation, had planned to cast **Henry Winkler** as male lead Danny Zuko, but that came to nothing because Winkler was keen to avoid typecasting after playing The Fonz in the 1950s-set TV series *Happy Days*. The role passed to **John Travolta**, who had played Doody in the touring stage production. **Olivia Newton-John** was always the first choice for the female lead Sandy Olsson, although director **Randal Kleiser** also scouted Carrie Fisher in case her screen test proved unsatisfactory.

Working with screenwriter **Bronte Woodard**, Carr moved the setting from the city to the suburbs and introduced some of his own schoolboy memories. He also toned down the stage play's language and sexual references. Dropping such show favourites as "Freddy, My Love", "Magic Changes" and "It's Raining On Prom Night", Carr commissioned new songs from **Barry Gibb** ("Grease") and **John Farrar** ("Hopelessly Devoted To You" and "You're The One That I

Want"), and contributed "Sandy" himself. However, the new tunes felt more like 1970s pop than 1950s pastiche, and **Patricia Birch**'s energetic choreography was similarly anachronistic.

The picture seemed to owe more to *American Graffiti* (1973) and *Happy Days* than to the low-budget, teenage drive-in fodder that had originally inspired Jacobs and Casey. And the inclusion of old-time stalwarts Joan Blondell, Eve Arden, Sid Caesar and Frankie Avalon only reinforced the feel of manufactured nostalgia, which was designed to appeal to those who hadn't personally experienced the birth of rock'n'roll. The critics picked up on this calculation and chastised the picture for smoothing away the original's rough edges in the name of family entertainment. They also sniped at the performance of "Olivia Wooden John", whose hesitancy was only exacerbated by Travolta's energetic magnetism and the vibrancy of the admirable ensemble. However, the indifferent notices proved an irrelevance. The chart success of the irresistibly catchy "You're The One That I Want" and "Summer Nights" guaranteed *Grease*'s enthusiastic reception, especially as film footage was culled for ready-made pop videos.

This thoroughly enjoyable movie grossed more than $150 million on its first run, becoming the most successful screen musical of all time. Although the disappointing 1982 sequel didn't fare so well, *Grease* had given Hollywood the idea that teen flicks could save the musical, and *Fame* (1980), *Footloose* (1983), *Flashdance* (1984) and *Dirty Dancing* (1987) all followed. However, their lack of originality and the fact that they were essentially dramas with musical interludes meant that they contributed more to the evolution of the pop promo than to the preservation of a declining genre.

# Guys And Dolls

## *dir* Joseph L. Mankiewicz, 1955, 158m

*cast* **Marlon Brando, Jean Simmons, Frank Sinatra, Vivian Blaine** *cin* **Harry Stradling** *m* **Frank Loesser**

"I was born to play Sky the way Gable was born to play Rhett Butler," **Gene Kelly** once lamented. "But the bastards at MGM refused to loan me out." In fact, it was East Coast supremo **Nicholas Schenck** who blocked the deal, in order to settle an old score with producer **Samuel Goldwyn**. Kelly's career never quite recovered from this set-back, but it's debatable whether his presence could have done much to improve this tumescent adaptation of a vibrant stage classic.

Writer **Damon Runyon** was the "laureate of the illiterate" and sixteen of the stories in his 1931 collection *Guys And Dolls* were filmed. It was "The Idyll Of Sarah Brown" that inspired composer **Frank Loesser**'s stage musical (with its book by **Jo Swerling** and **Abe Burrows**) and the subsequent film. Subtitled "A Musical Fable of Broadway", the show ran for 1,200 performances from November 1950 and prompted a bidding war that saw MGM, Paramount and Columbia drive Goldwyn up to a record $1 million.

Having failed to land Kelly, Goldwyn and writer-director **Joseph L. Mankiewicz** considered Tony Martin, Kirk Douglas, Robert Mitchum and Burt Lancaster for the role of inveterate gambler Sky Masterson, before Goldwyn came up with the preposterous idea of teaming Dean Martin and Jerry Lewis. They finally settled on **Marlon Brando**, even though he was reluctant to risk a singing part because he felt his voice sounded like "the mating call of a yak". **Frank Sinatra** was cast alongside him as Nathan Detroit, the cash-strapped organizer of the oldest established permanent, floating crap game in New York, who challenges Sky to seduce the Save-a-Soul missionary Sarah Brown (**Jean Simmons**) in order to fund his latest enterprise.

Eleven of the Broadway show's sixteen songs survived, with Loesser's genius for underworld argot bringing a wiseacre realism to the lyrics. Loesser was generally less comfortable with romantic ballads, and he was rightly vexed when one of his best, "I've Never Been In Love Before", was replaced with "A Woman In Love" because Brando hated performing it. Brando's vocals had to be cobbled together from the best takes, yet he still had the temerity to criticize Sinatra's delivery, which further strained their combustible relationship.

Sinatra had never forgiven Brando for stealing *On The Waterfront* (1954) and deeply resented his insistence on improvisation, which Sinatra felt undermined his own spontaneity. Eventually, he and "Mumbles"communicated solely through intermediaries. Yet it was Sinatra who gave the weakest performance. Realizing he'd been saddled with a supporting role, he put little effort into his renditions of "Adelaide" and "Sue Me". By contrast, **Vivian Blaine**, reprising the role of Nathan Detroit's long-suffering chanteuse fiancée, tried too hard. However, she did deliver "Adelaide's Lament" with the same panache that fellow stage alumnus **Stubby Kaye** brought to "Sit Down, You're Rockin' The Boat".

But the real problems with the film lay not with the cast or the songs, but with **Oliver Smith**'s over-stylized sets, which added artifice but little style or wit, and the writer-director's lack of trust in his material. Mankiewicz so overwrote his screenplay in a bid to invest it with dramatic legitimacy that Orson Welles told Abe Burrows that he had "put a tiny turd on every one of your lines".

Despite the indifferent notices and Brando's own contention that the picture was "nothing to get on your tricycle about", business boomed. *Guys And Dolls* more than doubled its $5.5 million investment and, in some countries, outperformed the legendary 1939 blockbuster *Gone With The Wind*. The musical has since remained a cult favourite, but it's still tempting to speculate about Gene Kelly's possible interpretation.

# Hallelujah!

### *dir* King Vidor, 1929, 101m, b/w

**_cast_ Daniel L. Haynes, Nina Mae McKinney, William E. Fountaine, Harry Gray _cin_ Gordon Avil _m_ various**

---

The most iconic moment in *The Jazz Singer* (1927) depicted **Al Jolson** in minstrel make-up singing "Mammy". Yet the first all-black musicals, produced just two years later, are now almost entirely forgotten. Fox and MGM produced *Hearts In Dixie* and *Hallelujah!* respectively because they hoped that the stereotypically presumed African-American senses of rhythm and exuberance might suit the talkies and prove profitable. However, both films forced talented black performers to accept the white conception of their ethnicity and environment, and to give blackface rather than naturalistic performances.

Although it has many critics because of its ponderous pacing and patronizing politics, *Hallelujah!* retains a certain dignity and a determination to do right by the people it portrays. It set the template for future black musicals and for many African-American dramas. Indeed, historian Donald Bogle claimed it as the forerunner to such pivotal domestic pictures as Gordon Parks's *The Learning Tree* (1969).

*Hallelujah!* fulfilled **King Vidor**'s long-held dream to direct an all-black film, but several members of the MGM board were against the project and only gave it the green light after Vidor agreed to contribute his fee to the budget. Even then, they refused to loan him any sound recording equipment for his location shoots in Tennessee and Arkansas. He had to pioneer dubbing techniques to produce the poor quality soundtrack – although, ironically, this reinforced the palpable sense of poverty that pervaded the proceedings.

Although its plantation setting is as romanticized as any Ruritanian kingdom and its extremes of emotion are almost operatic, *Hallelujah!* is tantamount to a neo-realist musical. The montage sequence showing the cotton gin transforming the Johnson family crop into cash is as powerful as anything by **Eisenstein** or **Dovzhenko**, and the film emphasizes the crucial link between faith and farming by using **Irving Berlin**'s "Waiting At The End Of The Road" to compare this reckoning with that of Judgement Day.

Vidor similarly contrasted religious fervour with sexual desire. From the moment Zeke (**Daniel L. Haynes**) kisses Rose (**Victoria Spivey**) as she plays the "Wedding March", he is associated with the divine and the diabolical, the spiritual and the sensual. Thus, when he becomes an itinerant preacher, Zeke breaks into a rhythmic patter and then into a dance as he addresses his flock. The more Zeke surrenders himself to the beat, the more the director intercuts shots of the treacherously alluring Chick (**Nina Mae McKinney**) in the congregation, and the sermon becomes a come-on that results in her being baptized and nearly seduced.

The use of music in these contrasting segments is surprisingly subtle. While Zeke is in the bosom of his family, the spirituals on the soundtrack suggest contentment, but that is replaced by an increasing abandonment to the erotic energy of syncopation once Chick has tempted him. Zeke needs to be purged before he can make a penitent return to the homestead, and his Damascene moment occurs during the chase through the bayou, which begins with Chick's plunge from the runaway cart and ends with Zeke killing Hot Shot (**William E. Fountaine**), the cardsharp who caused his first fall from grace.

Regrettably, Vidor divorced black life from the struggle to survive in a white-dominated world, which meant that *Hallelujah!* accentuated his own outsider idealism rather than presenting the authentic experience of the repressed. However, he drew fine performances from his inexperienced cast (Nina Mae McKinney's shift from child-woman to siren-victim had a particular influence on Lena Horne in 1943's *Stormy Weather* and Dorothy Dandridge in 1954's *Carmen Jones*). Unfortunately, *Hallelujah!* lost $120,000 on its $320,000 outlay and demonstrated to the studios that there was no money to be made in "black only" entertainment.

# High Society

## *dir* Charles Walters, 1956, 107m

**_cast_ Bing Crosby, Grace Kelly, Frank Sinatra, Celeste Holm, John Lund, Louis Calhern, Louis Armstrong _cin_ Paul C. Vogel _m_ Cole Porter**

Transferring from its triumphant run on Broadway, screwball comedy *The Philadelphia Story* (1940) had restored Katharine Hepburn to the Hollywood hierarchy and finally quashed her reputation for being "box-office poison". The MGM musical was similarly in the commercial doldrums when Charles Walters directed this variation of **Philip Barry**'s class satire in a bid to stem the tide of rock'n'roll. However, the story of blueblood Tracy Lord's inability to choose between fiancé George Kittredge, ex-husband C.K. Dexter-Haven and magazine reporter Mike Connor couldn't work the same magic twice. Teenagers were more interested in Elvis Presley's debut, *Love Me Tender* (1956), and even the first teaming of **Bing Crosby** and **Frank Sinatra** couldn't prise their parents away from the television.

Producer **Sol C. Siegel** was out to impress with his first outing for MGM since his move from Fox. He induced **Cole Porter** to compose his first original screen songs in eight years with an advance of $250,000, and offered similar fees to Crosby and Sinatra. Sinatra consented to a supporting role in order to work with his idol, Crosby, and even roused himself from the cocky lethargy that otherwise stifled his performance for their duet, "Well, Did You Evah?". Crosby

Frank Sinatra and Bing Crosby sing *High Society*'s only recycled song, "Well, Did You Evah?", which Cole Porter had originally written for Betty Grable in the 1939 Broadway version of *DuBarry Was A Lady*.

proved equally animated on "Now You Has Jazz", for which he was reunited with **Louis Armstrong** for the first time since *Pennies From Heaven* (1939).

Crosby was more eager to renew his acquaintance with **Grace Kelly**, with whom he'd had an affair in 1952. However, any hopes of rekindling the flames were doused by her announcement, a month before shooting began, that she was to marry Prince Rainier of Monaco. The picture became something of a grotesque parody of their real-life situation, particularly when Rainier was invited to the set on the day that Crosby and Kelly had to do a little smooching. No wonder he later banned the film from the Principality, claiming it "wasn't quite the thing".

Under Walters's expert stewardship, the five-week shoot was enjoyably relaxed, although the casual atmosphere encouraged a dramatic slackness that was exacerbated by **John Patrick**'s screenplay, which lacked the wit and bite of the source. Porter's score also missed the causticity of the original, but he produced pleasing ballads for Crosby ("I Love You, Samantha") and Sinatra ("Mind If I Make Love To You"), and a catchy catalogue song for Sinatra and **Celeste Holm** ("Who Wants To Be A Millionaire?"). However, the musical highlight was "True Love", which Porter had written for his late wife. Walters had planned to dub Kelly's vocals, but Crosby insisted on a proper duet. The song became Porter's first million-selling recording and earned Crosby his twentieth gold disc, but the rock revolution meant that it failed to reach number one.

While most critics commended Porter's songbook, they were less than enthusiastic about the picture itself, which confirmed MGM's shift from dance to more song-centric fare. Many shared *Saturday Review*'s contention that the cast exhibited a "glum cheeriness", which confirmed the unflattering comparisons with the zestful charm of *The Philadelphia Story*. The musical has gradually acquired classic status, thanks to repeated television screenings, but while it certainly has an air of effortless polish, it remains short on real style.

# High, Wide And Handsome

## *dir* Rouben Mamoulian, 1937, 110m, b/w

**_cast_ Irene Dunne, Randolph Scott, Dorothy Lamour, Elizabeth Patterson _cin_ Victor Milner _m_ Jerome Kern, Oscar Hammerstein II**

Hoping to repeat the success of Universal's *Show Boat* (1936), Paramount reunited actress **Irene Dunne** with songwriters **Jerome Kern** and **Oscar Hammerstein** for this musical reconstruction of the mid-nineteenth-century struggle between the sodbusters and the railroaders for control of the Pennsylvania oilfields. Hammerstein originally conceived the project as a musical comedy, but director **Rouben Mamoulian** had come from the stage version of George Gershwin's *Porgy And Bess* (1935) and was determined to couch everyday provincial reality in folk musical terms. He revised the screenplay and insisted on shooting on location in Chino, California to enhance the sense of period authenticity. The picture cost $2 million and proved to be a box-office disappointment. But, as critic Richard Roud suggested, its blend of social statement and showbiz escapism was "an extraordinary fusion of Brecht and Broadway". The film was less a reprise of *Show Boat* than was a rehearsal for the stage show *Oklahoma!* (1943), with which Mamoulian and Hammerstein transformed the American musical six years later.

Mamoulian was accused by some of spoiling a costume entertainment by including serious socioeconomic issues, and by others of ruining a pugnacious Western by dotting it with romance and operetta. In truth, he succeeded in combining the best elements of both genres and blended studio stylization and real locations to give the film a unique hybrid vitality. Some critics even found fault with the restrained staging of the musical numbers. But **Dorothy Lamour**'s torch song, "The Things I Want", and her saloon duet with Dunne, "Allegheny Al", were perfectly suited to 1850s performance styles. As was Dunne's circus ring reprise of "Can I Forget You?", which persuades her to return to **Randolph Scott** and rally his bid to lay an oil pipeline across hostile terrain in defiance of rail tycoon **Alan Hale**. The songs are neatly integrated into the storyline and are used to establish the relationship between the real and the romanticized, most notably in the medicine show opening and the farmyard sequence, in which the livestock join in with Dunne's song as she feeds them.

The connection between labour, landscape and community is reinforced by the pipe-laying sequences, which are worthy of John Ford and Howard Hawks in their depiction of progress on the American frontier and the camaraderie of professional men engaged in honest toil. *High, Wide And Handsome* is very much a tale of the land, with Peter (Scott) personifying its settled dependability and Sally (Dunne) its restless energy, which manifests itself in the eruption of oil that follows her nuptial rendition of the elegiac ballad, "The Folks Who Live On The Hill".

The pipeline, therefore, becomes a symbol of virility that will bring new life to a barren land and stimulate both the economy and the community. Mamoulian also gives it a sexual significance, as Peter is impotent before Sally and her circus family arrive to ensure both the final erection of the pipeline and the first triumphant gush of oil at the refinery. Rather than employing cheap phallic imagery, Mamoulian uses the couple's economic and erotic consummation to show how the romance of soil and soul fulfills America's belief in Manifest Destiny.

Recalling Frank Capra's contemporary fables in its exposure of hypocrisy and greed, *High, Wide And Handsome* also echoes the New Deal message of Busby Berkeley's backstage musicals by demonstrating that morality and amusement are not mutually exclusive. Indeed, Sally's vigour and resolve inspires the farmers to unite in a common enterprise, rather than trying to subsist in isolation. Unfortunately, post-Depression audiences were tired of such exhortations and the picture slipped into undeserved obscurity, even though its central premise of a cherished lifestyle coming under threat later became a recurrent theme in folk musicals from *Meet Me In St Louis* (1944) to *The Sound Of Music* (1965).

# The Jazz Singer

### *dir* Alan Crosland, 1927, 89m, b/w

**cast** Al Jolson, May McAvoy, Warner Oland, Eugenie Besserer, Otto Lederer *cin* Hal Mohr *m* various

No film has been more mythologized than *The Jazz Singer.* It's credited with launching a lucrative talkie boom that transformed Hollywood overnight, but the complacent hype bears little resemblance to the truth.

In 1926, Warner Bros spent $50,000 on the rights to **Samuel Raphaelson**'s play, *The Day Of Atonement*, as a dramatic project for Ernst Lubitsch. When the cash-strapped studio decided to rework it as a silent film with songs, George Jessel (who had headlined the Broadway play) was dropped in favour of **Al Jolson**, who had inspired Raphaelson's original story. Despite being billed as "The World's Greatest Entertainer", Jolson had misgivings about his ability to play the role of Jakie Rabinowitz, the cantor's son who alienates his father by choosing show business over his faith, changing his name to Jack Robin and romancing his non-Jewish co-star, Mary Dale (**May McAvoy**).

Shooting the silent scenes went smoothly throughout June 1927 and Jolson recorded his five songs in just nine days during August. He and composer **Louis Silvers** even made history with "Mother, I Still Have You", the first song written directly for the screen. However, it was what Jolson said between the standards "Dirty Hands, Dirty Face" and "Toot Toot, Tootsie" that secured his place in film folklore: "Wait a minute. Wait a minute. You ain't heard nothing yet!" Yet this trademark stage exhortation was much less audacious than the monologue that Jolson inserted between the verses of **Irving Berlin**'s "Blue Skies".

Opinion is still divided about whether the "Blue Skies" speech was scripted in advance. While off-screen pianist **Bert Fiske** may have been tipped off to play more softly as Jolson gushed about his love for his mother, **Eugenie Besserer**'s acute discomfort suggests that her screen son was ad-libbing, as does the nervous energy that makes his performance so electrically realistic. This casual intrusion of Jolson's own ebullient personality emphasized the artificiality of the film's silent sequences (which made up 65 percent of the action) and eventually persuaded Hollywood that the pantomimic art form

Al Jolson could never resist showboating, but his brio proved crucial in convincing Hollywood that talking pictures were the future of cinema.

was doomed. However, no such decision was reached in the immediate aftermath of the film's New York premiere, nor on the back of universal press acclaim or commercial success. The critics were more concerned with the sudden death of studio mogul **Sam Warner**, whose courage had ensured the picture's completion, and when the trade papers did get around to carrying reviews, they were decidedly mixed.

A shortage of venues capable of handling the new Vitaphone sound system meant that *The Jazz Singer* was seen by more people as a silent film, than as a talkie (and was, therefore, outperformed by the likes of *Wings*, *Seventh Heaven* and *Sunrise*). In fact, more audiences heard Jolson sing on the 1931 sound-on-film reissue, than via the original discs. It's impossible to gauge the exact percentages taken by each of these three versions, so while $2.6 million over four years represents an impressive return on a $422,000 budget, it hardly signifies an instant box-office smash.

At the inaugural Academy Awards, Warner Bros received an honorary statuette for its "pioneer outstanding talking picture, which has revolutionized the industry". But this merely perpetuated the myth about the film's sudden, industry-changing impact that had been generated by the press. *The Jazz Singer* was a landmark; its songs were surprisingly well integrated into the, admittedly old-fashioned, storyline and it even made intelligent use of off-screen sound. However, both Jolson's follow-up, *The Singing Fool* (1928), and the inferior remakes – with Danny Thomas (1953), Jerry Lewis (1959) and Neil Diamond (1980) – drew bigger audiences.

# The King And I

### *dir* Walter Lang, 1956, 133m

**_cast_ Yul Brynner, Deborah Kerr, Rita Moreno, Martin Benson, Terry Saunders, Carlos Rivas _cin_ Leon Shamroy _m_ Richard Rodgers, Oscar Hammerstein II**

**Rodgers and Hammerstein** were essentially the middlemen on *The King And I*. The project was first suggested by British stage star Gertrude Lawrence, who had read **Margaret Landon**'s fact-based novel, *Anna And The King Of Siam* (1944), about an English woman who was appointed governess to the King of Siam's children in the 1860s. Initially, the duo were reluctant to accept the commission, as they preferred writing character ensembles rather than star-led musicals. However, a private viewing of John Cromwell's 1946 film adaptation changed their minds, and they based their libretto on **Talbot Jennings** and **Sally Benson**'s screenplay.

The songwriters' relationship became strained, as they struggled to avoid racial stereotype and Oriental cliché, while also making Siamese characters and customs unpatronizingly accessible to Western audiences. Privately, lyricist Hammerstein despaired of Rodgers' tendency to take his genius for granted, while the composer resented the critics for lauding the lyrics but suggesting that his score wasn't up to scratch. Rodgers' avoidance of regional influences resulted in some rather conventional melodies: "I Whistle A Happy Tune" was an upbeat variation of "You'll Never Walk Alone", "Something Wonderful" reworked "What's The Use Of Wondering", and "Getting To Know You" revised the *South Pacific* reject, "Suddenly Lucky". However, "Hello Young Lovers", "We Kiss In A Shadow", "Shall We Dance?" and "I Have Dreamed" were undeniably memorable tunes, and "March Of The Siamese Children" had a novelty, variety and quaintness that was unprecedented in musicals' history.

Neither Rodgers nor Hammerstein had much to do with the stylized ballet, "The Small House Of Uncle Thomas", which was largely scored by dance arranger **Trude Rittman** and choreographed by **Jerome Robbins** (although rumours abound that it was actually supervised by an uncredited Vincente Minnelli). The ballet arose from a typical Hammerstein sub-plot, which involved the concubine Tuptim (**Rita Moreno**) and the Burmese emissary Lun Tha (**Carlos Rivas**). Although many have criticized this love story as a formulaic diversion, it introduced the key theme of liberty, while the relationship between monogamous English widow Anna Leonowens (**Deborah Kerr**, who was partially dubbed by **Marni Nixon**) and polygamous Siamese King Monghut I (**Yul Brynner**, in an Oscar-winning performance) merely provided the framing storyline.

Nevertheless, Anna and the King remain the most interesting couple in the Rodgers and Hammerstein canon, and Kerr and Brynner are splendidly matched. Their intellectual and cultural clashes are far more intriguing than the staple narrative of the pursuit of love in the face of dissenting social convention. The film was conceived as exotic costume escapism, and King Monghut's relationship with Anna centres more on her feisty resistance to his authority and "scientific" egotism than on her disappointment at his flawed nobility or his shameful realization of the rectitude of her accusations of barbarity. However, Hammerstein refused to dabble in the smug jingoism of exotic operetta, and chastised Anna for her democratic disdain for slavery, marital dominion and tyrannical absolutism with pointed references to British involvement in the slave trade and the American Civil War.

Moreover, by having Anna and the King harbour mutually intense feelings, the film challenged Hollywood's aversion to interracial attraction for the first time since Frank Capra's *The Bitter Tea Of General Yen* (1933). Even more daringly, it suggested that the couple had produced a child in their own image, as Prince Chulalongkorn (**Patrick Adiarte**) shows what he has learnt from his governess by abolishing the ancient practice of kowtowing as soon as he assumes his father's mantle. But while such boldness contributed towards an $8.5 million gross at the US box office, it led to *The King And I* being banned in Thailand (formerly Siam) for demeaning a proud nation.

# Kiss Me Kate

## *dir* George Sidney, 1953, 109m

### *cast* Kathryn Grayson, Howard Keel, Ann Miller, Tommy Rall, Bobby Van *cin* Charles Rosher *m* Cole Porter

Contrary to popular belief, this was not the first 3-D musical; Paramount pipped MGM to the post by a month with the little-seen Rhonda Fleming vehicle, *Those Redheads From Seattle* (1953). The vogue for stereoscopy ended almost as soon as it began, and few audiences got to appreciate the full effect of *Kiss Me Kate*'s **Kathryn Grayson** hurling objects at the lens or **Howard Keel** delivering a song on a runway that seemed to jut into the auditorium. However, even those who only saw the flat version recognized that this was Hollywood's best transfer of a **Cole Porter** show.

Coming between Broadway's *The Boys From Syracuse* and *West Side Story*, *Kiss Me Kate* was the second of three Golden Age musi-

Ann Miller at the peak of her powers in the sizzling "Too Darn Hot". Yet her screen career was over within three years as the musical declined.

cals to be based on Shakespeare's plays. Inspired by *The Taming Of The Shrew*, the stage musical was written by **Samuel and Bella Spewack** and later adapted for the screen by **Dorothy Kingsley**. Porter was not immediately chosen to create the score because a string of misfires had led to some considering him a spent force. However, when he was brought on board, he created a superior score that led to the show winning the Tony Award for the best musical of 1948.

*Kiss Me Kate* chronicles the romantic misadventures of actor Fred Graham (Keel) and his ex-wife Lilli Vanessi (Grayson), as they take on the roles of Petruchio and Katherine in their own musical version of *The Taming Of The Shrew*. Much more structurally complex than most contemporary musicals, *Kiss Me Kate* constantly blurred the line between reality and fantasy, which meant that the songs had to be integrated into the action. Porter, who specialized in witty, literate ditties, rose to the challenge. He distributed the emotion tunes and the showstoppers between the scenes depicting life and artifice, but allowed several lyrics to work as both exposition and entertainment, as the stage roles played by the protagonists impinged upon their personal feud.

Consequently, *Kiss Me Kate* ranks among Porter's most consistent and innovative efforts, with "Wunderbar" lampooning the waltz-time exuberance of Viennese operetta and the beguine "So In Love" starting and ending in different keys. Several of the play-within-the-film songs, including "I've Come To Wive It Wealthily In Padua" and "Where Is The Life That Late I Led?", stem directly from Shakespeare's text, yet Porter still managed to turn them into trademark catalogue songs. Thankfully, producer **Jack Cummings** respected the brilliance of the score and dropped only three of the original musical's seventeen songs – although he did have to amend some of the saucier lyrics to appease the Breen Office censors.

Keel and Grayson were reunited following their solid showing in *Show Boat* (1951) and *Lovely To Look At* (1952). Keel's customary swagger and tendency to overact suited his character in this film, but Grayson lacked the snap to make Lilli a suitably temperamental diva. They were both frequently upstaged by **Ann Miller**, who gave the performance of her career, whether duetting with **Tommy Rall** on "Why Can't Men Behave?", leading the ensemble in the **Hermes Pan**-choreographed romp "Tom, Dick And Harry" or hitting around five hundred taps per minute during the scintillating showcase, "Too Darn Hot". However, not even Miller could match the sensuality of **Bob Fosse** and **Carol Haney**'s dance duet in the gem "From This Moment On", which was full of the sinuous movements, knee slides and chic business with hats and clicking fingers that later characterized Fosse's choreography.

## *The Lion King*: from screen to stage

Most musicals move from stage to screen, but *The Lion King* reversed the trend. In 1997, **Julie Taymor** adapted the popular animated musical for the stage and it became the film's most impressive by-product. It opened at Florenz Ziegfeld's New Amsterdam Theater on Broadway and then at the Lyceum in London, before going on tour.

Drawing on **Hans Zimmer**, Mark Mancina and Lebo M's soundtrack, *Rhythm Of The Pridelands* (1995), to increase the song count, Taymor also devised stylized masks, costumes, puppets and kinetic sculptures to suggest Africa and its wildlife, rather than reproducing their Disneyfication. She achieved a celebration of performance that retained the spirit of the source while also bringing a new sense of theatrical artistry to the Broadway musical.

# The Lion King

***dir* Roger Allers, Rob Minkoff, 1994, 88m**
***voices* Jonathan Taylor Thomas, Matthew Broderick, James Earl Jones, Jeremy Irons, Moira Kelly, Whoopi Goldberg *m* Elton John, Tim Rice, Hans Zimmer**

After 25 years of mediocrities and misfires, Disney embarked on a spectacular run of musical kids' pics that included *The Little Mermaid* (1989), *Beauty And The Beast* (1991) – the first animated film ever to be nominated for the best picture Oscar – and *Aladdin* (1992), before *The Lion King* set artistic and commercial standards that the studio has since been unable to equal.

Originally conceived as a sort of National Geographic project entitled *King Of The Jungle*, this coming-of-age story has been variously interpreted as an allegory of modern times, a spiritual odyssey, a cartoon take on Shakespeare and an embodiment of Jungian archetypes. But its essence is contained in the "Circle Of Life" opening, as the film echoes Disney animal outings like *Dumbo* (1940) and *Bambi* (1942) in following a young creature trying to cope with the loss of a parent. *The Lion King* is fully aware of its studio heritage, hence its allusions to *Pinocchio* (1940), in which a confident youth learns humility and responsibility, and *101 Dalmatians* (1961) and *The Rescuers* (1977), in which different species cooperate to confound a common enemy.

This film was pitched to screenwriter **Irene Mecchi** as "*Bambi* in Africa meets *Hamlet*". However, Simba the lion cub's progress also recalls Shakespeare's *Henry IV* and *Henry V*, and it's easy to see Pumbaa the warthog and Timon the meerkat as Falstaffian mentors, with added elements of Laurel and Hardy, Abbott and Costello and Baloo the bear (especially as "Hakuna Matata" so consciously recalls the rebelliously hedonistic spirit of *The Jungle Book*'s "The Bare Necessities"). There's also a political and religious significance in Simba's rejection of Timon and Pumbaa's "no worries" indolence in favour of embracing his destiny. Indeed, with its firm emphasis on patriarchy, this is an exceedingly conservative film. It presumes that citizens are better off with their traditional rulers – to the point of championing primogeniture over democracy and meritocracy – and urges them to accept the decisions made on their behalf by their sapient and benevolent leaders. *The Lion King* was the first neo-conservative musical, and it would have made Uncle Walt proud.

This advocacy of a hierarchical class structure is reinforced by the demonstration that fathers can be faithful to their wives and indulgent towards their offspring without losing dignity or machismo. Some critics suggested that the casting of **James Earl Jones** as the voice of Mufasa implies that this appeal for hands-on fathering was specifically aimed at African-Americans. Further controversy was sparked by accusations of homophobia (in the implication that the villainous lion Scar was gay), xenophobia (Scar was voiced by English actor, **Jeremy Irons**) and gynophobia (in light of the subservient roles accorded to lionesses, Nala and Sarabi). Other critics complained that **Elton John** and **Tim Rice** should have composed songs based on traditional African music and culture, rather than writing transatlantic pop songs, like the Oscar-winning "Can You Feel The Love Tonight" and "I Just Can't Wait To Be King", which riffed on Busby Berkeley and Michael Jackson.

The violence of some scenes, particularly Mufasa's murder, concerned others. This was, indeed, the darkest Disney animation to date, with its in-jokes referencing such adult features as *Triumph Of The Will* (1935), *Gone With The Wind* (1939), *In The Heat Of The Night* (1967), *Scarface* (1983) and *Reversal Of Fortune* (1990). The studio reasoned that the 24-hour news media, movies and video games had conditioned 1990s kids to the grimmer realities of life – yet it avoided express references to the savannah food chain, and opted instead for typically cutesy critter graphics (despite vaunting the authenticity of such CGI sequences as the wildebeest stampede).

Audiences, however, seemed largely oblivious to the critics' concerns and *The Lion King* went on to gross $300 million on its estimated budget of $79,300,000. It also sold a record 55 million videos and spawned the straight-to-video sequels, *The Lion King II: Simba's Pride* (1998) and *The Lion King 1½* (2004).

# Love Me Tonight

## *dir* Rouben Mamoulian, 1932, 104m, b/w

**_cast_ Maurice Chevalier, Jeanette MacDonald, Charlie Ruggles, Charles Butterworth, Myrna Loy _cin_ Victor Milner _m_ Richard Rodgers, Lorenz Hart**

Musicals might have got bigger, more spectacular and more technically innovative, but plot, characterization, visuals and score were never better integrated into a seamless, magical whole than in this effervescent delight directed by **Rouben Mamoulian**.

*Love Me Tonight* was inspired by the 1924 Leopold Marchand and Paul Armont play, *The Tailor In The Chateau*. The story of a Parisian tradesman whose pursuit of an unpaid debt results in romance is whisper thin. However, the deft performances of **Maurice Chevalier**, **Jeanette MacDonald** and the exceptional ensemble combined with the glorious **Rodgers and Hart** score and Mamoulian's audiovisual ingenuity to give this musical fantasy a screwball charm that was only matched by the dance musicals of Fred Astaire and Ginger Rogers.

Although he began his film career with the musical *Applause* (1929), Mamoulian was reluctant to return to the genre. However, he was intrigued by Paramount's bid to prove that a musical film could be as valid and sophisticated as a Broadway show and he couldn't resist the opportunity to pit his talent against the studio's master of wit and elegance, Ernst Lubitsch. Mamoulian insisted that each of the nine distinctively staged musical numbers should be factored into the screenplay, so that they not only advanced the plot and developed the characters, but also subverted musical convention by forming bridges between the dialogue and the lyrics that were as subtly rhythmic as the cutting and the movement of the cast and camera. The scale of Mamoulian's achievement is evident from the first sixteen minutes, which effortlessly establish the key themes of town/country, night/day, rich/poor, old/new and two hearts becoming one.

The director drew on his 1927 stage production of *Porgy And Bess* for the opening "symphony of noises" sequence, in which the sounds of pavement-sweeping, boot-making, cobblestone-tapping and bell-ringing create an audio equivalent of the "city symphony" montages pioneered by the likes of Walter Ruttmann and Dziga

Vertov. This cityscape survey (borrowed from René Clair's French musicals) segues into Maurice Courtelin (Chevalier)'s "The Song Of Paree", which itself melds into "How Are You?" as the tailor promenades to his shop. Having attended to a couple of customers, he then breaks into "Isn't It Romantic?", which is subsequently carried into the street by a viscount, who passes it along to a cabby, a composer, some soldiers and a gypsy violinist before it's completed by Princess Jeanette (MacDonald) in her country chateau. In this one sequence, Mamoulian not only captured the time, place and mood of the entire picture, but also united Maurice and Jeanette in the audience's mind and transported them on a musical journey from *chanson* to operetta via a Tin Pan Alley ditty, a march and a gypsy folk song.

The action at the chateau is every bit as adept, with Mamoulian referencing a range of fairy tales, Chevalier and MacDonald's previous teamings and the classic German costume drama, *Der Kongress tanzt* (*The Congress Dances*, 1931). He also played mischievous games with the film speed and the sound effects, and revelled in the risqué dialogue, much of it involving **Myrna Loy**'s man-eating Countess Valentine. However, the music remains the animating force, whether it's Jeanette singing "Lover" to her horse, Maurice serenading her with "Mimi" or the titular duet which ends with a saucy split-screen shot of Maurice and Jeanette's heads on neighbouring pillows.

Moreover, in deference to the duality that dominates Hollywood musicals (see p.249), Mamoulian used mirror songs to unify the action, with "Maurice Enters The Castle" reprising "How Are You?" and his disguise as a baron being exposed in the passed-along tune, "The Son Of A Gun Is Nothing But A Tailor", which culminates in a top shot that anticipated Busby Berkeley's famous camera angle, as the footmen scurry off in star formation to spread the gossip.

*Love Me Tonight* epitomizes the saucy chic that characterized many Hollywood musicals before the imposition of the draconian Hays Code in 1934.

The picture's happy ending confounds expectations, with Mamoulian even out-montaging Sergei Eisenstein as Jeanette reverses the romantic roles by charging after the departing Maurice's train on her trusty steed. *Love Me Tonight* initiated the musical tradition of having one character leave behind the everyday to enter a neverland, and although it did only moderate business at the box office and was overlooked by the Academy, it has since been acknowledged as a musical masterclass.

# The Love Parade

**_dir_ Ernst Lubitsch, 1929, 110m, b/w**
**_cast_ Maurice Chevalier, Jeanette MacDonald, Lillian Roth, Lupino Lane, Eugene Pallete, E.H. Calvert, Edgar Norton**
**_cin_ Victor Milner _m_ Victor Schertzinger, Clifford Grey**

Drawing comparisons with Strauss, Mozart and Hans Christian Andersen, Jean Cocteau dubbed *The Love Parade* "a Lubitsch miracle". Yet **Ernst Lubitsch** only embarked upon his sound debut after the rare failure of his 1929 silent, *Eternal Love*. The director distrusted talkies, believing they limited camera fluidity and made the dramatic content too literal, but his pictures had always possessed an innate musicality and he saw the advantages of setting entire scenes to the rhythm of a score. He sought ways to translate the wit, elegance and innuendo of the "Lubitsch touch" into dialogue, music and contrapuntal sound and, in so doing, he not only subverted stage conventions, but also established many staples of the screen's newest genre.

In the opening sequence, a valet (**Lupino Lane**) lays a table and then pulls the cloth from beneath the meticulous place settings – and that's exactly what Lubitsch does with the film's operetta format. He sets up an escapist Ruritanian scenario, with its Art Deco designs and fairy-tale costumes, and then introduces a disgruntled hero, whose roguish presence brings a hint of ignobility to the rarefied art form. The disgruntled hero is Count Alfred Renard (**Maurice Chevalier**), who abandons his amorous existence in Paris to marry Queen Louise (**Jeanette MacDonald**) of Sylvania. Tiring of his role as a powerless spouse, Alfred is only dissuaded from divorce – much to the relief of his lovestruck valet and the queen's maid (**Lillian Roth**) – by the proud monarch's realization that her regal and romantic ambitions can only be achieved through reciprocity.

In adapting Leon Xanrof and Jules Chancel's 1919 play, *The Prince Consort*, screenwriters **Guy Bolton** and **Ernest Vadja** revised the typical operetta structure by reversing the gender roles of the romantic leads and removing the external source of opposition to their union by locating it within their own relationship. Through consistently uniting and dividing the lovers until they learned to compromise, Lubitsch not only brought a new adult sophistication to the musical comedy, but also initiated a tradition that would persist for the next thirty years.

The further genius of *The Love Parade* comes from its unlikely union of operetta and revue. In operetta, the music traditionally takes precedence over the lyrics and the songs are used to heighten mood and emotion. In a revue, however, the numbers are performed with the express intention of amusing or affecting. By blending the two styles, Lubitsch made the lyrics advance both the storyline and the character development, while also bringing a satirical edge to a format renowned for its conservatism and sentimentality.

Lubitsch integrated the songs into the action, rather than squeezing them into contrived diegetic pauses, and thereby established the convention of the central couple and their duet being the central focus of the Hollywood musical. Moreover, he managed to restore some movement to the motion picture by utilizing a tracking shot during the wedding sequence, which was choreographed throughout to the beat of a metronome, so that every gesture and every expression fitted the accompanying rhythm precisely.

The action also contains flashes of the customary Lubitsch drollery, most notably during "Paris, Stay The Same", in which Alfred takes his leave of the Parisian belles, while his valet salutes the maids and the dog bids *adieu* to the manicured poodles. A similarly inspired use of off-screen space occurs during the dinner sequence, in which everything we need to know about the unseen Alfred and Louise's demeanour is conveyed by their anxious, eavesdropping courtiers. Lubitsch even found a novel way to open up the scenes and avoid editorial problems – he shot the footage he was going to intercut on neighbouring sound stages linked by a single orchestra, so that he could crosscut on exactly the right notes.

Lubtisch's taste and ingenuity resulted in an exquisite, innovative and irresistible movie that the critics lauded and the Academy honoured with six Oscar nominations. However, so few cinemas were wired for sound in 1929 that most audiences only got to see it in a shorter silent version.

# Mary Poppins

## *dir* Robert Stevenson, 1964, 140m

**_cast_ Julie Andrews, Dick Van Dyke, David Tomlinson, Glynis Johns, Karen Dotrice, Matthew Garber _cin_ Edward Colman _m_ Richard M. Sherman, Robert B. Sherman**

Helen Goff (better known by her pen name **P.L. Travers**) thought movies were vulgar, so she was less than impressed when **Roy Disney** came to New York in the early 1940s hoping to secure the rights to her 1934 bestseller about a remarkable nanny, which was a firm favourite of his niece, Diane. **Walt Disney** had no more luck in the 1950s, but Travers finally relented in 1961, on the proviso that her book was not turned into a cartoon and that she was hired as a consultant. Having selected six episodes from *Mary Poppins* and *Mary Poppins Comes Back*, Walt Disney and the **Sherman brothers** drafted a scenario, to which Travers responded with a raft of candid observations. But Disney ignored her cavils and made the film his own way. Indeed, when Travers submitted suggested amendments to the rough cut, he snapped that she only had final approval over the script, not the entire picture.

Bette Davis and Mary Martin were considered for the title role, but Disney chose **Julie Andrews** after seeing her on stage in *Camelot*. Fresh from the 1963 Disney romp, *The Three Lives Of Thomasina*, **Matthew Garber** and **Karen Dotrice** were recruited to play the Banks children, while popular TV star **Dick Van Dyke** was cast as Bert – regardless of his Cockney deficiencies. Equally as important as the cast were the new artists hired to work with the established Disney staff, in order to bring some innovation to their expertise. As a result, the animated scenes had both ingenuity and beauty, with the animals in the "Jolly Holiday" sequence eschewing the studio's customary cuteness, while the pace and intricacy of the action demonstrated how far matting techniques had come since Gene Kelly danced with Jerry Mouse in *Anchors Aweigh* (1945).

The score was just as ingenious. It echoed *My Fair Lady*'s conscious diversity, sharing its Edwardian aura and borrowing its patter song style for **David Tomlinson**, as Mr Banks. The influence of Lerner and Loewe could be discerned in the shifts between operetta ballads like "Feed The Birds", music-hall frolics like the Oscar-winning "Chim Chim Cheree" and Tin Pan Alley standards like "Sister Suffragette", but echoes of the nursery songs from Rodgers and Hammerstein's *The Sound Of Music* could also be heard in "A Spoonful Of Sugar" and "Supercalifragilisticexpialidocious". There were even hints of *Snow White And The Seven Dwarfs* (1937) and *The Wizard Of Oz* (1939) in the storyline, as not only does an outsider transform the lives of those in her care, but Jane and Michael Banks also come to realize that "there's no place like home".

Although it exhibits fairy-tale elements, *Mary Poppins* is essentially a folk musical (see p.262), in which unruly siblings learn responsibility and uptight parents rediscover the cheerful optimism of their own childhoods. What's less appealing about this civics lesson is its regrettable tendency to idealize bourgeois mores, while romanticizing the poverty of the chimney sweeps and the Bird Woman. Less intrusive, however, is the personal slant. Walt and Roy Disney had been raised by a similarly humourless martinet father and an affectionate ineffectual mother (Mr Banks even sported Elias Disney's pencil moustache). Walt Disney also saw something of himself in Mary Poppins, as he could transform humdrum lives, albeit temporarily, with his special brand of magic.

He conceived the film as a summation of his achievements as an artist, showman and children's entertainer. It may have been overlong and may have lost its focus on Poppins in the final third, but it was a vast improvement on the studio's previous live-action musical, *Babes In Toyland* (1961). It took a then-massive $31 million at the US box office and won five Oscars from thirteen nominations, but Travers never accepted Disney's intepretation of her novels and always insisted that the film would have worked better with period tunes like "Ta Ra Ra Boom De Ay".

# Meet Me In St Louis

## *dir* Vincente Minnelli, 1944, 113m

**cast Judy Garland, Margaret O'Brien, Mary Astor, Lucille Bremer, Leon Ames, Tom Drake, Marjorie Main *cin* George Folsey *m* Hugh Martin, Ralph Blane**

Frustrated at missing out on the rights to the stage hit *Life With Father*, producer **Arthur Freed** found a ready-made replacement in the "Kensington" stories **Sally Benson** published in the *New Yorker*. Charmed by the sweetness of the autobiographical vignettes that were "like a Valentine in the palm of your hand", Freed originally conceived the project as a musical with period songs for director George Cukor. The MGM board had doubts about making a film with a non-linear structure, but **Louis B. Mayer** saw the venture as a costume equivalent to the long-running Andy Hardy series, and instead backed the screenplay that **Fred Finklehoffe** and **Irving Brecher** wrote for **Vincente Minnelli**.

Meyer sanctioned Freed's recruitment of Broadway art director **Lemuel Ayers** (who had designed *Oklahoma!*) and the construction of a 1903 St Louis street at a cost of more than $200,000. He also helped coax **Judy Garland** into accepting the part of Esther Smith, even though she was increasingly anxious to escape from juvenile roles. She was surrounded by dependable character actors **Mary Astor**, **Leon Ames**, **Harry Davenport** and **Marjorie Main**, as well as newcomers **Lucille Bremer**, **Joan Carroll** and **Margaret O'Brien** as her sisters. Freed and Mayer were committed to *Meet Me In St Louis* because it reaffirmed the key message from *The Wizard Of Oz* (1939): "There's no place like home". This was more relevant than ever with so many military personnel overseas, and Minnelli's "sentimental mood piece" revisited the contrasting concepts of youth/adulthood, fantasy/reality and faraway/home, while also placing patriotic faith in the rituals, inventions and values that America was fighting to uphold.

For all its seemingly simple positivity, this is also a film of contradiction and complexity. The spirited Smith women are determined to seize life, but they are also cheerfully subservient and domesticated. Conversely, their chauvinistic father despises the telephone, yet so aspires to the social mobility it symbolizes that he accepts a promotion that will uproot his entrenched family to New York. Ironically, this nostalgic saga is actually firmly rooted in modernity. Great store is set in technological advances and the comforts and conveniences of consumerism, while the World Fair finale celebrates the future with an optimism that would have cheered contemporary audiences, who were already beginning to anticipate peace.

Convinced she's not going to have herself a merry little Christmas, Tootie Smith (Margaret O'Brien) destroys the snow people she had modelled on her once-contented family.

The score blends 1900s standards such as Bob Cole's "Under The Bamboo Tree" and Kerry Mills's title ditty with 1940s pop tunes such as **Hugh Martin** and **Ralph Blane**'s "The Trolley Song", "The Boy Next Door" and "Have Yourself A Merry Little Christmas". The décor (shot in lustrous Technicolor) similarly combines authentic period details gleaned from Benson's stories and the paintings of Thomas Eakins with the inspired use of light, colour and composition that Minnelli had learned as a window dresser. This conscious theatricality also applies to choreographer **Charles Walters**' staging of the musical numbers, which largely remain within confined spaces, despite Minnelli's agile camera – although "The Trolley Song" has a more traditional production feel.

The film wasn't all cosy artifice, however. The youngest Smith daughter (O'Brien) imparts a sense of mischief and melancholy that turns disconcertingly dark during the Halloween and Christmas sequences. In the latter, after learning of her father's decision to quit St Louis, she launches into a furious assault on the snow people that she had built so lovingly in the garden. Such self-possessed shifts between innocence and experience earned O'Brien a special Oscar.

*Meet Me In St Louis* amassed receipts of $7,566,000 on its $1,707,561 budget. But, more significantly, by integrating the songs into the narrative to emphasize the emotional aspects of everyday life, it had an even greater impact on the Hollywood musical than *Oklahoma!* had exerted on Broadway.

# The Merry Widow

**_dir_ Ernst Lubitsch, 1934, 99m, b/w**

**_cast_ Maurice Chevalier, Jeanette MacDonald, Edward Everett Horton, Una Merkel, George Barbier _cin_ Oliver T. Mash _m_ Franz Lehár, Lorenz Hart, Gus Kahn**

When **Franz Lehár**'s operetta *Die lustige witwe* (*The Merry Widow*) opened in Vienna in 1905, it caused a sensation. It rapidly become an international success, and within months of the American premiere, the first of ten screen adaptations was released. MGM bought the rights in 1925, and Erich von Stroheim directed a silent reworking that subjected the slender storyline to a Freudian interpretation that unexpectedly helped it turn a substantial profit.

However, production chief **Irving G. Thalberg** detested Von Stroheim and was keen to remake the picture. His first attempts to mount sound productions foundered because the studio lacked a stable of musical talent capable of doing *The Merry Widow* justice. But in 1934, he persuaded **Maurice Chevalier** to headline a musical adaptation of Lehár's masterpiece, which tells the story of a disgraced count's bid to seduce a wealthy widow to prevent her from removing her fortune from the tiny kingdom of Marshovia. Chevalier wanted Metropolitan Opera diva Grace Moore to play the widow Sonia to his Count Danilo and was piqued when MGM not only denied his request, but also paired him with **Jeanette MacDonald** (whom he couldn't abide). Both Chevalier and MacDonald complained about the reunion, but she recognized his wit and charm and he admired the vulnerability and vivacity that he inspired in her.

Director **Ernst Lubitsch**, however, was less concerned with casting than with demonstrating that music was audible romance. He wanted the score to be as expressive and intimate as the dialogue and, to this end, he imbued the action with a continental sophistication that marked quite a departure from MGM's all-American approach to the genre.

Disregarding MGM's concerns that a frothy romance was being transformed into a satire on the risibility of sex (and cinema's depiction of it), Lubitsch exploited his contract's unprecedented levels of latitude by hiring **Lorenz Hart** and **Gus Kahn** to write new lyrics emphasizing the blatant eroticism of the lovers' growing attachment. He also anticipated the films of Fred Astaire and Ginger Rogers by using dance as an emotional barometer. Danilo and Sonia only realize their feelings for each other while dancing cheek-to-cheek to the "Merry Widow Waltz" in the private dining-room at Maxim's restaurant. However, a comedy of errors (which became another Fred'n'Ginger staple) then conspires to keep them apart until the same song reunites them at the Embassy Ball. They finally seal their passion in a glorious progress through the building that irradiates every room they enter, including a mirrored corridor.

Thus, for the first time, Lubitsch employed music as a metaphor for love rather than lust. He even shifted the gender emphasis by having Danilo succumb to Sonia, rather than resist her impassioned pursuit. However, the Hays Office censors were appalled by the way in which "filth" had been introduced into such a respectable art form and insisted on thirteen cuts being made to tone down Danilo's pleasure at his sexual prowess. In all, three minutes of footage were excised from the American release, and not restored until 1962. But such prudish butchery could do nothing to detract from the mastery of Lubitsch's direction, the mischievous majesty of the score or the effortless carnality of Chevalier and MacDonald's byplay.

Despite the success of the French-language version, *La veuve joyeuse* (which was filmed simultaneously with the same cast, *The Merry Widow* failed outside of the major American cities and lost $113,000, which persuaded MGM to rethink its approach to the genre. With screwball comedies and Busby Berkeley musicals concentrating on the middle and lower classes rather than the upper echelons, the days of the "naughty" operetta were numbered. Lubitsch abandoned the musical altogether, while Chevalier left Hollywood in 1935, and did not return for 25 years. MacDonald went on to become the studio's biggest singing star – in partnership with Nelson Eddy – but she never again exhibited the same spirit or sensuality.

# My Fair Lady

## *dir* George Cukor, 1964, 170m

**cast Audrey Hepburn, Rex Harrison, Stanley Holloway, Wilfrid Hyde-White, Gladys Cooper, Jeremy Brett *cin* Harry Stradling *m* Frederick Loewe, Alan Jay Lerner**

**George Bernard Shaw** so disliked the 1908 operetta of *Arms And The Man* that he refused to allow any further musical adaptations of his plays. Indeed, when producer **Gabriel Pascal** suggested that he could make a splendid musical out of *Pygmalion*, the story of a phonics professor who wagers that he can turn a flowergirl into a duchess, Shaw retorted, "I absolutely forbid such an outrage. If *Pygmalion* is not good enough for your friends with its own verbal music, their talent must be altogether extraordinary." Fortunately for Pascal, the songwriting team of **Alan Jay Lerner** and **Frederick Loewe** were sufficiently gifted. After Shaw's death, Pascal entrusted them with writing the libretto and score, and Loewe's genius for period idioms provided a quaintly restraining accompaniment to Lerner's self-consciously clever lyrics.

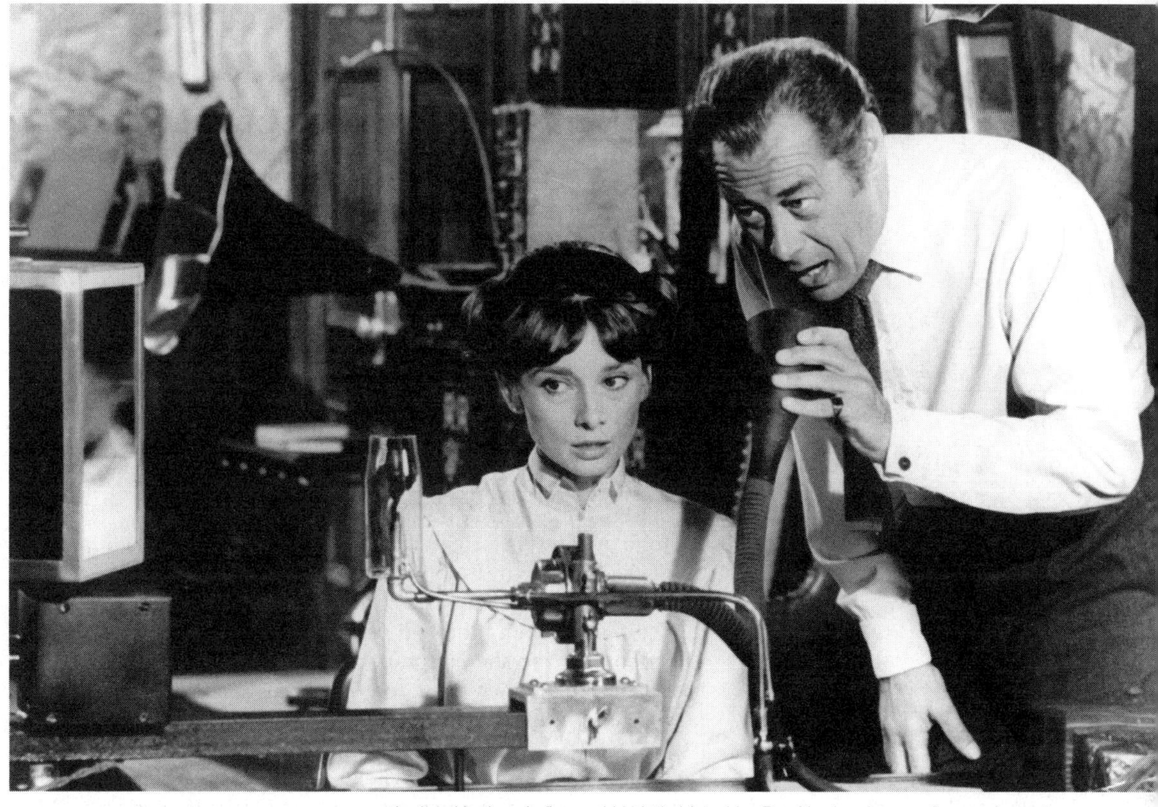

Audrey Hepburn's flowergirl is intimidated by Rex Harrison's recording equipment, which emphasizes the film's key thematic contrast between nature and nurture.

*My Fair Lady* is a combination of class and character comedy, in which the antipathy between Henry Higgins (**Rex Harrison**) and Eliza Doolittle (**Audrey Hepburn**) is exacerbated by the respective intellectual pomposity and social deprivation that prevent them from realizing their human connection. By showing how a street urchin with diction, but no education, could pass muster in society, Shaw had sought to expose the link between accent and perception. However, by sticking to Shaw's screenplay for Anthony Asquith and Leslie Howard's 1938 film of *Pygmalion*, Lerner realized that he could not only explore the economics of language, but also focus on the triumph of love over hierarchy.

Consequently, the score took its character from Shavian politics and its context from a romanticized London. Higgins's songs were cast as recitatives that allowed Lerner to keep Shaw's caustic wit from descending into musical cant. The technique also permitted the neat irony of suggesting that the linguist Higgins was out of his depth in a world of song, unlike the full-throated Cockney songbird and her roistering dustman father (**Stanley Holloway**). With its pleasing mix of Gilbert and Sullivan, operetta, music hall and Tin Pan Alley, the score was tantamount to a potted history of the genre, and its diverse approach to the past made it seem timeless.

Lerner always insisted that he wrote Higgins with Rex Harrison in mind, and Harrison had to learn to talk on pitch and rely on his innate sense of rhythm to stay on note. He opened the Broadway stage show in 1956, before reprising the role on the screen after Warner Bros secured the rights for an unprecedented $5.5 million. **Jack Warner** had been determined to cast Cary Grant as Higgins, but he declined, famously stating, "not only will I not play in it, but if Rex Harrison doesn't do it, I won't even go to see it".

**Julie Andrews** starred alongside Harrison in the stage production hailed as "the greatest musical of the twentieth century", but she was deemed a box-office risk and replaced with Audrey Hepburn for the film version. Although Hepburn's casting was the subject of much controversy, she epitomized Eliza's Cinderella spirit, and she had already played a similar role in *Funny Face* (1957). This time, however, she was not allowed to sing for herself. She acted the lyrics to "Wouldn't It Be Loverly?", "I Could Have Danced All Night" and "Show Me", while lip-synching to **Marni Nixon**'s playback. But she did so with as much musicality as Harrison musters for "I'm An Ordinary Man" and "I've Grown Accustomed To Her Face" or Holloway manages on "With A Little Bit Of Luck" and "Get Me To The Church On Time".

Much of this was due to **George Cukor**'s decision to place Eliza at the centre of the action, with **Cecil Beaton**'s costumes and **Gene Allen**'s sets consciously evoking her trade. Flashes of flowerful colour consistently reveal her presence and her growing influence on everyone she charms. The scheme enables her to stand out from the grime of Covent Garden, the fusty browns of Higgins's study and the colourless snobbery of the Ascot enclosure, and it also intimates that she is blooming in Higgins's hot house. While their alliance doesn't necessarily guarantee marital bliss, Higgins and Eliza, nevertheless, unite the worlds of academia and nature, technology and emotion, monochrome and colour, high society and the streets. Cukor also succeeds in binding Broadway to Hollywood, by taking a theatrical conception and energizing it with cinematic flourishes and star power in a manner that so many other transfers would seek to emulate over the next decade.

Deploring the fact that it wasn't shot on location in London, Lerner disliked this 70mm Super Panavision masterpiece.Yet *My Fair Lady* took $72 million at the US box office and converted eight of its twelve Oscar nominations. More significantly, it proved to be an impeccable amalgamation of script, score, lyrics, design and performance and it elevated the musical to a new level of literate, artistic entertainment that has yet to be surpassed.

# Nashville

## *dir* Robert Altman, 1975, 159m

### *cast* Henry Gibson, Karen Black, Ronee Blakley, Keith Carradine *cin* Paul Lohmann *m* Richard Baskin et al

**Robert Altman** decided that he wanted to make a musical after hearing **Keith Carradine** sing "It Don't Worry Me" and "I'm Easy" at a party, and he set **Joan Tewkesbury** to write an original scenario. But, as this was to be a typically extemporized collaboration, Altman also insisted that the cast composed their own songs, and many relied on the assistance of music supervisor **Richard Baskin**. His contribution to the fifty or so titles developed for the project is all the more remarkable considering his influences were Bartok, Gershwin and Satie, rather than American folk or country and western.

Shooting over 45 days on a $2 million budget, Altman amassed more than sixteen hours of footage and briefly considered releasing two features, *Nashville Red* and *Nashville Blue*. His hopes of producing a ten-hour mini series for ABC were also dashed when the film grossed only $7 million – despite reviews that compared Altman to everyone from Chekhov, Joyce, Dos Passos and Mailer to Fellini, Godard, Bertolucci and Astaire. Howard Koch, who co-wrote *Casablanca*, considered this study of "the famous somebodys crossing paths with the lowly nobodys in a city of dreams and illusions" to be "the *Citizen Kane* of this generation", while Molly Haskell proclaimed it to be "a Chaucerian musical pilgrimage whose Canterbury is Nashville". Certainly, a quasi-religious sense of America after the Fall pervades the picture, which was released midway between President Nixon's resignation and the start of the Bicentennial celebrations. Furthermore, it opened in the same month that *A Chorus Line* – also a story of showbiz aspirants in a microcosmic setting – premiered on Broadway and launched its own assault on the conventions of the stage musical.

*Nashville* is a denunciation of fundamentalism. It equates the conservatism and folksy *faux* humility of the country scene with the hypocrisy of the political establishment and indicts Nixon, Hollywood and Nashville for devaluing cherished American institutions. The multi-threaded narrative is also about the assassination of the Kennedys and Martin Luther King, the suppression and exploitation of women, debasement in the pursuit of ambition, and the public's acquiescence in the decline of political integrity and artistic ingenuity. But, most significantly, *Nashville* is about the death of the musical.

Altman felt that Nashville in the 1970s had the same feel as Hollywood in the 1940s, so MGM and Fox musicals such as *Meet Me In St Louis*, *The Harvey Girls*, *Down Argentine Way* and *Moon Over Miami* exerted a considerable influence on his approach. However, he also subverted the genre's love of symbolic celebration by contrasting *Centennial Summer*'s (1946) post-war sense of euphoria with the nation's despondency at the end of the Vietnam conflict. This sense of chaos and inertia is superbly conveyed in the airport and freeway sequences, which not only establish the cacophony that will eventually drown out the music, but also suggest that the songs are as superficial as their singers. Thus, *Nashville* treats music in much the same way that Kurosawa's *Rashômon* (1950) exploited diegetic truth; it posits that the traditional musical has no place in modern America because the generic gambits that sustained it are now extraneous to everyday life.

Everything about *Nashville* is designed to undermine musical convention. The customary duality is destroyed by presenting the characters in isolation or in threes and the lack of romantic contentment dashes any backstager notions of success. However, Altman reserves his special ire for the folk musical (see p.262). With everyone in town to satisfy their own ends, the usual sense of harmonious community is corrupted. Consequently, the myth that anyone can be a performer is shattered, because music no longer emanates spontaneously from the soul of the people. Instead, it is manufactured and packaged in order to make money, sustain celebrity or secure political power or sexual favour.

Stripped of its potential to touch hearts and change lives – let alone expose the psyche of the singer – music becomes an irrelevance. Whereas ambient sound was once suspended for the duration of a number, it now interrupts or obscures the music during the majority of the live spots; performance belongs in the artificial studio environment of the real world and not in a screen fantasy. In the late 1980s, Altman considered making a sequel called *Nashville 12*, but with the musical virtually extinct, there was nothing left to lampoon.

# Oklahoma!

## *dir* Fred Zinnemann, 1955, 145m

**cast** Gordon MacRae, Gloria Grahame, Shirley Jones, Gene Nelson, Charlotte Greenwood *cin* Robert Surtees *m* Richard Rodgers, Oscar Hammerstein II

**Fred Zinnemann**'s 1955 film version of *Oklahoma!* changed nothing and influenced nothing. Such was the delay in bringing Rodgers and Hammerstein's landmark 1943 show to the screen that many of its innovations – from integrating the score into the narrative to fashioning dream ballets – had become clichés both in Hollywood and on Broadway. Consequently, this laudably faithful transfer seemed old-fashioned and staid, although it is valuable as a record of the show that transformed the history of the stage and screen musical.

Theatre producer Theresa Helburn had conceived the idea for *Oklahoma!* during a 1941 revival of **Lynn Riggs**'s social realist drama, *Green Grow The Lilacs* (1931), which included not only interpolated folk songs, but also a square dance choreographed by Gene Kelly. Realizing that the story worked better as a "play for music" and keen to break the moulds of operetta and musical comedy, Helburn asked **Richard Rodgers** to musicalize the play. His lyricist partner, Lorenz Hart, was convinced that the project would fail, so Rodgers turned instead to **Oscar Hammerstein**, feeling intuitively that their contrasting styles would gel. Rodgers had to abandon his jazzy urbanity to accommodate Hammerstein's folksy lyrics, but he was eventually able to boast that "the orchestrations sound the way the costumes look". Rodgers was utterly convinced of the production's quality. "Do you know what is wrong with this show?" he asked stage director Rouben Mamoulian on opening night. "Nothing." Rival producer Mike Todd offered a very different opinion, "No girls, no gags, no chance". But Rodgers was ultimately proved right, as *Oklahoma!* ran on Broadway for 2,212 performances and visited over 150 venues nationwide before finally closing in May 1954.

Farm-girl Laurey Williams (Shirley Jones) and cowboy Curly McLain (Gordon MacRae) fall in love and help to create civilization on the untamed frontier.

Embittered by seeing so many of his earlier Broadway hits bowdlerized by movie producers, Rodgers was determined to make Hollywood wait for his masterpiece and then stipulated that his score had to remain intact. Zinnemann preserved the integrity of the score, but he opened out the action by shooting numbers like "Oh, What A Beautiful Mornin'" in authentic, atmospheric locations. He also introduced some sprightly action to "The Surrey With The Fringe On Top", a deft comic sensibility to "I Cain't Say No" and a quaint romanticism to "People Will Say We're In Love", while retaining the verve of Mamoulian's original stagings of "Kansas City", "Oklahoma" and "The Farmer And The Rancher".

However, Zinnemann's widescreen photography often diluted the intimacy of this turn-of-the-century pioneer tale about cowboy Curly McLain and his farm-girl sweetheart Laurey Williams, despite the use of audacious close-ups. Moreover, **Gordon MacRae** and **Shirley Jones** were somewhat anaemic as Curly and Laurey. Although their vocals were more than adequate, their acting deficiencies were exposed by the sharper edge that **Rod Steiger** and **Gloria Grahame** brought to their performances, as sinister farm hand Jud Fry and Laurey' best friend Ado Annie, and by the folksiness with which **Charlotte Greenwood** portrayed Aunt Eller.

With *Oklahoma!* Rodgers and Hammerstein had consciously created a musical in which the action and the score could be interwoven into a single rhythmic and dramatic pattern. The finest embodiment of this was choreographer **Agnes De Mille**'s highly praised dream ballet, "Laurey Makes Up Her Mind", which explored exclusively through dance Laurey's conflicting feelings for Curly and Jud. Hammerstein had envisaged something with a circus theme, but De Mille insisted that "nice girls dream rather dirty dreams". He replaced the stars with professional dancers, **James Mitchell** and **Bambi Lynn**, who were more able to convey emotions that shifted from naive romance to sinister doubt, as the music, movement, lighting and design merged in a uniquely expressive manner.

The ballet also helped *Oklahoma!* to create the template for the folk musical (see p.262). The dance routines – and indeed many of the everyday actions – adhered to the rhythms of life, while the songs were inspired by the sounds of nature. As a sodbuster and a cowpoke, the lovers represent both the stability of the soil and the restless energy of wanderlust, and by uniting, they bring a renewed sense of permanence, vigour and continuity to the wider community, thus creating civilization out of the chaos of the untamed frontier.

The story is set in 1907, the year in which Oklahoma was admitted to the Union, and its reaffirmation of liberty and individuality within a democratic system had a certain resonance for audiences watching the Broadway show in 1943, when American forces were attempting to restore order to a conflicted world. Even though Zinnemann's film was released at the height of the Cold War, it didn't have quite the same poignacy. The film offered little by way of innovation, despite being photographed in two new widescreen processes, Todd-AO and CinemaScope, and it suffered from the fact that Zinnemann was a dramatist rather than a pictorialist or a musical specialist. Consequently, the picture never had the impact of its stage predecessor, even though it grossed a more than respectable $7.1 million at the US box office. Time has since imparted a nostalgic glow on *Oklahoma!*, and the success of later Rodgers and Hammerstein films has helped this reverential, if uninspired screen adaptation acquire classic status.

# On The Town

## *dir* Gene Kelly, Stanley Donen, 1949, 98m

***cast*** **Gene Kelly, Frank Sinatra, Jules Munshin, Vera-Ellen, Betty Garrett, Ann Miller** ***cin*** **Harold Rosson** ***m*** **Leonard Bernstein, Roger Edens, Betty Comden, Adolph Green**

*On The Town* set a new agenda for the movie musical. After seven years working at MGM, **Gene Kelly** had realized that the techniques used to record song musicals were wholly inappropriate for filming dance. He was determined to capture the kinetic energy of live performance and, in order to do so, he had to reinvent the art of screen choreography.

Kelly set out to create a masterpiece, and he sought to give it a distinctly proletarian sensibility by concentrating on three average sailors and the hard-working city girls they meet during a 24-hour furlough. He even achieved a novel sexual equality by having **Betty Garrett** and **Ann Miller** move in on **Frank Sinatra** and **Jules Munshin**, while his own obsession with **Vera-Ellen**'s Miss Turnstiles owed as much to her cultural and sporting aptitude as to her celebrity or looks. Kelly and co-director **Stanley Donen** also challenged the conventions of Hollywood storytelling by shooting on location, dislocating the narrative and compressing time and space to give the action a sense of urgency that equated to modern urban living. They even included regular on-screen time checks to emphasize the immediacy of Kelly's race to find his girl before he has to return to his ship.

The filming of this landmark picture met opposition at every stage. Despite following **Arthur Freed**'s advice and purchasing the rights to the original 1944 Broadway show during pre-production, MGM chief **Louis B. Mayer** branded it "smutty" and "Communistic", and shelved the project until Kelly insisted on its revival. Freed himself has misgivings about **Leonard Bernstein**'s original score and teamed screenwriting lyricists **Betty Comden** and **Adolph Green** with associate producer **Roger Edens** to create something catchier and more cinematic.

Meanwhile, Mayer baulked at the expense of shooting in New York and limited Kelly and Donen to a mere five days on location. Yet they overcame bad weather and considerable technical difficulties relating to playback and synchronization to achieve an impressionistic "city symphony" that conveyed a tourist's excitement, while also capturing a sense of the everyday. Much of this was down to editor **Ralph E. Winters**, who packed three-and-a-half diegetic hours and eighteen locations into the two-and-a-half-minute opening number, "New York, New York".

This vibrancy also informed the other musical stagings. Kelly experimented with a dazzling variety of dance styles, including ballet, soft-shoe, tribal dance, tap and comic hoofing, and choreographed **Harold Rosson**'s camera to match the vigour of the routines. Kelly used all manner of dollies, cables and cranes to make the moving camera a partner in the dance rather than a detached spectator, and frequently shot in long takes to make innovative use of angle and space. On the rare occasions that he did cut away, he resumed the action with the dancers mid-movement, in order to disguise the edit and open up new spaces for the routine to enter.

Indeed, such was the emphasis on dance that all but Kelly and Vera-Ellen were replaced with professional dancers for the "Day In New York" ballet, which took a sizeable risk in asking audiences to accept that Kelly's macho, wisecracking sailor had a balletic soul. However, he pulled it off with typically bullish bravado and brought a new athleticism to screen dancing, which later came to characterize his unique brand of choreography.

The MGM brass felt that *On The Town* was too different from the usual studio fare and they were convinced it would fail. But the movie grossed $4.4 million on its $2 million budget and won the Oscar for the best scoring of a musical picture. Moreover, it proved conclusively that musicals didn't have to be about show people; they could focus on ordinary folk who sang and danced on actual streets because they had no other way of expressing themselves. Thereafter, the old backstage format went into abeyance for much of the decade – although *Singin' In The Rain* (1952) and *The Band Wagon* (1953) were glorious exceptions.

# The Pajama Game

## *dir* George Abbott, Stanley Donen, 1957, 101m

*cast* Doris Day, John Raitt, Carol Haney, Eddie Foy, Jr. *cin* Harry Stradling *m* Richard Adler, Jerry Ross

**Stanley Donen** is the unsung hero of the Hollywood musical. Gene Kelly was never as effective a director without him, and Donen's 1950s output was consistently superior to that of Charles Walters, George Sidney and Walter Lang – on occasion, he even surpassed the efforts of Vincente Minnelli. However, after *The Pajama Game* and *Damn Yankees* (1958), he all-but severed his links to the genre he had done so much to infuse with kinetic energy. Donen even had reservations about taking on *The Pajama Game*, as he preferred to direct original musicals that freed him from comparisons with the stage version and from the temptation to settle for proven material. However, realizing that several sequences could be translated to the screen without many changes, he asked Broadway director **George Abbott** to share the screen credit – although there was little actual collaboration involved.

Based on **Richard Bissell**'s novel *7½ Cents* (1953), the story of a union official's romance with a factory superintendent during a pay dispute had restored some of the fun that had disappeared from the Broadway musical during the Rodgers and Hammerstein era. It also caught the blue-collar mood of the sitcoms and domestic dramas that were then dominating America's TV schedules. Yet besides its wry social comment, the movie also borrowed tropes from the back-stager and folk musical traditions to ensure an element of escapism, and subverted the conventions of musical coupling by making the romantic leads, Babe (**Doris Day**) and Sid (**John Raitt**), as amusing as the comic juveniles, Hines (**Eddie Foy, Jr.**) and Gladys (**Carol Haney**).

After Warner Bros bought the film rights, Donen retained over a third of the original show's cast and eleven of the fifteen songs, making this one of Hollywood's most faithful transfers. Only Janis Paige, who had starred as Babe, was absent from the principals, but her replacement, Doris Day, turned in her best screen performance by combining elements of her established tomboy sass with the controlled feminist chic that would become her battle-of-the-sexes trademark. There was also just a chink of vulnerability in Day's persona, which she archly concealed with a brassy sexiness, that was never allowed to recur after she was reinvented as a screwball comedy icon.

Donen refused to prettify the remainder of the cast, whose physiques, fashion sense and hair styles unfussily complemented the studio realism of the Sleeptite Pajama Factory, the union offices, Babe's house and the riverside dive, Hernando's Hideaway. Moreover, the diversity of the score reflected the contrasts between the characters and conveyed the rhythms of working life, which Donen established in the pre-credit sequence and satirized by undercranking the camera to speed up the action during "Racing The Clock". Such neat touches exposed the static approach to filming musicals that followed MGM's heyday.

For "Hey There", Donen not only made clever use of a dictaphone to allow John Raitt to sing a duet with himself, but also turned the camera into a discreet participant in a scene that showed a man wrestling with his feelings. rather than a performer delivering a song. By shooting in a single take, Donen made a key psychological moment highly cinematic. Day's reprise of the song is equally inspired, with the red and green lights of the railway signal outside her window bathing the room in symbolic colour as her live rendition ends with sobs of frustration that choke the lyrics. In fact, Day's intelligent rendition of the song indicates just how wasted she had been in all those Warner Bros trifles.

Despite Day's fine performance, the film is stolen on three separate occasions by Carol Haney. Gene Kelly's former assistant not only sings with a pleasingly authentic ordinariness, but also erupts onto the screen in the glorious trio of "Once A Year Day", "Hernando's Hideaway" and "Steam Heat". The first routine innovatively exploited the undulating topography of Hollenbeck Park, where it was filmed, and shattered the Berkeleyesque uniformity of the chorus line, while the second deftly combined darkness, matchlight and nimble camera movements, and the third was a genuine showstopper. Sadly, Haney never became the star she deserved to be, because she died tragically young – depriving musicals of exuberant, innovative class just when they needed it most. However, she definitely left her mark on what Jean-Luc Godard branded "the first left-wing operetta".

## Bob Fosse's "Steam Heat"

The dance number "Steam Heat" proved to be one of the most spectacular set pieces in *The Pajama Game*, and it confirmed **Bob Fosse**'s choreographic reputation. Utilizing hissing radiators and clunking pipes, Fosse created a jazzy syncopated number for dancer **Carol Haney**, and reinforced the rhythms with finger-snapping, hand-clapping and foot-stomping. The stylized gyrations might have owed much to the great choreographer Jack Cole and the use of hats and props recalled Fred Astaire's routines, but the minimalist costumes, jerky body movements and expressive hand gestures became Fosse's signature schtick.

# The Pirate

## *dir* Vincente Minnelli, 1948, 102m

**cast** Judy Garland, Gene Kelly, Walter Slezak, Gladys Cooper *cin* Harry Stradling *m* Cole Porter

*The Pirate* ranks among the musical's most maligned masterpieces. It was inspired by Ludwig Fulda's 1911 play, *Der Seeräeuber*, which had been adapted by **S.N. Behrman** as a stage comedy in which an entertainer poses as a pirate in order to steal a Caribbean beauty from a duplicitous mayor. MGM acquired the rights and producer Arthur Freed drafted in scriptwriters **Frances Goodrich** and **Albert Hackett** to collaborate with **Cole Porter** and director **Vincente Minnelli**. They integrated the score into the scenario, in order to lampoon the conventions of operetta while also celebrating their theatricality.

Refusing to shoot on location, Minnelli had art director **Jack Martin Smith** blend Latin American and West Indian design styles to achieve the conscious artificiality that was to be the film's *leitmotif*, as this 1830s romance is a study in illusion. Manuela (**Judy Garland**) thinks she is in love with the infamous pirate Macoco, but she's really only enamoured of his dashing image in a book. Unsurprisingly, she falls for Serafin (**Gene Kelly**), a ham actor masquerading as her hero, rather than the buccaneer himself, who is actually the corpulent aristocrat, Don Pedro (**Walter Slezak**), that she is supposed to marry.

It takes Manuela's entry (under Serafin's hypnosis) into a dream world to reveal her suppressed desires and belt out "Mack The Black" with a passion that thrills both the onscreen bystanders and the film audience. The viewers not only share her willingness to be transported to a place of escape and romance, but are similarly ready to be mesmerized by the action on the screen. The picture is, therefore, a classic Hollywood paean to show business. It's also a fine example of the fairy-tale musical (albeit one with a little backstager morality thrown in), as Manuela chooses the itinerant troubadour over the seeming respectability of wealth, while Serafin appears content to abandon his philandering ways to settle down with his true love.

The production itself ended less happily, however. *The Pirate* placed huge demands on Garland, as she not only had to combine dramatic intensity with comic finesse, but she also had to sing Porter's songs with passion and keep step with Kelly in the dance numbers. And all at a time when she was struggling to cope with the birth of her daughter Liza, the terminal decline of her marriage to Minnelli and the onset of a nervous breakdown that she kept at bay with pills. Consequently, she succumbed to the strain and missed 99 out of 135 shooting days before checking into a sanatorium.

Despite all this, Garland somehow managed to produce a fine performance, excelling particularly on "Love Of My Life", "You Can Do No Wrong" and "Mack The Black". She even held her own with Kelly on the reprise of "Be A Clown", the original rendition of which he had insisted on performing with the African-American Nicholas Brothers, despite knowing that the number would be cut in the Deep South. Garland's luminous display owed much to **Harry Stradling**'s chivalrously sensitive cinematography, which managed to make her look as glamorous as the sumptuous sets. These were at their Technicolor best in "Nina" and "The Pirate Ballet", which were impeccably edited by **Blanche Sewell** to capture the full exuberance of Kelly's mischievous impersonations of Douglas Fairbanks and John Barrymore.

Unfortunately, neither the glorious artistry nor the gleeful fantasy found public favour and *The Pirate* became Garland's only MGM movie to lose money. Freed suggested that it was twenty years ahead of its time. But **Louis B. Mayer** shared *Time* magazine's verdict that the picture was "entertainment troubled by delusions of art" and he rushed Kelly and Garland into *Easter Parade* (1948) in a bid to restore their wholesome reputations.

# The Rocky Horror Picture Show

### *dir* Jim Sharman, 1975, 95m

**_cast_ Tim Curry, Susan Sarandon, Barry Bostwick, Richard O'Brien _cin_ Peter Suschitzky _m_ Richard O'Brien**

Were it not for **Tim Deegan** and **Denise Borden**, *The Rocky Horror Picture Show* would not be part of this canon. Faced with a critical and commercial catastrophe in the US, 20th Century-Fox was planning to consign this B-movie homage to video when marketing executive Deegan persuaded theatre owner Borden to screen the film as a midnite matinee at the Waverly in Greenwich Village, New York. But what turned a curio into a cult were the audience members who began attending the screenings in character costume and shouting out ad-libbed responses to the dialogue. *Rocky* thus became a refuge for outsiders and exhibitionists, who identified with the movie's motto "Don't Dream It, Be It", and it's been a countercultural phenomenon ever since.

*The Rocky Horror Show* originally opened in the sixty-seater Theatre Upstairs at London's Royal Court in 1973. It was the brainchild of struggling actor **Richard O'Brien**, who played Riff Raff, as well as writing the scenario and score. But much credit should also go to **Richard Hartley**, who helped O'Brien produce a song demo and persuaded the Court to mount the production, and director **Jim Sharman** and designer **Brian Thomson**, who were responsible for the look of the stage and screen incarnations. Pop maverick Jonathan King also merits mention for releasing the cast album that prompted US record mogul Lou Adler to open the show in Los Angeles, which, in turn, led to the movie deal with Fox.

Dressed to kill: Richard O'Brien and Patricia Quinn (whose hairstyle was inspired by Elsa Lanchester's in *Bride Of Frankenstein*, 1935).

To most fans, the film's appeal lies in O'Brien's songs and storyline, which fondly lampooned the sci-fi and horror cheapies that had been churned out since the 1950s by companies like Universal and American International Pictures (AIP), and the British trio of Hammer, Amicus and Tigon. However, the performances have become equally iconic, especially **Tim Curry**'s bravura turn as Frank N. Furter, a transvestite from the planet Transexual in the galaxy of Transylvania. Next to his scene-stealing strutting in numbers like "Sweet Transvestite", it's easy to overlook the sly underplaying of **Barry Bostwick** and **Susan Sarandon**, as the straight-laced Brad Majors and his fiancée, Janet Weiss. Their respective renditions of "Dammit, Janet" and "Touch-a, Touch-a, Touch Me" rank among the musical highlights, alongside the superb opener, "Science Fiction, Double Feature", which namechecks movies and stars more renowned for their kitsch value than their quality.

However, the film's undoubted showstopper is "The Time Warp", which engulfs Brad and Janet as they enter Dr Furter's old dark house after their car breaks down during a storm. Such is the comic gusto displayed here by O'Brien (as the hunchbacked henchman, Riff Raff), **Patricia Quinn** (as Frank's incestuous sister, Magenta) and **Charles Gray** (as the narrator) that the score struggles to recapture its ingenuity and exuberance. The plot similarly begins to meander as the emphasis shifts away from Brad and Janet and onto rebel biker Eddie (**Meatloaf**) and Frank's Frankensteinian vision of idealized manhood, Rocky (**Peter Hinwood**), and viewers not being bouyed along by participating audiences at ritualistic fancy-dress screenings will find time hanging increasingly heavy.

Rejecting a substantial budget and the prospect of Mick Jagger playing Frank, Sharman remained largely loyal to the original cast, and shot the film for $1 million in eight weeks at the old Hammer studios at Bray and the nearby Gothic pile, Oakley Court. However, it opened to disastrous Stateside reviews. Conservative critics expressed their disgust at a musical that not only parodied the all-American genre, but also demonstrated such an unflinchingly positive attitude to what they considered to be sexual deviancy. But the British press were less squeamish about *Rocky*'s blend of audiovisual pastiche and good honest smut and the film was soon hailed as a progenitor of punk. Late-night screenings at arthouses, grind houses and university campuses across America eventually rescued *Rocky* from obscurity – and the Waverly Theatre sequence in *Fame* (1980) added to its kudos.

The mania that accompanies the famous sing-along screenings has since seen *Rocky* gross over $135 million. But even its cast members (many of whom prefer the vitality and viscerality of the stage original) are somewhat at a loss to explain its enduring allure. One key factor is the film's subtext, which revolves around notions of stardom and MGM's attitude to its own troubled creation, Judy Garland. Sharman had even planned to shoot the action prior to Frank's entrance in monochrome and then switch to colour, as in *The Wizard Of Oz* (1939). But the ploy proved too expensive, and he had to content himself with following *Oz*'s lead of having several actors play characters in both the everyday and the fantasy sequences.

# Seven Brides For Seven Brothers

***dir*** **Stanley Donen, 1954, 102m**

***cast*** **Jane Powell, Howard Keel, Jeff Richards, Russ Tamblyn, Tommy Rall, Marc Platt, Matt Mattox** ***cin*** **George Folsey** ***m*** **Gene De Paul, Johnny Mercer**

In these supposedly politically correct times, it's hard to imagine that a story centred on the abduction and incarceration of six virginal women by a sextet of uncouth youths could still be considered family entertainment. Yet *Seven Brides For Seven Brothers* retains an innocent appeal that overcomes its blatant chauvinism. Its cinematic shortcomings have been overlooked, and it consistently outperforms musicals with greater artistic sensibility, more melodic scores and more accomplished performances – but that's popular taste for you.

MGM bought the rights to Stephen Vincent Benet's short story, "The Sobbin' Women", and offered the project to director **Stanley Donen** in the hope of persuading him to sign a new contract. He collaborated with screenwriters **Frances Goodrich** and **Albert Hackett** in toning down the plot line that translated Plutarch's account of the rape of the Sabine women to 1850s Oregon. Producer **Jack Cummings** was keen to interpolate a score of folk standards, but Donen couldn't find any that would integrate satisfactorily into the narrative and promptly hired **Gene De Paul** and **Johnny Mercer**.

They produced songs with lyrics full of natural imagery, earthily prudish euphemisms, and crude grammar and melodies that were ingeniously orchestrated with banjos, accordions and harmonicas by the Oscar-winning duo of **Saul Chaplin** and **Adolph Deutsch**.

Baritone **Howard Keel** and soprano **Jane Powell** were chosen for the lead roles of Adam and Milly Pontipee, but the stiff and frequently undemonstrative Keel soon came to resent being goaded into giving a performance and tried to have Donen replaced. But Keel's temperament was the least of Donen's problems. MGM had little faith in the picture and accorded it a meagre budget that confined the shoot to Culver City. As with *Brigadoon* (1954), the decision to mount an outdoor story on stylized sound stages backfired and, while it might have saved a few dollars, it proved a false economy. The use of actual locations under the opening credits only exacerbated the artificiality of what followed. The fabricated scenery is strikingly evident during "Wonderful, Wonderful Day" and "Lament", while the back projection used as the brothers sneak out of town and as the newlyweds depart after their shotgun weddings is shoddy in the extreme. Donen also bitterly regretted the parsimony that prevented him from turning "Spring, Spring, Spring" into a production number filled with natural images of the changing seasons.

One advantage of all the penny-pinching, however, is that it heightened the authenticity of **Edwin Willis** and **Hugh Hunt**'s interiors and **Walter Plunkett**'s costumes (the brides' dresses were made from quilts found in a Salvation Army thrift shop). Even **George Folsey**'s Ansco Color photography has an unrefined austerity that suited the period and the backwater setting. Sufficent funds were found to film in both CinemaScope and Hollywood ratios, as not all cinemas could accommodate the widescreen format. It's intriguing to compare the compositions in each version, because Donen used the additional space more intuitively than many of his contemporaries. He also defied editing restrictions (because of the costs involved in multiple set-ups) and the frequency of the cuts increased the picture's pace without disrupting the balance of the *mise en scène*.

The "Barn-Raising" ballet epitomizes Donen's approach. Choreographed as a frontier reality, not a dream interlude by **Michael Kidd**, this pioneering segment didn't recapitulate past events or explore the characters' psychology through symbolic action. Instead, it showed the local girls becoming attracted to the strapping Pontipee brothers as they demonstrate not only their

Prostestant work ethic, but also their ability to take care of themselves in a rowdy brawl. The eight-minute sequence was also intricately structured to establish the innocent thrill of the picnic, the percussive rhythms of manual labour and the knockabout machismo of the fist fight. There wasn't room for the pretty escapism of previous ballets, just the careful colour-coding of the future lovers and the dazzling combination of jazz, ballet, acrobatics, slapstick and Wild West posturing that anticipated the gangland strutting of the Sharks and the Jets in *West Side Story* (1961) and harked back to the collapsing building in Buster Keaton's *Steamboat Bill, Jr.* (1928).

The success of *Seven Brides* took the studio by surprise, as it demonstrated the popularity of original musicals at a time when the genre was becoming increasingly dependent on remakes and Broadway transfers. But while it established Donen as a major talent, it failed to turn Keel and Powell into the new Nelson Eddy and Jeanette MacDonald, because their controlled, sub-operatic styles were already slipping out of fashion as crooners, swingers and rockers began to dominate the airwaves.

# Shall We Dance

**_dir_ Mark Sandrich, 1937, 101m, b/w**

**_cast_ Fred Astaire, Ginger Rogers, Edward Everett Horton, Eric Blore, Jerome Cowan, Ketti Gallian, Harriet Hoctor _cin_ David Abel _m_ George Gershwin, Ira Gershwin**

**George Gershwin** had previously worked with **Fred Astaire** and **Ginger Rogers** on Broadway, but he hadn't written a screen score since the undistinguished *Delicious* (1931), and was concerned that he would be responsible for the duo's first flop. However, in the end, he felt that he'd wasted too many good songs on the moderate singers and was dismayed by how little space director **Mark Sandrich** accorded gems like "(I've Got) Beginner's Luck" and the Oscar-nominated "They Can't Take That Away From Me". Although the songtrack was splendid, Gershwin still had the misfortune to participate in what was considered Fred'n'Ginger's first disappointment.

The box-office takings slipped slightly, and the critics complained that the comic byplay between **Edward Everett Horton** and **Eric Blore** was becoming stale and that "the Great White Sets" had grown grandiose. They also detected self-indulgence in the picture's length and in its bid to marry art with entertainment. But mostly, they couldn't fathom why Rogers and Astaire opted to dance unconvincingly with **Pete Theodore** and **Harriet Hoctor** rather than glide through their customary romantic duets. Yet while the plot may be slightly asinine and the routines may have striven for novelty rather than intimacy, *Shall We Dance* has been unfairly maligned.

Adapted from a story by **Lee Loeb** and **Harold Buchman**, the film was Astaire and Gershwin's response to Rodgers and Hart's Broadway hit, *On Your Toes* (1936), which Astaire had rejected because it didn't conform to his screen image. Indeed, Astaire's masquerade as a Russian ballet star in the film reflected Gershwin's classical-populist ambitions more than his own. Nevertheless, his solos, "Slap That Bass" and "Shall We Dance", saw Astaire contrasting jazz hoofing with pseudo-ballet, if only to mock European pomposity and inverted American snobbery.

Shall we dance? Ginger forgets to serve the divorce papers after she sees the masked tribute that Fred has staged for her in his latest revue.

The slender storyline sees Rogers (as Linda Keene) and Astaire (as Peter Peters) deciding to marry and then divorce to quash press speculation about their relationship. It might have got off to a livelier start had RKO been prepared to spend $55,000 on a Parisian set for "Hi-Ho", in which Peter was to have become obsessed with Linda's image on countless billboards. However, the number was dropped and the multiple-Linda concept was reserved for the finale

– even though Busby Berkeley had already used the identical mask idea for "I Only Have Eyes For You" in *Dames* (1934). In fact, *Shall We Dance* is unusual for the extent of its borrowing: the flip book recalls *Footlight Parade* (1933), the Constructivist engine-room sequence echoes *Modern Times* and the seasickness gags were regurgitated from *Anything Goes* (both 1936).

However, there was daring originality in the decision to make "They All Laughed" the longest-delayed first dance in the couple's canon (although they had earlier strutted the deck of a transatlantic liner to the mischievous instrumental "Walking The Dog"). And it was well worth the wait, as Astaire and Rogers traded steps in a typical challenge routine that culminated in them leaping atop a piano. Their rollerskating high jinks to "Let's Call The Whole Thing Off" were even more flamboyant, although their effortless ease belied the fact that the number took 32 hours to rehearse and thirty takes to complete (during which time the twosome danced over eighty miles).

Instead of Linda realizing her love for Peter as they dance together, the penny finally drops as she watches him on stage with second-rate ballerina Harriet Hoctor and the masked chorines in a finale that was clumsily choreographed by **Harry Losee** after RKO failed to intice the legendary dancer Leonard Massine. The action ended with Fred'n'Ginger together, but the film was released amid rumours that the partnership was under strain, which were only confirmed when they made *A Damsel In Distress* (1937) and *Vivacious Lady* (1938) apart. The duo later reunited for three more pictures, but this was the last outing in their trademark style.

# Show Boat

## *dir* James Whale, 1936, 113m, b/w

**_cast_ Irene Dunne, Allan Jones, Helen Morgan, Paul Robeson, Charles Winninger, Helen Westley _cin_ John Mescall _m_ Jerome Kern, Oscar Hammerstein II**

Premiering on December 27, 1927, *Show Boat* was the first musical to tackle a serious subject in an adult manner. Its discussion of race and prejudice is neither sensational nor sentimental, even though it's couched in the terms of the Americanized operetta. Both the stage and screen versions managed to transpose the backstager into an historical context and showed that while blacks and whites were socially segregated, they were culturally interdependent. It also proved that white Jewish composers were capable of producing pseudo-black music for a mixed-race cast. But perhaps most significantly, *Show Boat* broke with the tradition of the musical numbers being merely a diegetic diversion: they were integrated into the narrative and the peripheral figures within the scene became the chorus. The songs were mostly private expressions rather than public performances, so they were written in character idiom. Yet composer **Jerome Kern** still combined ragtime syncopation, minstrel melody and spiritual soul to create an American variation on Viennese operetta. This gave the score an innovative musi-

The son of a former slave, Paul Robeson brought integrity and intelligence to the role of Joe, which he had played in both the first London run and the 1932 Broadway revival.

cal unity whose influence has since proved incalculable.

Kern had acquired **Edna Ferber**'s source novel soon after its publication in 1926. And after persuading theatre producer **Florenz Ziegfeld** to mount the production, he hired 28-year-old lyricist **Oscar Hammerstein** to write the libretto, as he knew Hammerstein would tackle the thorny issue of miscegenation with forthright tact. *Show Boat* became the longest-running stage hit of the 1920s, and it confirmed Broadway's conversion to an indigenous style of musical theatre by tracing the evolution of the American popular song. It then went on to make a similar mark on Hollywood.

Ferber's story about gambler Gaylord Ravenal and Mississippi riverboat singer Magnolia Hawks was first made into a film in 1929. Universal had already completed the part-talkie version when studio boss **Carl Laemmle** decided to splash out $100,000 on the musical rights. But rather than integrating the numbers into the picture, he instead added an eighteen-minute musical prologue comprising the highlights of Kern and Hammerstein's score. It soon became clear that the studio had botched the job, so in 1936, **James Whale** (who was then best known for horrors like *Frankenstein*, 1931, and *The Old Dark House*, 1932) was asked to direct a new adaptation of *Show Boat*, using a revised Hammerstein screenplay.

Much more the work of a dramatist than a showman, Whale's interpretation has often been accused of lacking musical panache. But it has a sense of realism that only heightens the story's social and emotional impact. Moreover, the action was paced to roll along like the Mississippi, in order to reflect the unchanging lives of these dignified show people. Kern and Hammerstein have also been criticized, for patronizing their black characters. However, their song "Ol' Man River" is unique in American music for being a spiritual that is not only a personal credo, but also a social commentary: the melancholic sense of resignation in the lyrics embraces both the Jewish and the African-American experience. "Can't Help Lovin' Dat Man" similarly combines literary and theatrical stereotyping with a deeply moving affirmation of human emotion. This prompts the supposition that the songwriters were simultaneously exploiting and parodying white attitudes and assumptions about African-Americans that had been reinforced by showbusiness staples such as minstrelsy and the coon show.

The cast appreciated the sensitivity and excellence of the score and responded with some outstanding performances. Each principal had previously played their part on stage, although the sole survivors from the Broadway original were **Charles Winninger**, as Cap'n Andy, and **Helen Morgan**, as Julie LaVerne, the mulatto singer whose marriage to a white man causes her to be dismissed from the *Cotton Blossom*. Morgan's renditions of "Bill" and "Can't Help Lovin' Dat Man" are achingly poigant, while **Paul Robeson** (as Joe the stevedore) brings power, pathos and pride to "Ol' Man River". As Magnolia and Gaylord, **Irene Dunne** and **Allan Jones** make the most of songs like "Gallivantin' Around" and "I Have The Room Above". There's hardly a false note in the entire score, and the three numbers that were written especially for the film complement the nine that were retained from the stage show.

*Show Boat*'s revised plotline does become a little melodramatic towards the end, but this does not diminish the film's overall grandeur, gloss and humanity. It is unfortunate, therefore, that MGM bought and suppressed Whale's version when Arthur Freed embarked on a Technicolor remake in 1951. Too few people have had the opportunity to appreciate the infinite superiority of a monochrome version that has been all but forgotten.

# Silk Stockings

## *dir* Rouben Mamoulian, 1957, 117m

*cast* Fred Astaire, Cyd Charisse, Janis Paige, Peter Lorre
*cin* Richard Bronner *m* Cole Porter

*Silk Stockings* was a film of firsts and lasts. Inspired by Ernst Lubitsch's classic screen comedy, *Ninotchka* (1939), it was adapted from **Cole Porter**'s final Broadway show and marked **Arthur Freed**'s first outing as an independent producer at MGM. But, most crucially, it spelt the end of **Rouben Mamoulian**'s movie career and proved to be Astaire's last musical film for a decade.

The critics seemed to sense this twilight aura and delivered mostly misguided pronouncements about the picture's supposed pro-capitalist and anti-intellectual attitudes. Especial ire was reserved for **Cyd Charisse** as Ninotchka, who was unfavourably compared to Greta Garbo who had excelled in the role of the dour Russian emissary in Lubitsch's sparkling original. But such reproach simply missed the point. Mamoulian had no intention of duplicating either *Ninotchka* or the stage version of *Silk Stockings*. Instead, he sought to turn a song show into a dance film, in which Astaire and Charisse's duets carried more dramatic and psychological significance than the text.

It wasn't an easy task, however. The MGM suits blamed Mamoulian for the losses incurred by *Summer Holiday* (1948) and only hired him at Freed's insistence. Neither Leonard Spigelgass nor Harry Kurnitz's draft screenplays were up to scratch, and **Leonard Gershe** was accorded only a couple of weeks to rectify the situation. Nevertheless, by editing as he shot, Mamoulian not only wrapped on schedule, but he also kept the budget down to $1,853,463. Meanwhile, Astaire had misgivings about Mamoulian's abilities and his own May-December teaming with Charisse. He was also concerned about the ailing Porter's commitment to the project. But Porter's thirteen tunes boasted a classic catalogue song in "All Of You" and two well-judged new numbers for Astaire, including "The Ritz Roll And Rock" in which he combined the coat tails of his deco past with the doo-wop of the pop present. The score also provided **Janis Paige** with the risqué gems "Silk And Satin" and "Josephine", and the mischievously self-reflexive "Stereophonic Sound".

The excesses, crassness and cultural insensitivity of Hollywood and the decadent West were as much the subject of *Silk Stockings* as Soviet hypocrisy and repression. The film is full of self-deprecating humour, with swimming star Peggy Dayton (Paige) arriving in Paris to shoot *War And Peace*, but ending up making a musical about Napoleon's love life, entitled *Not Tonight*. Moreover, the jazzing up of the Soviet anthem "Ode To A Tractor" lampooned Hollywood's habit of bowdlerizing show scores, as well as positing the superiority of American music over everyone else's. In fact, the film's fascination lies in these contrasts and contraditions, because they go beyond the traditional parameters of studio escapism. It consistently subverts backstager expectations, both by questioning the customary endorsement of entertainment over art and by dispensing with the usual interdependence of the lovers' fate and the success of the show.

The picture has a tendency to laugh *at* communism and *with* capitalism, and the broad satire doesn't always suit the Cold War context. But although Mamoulian ridicules the Marxist emphasis on utility over beauty, he also exposes the dehumanizing impact of faddish materialism and vulgar populism on the complacent West. He even raises the notion of the male gaze, for while Ninotchka seems to sing "Without Love" from a position of subservience, she still resents the objectifying of women for male gratification and denounces Peggy's suggestive and demeaning performances. It says much for Mamoulian and Charisse's artistry, therefore, that the sensual "Silk Stockings" routine – in which Ninotchka abandons idealogy for lingerie – is a dreamy psychological insight and not a voyeuristic tease.

Mamoulian explores emotion through dance throughout the film. Charisse resists Astaire's eagerness and charm until they dance to "All Of You", but she then succumbs to the artifice of the film sets, as he glides her on a tour through his land of make-believe to "Fated To Be Mated". Even when she dances "The Red Blues" in a stylized Russian reality of greys, blues and khakis, it's movement that conveys her mindset rather than the dialogue or lyrics. As ever, Mamoulian makes such transitions between reality and artifice, drama and music, comedy and romance with exquisite, rhythmic ease, and stages the musical sequences with effortless precision. Thus, while *Silk Stockings* may have seemed somewhat studio-bound after *Funny Face* (1957), it still made a successful return at the box office and ranks among MGM's later musical glories.

# Singin' In The Rain

## *dir* Gene Kelly, Stanley Donen, 1952, 103m

**_cast_ Gene Kelly, Donald O'Connor, Debbie Reynolds, Jean Hagen, Cyd Charisse, Millard Mitchell _cin_ Harold Rosson, John Alton _m_ Nacio Herb Brown, Arthur Freed, Roger Edens, Betty Comden, Adolph Green**

In 1982, *Singin' In The Rain* came second only to *Citizen Kane* (1941) in *Sight & Sound*'s decennial poll of the best films of all time. The ultimate self-reflexive, mythologizing genre picture, *Singin' In The Rain* is a history of the MGM musical and of lyricist-producer **Arthur Freed**'s part in its evolution. Consequently, it's anything but original. It's essentially a Stateside variation on *An American In Paris*

(1951), with Hollywood replacing the City of Light, movies supplanting paintings and Freed and **Nacio Herb Brown**'s songbook superseding that of the Gershwins. Moreover, the emphasis is on performance rather than psychology, and on representation rather than evocation; the picture was perceived as studio prose instead of auteur poetry, as musical entertainment not screen art.

*Singin' In The Rain*'s enduring appeal lies in its reconstruction of a bygone age of cinematic innocence. It tells the story of the industry's difficult transition from silent to sound pictures, and focuses on the problems experienced by matinee idol Don Lockwood (Gene Kelly) and his squeaky-voiced leading lady Lina Lamont (Jean Hagen) when their studio decides to turn *The Duelling Cavalier* into a talkie. Most of the film's humorous incidents relating to the problems of recording sound for the first time were based on fact, and several of the characters were modelled on Hollywood legends. The songs were similarly lifted from past MGM hits, while dance routines like "Beautiful Girl" borrowed from other studios and paid homage to both Busby Berkeley's kaleidoscopic patterns and the fashion shows mounted in *Roberta* (1935) and *Cover Girl* (1944). Even the supposedly original "Make 'Em Laugh" unintentionally plagiarized Cole Porter's "Be A Clown" from *The Pirate* (1948). Many of the props were also recycled, although much of the primitive sound equipment had

Gene Kelly looks admiringly at 19-year-old Debbie Reynolds, who remains convinced to this day that her co-star didn't want her in the picture and that she was "being thrown to the lions".

to be researched and re-created, as it had become obsolete in the 25 years since talkies had taken over Tinseltown.

In creating a dance picture set in the wake of *The Jazz Singer* (1927), Kelly and co-director **Stanley Donen** could play lots of audiovisual games, in which sound and image were frequently out of sync. The opening montage chronicling Don Lockwood's early career, for example, bears no resemblance to the story he spins for the listening radio audience. But the slyest in-joke lay in the dual deceit of having Hagen actually deliver some of her own dialogue, which was supposedly being dubbed in the film by **Debbie Reynolds**' aspiring actress Kathy Selden. Reynolds' singing voice was, in turn, dubbed by uncredited vocalist **Betty Noyes**.

Nineteen-year-old starlet Reynolds had a tough time during the shoot, as Kelly rehearsed her hard to atone for the deficiencies in her dance technique. He had no such problems with **Donald O'Connor**, however, whose knockabout performance on "Make 'Em Laugh" ranks as highly as Kelly's own in "Singin' In The Rain". Kelly's signature number not only celebrated Don's new love for Kathy, but also his realization that *The Duelling Cavalier* could be saved by transforming it into a musical comedy. The exhilarating routine revisited the old backstager tactic of linking courtship with the success of the show and having entertainment triumph over art. It also alluded to the fairy-tale tradition (see p.257) of having a footloose character find stability by emancipating a timid lover. But, most significantly, the number typified the film's bold exploitation of the confines of the sound stage and frame, its unique ellision of time and space, and its use of film iconography and technical magic to tell a story in a fluent and wholly cinematic manner.

On the other hand, the "Broadway Rhythm" ballet exposed Kelly's limitations as a director. His use of light, colour and design during the lengthy sequence was markedly less innovative than Vincente Minnelli's staging of similar dream ballets in *The Pirate* and *An American In Paris*. Moreover, the number was less narratively taut than the "Slaughter On Tenth Avenue" routine that Kelly had designed for *Words And Music* (1946). However, the ballet did make a star out of dancer **Cyd Charisse**, who plays the vamp that dumps Kelly's wan-nabe hoofer for a diamond-toting mobster. *Singin' In The Rain* has lost little of its popularity since its rapturous critical and commercial reception, but it proved to be the peak of Kelly's creativity. His career rather tailed off after this, and he left MGM five years later.

# Snow White And The Seven Dwarfs

## *dir* David Hand, 1937, 82m

*voices* Adriana Caselotti, Harry Stockwell, Lucille LaVerne, Moroni Olsen *m* Frank Churchill, Larry Morey

Even though the teenage **Walt Disney** had been impressed by a multi-screen, live-action version of *Snow White* in 1917, he had always hoped to make *Alice In Wonderland* his first "Feature Symphony". However, he lost his nerve in the face of rival live-action adaptations made in 1931 and 1933. Plans to animate *Rip Van Winkle* and *Babes In Toyland* were similarly thwarted, as Paramount and RKO respectively refused to release the rights. By 1934 the spiralling cost of producing cartoon shorts and the difficulty of distributing them to venues reliant on double bills finally persuaded Disney to embark upon a full-length retelling of the Brothers Grimm's classic 1812 fairy tale.

A handful of animated features had been completed since the Argentinian Quirino Cristiani issued the first, *El Apóstol* (*The Apostle*), in 1917. But none had been made in either English or colour, and the sceptics soon branded the enterprise "Disney's Folly". Even Walt's brother Roy had his doubts, especially as the proposed $250,000 budget rose over three years to $1,488,423, in order to engage the 32 animators, 102 assistants, 167 in-betweeners, 20 layout artists, 25 watercolourists, 65 effects animators and 158 inkers and painters required to produce the film's two million illustrations in their 1,500 different hues.

It didn't help that the production progressed almost by trial and error in its early stages. Thousands of sketches and watercolours were produced for the endless script and character conferences that Disney called to ensure that Snow White emulated "a Janet Gaynor type", the Prince resembled Douglas Fairbanks, and the Wicked Queen became "a mixture of Lady Macbeth and the Big Bad Wolf". The crew also had to surmount considerable technical challenges. A larger field size had to be introduced to achieve greater graphic detail, which necessitated the manufacture of enlarged cels and the recalibration of the cameras to accommodate them. Rotoscoping or tracing from live-action was also utilized to enhance the realism of the human characters (with dancer Marge Champion posing for Snow White), while Disney's trusted lieutenants **William Garity** and **Ub Iwerks** developed the multi-plane camera to ensure a consistency of image depth during tracking shots and pans.

Despite all these early difficulties, Disney's vision never faltered. He cast the 19-year-old unknown **Andrea Caselotti** as the voice of Snow White, and she produced delightful renditions of "Some Day My Prince Will Come" and "I'm Wishing". But the main musical burden fell on the dwarfs, whom Disney insisted had their own names and distinctive characters – although he was forced to misquote Shakespeare in order to convince his team that Dopey didn't sound too modern a moniker for a character in a timeless fantasy.

Disney was also determined to have a plot-driven score, and he got **Frank Churchill** to produce some 35 songs before he finally settled on the eight that comprised the soundtrack. Sung by the dwarfs to accompany such mundane tasks as cleaning the house, washing for dinner and marching home from the mines, "Whistle While You Work", "Bluddle-Uddle-Um-Dum" and "Heigh-Ho" kept the action moving and even the youngest audience members transfixed. However, tunes like "Music In Your Soup" and "You're Never Too Old To Be Young" were dropped, along with more sinister sequences that would have shown a skeleton dance and Snow White's mother dying in childbirth.

Although some critics complained that it lacked the wit of a Mickey Mouse or Donald Duck cartoon, *Snow White* proved an instant success, grossing $4.2 million in the States alone. Sergei Eisenstein proclaimed it the "greatest film ever made" and the Academy presented Disney with a special award, comprising one full-sized Oscar and seven miniatures. Translated into ten languages and released in 46 countries, the picture has since been reissued eight times and sold millions of copies on video and DVD. But, for some, it remains merely novel and magical, while its successor, *Pinocchio* (1940), comes closer to genuine art.

# The Sound Of Music

## *dir* Robert Wise, 1965, 174m

**_cast_ Julie Andrews, Christopher Plummer, Eleanor Parker, Richard Haydn, Peggy Wood, Charmian Carr _cin_ Ted McCord _m_ Richard Rodgers, Oscar Hammerstein II**

"No musical with swastikas in it will ever be a success," Billy Wilder told **Ernest Lehman**, when he heard that he was adapting **Rodgers and Hammerstein**'s final collaboration for the screen. Gene Kelly was even less enthusiastic, telling Lehman "to go find somebody else to direct this shit". However, a Welsh housewife named Myra Franklin would have disagreed with Wilder when she entered the *Guinness Book Of Records* in 1988 for having seen *The Sound Of Music* 940 times. But then this production confounded showbiz sages from the start.

Broadway director **Vincent Donehue** acquired the rights to the 1956 feature, *Die Trappe-Familie*, which was based on the true story of a nun who married an Austrian captain and helped his singing offspring escape from the Nazis during World War II. Initially, the Von Trapps were to sing folk songs and hymns, but when Rodgers and Hammerstein were asked to contribute an original song, they insisted on composing the entire score. However, Hammerstein allowed **Howard Lindsay** and **Russel Crouse** to write the stage play, and although they stuck to his key themes, the narrative's contrivances and melodramatics conspired to make the score seem trite. It was still well integrated into the narrative, but its contents were rather conventional. The majority of the melodies recalled operetta or folk and were short of complexity and innovation. Moreover, there were no ballets or soliloquies to offer variation from the string of hummable tunes, like "Do-Re-Mi", "My Favourite Things" and "The Lonely Goatherd", whose wholesomeness was out of step with both contemporary Broadway and rock'n'roll.

Nevertheless, the show was a success, and it won six Tony Awards. The critics deemed it Rodgers and Hammerstein lite, but the lyricist's death in 1960, nine months after the Broadway opening, gave the production a nostalgic allure that Fox's 1965 movie inherited. **Robert Wise** signed up as director without having seen the stage show that associate producer, **Saul Chaplin**, detested. However, they were both seduced by Lehman's screenplay and the prospect of working with **Julie Andrews**. She was always Wise's first choice for Maria, although Audrey Hepburn and Doris Day had been mooted, and **Christopher Plummer** finally agreed to play Captain Von Trapp. He later dubbed the picture "The Sound of Mucus", but his stiff presence, especially while lip synching to the singing of vocalist Bill Lee, is one of its major weaknesses.

The film was easily the most cinematic Rodgers and Hammerstein transfer. There was less emphasis than before on static performance and Wise achieved a greater sense of interaction between the characters and their environment, which reinforced the contrasts

Despite its cosy domesticity, *The Sound Of Music* is essentially an operettic fantasy in the tradition of Jeanette MacDonald costume romps such as *The Firefly* (1937).

between the confined abbey and the Alpine expanses, and between Austria before and after the Anschluss. However, a fatal whimsicality pervades the picture and bolsters the risible equation of song with freedom, as though the Nazis would be less evil if, like Maria, they surrendered to the power of music. The original score contained harder-edged numbers like "How Can Love Survive?" and "No Way To Stop It", but they were dropped from the film (leaving 1972's *Cabaret* to prove that the National Socialists could sing – and that they knew some pretty sinister songs).

This is a fairy-tale musical, with a folk soul. And despite its romanticism, the emphasis is firmly placed on family unity, the sovereignty of the land and tradition's ability to withstand change and pernicious ideology. It also employs the classic musical tactic of having Maria help the Captain to reconnect with his family, while he helps her find a purpose in caring for his children. Thus, a free spirit puts down roots, while a stoic rediscovers his suppressed self by agreeing to sing at the Salzburg Folk Festival. In this case, resorting to the backstager gambit of linking the fate of the romantic leads to the success of the show takes on a greater urgency, as lives depend on the Von Trapps turning their performance into a disappearing act.

*The Sound Of Music* is often labelled a fresh and youthful picture, but it's very much the work of a man who knew he was dying. Hammerstein's nostalgic lyrics are tinged with the regrets of an author who isn't sure what the future holds, and his evocation of bygone wars and moral rectitude at a time of uncertainty goes some way to explaining the film's extraordinary popular appeal. It proved virtually critic-proof and took around $80 million on an $8,250,000 outlay. It has become a cultural phenomenon, whose depiction of resistance to a tyrannical regime helped redefine America's self-worth following the Cuban Missile Crisis, JFK's assassination, the exposure of racism by the Civil Rights movement and the escalation of the conflict in Vietnam.

However, these notions of liberty and patriotic pride did not go down well in Cold War Germany, where Hollywood's patronizing approach to Nazism and the concept of Heimat condemned the most commercially successful musical of all time to ignominious failure. Clearly the vanquished and divided population didn't concur with Rodgers' contention "that anyone who can't, on occasion, be sentimental about children, home or nature is sadly maladjusted".

# South Pacific

## *dir* Joshua Logan, 1958, 171m

***cast*** **Rossano Brazzi, Mitzi Gaynor, John Kerr, Ray Walston, Juanita Hall, France Nuyen** ***cin*** **Leon Shamroy** ***m*** **Richard Rodgers, Oscar Hammerstein II**

*South Pacific* ranked among Broadway's greatest musicals and not even **Joshua Logan**'s cack-handed direction could totally diminish its impact on screen. Primarily based on two stories – "Our Heroine" and "Fo' Dolla" – from **James A. Michener**'s *Tales Of The South Pacific* (1947), the 1949 stage show was commissioned for the operatic bass Ezio Pinza, and was showbiz legend Mary Martin's finest hour. It earned songwriting team **Rodgers and Hammerstein** their second Pulitzer Prize for Drama, but it was more conventionally operatic than their previous shows, despite inverting the traditional principal/juvenile plot lines. It also virtually abandoned dance and held back the star duet until the audience became accustomed to Martin and Pinza's contrasting singing styles.

It was, therefore, a tricky picture to cast. After buying the screen rights and keeping Logan on as director, 20th Century-Fox secured **Rossano Brazzi** as French plantation owner Emile de Becque. Rodgers suggested that Doris Day should play Nellie Forbush, but Logan felt that her persona wasn't suitable for the role of a nurse enduring the conflicts of passion and prejudice during World War II. They announced a search for a star, and Jean Simmons, Ginger Rogers, Audrey Hepburn, Elizabeth Taylor and Shirley Jones were all considered before **Mitzi Gaynor** was unveiled. The studio then apportioned a budget of $6 million, scouted locations on the Hawaiian island of Kauai and borrowed free uniforms, equipment and extras from the US Navy.

Surviving virtually intact, the score retained its innovative glory – "A Cockeyed Optimist" dispensed with verses, and "Some Enchanted Evening" and "A Dual Soliloquy" owed more to operatic arias and recitatives than American pop music. Rodgers even ventured into pastiche blues for "I'm Gonna Wash That Man Right Outta My Hair", although he reverted to his preferred waltz-time for "A Wonderful Guy". The score also boldly exploited character and social background: Nellie's solos were upbeat and optimistic, Emile's were melancholic and romantic, Lieutenant Cable's (**John Kerr**) were idealistic and naive, Bloody Mary's (**Juanita Hall**) were full of indigenous poetry and acquired wit, and the Marines' were coarse and droll.

Once again, Hammerstein had been inspired by incompatible couples, but this time it was racial prejudice that kept his characters apart. His call for racial acceptance wasn't immediately heeded by either Lieutenant Cable, who is eventually willing to forget the prejudices he had been so "Carefully Taught" by his unbrotherly folks in Philadelphia, or Nellie, who struggles to overcome her Arkansas intolerance and only accepts her French lover's half-Polynesian offspring at the close. Although most critics were willing to accept another of Hammerstein's homilies on harmony, others attacked his smug moralizing. They complained that he used Cable's death in combat to avoid confronting the contentious issue of miscegenation that would have arisen had he and Liat (**France Nuyen**) lived happily ever after.

However, such thematic controversies were the least of the film's problems. Rodgers and Hammerstein produced *South Pacific* themselves, which somewhat explains its lack of pictorial grace or distinctive visual style. Like Logan, they were essentially men of the theatre, and they were primarily concerned with doing near-verbatim justice to their creation. Therefore, they placed undue emphasis on the performance of the songs and insisted on them being filmed as hermetic showcases, rather than contextual expressions of characters' emotions. This seems particularly odd from writers who took such pains to integrate their tunes into their storylines. This tactic was further undermined by the fact that so many of the principals were dubbed. Brazzi and Kerr were dubbed by **Giorgio Tozzi** and **Bill Lee**, respectively, and **Muriel Smith** was hired to dub Hall, whose voice had apparently deteriorated since her award-winning turn in the Broadway original.

If the singing was stilted, the dance routines were even more reminiscent of the early talkies. It was bad enough that **LeRoy Prinz**'s ethnic choreography frequently felt patronizing, but the static camera's failure to utilize either the widescreen space or the authentic locations – particularly during exuberant pieces like "There Is Nothing Like A Dame" – robbed the action of some much-needed kineticism. When he did open out the action, Logan invariably staged travelogue sequences, rather than allowing his characters to interact with their environments. And any hopes of capturing the text's mystique were dashed by Logan's abysmally misjudged use of tints.

Seeking to bring some ethereal magic and theatrical intimacy to the vibrant Technicolor vistas, Logan respectively shrouded "Bali Ha'i", "Some Enchanted Evening" and "A Cockeyed Optimist" in fuchsia, metallic blue and canary yellow mists that he had been assured could be removed in the lab before the film's release. But, fifty years later, they still remain, despite Logan's embarrassment and Hammerstein's fury. Ultimately, the garish visuals did nothing to harm *South Pacific*'s commercial prospects. It grossed over $17 million and landed an Oscar for its sound, while the soundtrack album spent 31 weeks at number one. However, it's now almost impossible to watch this musical landmark without lamenting the missed opportunities and avoidable mistakes.

# A Star Is Born

## *dir* George Cukor, 1954, 182m

***cast*** **Judy Garland, James Mason, Jack Carson, Charles Bickford** ***cin*** **Sam Leavitt** ***m*** **Harold Arlen, Ira Gershwin**

*A Star Is Born* is the finest MGM musical the studio never made. Produced by Warner Bros, it's a veritable *film à clef*, as **Judy Garland**'s real-life rise to stardom echoed that of her character, Esther Blodgett. The actress would also have found its depiction of addiction, unprofessionalism and the stresses placed upon showbiz marriages all too familiar.

Although this was a courageous and deeply personal study of stellar burnout, it was also a sour riposte to the celebratory nostalgia of *Singin' In The Rain* (1952). Garland may well have stomped through puddles to "Lose That Long Face", but Gene Kelly's Golden Age optimism had begun to evaporate, and the decline of fading movie star Norman Maine (**James Mason**) in *A Star Is Born* evoked *The Band Wagon*'s (1953) melancholic end-of-an-era aura. Indeed, the tragic denoument shattered the backstager truism that the romantic union of the stars guarantees the success of the show. After this picture, Hollywood's vision of itself would never be the same again, and cynical exposés like *Pal Joey* and *The Joker Is Wild* (both 1957) became the norm.

With Garland's career back on track after her 1951 triumphs at the Palace Theatre in New York and the London Palladium, her third husband, producer **Sid Luft**, thought that a remake of William Wellman's 1937 drama, *A Star Is Born*, would make the perfect movie comeback. But while the part of Esther Blodgett almost wrote itself, screenwriter **Moss Hart** had to borrow from director **George Cukor**'s 1932 saga, *What Price Hollywood?*, for Norman Maine, who bore traces of everyone from John Bowers, John McCormick and Marshall Neilan to John Barrymore and Al Jolson. Despite Garland's entreaties, Cary Grant rejected the role of the monstrous, drunken has-been, which finally went to **James Mason**.

Grant may have been reluctant to play second-string to Garland, who was given the confidence to dominate proceedings by the ever-empathetic Cukor, and summoned up a performance that would have been unthinkable during her later years at MGM. She delivered the anthemic "The Man That Got Away" in a single take and demonstrated her gift for mimicry and her genius for feel-good in "Somewhere There's A Someone", in which she created an entire production number simply with the props to hand in her sitting room.

Although songwriters **Harold Arlen** and **Ira Gershwin** played to Garland's strengths with the likes of "Gotta Have Me Go With You", "It's A New World" and "Here's What I'm Here For", it was **Leonard Gershe** and **Roger Edens**' arrangement of the eighteen-minute "Born In A Trunk" that stopped the show. Garland rattled through the medley of standards that gave a foretaste of the more camp, more theatrical style that she later adopted for her legendary cabaret performances. The role also gave Garland the chance to prove she was a dramatic actress, as well as an all-round entertainer, and plenty of raw emotional power went into the *tour de force* performance that *Time* magazine correctly identified as "the greatest one-woman show in modern movie history".

Aware of Garland's off-screen problems, contemporary audiences must have known that they were witnessing the passing of the old Judy, but Cukor also used the state-of-the-art CinemaScope frame to suggest that the movie business was itself at a crossroads. The opening shots present Hollywood as a glamorous distant dream that becomes a pressurized nightmare when viewed up close, and Cukor utilized similar matches and contrasts to show Norman and Esther working towards a common goal. However, once Esther becomes famous (under the stage name Vicki Lester), into parallel sequences designed to reveal that stars are ordinary people whose heightened sense of ego makes their highs higher and their lows unendurable.

Cukor further demythologized Tinseltown by including shots of television sets in the pivotal scenes in which Norman is fired and then humiliates himself at the Oscars. He did so in order to imply that cinema had not only lost its battle with the small screen, but was now increasingly dependent upon it for publicity. This despondent message may have counted against *A Star Is Born* at the Academy Awards, as Garland lost the best actress category to Grace Kelly in the similarly themed *The Country Girl*. But that probably owed more to **Jack Warner**'s philinistic decision to cut 27 minutes of her performance, despite a successful round of previews. The film underwent a miraculous restoration in 1983 and was reclaimed as a masterpiece. But back in the mid-1950s, its meagre $1 million profit, after an expensive ten-month shoot and exaggerated rumours of Garland's unreliability, ensured that she didn't make another film for six years.

# Summer Holiday

## *dir* Rouben Mamoulian, 1948, 92m

**cast** Mickey Rooney, Gloria De Haven, Walter Huston, Frank Morgan *cin* Charles Rosher, Charles Schoenbaum *m* Harry Warren, Ralph Blane

One of the musical's forgotten masterpieces, *Summer Holiday* was a sly satire on the ongoing investigation into Communism in Hollywood by the House Un-American Activities Committee (HUAC). Yet the film was also part of the Americana boom that followed in the wake of *Meet Me In St Louis* (1944).

Producer **Arthur Freed** had long been keen to work with **Rouben Mamoulian**, so when plans for *Jumbo* and *The Belle Of New York* stalled, he suggested a musical variation of **Eugene O'Neill**'s

1933 play *Ah, Wilderness!* Although a great admirer of the play, Mamoulian was initially unconvinced that the doings of the Miller family in Danville, Connecticut in 1906 were the stuff of screen musicals. However, he soon realized that he could enhance the emotional impact of the original text by integrating songs to do the work of the dialogue. He understood that a musical play could tell the story "in richer, more colourful and more imaginative terms, without sacrificing any of its true values", and that such an approach could impart "more beauty and excitement than was there before".

As the feature was to be filmed on the old Andy Hardy set, it was fitting that 27-year-old **Mickey Rooney** was cast as Richard Miller, the teenager with radical inclinations and an inquisitive zest for life. The MGM executives were keen to reassert a certain sexual innocence to counter headlines about Rooney's marital misadventures and they hoped that the project would smooth his transition to adult roles, much as *Meet Me In St Louis* had done for Judy Garland.

Although it took two weeks to rehearse, the glorious opening number was a masterclass in scene-setting. Mamoulian exploited Nat Miller's (**Walter Huston**) rendition of "Our Home Town" to capture a sense of place through the town's architecture, atmosphere and principal inhabitants, and the number leads seamlessly into Richard's delightful soda-shop date with his sweetheart Muriel McComber (**Gloria DeHaven**). Necessitating twelve days of shooting in the stifling heat of a Pasadena park, the Independence Day picnic sequence proved equally impeccable, with its dazzling use of tableaux, montage, dissolves, pans and top shots.

However, the most intricate scene to execute was Richard's bar-room encounter with the vampish Belle (**Marilyn Maxwell**). A triumph of visual ingenuity, its subtle shifts in costume, colour and décor required eight days of filming to accommodate the 89 different camera and lighting cues. Yet the manner in which Belle's dress and demeanour change as Richard becomes increasingly inebriated epitomizes Mamoulian's audiovisual genius. Moreover, the use of different shades of red, as Belle's reputation as a scarlet woman becomes clear, contrasts strikingly with the predominant palette of yellows, beiges and greens that Mamoulian borrowed from the Americana paintings of Grant Wood, Thomas Benton and John Curry.

The MGM front office resented Mamoulian's artistic autonomy and exacted their revenge by removing three songs from the final print: Huston's first rendition of "Spring Is Everywhere", DeHaven's solo, "I Wish I Had A Braver Heart", and the reportedly exquisite "Omer And The Princess", which had been designed by costumer **Walter Plunkett** in the style of a Persian print. The studio then shelved the picture for eighteen months and, when it was eventually released, the critics chimed in with the in-house verdict that it was short on pizzazz and long on period kitsch. Consequently, it lost $1,460,000 and decimated Mamoulian's reputation, and he only returned to Hollywood a decade later for *Silk Stockings* (1957). In fact, *Summer Holiday* was anything but a hokey piece of sentimental pictorialism. It was more concerned with the transition from youth to adulthood than with freezing a moment in time, and it depicted the impatient and rebellious Richard consistently debunking notions of bourgeois idealism. Indeed, some of Mamoulian's more pereceptive contemporaries recognized the picture's iconoclasm and followed his lead away from the genre's more conventional formats.

# Swing Time

## *dir* George Stevens, 1936, 103m, b/w

*cast* **Fred Astaire, Ginger Rogers, Victor Moore, Helen Broderick** *cin* **David Abel** *m* **Jerome Kern, Dorothy Fields**

*Swing Time* is a workaday *Top Hat* (1935). The romance is just as glorious, but its smooth 1920s surfaces have been scuffed by life in the 1930s. Almost entitled *I Won't Dance* or *Never Gonna Dance*, the picture saw **Fred Astaire** and **Ginger Rogers** return to Art Deco escapism after the comparative realism of *Follow The Fleet* (1936). However, any glamour was restricted to **John Harkrider**'s fabulous nightclub sets, as director **George Stevens** recognized times were tough and realistically had Astaire's dancing gambler, Lucky Garnett, riding the rails and Rogers' Penny Carroll grateful for work at a crummy dance school.

Despite opening with a society wedding, as Lucky leaves socialite Margaret Watson (**Betty Furness**) waiting at the altar, *Swing Time* depicts a bourgeois world where nothing can be taken for granted. Indeed, its little ironies even extend to the songs: Astaire pretends not to be able to dance in "Pick Yourself Up"; Rogers has shampoo in her hair when she's serenaded with the Oscar-winning ballad "The Way You Look Tonight"; and the climactic duet, "Never Gonna Dance", sees the duo drifting agonizingly apart, just as they were in fact doing off screen.

Scripted by **Allan Scott** (who worked on six Astaire-Rogers pictures) and **Howard Lindsay** (who had directed Astaire on stage in *The Gay Divorce* in 1932), *Swing Time* was essentially a book musical, with the songs deftly integrated into the screwball storyline. Having previously worked with Rogers and Astaire on *Roberta* (1935), songwriters **Jerome Kern** and **Dorothy Fields** knew precisely what was expected of them and their tunes dominated the American music charts for weeks. But even at the time, Kern's music was considered slightly old-fashioned, and arranger **Robert Russell Bennett** and rehearsal pianist **Hal Borne** deserve much of the credit for jazzing up the score to some of the stars' finest routines.

Fred picks himself up, dusts himself off and starts all over again, as Ginger puts him through his paces at the Gordon Dancing Academy.

An inverted challenge song with Rogers taking the lead, "Pick Yourself Up" bubbles with the characteristic energy and confidence that allowed the duo to attempt both comic steps and audacious lifts with effortless exuberance. "Waltz In Swing Time" represents a moment of pure moonlit magic, which glides by as the routine's unexpected intricacies unfold. It serves no narrative purpose, but allows Rogers and Astaire to showcase their athletic, rhythmic genius and irresistible physical chemistry. Such qualities are also evident in "A Fine Romance" – dubbed "a sarcastic love song" by Fields and Kern – which the pair sing in a snowy park, with Rogers looking peeved in a fur coat and Astaire in a bowler hat playing the innocent like Stan Laurel. Finally, "Never Gonna Dance" proved to be not just the summation of *Swing Time*, but also of Fred'n'Ginger on film. A rare male torch song that's both witty and melancholic, "Never Gonna Dance" epitomizes the passionate, yet chic exchange of emotions that only Rogers and Astaire could express. However, the routine was also hard work; the last 16 bars required 47 takes, and Rogers' feet were bleeding from around the 25th.

Astaire has a fine solo slot with "Bojangles Of Harlem", which proved to be the most controversial number of his career. It's easy to condemn his use of blackface, but this is a genuine homage from one great artist to another, with affectionate lyrics by **Dorothy Fields** (who had collaborated with Bill "Bojangles" Robinson on 1935's *Hooray For Love*). It's a pop ballet that anticipated Vincente Minnelli and Gene Kelly's dream ballets, with the three giant silhouettes (which were his own shadows cast on giant screens by trick photography) dancing behind Astaire providing a link between the minstrel show and cinema, between dance history and his own dance style.

Despite its musical triumphs, *Swing Time* didn't do as well commercially as previous Astaire-Rogers outings. It's now regarded by some as their finest feature, but some contemporary critics highlighted the flaws in the derivative plot and bemoaned the frivolous romantic contrivances. Rogers was also aware of these shortcomings and was becoming increasingly frustrated by having to play second fiddle to Astaire. Stevens, who was among Hollywood's most versatile directors, sympathized with her plight and convinced her that she could become a dramatic star in her own right. Consequently, Fred'n'Ginger agreed to take a brief break after their next assignment, *Shall We Dance* (1937), and they never quite recaptured the magic of *Swing Time*.

# Top Hat

## *dir* Mark Sandrich, 1935, 101m, b/w

***cast*** **Fred Astaire, Ginger Rogers, Edward Everett Horton, Helen Broderick** ***cin*** **David Abel** ***m*** **Irving Berlin**

---

Refusing to stray from the upper echelons of leisured society, *Top Hat* is a Jazz Age film that somehow found itself brightening up the tail end of the Depression. It is a treatise on innocent wish-fulfilment, in which people with impeccable manners and sartorial style drift through an Art Deco neverland while managing to make life and love look ridiculously easy.

**Fred Astaire** was reluctant to embark upon this fourth pairing with **Ginger Rogers**, as he still feared becoming part of another team following his stage success with his sister, Adele. However, the unprecedented creative freedom he was offered convinced him to sign up for this peerless screwball musical, which bore many similarities to the earlier Astaire-Rogers vehicle *The Gay Divorcee* (1934). This similarity was no coincidence, as *Top Hat* scenarist **Dwight Taylor** had written the libretto for the original 1932 stage show, *The Gay Divorce*.

*Top Hat* is the classic Fred'n'Ginger scenario. The pair meet accidentally and although he is smitten on sight, she finds him irksome and resists his attentions until their first dance. "Isn't This A Lovely Day (To Be Caught In The Rain)?" is a typical challenge dance, in which Rogers gives as good as she gets (in keeping with her feisty character) until she allows herself to be impressed by Astaire's grace and agility. But true love is never allowed to run smoothly and a comic misunderstanding then conspires to keep the couple apart. Rogers' fashion model Dale Tremont mistakes Astaire's Broadway dancer Jerry Travers for her best friend Madge Hardwick's (**Helen Broderick**) dithering husband, Horace (**Edward Everett Horton**), who is really the English backer of Jerry's West End revue.

This mistaken identity idea came from Alexander Farago and Aladar Laszlo's play, *A Scandal In Budapest* (1911), which RKO had bought for $10,000. The fashion designer sub-plot was another interpolation, from James H. Montgomery's 1919 play, *Irene*. Astaire's choreography also owed something to past stage musicals. He had led a evening-dressed chorus through the "High Hat" routine in *Funny Face* (1927) and used his cane to machine-gun down a similarly attired ensemble in "Say, Young Man Of Manhattan" in *Smiles* (1930). The score, however, was wholly original. This was **Irving Berlin**'s first screen musical and he attended all of the initial script conferences to ensure that his songs were specifically tailored to both the storyline and Fred'n'Ginger's talents – making this the most integrated movie musical of the period.

"No Strings", for example, comes about because the free-spirited Jerry is keen to evade Horace's suggestion that he marries and settles down. But, ironically, the song also leads to his first meeting with Dale (after his tap dancing awakes her in the hotel room below), which completely changes his mind. His subsequent soft-shoe sand lullaby similarly intrigues her, as she settles back to sleep on her satin pillows. Even the stage number "Top Hat, White Tie And Tails", which begins with a line about an invitation to a formal party, follows Jerry's invitation to Venice, and he smugly sidles onto the stage still clutching the telegram.

Dale finally loses her heart in a second, more intensely passionate duet, "Cheek To Cheek", which is made all the more deliciously illicit as she dances it thinking that Jerry is a married man. Even after she learns that he is single (thanks to their unchaperoned gondola ride), the misunderstandings continue, and they dance "The Piccolino" under the impression that she has just wed a foppish Italian dressmaker (**Erik Rhodes**). It's only in the closing sequence that the narrative contrivances are happily resolved by the revelation that Dale was married by Horton's valet (**Eric Blore**), who was posing as a clergyman.

Everything about *Top Hat* was meticulously conceived, although no amount of perfectionism could prevent Rogers' dress from famously shedding ostrich feathers (much to Astaire's fury) during the numerous takes of the Oscar-winning "Cheek To Cheek". **Van Nest Polglase** and **Carroll Clark**'s Venetian sets were particularly splendid, evoking the "white telephone" romances that were then popular in Italy. Although the censors insisted on a number of cuts – and the songs "Wild About You", "You're The Cause" and "Get Thee Behind Me, Satan" were excised to brisken the action – *Top Hat* so appealed to American audiences that the $620,000-picture took $3.2 million at the box office and remained RKO's most profitable musical for years to come.

# West Side Story

## *dir* Robert Wise, Jerome Robbins, 1961, 151m

*cast* Natalie Wood, Richard Beymer, Russ Tamblyn, Rita Moreno, George Chakiris, Tucker Smith, Simon Oakland *cin* Daniel Fapp *m* Leonard Bernstein, Stephen Sondheim

For a musical that is now regarded as a masterpiece, *West Side Story* took quite a buffeting from critics in the early years. The majority of the Broadway notices were positive, but the naysayers were vocal and acerbic: one branded the show "a juke-box Manhattan opera", while others identified either a lack of humanity and humour or an excess of posturing and ferocity. Many found the pace and the storyline overly abrasive, while others suggested that the treatment of race and gang rivalry was too superficial and sentimental to engender true tragedy. But the reception accorded to United Artists' 1961 film couldn't have been more different. The reviews were almost unanimously ecstatic and the picture scooped ten Academy Awards.

There were, however, some dissenting voices. Composer **Leonard Bernstein**, lyricist **Stephen Sondheim** and librettist **Arthur Laurents** all disliked the film, while critic Pauline Kael dismissed it as "a piece of cinematic technology" whose dancing tries "so hard to be great it isn't even good". Bernstein's score was criticized for pastiching everyone from Friml, Herbert and Romberg to Kern, Rodgers and even Stravinsky. The stereotypical characterization and platitudinous dialogue were similarly castigated, as was the unpersuasive juxtaposition of street realism and studio artifice and the mediocre performances of **Richard Beymer** and **Natalie Wood**.

Yet *West Side Story* is unquestionably an artistic landmark – a concept musical, with a danced opening and a mimed finale, that aspired higher than most of the musicals before it. It was conceived, choreographed and directed by **Jerome Robbins**, who originally planned to set Shakespeare's *Romeo And Juliet* amongst New York's Catholics and Jews. But the focus eventually shifted to the tensions between the city's Americans and Puerto Ricans, in order to exploit the poetic argot and ethnic energy of 1950s urban life.

Although Sondheim's lyrics reflected the angst and inarticulateness of disenfranchised youth, Robbins was intent on having the characters primarily express themselves through dance, and the routines "Prologue", "Dance At The Gym", "Cool", "Rumble" and "Somewhere" formed the core of the action. Introducing jive and rock steps to Broadway, Robbins also gave the dance numbers an aspirational twist by using raised arms and legs to symbolize the determination to get out of the ghetto. However, what proved seismic on stage felt more contrived on screen. Having fought to retain artistic control, despite his cinematic inexperience, Robbins deeply resented having to rethink his acclaimed choreography to suit the expanses of the real West 68th Street, and what associate producer **Saul Chaplin** had envisaged as "a little black-and-white picture" soon assumed blockbuster proportions.

Despite the effective opening swoop from the sky to ground level, Robbins made little use of camera movement or depth of field. Moreover, his insistence (after an unprecedented ten weeks of rehearsals) on experimenting with alternative angles with a disregard for continuity convinced co-director **Robert Wise** (who had made his name as an editor) that the routines would not cut together. Therefore, with costs rising and time slipping away, Robbins was dismissed – much to the relief of many cast members, who found him an egotistical taskmaster – leaving Wise to finish the picture alone. He overused close-ups in his interpretation of the choreography, and his pursuit of "dramatized realism" transformed a dance show into a song film. Unsurprisingly, neither Wise nor Robbins mentioned the other in their Oscar acceptance speeches.

Beymer and Wood, who play the romantic leads Tony and Maria, were scarcely more compatible (although she failed in her attempts to have him removed from the role). With their vocals provided by **Jimmy Bryant** and **Marni Nixon** respectively, their performances rarely suggested a reckless passion that could culminate in slaughter, and they were both easily upstaged by the supporting cast of **Russ Tamblyn**, **George Chakiris** and **Rita Moreno** (who was dubbed by **Betty Wand**).

*West Side Story* added a bestselling soundtrack album and a $20 million gross to its impressive Oscar haul, but perhaps more importantly, it also introduced "dance movement" to the screen and suggested new topics for the genre to explore. The film offered a starkly contrasting view of American youth to those presented in either the Mickey Rooney and Judy Garland barnyard musicals or the rock vehicles of Elvis Presley. However, its release coincided with the decline of the traditional musical format and the arrival in Hollywood of *nouvelle vague* techniques that quickly dated the film's melodramatic conventionalism and patronizing social propaganda. Yet another stage show that was considered ahead of its time had been made into a calcified movie version lacking in courage, creativity and class.

# The Wizard Of Oz

## *dir* Victor Fleming, 1939, 101m, b/w and colour

**_cast_ Judy Garland, Ray Bolger, Bert Lahr, Jack Haley, Frank Morgan, Margaret Hamilton, Billie Burke _cin_ Harold Rosson _m_ Harold Arlen, E.Y. Harburg**

Few films have attracted as many rumours, anecdotes and statistics as *The Wizard Of Oz*. Prime among them is the contention that MGM chief **Louis B. Mayer** was so keen to secure Shirley Temple for the lead role of Dorothy Gale that he was prepared to lend Clark Gable and Jean Harlow to 20th Century-Fox in return. Yet this is pure Hollywood myth. Associate producer **Arthur Freed** had always viewed the project as a star-making vehicle for 16-year-old **Judy Garland** and even overruled senior producer **Mervyn LeRoy**'s preference for Deanna Durbin.

More accurate are assertions that actor Buddy Ebsen had to be replaced because he had an allergic reaction to his Tin Man make-up, and that numerous writers and directors, including George Cukor and King Vidor, made uncredited contributions to the finished film. However, **Victor Fleming** still merits his sole directorial credit, if only for spending countless nights traipsing back from the *Gone With The Wind* (1939) set for nocturnal editing sessions with **Blanche Sewell**. Despite all these changes of personnel, the film exhibits a remarkable creative unity, which owes much to MGM's trademark perfectionism and the consistent excellence of **Ray Bolger** (The Scarecrow), **Jack Haley** (The Tin Man) and **Bert Lahr** (The Cowardly Lion), whose deft professionalism made it seem as though Garland was carrying the entire picture.

Another signigicant unifying factor was **Harold Arlen** and **Yip Harburg**'s pioneering soundtrack. This not only proved an appropriate summation of the genre in the 1930s, but also anticipated the integrated musicals of the post-war era, when songs played a pivotal part in telling the story rather than merely providing entertaining digressions from it. However, Freed had to fight to keep the film's best-known tune, "Over The Rainbow", which the executives wanted to cut because it delayed Garland's entry into the multi-coloured neverland of Oz on which they had lavished so much expense.

### Behind the rainbow

Bringing *The Wizard Of Oz* to the screen was a massive logistical undertaking. A team of 150 painters applied 62 different colours to the Oz backdrop, which measured a massive 600m x 12m. Months of work also went into creating 65 individual sets and 4000 costumes for the 1000-strong cast, which included 350 midgets (many of whom came from Leo Singer's celebrated vaudeville troupe). The stars rehearsed for 12 weeks before spending 136 days in principal photography, which was particularly rough on Bert Lahr, as his Cowardly Lion costume weighed nearly 45kg. Terry, the cairn terrier who played Dorothy's dog Toto, also found the shoot tough going, as the giant fans used to create the wind effects kept blowing him over.

Despite assigning a budget of $2,777,000, MGM always considered *Oz* to be a commercial risk, which could only be justified by allowing Technicolor to conduct some vital camera experiments before shooting began on *Gone With The Wind*. However, the recent success of Disney's *Snow White And The Seven Dwarfs* (1937) had alerted the studio to the potential of the juvenile market and **L. Frank Baum**'s novel, *The Wonderful Wizard Of Oz* (1900), seemed an obvious choice, especially as it had frequently been mentioned by fans suggesting potential projects. Several screen adaptations had already been made, including Larry Semon's 1925 silent version featuring Oliver Hardy as the Tin Woodsman, but Fleming's picture remains far and away the best.

A moment of monochrome magic as 17-year-old Judy Garland sings what would be her signature tune for the remaining thirty years of her life.

Like *Snow White*, *The Wizard Of Oz* has its genuinely scary moments, and the talking trees, the flying monkeys and the Wicked Witch's dire threats contributed to it originally being given an adults only rating by the British censor. Crucial to all of these sequences – and the tornado, skywriting broomstick and melting Wicked Witch scenes – was the technical ingenuity of **Buddy Gillespie**'s special effects unit. Equally exemplary were **Adrian**'s costumes and **Jack Dawn**'s make-up, which together made the characters seem both pantomimic and credible. However, the key to the film's enduring visual appeal lies in cinematographer **Harold Rosson**'s use of colour, which transforms the sepia Kansas countryside into the dazzling, Technicolor land over the rainbow, complete with its yellow brick road, ruby slippers, Emerald City and horse of different colour.

The picture's themes have also contributed to its longevity. The cosy notion that "there's no place like home" consoled contemporary viewers who were nostalgic for the places they'd been forced to leave in order to find work during the Depression, and it took on renewed significance during World War II. Such timeless sentiments have since been reinforced by the feature's optimistic and aspirational subtext and its advocacy of acceptance (which has made it a particular favourite of gay audiences). However, despite its propitious ideas and the care lavished upon it, *The Wizard Of Oz* drew a mixed critical response and grossed only $3 million on its first release. And it wasn't until its reissue in 1948 and 1954, and its sale to television in 1956, that the picture turned a respectable profit and became a firm family favourite. *The Wizard Of Oz* now stands as a celebration of the magic of childhood and the vitality of the imagination – treasures that the makers of contemporary kids' pics seem to have forgotten.

# Yankee Doodle Dandy

### *dir* Michael Curtiz, 1942, 126m, b/w

**_cast_ James Cagney, Joan Leslie, Walter Huston, Richard Whorf _cin_ James Wong Howe _m_ George M. Cohan**

Even if it had not brought **James Cagney** his only Oscar, this musical biopic of **George M. Cohan** would still have been his favourite film. Cagney had idolized the man known as the "Prince of the American Theatre" since his youth, and had borne no grudges when he had once rejected him at an audition. Hungarian-born director **Michael Curtiz** was equally proud of his achievement, and in his unique, language-mangling way, he declared *Yankee Doodle Dandy* to be "the pinochle of my career".

Although renowned as an actor, producer, director, playwright, librettist, songwriter and showman, Cohan was a jack who never mastered his trades. However, as this film shows, he introduced American populism to the legitimate musical stage. His scenarios were stridently sentimental, briskly comic and conspicuously bereft of plot complications and psychological subtleties. He also composed songs like "Give My Regards To Broadway" and "Yankee Doodle Boy", which are both ably performed by Cagney, and their catchy melodies and simple, direct lyrics caught the national mood as effectively as his World War I hit, "Over There".

Despite columnist Sidney Skolsky pointing out the similarities between the two pugnacious Irish-Americans in the mid-1930s, Cagney had not been the first choice for the lead role. MGM had originally acquired the Cohan story for Mickey Rooney, but the

Both Mickey Rooney and Fred Astaire had turned down Cohan biopics, but neither would have captured his cocky pugnacity with quite the same swagger as the inimitable James Cagney.

project collapsed over a final cut dispute. Cohan then suggested that Fred Astaire should play him, but Astaire insisted that he was ill-suited to Cohan's buck-and-winging style and the idea was shelved. Producer **William Cagney** later revived it as a way to bolster his brother's reputation in the face of accusations that he was a Communist, and Warner Bros enticed Cohan with promises of $100,000 and full script and cast approval.

Cohan spent many weeks reminiscing about his life in vaudeville and on Broadway with screenwriter **Robert Buckner**. However, James Cagney felt that the resulting script lacked humour and humanity, and he persuaded *Casablanca* scribes **Julius and Philip Epstein** and gag writer **Edward Joseph** to doctor it. The final film script included few of Cohan's failures, but he was a vain man and he wholly approved of any changes that air-brushed out his personal or professional failings. His unpopularity on Broadway after he opposed the 1919 Equity Strike was ignored, and his break with business partner Sam Harris (**Richard Whorf**) was cornily sanitized. Even his marriages to Ethel Levey and Agnes Nolan were merged into a single, blissful liaison with a fictional wife, who was dubbed Mary (**Joan Leslie**) after the famous song, "Mary's A Grand Old Name", that earned Cohan his break on Broadway in 1906.

The theatrical re-creations were the most authentic aspect of the picture, as they slickly reproduced the look and feel of the original stage productions. Cagney did a fine job of duplicating Cohan's stage persona, but he never had any intention of impersonating his hero or trying to understand his myriad contradictions. He did, however, consult friends who had worked with Cohan, including Spencer Tracy and Pat O'Brien, and used their insights to create a character that owed as much to the inimicable Cagney style as it did to Cohan's own.

America entered World War II on the first day of filming, and Curtiz used the fate of the vaudeville family act, The Four Cohans, to emphasize the importance of unity in times of crisis. The picture's New York premiere on 29 May 1942 was given a similarly propagandist slant, as Warner Bros were acutely aware of the benefits of patriotic publicity; *Yankee Doodle Dandy* went on to gross nearly $4,750,000 and raised the same amount again in war bonds. But Cohan's response is perhaps the most interesting: after a private screening of the film he apparently said either "My God, what an act to follow!" or "It was a good movie. Who was it about?".

# Yolanda And The Thief

## *dir* Vincente Minnelli, 1945, 106m

**cast Fred Astaire, Lucille Bremer, Frank Morgan, Mildred Natwick *cin* Charles Rosher *m* Harry Warren, Arthur Freed**

**Vincente Minnelli** once described *Yolanda And The Thief* as "a fantasy that just didn't perfectly come off". Ever since its disappointing showing at the American box office, the picture has been deemed a disaster and it rarely figures prominently in histories of the genre. However, it was an audacious experiment in dance and design that not only confirmed Minnelli's status as a visionary artist, but also sent the Hollywood musical in an entirely new direction.

Producer **Arthur Freed** found his inspiration in a magazine story by **Ludwig Bemelmans**, who collaborated with **Irving Brecher** on the screenplay that reworked the operetta tradition of pinning a country's future on the romantic fortunes of its most significant citizen. The script also provides a classic example of the fairy-tale musical (see p.257), as love not only affords heiress Yolanda Aquaviva the opportunity to escape from the confines of her supposedly idyllic existence, but it also prompts the scheming Johnny Riggs to forget his wanderlust and settle down. Despite Judy Garland lobbying for the role, Freed's protégée, **Lucille Bremer**, was cast as Yolanda, opposite **Fred Astaire** as Johnny. The pair had previously performed well together in 1944 on the *Ziegfeld Follies* routines "Limehouse Blues" and "This Heart Of Mine", the latter of which anticipated *Yolanda And The Thief*'s tale of an unscrupulous con man.

The opening sequence in Yolanda's convent school was drawn from Bemelmans' famous *Madeline* books, while art director **Jack Martin Smith** took his cue for the baroque architecture in the fictional South American country of Patria from the paintings of Tiepolo. Choreographer **Eugene Loring** imported ideas from Salvador Dali and Jean Cocteau for "Dream Ballet", while **Irene Sharaff** conceived the undulating black-and-white striped floor in "Coffee Time" solely to set off her *café au lait* costumes. But Minnelli imposed a miraculous unifying vision on these diverse visual influences. Pre-empting the self-reflexivity of the *nouvelle vague*, he gloried in the filmic qualities of his creation, employing colours and compositions of such self-conscious artificiality that the audience can never forget that they're watching a motion picture rather than a slice of real life.

*Yolanda* brims with a sexual energy that defied the strictures of the Production Code. Yolanda's carriage ride to meet Johnny at his hotel emphasizes her repressed passion, which was both reinforced and subverted by Minnelli's decision to shoot Astaire's serenade through the strings of a harp. This not only implied her moral imprisonment, but also her willingness for his fingers to play her in a similar manner. Minnelli's emphasis on artifice, eroticism and psychology culminated in Loring's sixteen-minute dream ballet, which borrowed liberally from conceits devised for the stage productions of *Oklahoma!* and *Lady In The Dark*. But the combination of Loring's ingenuity, Astaire's grace and Minnelli's genius for Technicolor stylization gave this surreal interlude such a mesmeric beauty and disconcerting ethereality that it rivalled anything later achieved by Gene Kelly.

The picture wasn't just artistically daring, however. It also packed a political punch. *Yolanda* has too often been lumped with the "Good Neighbour" musicals that Hollywood churned out to keep Central and South America onside during World War II. In fact, it slyly insinuated the interdependence of the Americas, rather than following the "quaint, exotic and exploitable" line that Fox established in the likes of *Down Argentine Way* (1940). *Yolanda* also parodied this patronizing attitude; by having Johnny pose as Yolanda's guardian angel, the film exposed the cynical reasons for the USA's overtures of friendship and its reluctance to enter into anything other than an alliance of convenience.

Despite receiving positive reviews, *Yolanda And The Thief* missed the mood of post-war audiences, who regarded Latin escapism as passé and preferred all-American entertainments that didn't make too many intellectual demands. The picture's failure cost Bremer her career and prompted Astaire to retire temporarily the following year. However, Freed courageously persevered, as he had recognized the pioneering qualities that would become the artistic cornerstones of the distinctive MGM style over the next decade.

# The Icons:

## singing stars & unsung talent

The magic of the MGM musical is encapsulated in this wondrously romantic panorama of the City of Light in Vincente Minnelli's multi-Oscar-winning masterpiece, *An American In Paris* (1951).

# The Icons: singing stars & unsung talent

## Julie Andrews

Actor, b. 1935

Joining her mother and stepfather's vaudeville act at 10, Julie Andrews had made her West End debut (in the 1947 *Starlight Roof* revue) and become a regular on radio's *Educating Archie* while still in her teens. Indeed, she was only 19 when she reached Broadway in Sandy Wilson's *The Boy Friend* (1954). Two years later, she excelled as Eliza Doolittle in *My Fair Lady* and, in recognition, **Lerner and Loewe** created the role of Guinevere for her in *Camelot* that same year. Amidst much controversy, she lost out on both screen versions (1964 and 1966 respectively) and had to content herself with an Oscar-winning performance in Disney's *Mary Poppins* (1964, see Canon).

Fresh from playing a nanny, she became a governess in *The Sound Of Music* (1965, see Canon) – her second **Rodgers and Hammerstein** experience, after starring in the 1957 TV version of *Cinderella* – and her four-octave range and precise delivery went down equally well in *Thoroughly Modern Millie* (1967). Andrews was keen to avoid musical typecasting. But the public spurned non-musical outings like **Alfred Hitchcock**'s *Torn Curtain* (1966), and then seemed no better disposed to the Gertrude Lawrence biopic *Star!* (1968) and the wartime spy spoof, *Darling Lili* (1970), despite their accomplished scores.

After a lengthy spell off screen, Andrews was helped to shake her "goody-goody" image and establish herself as a comedienne by second husband **Blake Edwards** in *10* (1979), *S.O.B.* (1981) – in which she famously went topless – and *Victor/Victoria* (1982), in a cross-dressing role that she reprised on Broadway in 1995. Regrettably, this proved to be her last major singing engagement, as, three years later her vocal chords were damaged during throat surgery to remove non-cancerous nodules.

Julie Andrews struggled to ditch the wholesome image peddled in films like *Thoroughly Modern Millie*. "Sometimes I'm so sweet," she once said, "even I can't stand it."

### Thoroughly Modern Millie
**dir George Roy Hill, 1967, 138m**

Producer Ross Hunter set out to create a classic, but overdoes just about everything in this Jazz Age pastiche, in which genial gold-diggers Julie Andrews and Mary Tyler Moore find themselves residing in a New York hostel run by white slaver, Beatrice Lillie. The blend of Jimmy Van Heusen–Sammy Cahn originals and period hits works well enough and allows Carol Channing to cameo on "Jazz Baby" and "Do It Again". But the knowing schtick eventually begins to grate.

### Star!
**dir Robert Wise, 1968, 175m**

One of the most infamous commercial calamities in the genre's history, this elephantine Gertrude Lawrence biopic not only suffers from the miscasting of Julie Andrews and Daniel Massey (as Noel Coward), but it also makes a hash of standards by the likes of Porter, Gershwin and Weill. In a desperate bid to recoup some of its $12 million outlay, Fox trimmed and reissued the picture as *Those Were The Happy Times* – but no one was fooled.

### Victor/Victoria
**dir Blake Edwards, 1982, 133m**

A surfeit of clumsy comedy wracks this remake of Reinhold Schünzel's *Viktor und Viktoria* (1933), in which Julie Andrews, playing a struggling singer who masquerades as a female impersonator in 1930s Paris, causes a rift between Chicago nightclub boss James Garner and his feisty moll, Lesley Ann Warren. Robert Preston's performance as a gay confidante and a flagrant chorus-line routine caused offence, while the Henry Mancini–Leslie Bricusse score was undistinguished. Yet this plays its generic games rather slickly.

## Harold Arlen

Composer, 1905–86

**Ethel Waters**, for whom he wrote "Stormy Weather", called Harold Arlen "the Negro-ist white man" she'd ever known. His residency at the Cotton Club (1930–34) certainly imbued his music with a bluesy melancholia. Yet his first published song was "Get Happy", which **Judy Garland** performed with such élan in *Summer Stock* (1950). Arlen would prove to be one of Garland's key collaborators, providing the scores for *The Wizard Of Oz* (1939, see Canon), *A Star Is Born* (1954, see Canon), *Gay Purr-ee* (1962) and *I Could Go On Singing* (1963).

Breaking into movies with *Take A Chance* (1933), Arlen had to be content with contributions to Eddie Cantor's *Strike Me Pink* (1936), Al

Jolson's *The Singing Kid* (1936) and the Busby Berkeley duo, *Gold Diggers Of 1937* and *Stage Struck* (both 1937). Rarely sticking to the 32-bar format, he came up with the occasional surprise, like **Groucho Marx**'s "Lydia The Tattooed Lady" in *At The Circus* (1939). He also enjoyed Broadway success with the revue *Life Begins At 8:40* (1934), the anti-war satire *Hooray For What!* (1937) and feminist show, *The Bloomer Girl* (1944).

His star rose with *Oz* and he drew Oscar nominations for songs in *Blues In The Night* (1941), *Star Spangled Rhythm* (1942), *Cabin In The Sky*, *The Sky's The Limit* (both 1943), *Up In Arms* and *Here Come The Waves* (both 1944). His stage shows for Ethel Waters and Lena Horne were also admired. But later outings were less impressive and his final years were blighted by Parkinson's disease.

## Fred Astaire

Actor, Choreographer, 1899–1987

Fred Astaire embodied the world of the musical and exuded its grace, rhythm and romance. Jerome Kern claimed that "Fred Astaire can't do anything bad". Irving Berlin described him as "pure gold' and Ira Gershwin avowed that his brother George's last words were, "Fred Astaire". Yet Astaire himself was very temperate about his gifts: "I just put my feet in the air and move them around."

Astaire was debonair and gentlemanly, confident and optimistic; yet he was always modest and genial. He dressed impeccably, walked with infectious cadenced poise and sang with unassuming intimacy. He was an excellent pianist and drummer and his sure sense of melody and metre stemmed from an innate musicality. He integrated songs into his films as though they were soliloquies and such was his finesse and urbanity that everything he did seemed generous-spirited and spontaneous. Astaire made dancing seem like a natural part of daily life rather than an aesthetic or athletic display, but he was also a perfectionist who worked hard to achieve his effortless ease.

He started out with his sister **Adele** in 1905 and they endured the buffetings of vaudeville to co-star in eleven Broadway hits between 1916 and 1931. Complete with their trademark runaround exit, they excelled in *Lady, Be Good!* (1924), *Funny Face* (1927) and *The Band Wagon* (1931). Yet when Paramount screen-tested them in 1928, Fred's report notoriously read: "Can't act. Can't sing. Balding. Can dance a little." Consequently, they made just one 1931 Vitaphone short together before Adele retired. Fred's career was decidedly at the crossroads when he followed his solo show, *The Gay Divorce* (1932), with his first feature bow in MGM's *Dancing Lady* (1933).

However, in his second picture, *Flying Down To Rio* (1933), Astaire was paired with **Ginger Rogers** (see p.225) for the climactic production number, "The Carioca", and the subsequent dance craze persuaded RKO to reunite them in *The Gay Divorcee* (1934). Such was their delicacy, style and sexual frisson in "Night And Day" that they seemed destined to dance together (even though Astaire was reluctant to become part of another team so soon after Adele).

Fred'n'Ginger only played the romantic leads in three musicals – *Top Hat* (1935, see Canon), *Swing Time* (1936, see Canon) and *Shall We Dance* (1937, see Canon). They were merely the comic and soubrette in *Roberta* (1935) and *Follow The Fleet* (1936) and were married in *The Story Of Vernon And Irene Castle* (1939) and *The Barkleys Of Broadway* (1949), while *Carefree* (1938) was more a screwball comedy than a musical.

The storylines were unashamedly formulaic – Fred falls in love at first sight, only to be spurned and then re-find Ginger by coincidence. The Astaire and **Hermes Pan** devised duets were unique in that they almost invariably arose from animosity not amorousness. Rogers begins to yield during the dance, but a spat or misunderstanding inevitably follows and a contrived solution to their problems has to be found before they patch for the happy ending. Their routines were infinitely varied and belied the effort that went into them. They often danced on single sets, so as not to distract from the steps, and were invariably shot in full figure with the camera positioned atop the "Astaire dolly" to follow the action rather than participate in it.

Rogers' vexation at playing Trilby to Astaire's Svengali prompted their separation in 1939 and he struggled to find a suitable replacement. Joan Fontaine in *A Damsel In Distress* (1937), Eleanor Powell in *Broadway Melody Of 1940* (1940), **Rita Hayworth** in *You'll Never Get Rich* (1941) and *You Were Never Lovelier* (1942), Paulette Goddard in *Second Chorus* (1942) and Joan Leslie in *The Sky's The Limit* (1943) all failed to fit the bill, and Astaire's best teamings in this period were with **Bing Crosby** in *Holiday Inn* (1942) and *Blue Skies* (1946). Following the lukewarm reception of MGM's *Yolanda And The Thief* (1945, see Canon) and *Ziegfeld Follies* (1946), in which he was creditably partnered by **Lucille Bremer**, Astaire decided to retire.

In 1948, an indisposed Gene Kelly requested Astaire step into his shoes for *Easter Parade* (see Canon) and the fourth phase of his peerless career began. On average, he was 26 years older than co-stars Judy Garland, Vera-Ellen, Betty Hutton, Jane Powell, Cyd Charisse, Leslie Caron and Audrey Hepburn. But Astaire's energy and élan meant that he never appeared his age and he settled into playing mentors to protégées who came to prominence through his own talent. He was almost akin to a musical Cary Grant in *Three Little Words*, *Let's Dance* (both 1950), *Royal Wedding* (1951), *The Belle Of New York* (1952), *The Band Wagon* (1953, see Canon), *Daddy Long Legs* (1955), *Funny Face* and *Silk Stockings* (both 1957, see Canon).

Finding ideas and worthwhile roles harder to come by, Astaire ceased to make musicals in 1957, although he racked up forty awards for his trio of TV specials with **Barrie Chase** and proved that he still had the old magic in *Finian's Rainbow* (1968). Fifty years after he went out at the top, Fred Astaire remains the single most significant figure in the genre's history.

### A Damsel In Distress
**dir George Stevens, 1937, 101m, b/w**

A solo Astaire is ably supported by Joan Fontaine, Gracie Allen and George Burns in this effortlessly entertaining P.G. Wodehouse frippery, which saw Fred relishing the Gershwin classics, "A Foggy Day In London Town", "Nice Work If You Can Get It" and "I Can't Be Bothered Now". It proved a commercial misfire, despite Hermes Pan winning the last ever dance direction Oscar for setting "Stiff Upper Lip" in a funhouse.

### The Story Of Vernon And Irene Castle
**dir H.C. Potter, 1939, 93m, b/w**

The Castles exerted a major influence on Fred Astaire's dance style, but this anachronistic biopic (which included Oscar Hammerstein among its scenarists) proved an unsatisfactory way to conclude his RKO partnership with Ginger Rogers. Irene Castle's tutting on-set presence further restricted stars already uncomfortable with matching their subjects' technique, although they did kick loose during the spirited montage sequence, while dancing across a giant map of America.

### Daddy Long Legs
**dir Jean Negulesco, 1955, 126m**

Fred Astaire missed his step in this oft-told story of an orphan who falls for her mysterious benefactor. The 55 year-old looked decidedly ill at ease both partnering Leslie Caron (who was 31 years his junior) through Roland Petit's precious ballets, "The Daydream" and "Dancing Through Life", and leading a school chorus through "Sluefoot". But there's real charm in his delivery of Johnny Mercer's Oscar-nominated "Something's Gotta Give" and plenty of peerless style in his drum solo, "History Of The Beat".

### Finian's Rainbow

**dir Francis Ford Coppola, 1968, 145m**

Burton Lane and Yip Harburg's 1947 Broadway satire about an Irish emigrant who steals a leprechaun's crock of gold ruffled a few feathers with its sub-plot about a bigoted Southern senator who turns black after misusing three wishes. But the moment had passed by the time Francis Ford Coppola turned this biting morality tale into whimsical escapism and, thus, Fred Astaire's last musical proved something of a damp squib.

## Busby Berkeley

Choreographer, Director, 1895–1976

Dance was considered a minor element of the musical before Busby Berkeley introduced his unique form of visual jazz. Born into a showbiz family, he devised his first precision routines on the parade grounds of World War I. In the absence of formal training, these military drills were his sole qualification for directing amateur shows back in the States. Yet he got through on instinct and imagination and eventually found himself on Broadway, choreographing such **Rodgers and Hart** hits as *A Connecticut Yankee* (1927) and *Present Arms* (1928).

After working on twenty productions in five years, Berkeley was lured to Hollywood (despite a suspicion of talkies) to choreograph Eddie Cantor's *Whoopee!* (1930). Once again his lack of experience proved no hindrance, as he kept in mind art director **Robert Day**'s advice that the camera has only one eye and, dispensing with the traditional three-camera strategy, he shot his elaborate set-ups with a single, mobile camera.

Berkeley is credited with coining the chorine close-up and the top shot in this picture, but both **Maria Gombarelli** and **Albertina Rasch** had already employed it on *The Cocoanuts* (1929) and *Lord Byron Of Broadway* (1930) respectively. However, no one could match the ingenuity and audacity that Berkeley brought to the routines in *Cantor's Palmy Days* (1931), *The Kid From Spain* (1932) and *Roman Scandals* (1933).

With the genre in the doldrums, Berkeley was considering a return to New York when **Darryl F. Zanuck** brought him to Warner Bros, where he secured his place in musicals history with *42nd Street*, *Gold Diggers Of 1933* and *Footlight Parade* (all 1933, see Canon).

Fashioning shades of black and white into endlessly varying arrangements of circles and lines, Berkeley didn't so much choreograph dancers as utilize them as live set dressings. His tendency to subordinate individuality to the grander design was denounced by some as fascistic and he has since been much castigated for reducing the female form to a dehumanized prop. But others have identified a social dimension to Berkeley's kaleidoscopic, geometric designs, as he encouraged Depression audiences to unite in the common cause while darkly parodying their everyday reality.

Zanuck gave Berkeley free rein and he was nominated four times for the dance direction Oscar. But while *Wonder Bar*, *Fashions Of 1934*, *Dames* (all 1934) and *Gold Diggers Of 1935* (1935) – which Berkeley also directed – had their extravagant moments, the Production Code, reduced budgets and changing tastes clipped his wings.

He was even more tightly reined in at MGM, despite impressive work on the **Mickey Rooney** and **Judy Garland** barnyards *Babes In Arms* (1939), *Strike Up The Band* (1940), *Babes On Broadway* (1941) and *Girl Crazy* (1943), and **Gene Kelly**'s debut, *For Me And My Gal* (1942). He found more latitude at Fox, where **Carmen Miranda**'s "The Lady In The Tutti-Frutti Hat" in *The Gang's All Here* (1944) epitomized Berkeley's blend of cinematic panache and burlesque vulgarity.

Having already escaped a prison sentence following a fatal motoring accident in 1935, Berkeley narrowly avoided being committed to an institution after a suicide attempt brought on by his mother's death in 1946. Warner Bros afforded him a choreographic comeback with Doris Day's breakthrough, *Romance On The High Seas* (1948), and MGM let him direct *Take Me Out To The Ball Game* (1949). But he became embroiled in **Judy Garland**'s mental collapse and his career seemed over when he was removed from *Annie Get Your Gun* (1950, see Canon).

Defying the odds, he stayed on to stage showstoppers in *Two Weeks With Love* (1950), *Call Me Mister* (1951) and *Rose-Marie* (1954), as well as Bobby Van's remarkable hopping turn in *Small Town Girl* (1953). However, the Hippodrome-inspired aquacades he concocted for the **Esther Williams** vehicles, *Million Dollar Mermaid* (1949) and *Easy To Love* (1953) proved to be Berkeley's last hurrah, as the genre he'd done so much to define went into decline – although he did return to supervise the production numbers in Billy Rose's *Jumbo* (1962).

### Gold Diggers Of 1935
**dir Busby Berkeley, 1935, 95m, b/w**

There's not much to a storyline that sees medical student Dick Powell entice Gloria Stuart away from snuffbox expert Hugh Herbert at Alice Brady's New England hotel. However, Berkeley's choreography is quite extraordinary. The sight of 56 chorines playing white pianos that waltz around a cavernous stage thanks to hidden, black-clad stagehands is surreally mesmerizing. Party girl Wini Shaw's tragic misadventures against a stylized Manhattan skyline in Harry Warren and Al Dubin's Oscar-winning "Lullaby Of Broadway" ranks among Berkeley's finest achievements.

### Ziegfeld Girl
**dir Robert Z. Leonard, 1941, 131m, b/w**

Although Lana Turner, Hedy Lamarr and Judy Garland took the plaudits for this soapy MGM stab at backstage realism, the trio most responsible for its musical fascination was comprised of art director Daniel B. Cathcart, costumer Adrian and choreographer Busby Berkeley, whose staging of Antonio and Rosario's Latin routine, Tony Martin's "You Stepped Out Of A Dream" and Garland's "Minnie From Trinidad" are among his most cinematic efforts.

### The Gang's All Here
**dir Busby Berkeley, 1943, 103m**

Few remember Alice Faye's enchanting delivery of Harry Warren and Leo Robin's "A Journey To A Star" or "No Love, No Nothing" in her last starring musical before a seventeen-year screen retirement. This was all about Berkeley's first directorial experiments with colour and Edward Cronjager's glossy imagery reinforcing the gloriously garish excesses of Carmen Miranda's "The Lady With The Tutti Frutti Hat" (complete with its mammoth fruit headdress and line of banana-waving chorines) and the kaleidoscopic patterns, neon-lit hoops and rainbow-dappled water effects of the "Polka Dot Polka" finale.

## Irving Berlin

Songwriter, 1888–1989

In a career spanning fifty-five years, Irving Berlin wrote over fifteen hundred songs and supplied the score for nineteen films, earning seven Oscar nominations in the process. He was one of the few songwriters to be billed above the stars and is considered by many to have invented the popular song style that dominated Broadway and Hollywood throughout the twentieth century. Not bad for the Russian-born son of an émigré cantor, who never learned to read or write music and could only play the piano in the key of F sharp.

A former singing waiter, Berlin had his first hit with "Alexander's Ragtime Band" (1911), which launched a nationwide ragtime craze and led to him producing Broadway's first syncopated dance score for *Watch Your Step* (1914). He always considered himself a jobbing composer and preferred writing revues for his own Music Box Theatre than book shows, which he treated with the same suspicion as he did recordings, radio and talkies – even though his "Blue Skies" was the first song heard in *The Jazz Singer* (1927, see Canon).

Eventually the financial lure of Hollywood proved too great, although early ventures *The Cocoanuts* (1929), *Mammy*, *Puttin' On The Ritz* (both 1930) and *Reaching For The Moon* (1931) all proved unhappy experiences. But Berlin was tempted back following the Broadway success of *As Thousands Cheer* (1935) and he not only scored with the **Astaire'n'Rogers** trio of *Top Hat* (1935, see Canon), *Follow The Fleet* (1936) and *Carefree* (1938), but also had 23 of his songs included in Fox's *Alexander's Ragtime Band* (1938). And even greater success was to follow. Having composed the US wartime anthem, "God Bless America", the fiercely patriotic Berlin went on to produce the conflict's most enduring ballad, "White Christmas", for **Bing Crosby** in *Holiday Inn* (1942) and the stage and screen versions of *This Is The Army* (1942/1943).

Irving Berlin mostly played the piano on the black notes. He even had a special piano that automatically transposed to other keys from his favoured F sharp.

Berlin had always been adept at matching words, music and situations and his happy knack for hits gave *Blue Skies* (1946), *Easter Parade* (1948, see Canon) and *White Christmas* (1954) irresistible nostalgic appeal. Yet there were those who doubted that anyone could be so versatile and prolific and rumours that Berlin bought songs from unknowns and passed them off as his own fuelled the plot of *Rhythm On The River* (1940).

Berlin's first book show, *Louisiana Purchase,* was filmed in 1941 and *Annie Get Your Gun* (1950, see Canon) and *Call Me Madam* (1952) followed. But *There's No Business Like Show Business* (1954) proved to be his screen swan song. Having penned the title song for the **Marlon Brando** vehicle, *Sayonara* (1957), Berlin convinced himself that he couldn't adapt to the new rock'n'pop phenomenon and went into a long and reclusive retirement.

Fully aware of the value of a showstopper, Berlin was the most artless of the major composers, and his reluctance to attempt integrated scores led some critics to disparage his contribution to the development of musical theatre. But, as **Jerome Kern** once said, "Irving Berlin has no place in American music. He is American music."

### Alexander's Ragtime Band
**dir Henry King, 1938, 105m, b/w**

Chronicling the development of American popular music between 1915 and 1938 – as well as the ups and downs of Alice Faye's relationships with bandleader Tyrone Power and tunesmith Don Ameche – this Fox smash established the vogue for catalogue movies, in which the songbooks of Tin Pan Alley's finest were shoehorned into scenarios of varying complexity. The mellifluent Faye excels in this Irving Berlin Americana masterclass, while Ethel Merman provides some pleasingly contrasting oomph.

### Blue Skies
**dir Stuart Heisler, 1946, 104m**

One of the top ten grossing musicals of the decade, this Berlin songfest reunited Bing Crosby and Fred Astaire, as a nightclub owner and his hoofer pal who each holds a torch for Joan Caulfield. They team beautifully on "A Couple Of Song And Dance Men", while Astaire performs with eight images of himself for "Puttin' On The Ritz", which was designed by Hermes Pan as a swan song for Astaire before he retired to play golf, breed racehorses and supervise his chain of dance studios.

## Eddie Cantor

Actor, 1892–1964

Orphaned at 2 and raised by his Russian grandmother, Eddie Cantor started out singing on street corners and in a Coney Island café, where **Jimmy Durante** was his pianist. After a blackface stint in vaudeville, he toured with Gus Edwards's Kid Kabaret alongside George Jessel, before signing to **Florenz Ziegfeld** for four incarnations of the *Follies* (1916–19) and the hit shows, *Kid Boots* (1923) and *Whoopee!* (1928). The first was filmed silently in 1926 and Cantor guested in *Glorifying The American Girl* (1929) before reworking *Whoopee!* (1930) with producer **Samuel Goldwyn**.

An energetic comic and a dab hand with saucy lyrics, the banjo-eyed Cantor bounced back from the Wall Street Crash to become one of America's best-paid entertainers, through his long-running radio show and musical comedies like *Palmy Days* (1931), *The Kid From Spain* (1932), *Roman Scandals* (1933), *Kid Millions* and *Strike Me Pink* (both 1934). Regular co-stars **Lyda Roberti** and **Ethel Merman**, and the alluring Goldwyn Girls (choreographed by Busby Berkeley), also helped boost ticket sales.

In 1935, Cantor fell out with Goldwyn and while *Ali Baba Goes To Town* (1938) made money for Fox, later vehicles with **Joan Davis**, *Show Business* (1944) and *If You Knew Susie* (1948), performed poorly. Transferring to television, he remained popular until a heart attack hastened his retirement in 1952, only being drawn out briefly to dub Keefe Brasselle's songs for the wretched biopic, *The Eddie Cantor Story* (1955). Cantor received an Honorary Oscar in 1956, but, shamefully, he's steadily fallen into cinematic obscurity.

### Whoopee!
**dir Thornton Freeland, 1930, 93m**

Produced by Samuel Goldwyn and Florenz Ziegfeld and filmed in two-colour Technicolor, Eddie Cantor's first hit movie saw him playing a hypochondriac on an Arizona ranch. But it's mostly remembered for the Walter Donaldson and Gus Kahn tune "Making Whoopee" and the debut dance designs of Busby Berkeley, who built his first abstract pattern around a very young Betty Grable.

## Cyd Charisse

Actor, 1923

**Fred Astaire** once declared, "That Cyd! When you dance with her you stay danced with." The long-legged, classically trained Tula Finklea began with the Ballet Russe before changing her name to Lily Norwood for her screen debut in *Something To Shout About* (1943). However,

**Arthur Freed** opted for the more glamours Cyd Charisse for her appearance alongside Astaire (who branded her "beautiful dynamite") in *Ziegfeld Follies* (1946). She was more prominent in *The Harvey Girls* (1946), before being teamed with Margaret O'Brien in *Three Wise Words* (1946) and *The Unfinished Dance* (1947) and Ricardo Montalban in *Fiesta* (1947), *On An Island With You*, *The Kissing Bandit* (both 1948) and *Sombrero* (1953).

Keen to show that Charisse was more than an elegant *danseuse*, **Isabel Lennart** wrote *Meet Me In Las Vegas* (1956) for her and she dazzled in the thirteen-minute "Frankie And Johnny" ballet. But the studio doubted her acting prowess and continued to showcase her in speciality routines like "Smoke Gets In Your Eyes" in *Till The Clouds Roll By* (1946), the "On Your Toes" spot in *Words And Music* (1948) and the "One Alone" *pas de deux* in *Deep In My Heart* (1954).

However, MGM finally recognized her ability to steal a picture and she was cast alongside **Gene Kelly** in *Singin' In The Rain* (1952, see Canon), *Brigadoon* (1954), *It's Always Fair Weather* (1955) and *Invitation To The Dance* (1956) and with Astaire in *The Band Wagon* (1953, see Canon) and *Silk Stockings* (1957, see Canon). As the genre slipped into abeyance, Charisse left MGM following *Party Girl* (1958) and made *Five Golden Hours* and *Black Tights* (both 1960) in Europe.

## Maurice Chevalier

Actor, 1888–1972

A child acrobat, longtime partner of the legendary Mistinguett and ex-POW, Maurice Chevalier became a cabaret celebrity in 1917 by adopting the straw-hatted boulevardier persona that would become his trademark. He made thirteen silents, but it took sound to put across his nonchalant suavity. Despite a limited vocal range and a tendency to go off tempo or key, he sang with an evident enjoyment and saucy insouciance that made him irresistible, especially as he often seemed to be directly addressing the audience.

His Paramount debut came in *Innocents Of Paris* (1929), which featured the massive hit, "Louise". But, although he was boosted as "the French Al Jolson", his roguish manner and suggestive swagger were best seen in a series of Ruritanian

Even in his Ruritanian operettas like *Love Me Tonight* (1932) with Jeanette MacDonald (right), Maurice Chevalier always retained the vaudeville persona that had made him the toast of Paris.

operettas with **Jeanette MacDonald** (see p.216): *The Love Parade* (1929, see Canon); *Monte Carlo* (1930); *One Hour With You* (1931); *Love Me Tonight* (1932, see Canon); and *The Merry Widow* (1934, see Canon). However, it wasn't an easy partnership and he soon grew tired of playing debonair lovers in lesser vehicles like *Playboy Of Paris* (1930) and the **Claudette Colbert** duo, *The Big Pond* (1930) and *The Smiling Lieutenant* (1931).

He quit Hollywood following *Folies Bergère* (1935) and sought more challenging projects like Robert Siodmak's *Pièges* (*Personal Column,* 1939) and René Clair's *Le silence est d'or* (*Silence Is Golden,* 1947), although he still headlined such musicals as Julien Duvivier's *L'homme du Jour* (*The Man Of The Hour,* 1936) and the British twosome, *Break The News* (1936) and *The Beloved Vagabond* (1937). Surviving accusations of Nazi collusion, Chevalier toured extensively with his one-man show before his Hollywood resurgence in *Gigi* (1958, see Canon), *Can-Can* (1960) and *Fanny* (1961).

### The Smiling Lieutenant
**dir Ernst Lubitsch, 1931, 88m, b/w**

Inspired by Oscar Straus's *A Dream Waltz*, this Oscar-nominated, but little-seem gem has Austrian guards officer Chevalier switching his affections from confident musician Claudette Colbert to prim princess Miriam Hopkins. The dialogue and ditties are splendid, but Lubitsch seemed more preoccupied with demonstrating how sound and pantomimic innuendo could make excellent bedfellows.

### Folies Bergère
**dir Roy Del Ruth, 1935, 84m, b/w**

The story of a womanizing baron who hires an impressionist to divert his knowing wife was remade as *That Night In Rio* (1941) and *On The Riviera* (1951). Maurice Chevalier knocks Don Ameche and Danny Kaye into a straw hat with this glinting display of insouciant sauciness, which was enhanced by Dave Gould's Oscar-winning choreography, and the respectively sultry and sassy support of Merle Oberon and Ann Sothern.

## Bing Crosby

Actor, 1904–77

Over the course of a 55-year career, Bing Crosby recorded more than 2,600 different songs and sold in excess of 350 million records He commanded a loyal radio following, appeared in 24 shorts and 81 features, and his TV Christmas specials became a national institution – all of which reinforced the folksy image that made him something akin to a knowing, musical James Stewart.

Starting out as one of **Paul Whiteman**'s Rhythm Boys, Crosby debuted in *The King Of Jazz* (1930). A series of **Mack Sennett** shorts followed before *The Big Broadcast* (1932) established his on-screen presence and he spent the next quarter-century as Paramount's most bankable star. His relaxed approach suited him to a series of comedies with songs, in which he demonstrated that no matter how serious life seemed there was no problem that couldn't be solved with a quip and a croon. His films were packed with self-deprecating and often zany humour, which regularly saw him break the fourth wall and make references to contemporary events, film conventions and Hollywood politics.

His geniality fitted his everyman persona, but Crosby was also surprisingly versatile and he credibly played the mate on screwball heiress **Carole Lombard**'s yacht in *We're Not Dressing*, a college dean in *She Loves Me Not* (both 1934), a riverboat gambler in *Mississippi* (1935), a priest in *Going My Way* (1944), for which he won the best actor Oscar, and *The Bells Of St Mary's* (1945), and a doctor in *Welcome Stranger* (1947). He could do backstagers (*Going Hollywood*, 1933, and *Birth Of The Blues*, 1941), Broadway adaptations (*Anything Goes*, 1936), pseudo-operettas (*Waikiki Wedding*, 1933, and *Rhythm On The Range*, 1936), flagwavers

(*Here Come The Waves*, 1944) and biopics like *The Star Maker* (1939) and *Dixie* (1943), about Gus Edwardes and Dan Emmett respectively.

The petite blonde **Mary Carlisle** had played Crosby's love interest in such early outings as *College Humour* (1933), *Double Or Nothing* (1937) and *Dr. Rhythm* (1938). But his leading ladies became more varied in pictures like *Here Is My Heart* (1934), *Two For Tonight* (1935), *Pennies From Heaven* (1936) and *Paris Honeymoon* (1939), which were flimsy entertainments designed solely to let Bing sing. Yet they proved consistently commercial and he continued to figure prominently on the box-office charts with pleasing diversions like *If I Had My Way*, *Rhythm On The River* (both 1940), *Just For You* (1952) and the period pieces, *The Emperor Waltz* (1948) and *A Connecticut Yankee In King Arthur's Court* (1949).

He started landing more substantial material after *Sing, You Sinners* (1938) and was teamed with **Bob Hope** and **Dorothy Lamour** for the *Road To…* series (1940–62), Fred Astaire in *Holiday Inn* (1942) and *Blue Skies* (1946), Danny Kaye in *White Christmas* (1954) and Frank Sinatra in *High Society* (1956, see Canon) and *Robin And The 7 Hoods* (1964). He even attempted legit roles and courageously played against type in *The Country Girl* (1954). But Hollywood was changing and Crosby contentedly saw out his contract with cosy vehicles like *Mr Music*, *Riding High* (both 1950), *Here Comes The Groom* (1951) and a reworking of *Anything Goes* (1956).

### Anything Goes
**dir Lewis Milestone, 1936, 92m, b/w**

Bing Crosby romances Ida Lupino in this genially silly shipboard comedy of errors, which co-stars Charles Ruggles as a crook disguised as a cleric. But Ethel Merman stole the show, belting out the Cole Porter classics "I Get A Kick Out Of You", "You're The Top" and "Anything Goes" that she'd performed on Broadway. Crosby returned alongside Donald O'Connor for the heavily revised 1956 remake, in which they recruit Mitzi Gaynor and Zizi Jeanmaire for their new show.

### Holiday Inn
**dir Mark Sandrich, 1942, 101m, b/w**

Such is the popularity of Irving Berlin's Oscar winner "White Christmas" that it's easy to overlook Bing Crosby's other nine songs and Fred Astaire's six in this New England charmer, based around America's national holidays and the stars' infatuation with Marjorie Reynolds. Such was Astaire's perfectionism that he lost 14lbs during the shoot, much of it during the explosive "Let's Say It With Fire-Crackers" routine, which required 38 takes.

## Doris Day

Actor, b. 1924

Doris Day turned to singing after a car crash ended her dance training at 15. Changing her name from Von Kappelhoff, she sang with Bob Crosby and Les Brown's bands before making an immediate impression after replacing a pregnant Betty Hutton on *Romance On The High Seas* (1948). Warner Bros boosted its new star in such enjoyable, but lightweight musicals as *My Dream Is Yours*, *It's A Great Feeling* (both 1949), *Lullaby Of Broadway* (1951), *April In Paris* (1952) and *Lucky Me* (1954). But while the critics baulked, audiences flocked to her tomboyish teamings with **Gordon MacRae** (*Tea For Two*, 1950; *On Moonlight Bay*, 1951; *By The Light Of The Silvery Moon*, 1953) and the biopics *Young Man With A Horn* (1950, Bix Beiderbecke), *I'll See You In My Dreams* (1952, Gus Kahn) and *Love Me Or Leave Me* (1955, Ruth Etting).

Despite singing the Oscar-winning "Secret Love" in *Calamity Jane* (1953), Day became less reliant on musicals like *Young At Heart* (1955), *The Pajama Game* (1957, see Canon) and *Jumbo* (1962), as she tried other genres – although she still had hits with "Que Sera, Sera" from **Alfred**

Hitchcock's *The Man Who Knew Too Much* (1956) and the theme to *Move Over, Darling* (1963), one of her many battle-of-the-sexes comedies. Few singers made such a successful transition to non-musical projects. But Day was able to pass from girl-next-door to professional virgin (and enhance her popularity in the process), as she embodied the carefree radiance and honest optimism that American womanhood felt it ought to aspire to in the post-war world.

### On Moonlight Bay
**dir Roy Del Ruth, 1951, 95m**

Booth Tarkington's *Penrod* stories provided the inspiration for this period charmer, in which Doris Day abandons her tomboy ways after falling for hunk neighbour Gordon MacRae – her efforts are scarcely helped by father Leon Ames and housekeeper Mary Wickes. While ably performed, the songs are essentially ornamentation, but this is as agreeable as its sequel, *By the Light Of The Silvery Moon* (1953), in which the newlyweds have to cope with Ames's supposed dalliance with a French actress.

### Young At Heart
**dir Gordon Douglas, 1954, 117m**

This musicalization of *Four Daughters* (1938) might have worked better if Warner Bros hadn't soaked the cynical storyline in syrup. Ultimately, Frank Sinatra and Doris Day are just too different to make a credible couple, although her vocals on "Hold Me In Your Arms" and "Ready, Willing And Able" and his on "Someone To Watch Over Me" and "One For My Baby" are estimable.

### Love Me Or Leave Me
**dir Charles Vidor, 1955, 122m**

James Cagney excels as Martin "The Gimp" Snyder in this biopic of Ruth Etting, which continued Doris Day's graduation from girl-next-door roles. Despite the film's determined bid to scuff the showbiz veneer, Day's interpretation owed little to life. Still, she handled such Jazz Age standards as "Mean To Me" and "Ten Cents A Dance", as well as Nicholas Brodszky and Sammy Cahn's Oscar-nominated "I'll Never Stop Loving You", with sincere charm. The soundtrack album spent seventeen weeks at number one.

## Walt Disney

Producer, 1901–1966

From the moment that **Mickey Mouse** spoke in *Steamboat Willie* (1928), Walt Disney demonstrated an intuitive understanding of movie musical magic. He refined his ideas in the *Silly Symphony* series, which brought him a clutch of Oscars and the confidence to attempt the 1937 feature, *Snow White And The Seven Dwarfs* (see Canon). Further emboldened by its success, he embarked on *Fantasia* (1940), which sought to use cartooning to interpret various classical pieces. However, attempts to repeat the trick with *Make Mine Music* (1946) and *Fantasia 2000* (1999) proved less auspicious.

Yet these were rare misfires in Disney's quest for perfection. And though his messages were highly conservative, the films were technically, visually and diegetically innovative, with the "Heffalumps And Woozles" sequence in *Dumbo* (1941), for example, anticipating the dream ballet that would become the trademark of the MGM musical.

Disney could charm audiences with the likes of *Pinocchio* (1940) or tug at the heartstrings with the touchingly naturalistic *Bambi* (1942). But he was also conscious of animation's propaganda potential and contributed the Good Neighbour musicals *Saludos Amigos* (1943) and *The Three Caballeros* (1945) to the war effort.

In the early 1950s, Disney began producing live-action features. But while musicals like *Babes In Toyland* (1961) and *The Happiest Millionaire* (1967) underwhelmed, he scored with the live-cartoon combinations *Song Of The South* (1946) and *Mary Poppins* (1964, see Canon). His studio also continued to produce regular cartoons that have since become classics, including *Cinderella*

(1950), *Alice In Wonderland* (1951), *Peter Pan* (1953), *Lady And The Tramp* (1955), *Sleeping Beauty* (1959) and Uncle Walt's last personally supervised masterpiece, *The Jungle Book* (1967).

The studio lost form after *The Aristocats* (1970), with the likes of *The Rescuers*, *Pete's Dragon* (both 1977), *The Fox And The Hound* (1981), *Basil, The Great Mouse Detective* (1986) and *Oliver And Co.* (1988) struggling to duplicate the catchy, feel-good melodies that had characterized the earlier outings. But Disney never lost its graphic and storytelling genius and **Michael Eisner** and **Jeffrey Katzenburg** restored its reputation for cartoon excellence with *The Little Mermaid* (1989), *Beauty And The Beast* (1991) and *Aladdin* (1992), which boasted Oscar-winning songs by **Howard Ashman** and **Alan Menken**. Subsequently, pop stars like Elton John and Phil Collins have contributed to computer-generated hits like *The Lion King* (1994, see Canon) and *Tarzan* (1999).

### Pinocchio
**dir Ben Sharpsteen, Hamilton Luske, 1940, 88m**

Disney's second animated feature studs this joyous (and occasionally judiciously sinister) retelling of Carlo Collodi's classic fairy tale with such marvellous Leigh Harline and Ned Washington songs as the Oscar-winning "When You Wish Upon A Star" (which became the studio's theme tune), "Give A Little Whistle", "Hi-Diddle-Dee-Dee (An Actor's Life For Me)" and "I've Got No Strings".

### The Jungle Book
**dir Wolfgang Reitherman, 1967, 78m**

Adapted from the stories of Rudyard Kipling, the last animated feature on which Walt Disney worked boasts one of the studio's finest scores, with Phil Harris and Louis Prima respectively revelling in those Sherman brothers belters, "The Bare Necessities" and "I Wanna Be Like You".

## Deanna Durbin
Actor, b. 1921

Born in Canada but raised in California, Deanna Durbin failed to impress MGM's Louis B. Mayer when she was teamed with **Judy Garland** in the 1936 short, *Every Sunday*. So, she was snapped up by Universal, where she became an overnight sensation and saved the studio from bankruptcy with her bravura performance in *Three Smart Girls* (1937).

She would make five more Universal features under the guidance of German-born director **Henry Koster**, who brought European charm to her all-American exuberance. But it was ten-time producer **Joe Pasternak** who moulded her lyrical soprano and perky personality in a way that combined her contemporary style with classical phrasing, most notably in tandem with Leopold Stokowski in *One Hundred Men And A Girl* (1937).

Only Garland and **Shirley Temple** could match Durbin's spirited warmth in films like *Three Smart Girls Grow Up* (1939), *It's A Date* (1940) and *Nice Girl?* (1941). She quickly moved from playing Cupid to having crushes and her first kiss, with **Robert Stack**, in *First Love* (1939) became headline news, especially as she then had the world's biggest fan club.

Durbin was also a talented actress who delivered dialogue with a fluency and intelligence that echoed the disciplined clarity of her singing and made her a match for **Charles Laughton** in *It Started With Eve* (1941) and *Because Of Him* (1946). Indeed, non-musicals like *Christmas Holiday* (1944) and *Lady On A Train* (1945) suggested that she could easily have graduated from musicals to dramatic renown. But when Pasternak left for MGM, Durbin was assigned more routine (if still enjoyable) vehicles, like *The Amazing Mrs Holliday* and *His Butler's Sister* (both 1943), *I'll Be Yours* and *Something In The Wind* (both 1947), *Up In Central Park* (1948) and *For The Love Of Mary* (1949). By 1950, however, Durban's screen persona had begun to feel old-fashioned and she was struggling with her weight. And so, after 22 features, she retired at the age of 26.

She only made one film in colour, *Can't Help Singing* (1944), in which she introduced **Jerome Kern**'s "More And More", one of her four Oscar-nominated songs – the others coming in *That Certain Age* (1938), *Spring Parade* (1940) and *Hers To Hold* (1943). In fact, Durbin had more hits (twenty-three) on radio's *Your Hit Parade* than either Judy Garland (thirteen) or Betty Grable and Doris Day (twelve each). Yet on quitting Universal, she declared, "I can't run around forever being a Little Miss Fix-It who bursts into song – the highest paid star with the poorest material."

### Three Smart Girls

**dir Henry Koster, 1936, 84m, b/w**

A debuting Deanna Durbin joins screen siblings Barbara Read and Nan Grey in a scheme to keep divorced dad Charles Winninger out of gold-digging Binnie Barnes' clutches in this cheerful domestic delight. The 14-year-old soprano dominates with numbers like "My Heart Is Singing" and "Someone To Care For Me". Producer Joe Pasternak repackaged the picture as *Three Daring Daughters*, for Jane Powell and Jeanette MacDonald in 1948.

### One Hundred Men And A Girl

**dir Henry Koster, 1937, 84m, b/w**

This is probably the best of Hollywood's periodic bids to slip a little classical music into lowbrow entertainment. Both Durbin and Leopold Stokowski handle the Mozart, Verdi, Liszt and Tchaikovsky with the same finesse that Adolphe Menjou and the supporting cast bring to the unrelentingly upbeat story of a teenager's determination to find a conductor for her trombonist father's orchestra of unemployed musicians.

## Alice Faye

Actor, 1915–98

In true *42nd Street* (1933, see Canon) fashion, 18-year-old band vocalist Alice Faye made her screen debut in *George White's Scandals* (1934) at the suggestion of her mentor, crooner **Rudy Vallee**, after its star, Lilian Harvey, walked off the set.

Resembling a cuddly Jean Harlow, Faye averaged four musicals a year in her early career, although the likes of *She Learned About Sailors* and *365 Nights In Hollywood* (both 1934) are now largely forgotten, despite her ability to deliver coy lyrics, like those of "I Didn't Know" in George White's *1935 Scandals* (1935), with a certain allure.

She took more prominent supporting roles in *Sing, Baby, Sing* (1936) and *Wake Up And Live* (1937) before attracting attention in *On The Avenue* (1937), with a knowing rendition of **Irving Berlin**'s "I've Got My Love To Keep Me Warm". But she only became Fox's leading musical star in *In Old Chicago* and *Alexander's Ragtime Band* (both 1938) after her deep, smooth contralto (as capable of bluesy ballads as showstoppers) persuaded such luminaries as Berlin, **Cole Porter** and **George Gershwin** to declare her the best female singer in Hollywood.

Faye's films guaranteed pacy, polished entertainment with quality songs and a genial lead performance. She initially played girls who had worked hard to survive the Depression and were determined to have their share of the New Deal, whether gold-digging in *Every Night At Eight* or stealing the limelight in *King Of Burlesque* (both 1935), writing the show in *You Can't Have Everything* or battling to keep it on the road in *You're A Sweetheart* (both 1937).

But **Darryl F. Zanuck** preferred the softer

side she had exhibited opposite **Shirley Temple** in *Poor Little Rich Girl* and *Stowaway* (both 1936). Consequently, in the majority of her 31 musicals for Fox, she was cast as submissive types who were rarely in control of their own destiny. Few musical heroines suffered quite as much, and there were always plenty of tears before she finally found love with the likes of Don Ameche or John Payne in such backstagers as *Sally, Irene And Mary* (1938) and *The Great American Broadcast* (1941) period pieces like *Little Old New York* (1940) and *Hello, Frisco, Hello* (1943), the Fanny Brice *film à clef, Rose Of Washington Square* (1939), and the biopic, *Lillian Russell* (1940).

Faye resented having to play "a painted, doll-like dummy" and, after appendicitis forced her to drop out of *Down Argentine Way* (1940), the emergence of **Betty Grable** hastened the end of her tenure. She still showed to advantage in *Tin Pan Alley* (1940), *That Night In Rio* and *Weekend In Havana* (both 1941). But, having excelled in Busby Berkeley's *The Gang's All Here* (1943), she fell out with Zanuck after he cut her screen time in the thriller, *Fallen Angel* (1945). Besides occasional radio and television shows alongside bandleader husband Phil Harris (having previously divorced Tony Martin), she remained out of the spotlight until she made an ill-judged comeback in the mediocre 1962 remake of *State Fair.*

### On The Avenue
**dir Roy Del Ruth, 1937, 89m, b/w**

Socialite Madeleine Carroll forgives Dick Powell for his satirical revue and they fall in love. Jilted chanteuse Alice Faye, however, finds enough solace in tunes like "This Year's Kisses" from Irving Berlin's unsung score to even forgive Harry Ritz for his wicked impersonation. Marilyn Monroe and Yves Montand headlined George Cukor's loose remake, *Let's Make Love* (1960), which featured cameos from Gene Kelly, Bing Crosby and Milton Berle.

## Bob Fosse

Actor, Choreographer, Director, 1927–87

A student of ballet, tap and acrobatic dance, Bob Fosse started out at 13 in The Riff Brothers act that toured the vaudeville and burlesque houses where he absorbed the vulgar energy that would later characterize his work. He owed much to second wife, **Joan McCracken**, who not only guided him to a contract with MGM – where he danced in *Give A Girl A Break, The Affairs Of Dobie Gillis* (both 1953) and *Kiss Me Kate* (1953, see Canon) – but also landed him the post of choreographer on **George Abbott**'s *The Pajama Game* (1954) and *Damn Yankees* (1955). His staging of the showstoppers "Steam Heat" and "Whatever Lola Wants" led to Hollywood commissions for *My Sister Eileen* (1955) and the 1957 and 1958 screen versions of his Abbott stage triumphs.

Discarding McCracken, Fosse began a liaison with **Gwen Verdon**, who became his Muse as he transformed the dance musical by introducing slinky sophistication to the sexual suggestiveness of routines characterized by precise, sinuous, sometimes disjointed movements and their use of props (particularly hats).

Universal afforded him his directorial debut on *Sweet Charity* (1968), but many critics took against the gimmicky camerawork he used to capture the kineticism of **Shirley MacLaine**'s performance and the film flopped. However, he bounced back to become the first person to land the Tony/Emmy/Oscar hat-trick in the same year, with *Pippin, Liza With A Z* and *Cabaret* (1972, see Canon). Further Broadway success followed with *Chicago* (1975), while he took the Palme d'Or at Cannes for the autobiographical *All That Jazz* (1979), in which he summed up his musical philosophy in the supremely cynical "Razzle Dazzle 'Em".

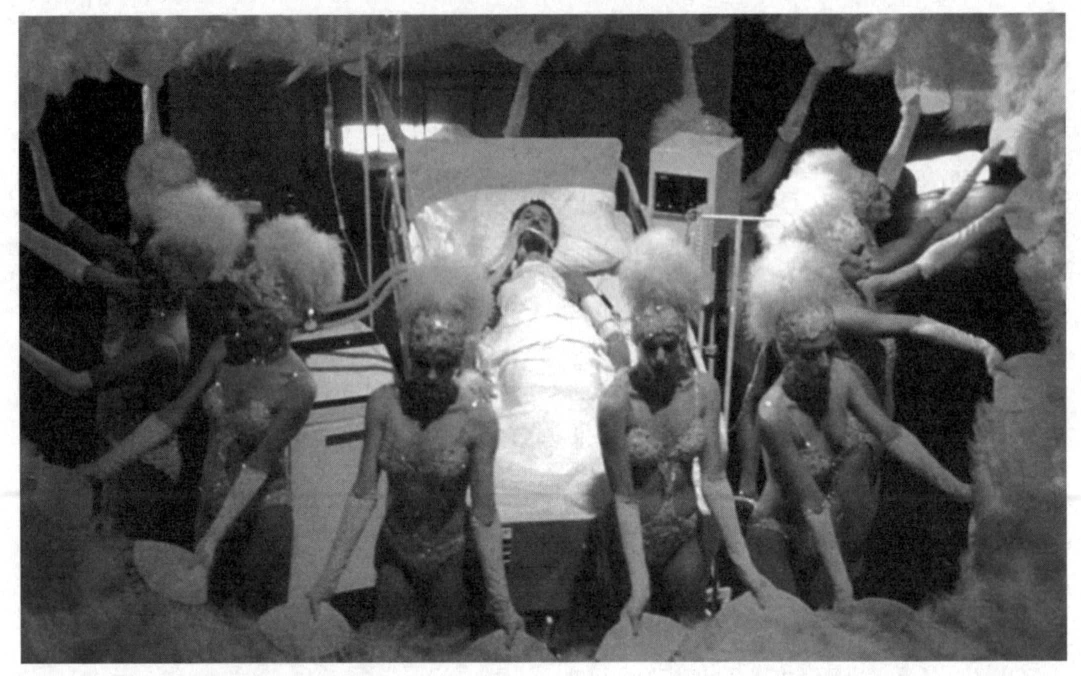

Bob Fosse opened his heart in *All That Jazz*, a scathingly forthright musical *à clef* that contains some of the most surreal numbers in the history of the genre.

## My Sister Eileen

**dir Richard Quine, 1955, 108m**

The 1942 comedy, *My Sister Eileen*, spawned both the Leonard Bernstein Broadway musical *Wonderful Town* (with its book by Comden and Green) and this amusing Jule Styne and Leo Robin remake, which boasted Bob Fosse's first solo choreography. It also featured Betty Garrett and Janet Leigh, as the Ohio girls loose in Greenwich Village, and a crooning-and-hoofing Jack Lemmon!

## Sweet Charity

**dir Bob Fosse, 1969, 133m**

Bob Fosse's discovery of zoom lenses undermined this Cy Coleman and Dorothy Fields musicalization of Federico Fellini's *Nights Of Cabiria* (1957), which he had guided to Broadway success in 1966. The modish technique and her teaming with Chita Rivera and Paula Kelly only emphasized Shirley MacLaine's inability to duplicate Gwen Verdon's stage magnestism, despite her bullish efforts on "Hey, Big Spender", "If They Could See Me Now", "There's Got To Be Something Better Than This" and "I'm A Brass Band".

## All That Jazz

**dir Bob Fosse, 1979, 123m**

Converting four of its nine Oscar nominations, this savagely honest assessment of Bob Fosse's achievement and the rigours of musical creation frequently lapses into self-pity, self-loathing and self-indulgence. But the staging of the opening "On Broadway" sequence is as superbly subtle as the finale, in which Ben Vereen leads a production number while Roy Scheider undergoes open-heart surgery, is in brilliant bad taste.

## Arthur Freed

Lyricist, Producer, 1894–1973

Between 1929 and 1960, Arthur Freed *was* the MGM musical. In addition to placing 105 of his own songs in more than 30 features, he also produced 39 musicals, many of which rank among the genre's undisputed masterpieces.

With **Roger Edens** and **Lela Simone** acting as his inspired lieutenants, Freed oversaw such classics as *Meet Me In St Louis* (1944, see Canon), *Easter Parade* (1948, see Canon), *On The Town* (1949, see Canon), *An American In Paris* (1951, see Canon), *Singin' In The Rain* (1952, see Canon), *The Band Wagon* (1953, see Canon) and *Gigi* (1958, see Canon). He was responsible for enduring favourites like *For Me And My Gal* (1942), *The Harvey Girls* (1946), *Annie Get Your Gun* (1950, see Canon) and *Silk Stockings* (1957, see Canon), as well as originals like *Yolanda And The Thief* (1945, see Canon), *The Pirate* and *Summer Holiday* (both 1948, see Canon), which were so far ahead of their time that they're only now receiving their critical due.

Freed started out as a song plugger and worked on stage with the Marx Brothers and Bing Crosby before teaming with composer **Nacio Herb Brown**. Two of their tunes, "You Were Meant For Me" and "The Wedding Of The Painted Doll", featured in MGM's first musical, *The Broadway Melody* (1929), and they went on to produce "Singin' In The Rain" for *The Hollywood Revue Of 1929*, "Temptation" for Bing Crosby in *Going Hollywood* (1933), "All I Do Is Dream Of You" for Joan Crawford in *Sadie McKee* (1934), "You Are My Lucky Star" for Eleanor Powell in *Broadway Melody Of 1936* (1935) and "Would You?" for Jeanette MacDonald in *San Francisco* (1936).

But Freed's ambition was to produce, and he took numerous uncredited jobs behind the scenes to develop an appreciation of every aspect of filmmaking. **Louis B. Mayer** rewarded him with an associate producer's berth on *The Wizard Of Oz* and afforded him his producing debut on *Babes In Arms* (both 1939), the first of four Mickey Rooney and Judy Garland barnyards. Mayer soon gave him permission to produce pictures his own way, and although fellow unit heads **Joe Pasternak** and **Jack Cummings** would occasionally outperform Freed at the box office, they rarely surpassed his artistic achievements.

Freed knew instinctively which stars, directors, songwriters, scenarists, choreographers and designers were best suited to render a project in the **Freed Unit**'s distinctive style. But his real genius lay in fostering a working environment where its unrivalled talents could shine. Freed considered the Unit to be heir to the tradition and spirit of vaudeville and had an unshakeable faith in the ability of his musicals to entertain and improve the world through their glamour, energy and conservative values. Thus, the Ziegfeld in him was balanced by a preference for songs that furthered the plot or explored character psychology and dance routines that were a synthesis of colour, décor and space. Artists like **Vincente Minnelli**, **Fred Astaire** and **Gene Kelly**, therefore, were given the latitude to integrate routines or indulge in showstoppers to tell their stories most authentically through music and movement.

Freed's emphasis on song, scope, spectacle and style helped him transfigure the musical from an escapist entertainment into an art form, and for this he will forever rank among the genre's pivotal figures.

### Broadway Melody Of 1936
**dir Roy Del Ruth, 1935, 110m, b/w**

Gossip columnist Jack Benny's testy relationship with producer Robert Taylor provides the core of this MGM backstager. But its appeal lies in Nacio Herb Brown and Arthur Freed's score, whose standouts are Frances Langford's charming rendition of "You Are My Lucky Star" and Eleanor Powell's exhilarating tap displays on "I've Got A Feeling You're Fooling", "Sing Before Breakfast" and the "Broadway Rhythm" finale.

### Kismet
**dir Vincente Minnelli, 1955, 113m**

"Stranger In Paradise" and "Baubles, Bangles And Beads" were the hits of this Broadway adaptation, fashioned by Bob Wright and Chet Forrest from some variations on Borodin. While Dolores Gray afforded Howard Keel alluring support, this Arthur Freed production succumbed to the kitsch of Preston Ames' lavish designs, and Vincente Minnelli's direction proved as uninspiring as Jack Cole's choreography.

### Bells Are Ringing
**dir Vincente Minnelli, 1960, 127m**

Arthur Freed's last musical and Judy Holliday's final film re-created her 1956 stage success, as the Susanswerphone operator who falls for playwright client, Dean Martin. The majority of Jule Styne and Comden and Green's score remained intact, with "Just in Time" and "The Party's Over" being the best-known tunes. For all the story's sweetness, Holliday's knockout performance and Bob Fosse's serviceable choreography, Vincente Minnelli's direction betrayed his indifference.

## Judy Garland

Actor, 1922–69

According to Hollywood legend, there was a mix up when **Louis B. Mayer** ordered a minion to ditch "the fat one" after seeing Deanna Durbin and Judy Garland in the 1936 short, *Every Sunday*. But the studio didn't rue any misunderstanding for long, as it was about to abandon the operetta-based pictures that would have suited Durbin. Moreover, Arthur Freed's musical director, **Roger Edens**, quickly recognized Garland as the voice of the future, going so far as to describe her discovery as "the biggest thing to happen to the MGM musical".

Yet at no stage was Garland ever in control of her life or career. Part of the Gumm Sisters vaudeville act at 3, she was successively a meal ticket for her mother, Mayer and third husband, **Sid Luft**. And each one betrayed her. After a loan-out to Fox for *Pigskin Parade* (1936) clued the studio how best to exploit her peerless talent, MGM conspired with her mother a regimen of appetite suppressors and uppers/downers that enabled Garland to cope with the hectic schedule the studio devised.

Having stolen *Broadway Melody Of 1938* (1937) with her rendition of "You Made Me Love You" to Clark Gable's photo, Garland endured *Everybody Sing* and *Listen, Darling* (both 1938) before finding her juvenile soulmate in **Mickey Rooney**, with whom she'd appeared in *Thoroughbreds Don't Cry* (1937). As well as three entries in his long-running teen series (*Love Finds Andy Hardy*, 1938; *Andy Hardy Meets Debutante*, 1940; *Life Begins For Andy Hardy*, 1941), they also made a quartet of infectious barnyard musicals – *Babes In Arms* (1939), *Strike Up The Band* (1940), *Babes On Broadway* (1941) and *Girl Crazy* (1943) – in which his brash enthusiasm was perfectly complemented by her disarming seriousness and unaffected geniality.

But it was *The Wizard Of Oz* (1939, see Canon) that made Garland a legend. In addition to revealing her to be a fine actress and a decent dancer, it demonstrated her rare ability to personalize a song. "Over The Rainbow" (the first of six Oscar-nominated songs she would introduce) particularly emphasized the moving intensity with which she sang. Born out of an identification with and commitment to her material, Garland's intimate style enabled her to forge a unique bond with her audience. Moreover, it suggested that she was no longer a child star and, after *Little Nellie Kelly* (1940), she received more grown-up roles in *Ziegfeld Girl* (1941), *For Me And My Gal* (1942) opposite a debuting **Gene Kelly**, and *Presenting Lily Mars* (1943).

Garland's misgivings about her next film had less to do with her character than its episodic structure and the inexperience of its director. Yet *Meet Me In St Louis* (1944, see Canon) not only changed the nature of the Hollywood musical, but it also put her in thrall to second husband **Vincente Minnelli**, who directed her non-musical, *The Clock* (1945), and her guest slots in *Ziegfeld Follies* and *Till The Clouds Roll By* (both 1946). But the marriage had soured before she and Kelly reunited on Minnelli's *The Pirate* (1948, see Canon). Moreover, her relationship with the studio was deteriorating and, although Garland had excelled in *The Harvey Girls* (1946), *Easter Parade* (1948, see Canon) and *In The Good Old Summertime* (1949), MGM took the unprecedented step of publicizing her erratic behaviour and dependence upon medication after it removed her from *The Barkleys Of Broadway* (1949).

A star is born: Liza Minnelli was only a few months old when she made her screen debut as her mother Judy Garland's bouncing baby in the finale of *In The Good Old Summertime*.

Even then, the studio refused to allow her an extended rest period, as it had "$14 million tied up in her". Despite happy teamings with Rooney in *Words And Music* (1948) and Kelly in *Summer Stock* (1950), Garland's insecurities resurfaced and her contract was terminated after her unreliability led to dismissal from *Annie Get*

*Your Gun* (1950, see Canon) and *Royal Wedding* (1951). Pressure to live up to her reputation undoubtedly precipitated the emotional turmoil that resulted in several suicide attempts over the next two decades. But Garland could also be capricious, controlling and malicious, and columnist Louella Parsons was not alone in criticizing her diva-like antics and childish need for sympathy and approbation.

However, the majority of Garland's co-workers remained loyal, with Roger Edens coaxing her through the nineteen-week comeback stint at New York's Palace Theatre that enabled Sid Luft to land her *A Star Is Born* (1954, see Canon) at Warner Bros. But not even a best actress nomination could convince Hollywood to give her another chance and Garland didn't return to the screen until her Oscar-cited supporting role in *Judgement At Nuremberg* (1961).

Garland was mainly seen in concert in the 1960s. Her 1961 triumph at Carnegie Hall was described as "the greatest night in show business history" and the bestselling double album won five Grammys. But she did sing on screen again, amusingly voicing a cat in the cartoon *Gay Purr-ee* and playing a singer with issues in *I Could Go On Singing* (both 1963). Her subsequent TV series, which ran from 1963 to 1964, flopped. She was also heckled by London audiences a year before she died in June 1969 of what was presumed to be an accidental overdose of barbiturates. As Ray Bolger said at her funeral, "She just plain wore out."

### Strike Up The Band
**dir Busby Berkeley, 1940, 120m, b/w**

Judy Garland helps Mickey Rooney form a school band to enter a Paul Whiteman radio contest in this MGM barnyard, which dispensed with all but the title track from George and Ira Gershwin's stage hit. Friction existed between the free-spirited Garland and her perfectionist director, who shot "Do The La Conga" in a single take after thirteen days of rehearsal. The fruit orchestra sequence, however, was devised by Vincente Minnelli and delightfully animated by George Pal.

### Girl Crazy
**dir Norman Taurog, 1943, 99m, b/w**

Bert Wheeler and Robert Wolsey had headlined RKO's 1932 adaptation of the Gershwins' 1930 stage hit. But MGM reunited Mickey Rooney and Judy Garland for its version of the story, in which some students try to save their Arizona college by mounting a musical rodeo. The shoot proved extremely fractious, with Busby Berkeley being fired after ructions on the "I Got Rhythm" finale. But Garland still shines on "Embraceable You" and "But Not For Me", while Rooney handles their duet ("Could You Use Me?") and the June Allyson nightclub routine, "Treat Me Rough", with equal aplomb.

### In The Good Old Summertime
**dir Robert Z. Leonard, 1949, 102m**

Producer Joe Pasternak musicalized Ernst Lubitsch's *The Shop Around The Corner* (1940) for this genial MGM venture into Americana. The serviceable score was astutely animated by choreographer Robert Alton. But this was essentially a singing screwball that showcased Judy Garland's comic gifts, as the bookstore clerk who's unaware that her cherished pen pal is really detested co-worker, Van Johnson.

### Summer Stock
**dir Charles Walters, 1950, 109m**

Gene Kelly's ingenious dance with a newspaper and a squeaky floorboard to Harry Warren and Mack Gordon's "You Wonderful You" would have been the highlight of this latterday barnyard, had producer Joe Pasternak not recalled a slimmed-down Judy Garland to don a tuxedo and fedora and rattle through Charles Walters' ballsy staging of Harold Arlen and Ted Koehler's "Get Happy". Unfortunately, this powerhouse performance – shot three months after the picture wrapped – proved to be her final number for MGM.

## George Gershwin

Composer, 1898–1937

When the novelist John O'Hara heard of George Gershwin's death from a cystic brain tumour in 1937, he said "I don't have to believe it if I don't want to." No composer, before or since, has made such a lasting impact on so many aspects of American music.

Gershwin was still studying piano when he became Tin Pan Alley's youngest-ever song plugger at 15. In 1919, he made his full Broadway debut with *La La Lucille* and scored the biggest hit of his career when **Al Jolson** adopted "Swanee", a combination of classical and popular elements that was full of the rhythmic surprises that would recur throughout Gershwin's career. From 1920 to 1924, he wrote for *The George White Scandals*, whose urban modernity perfectly suited his composing style. However, his "Blue Monday Blues" was considered too downbeat for the 1922 edition. But bandleader **Paul Whiteman** recognized its merits and commissioned an extended piece based upon it. This was *Rhapsody In Blue* and Whiteman performed Ferdie Grafé's fine arrangement in the 1930 screen revue, *King Of Jazz*.

By then, Gershwin had begun writing with his older brother, **Ira**, and had notched up a series of Broadway hits, including *Lady, Be Good* (1924), *Funny Face* and *Rosalie* (both 1927), *Strike Up The Band* and *Girl Crazy* (both 1930), which were packed with standards that would resurface in countless films. But when Hollywood beckoned, Gershwin loathed his experiences on *The Song Of The Flame* (1930) and *Delicious* (1931) and returned to New York determined to create a new kind of musical comedy, with a political edge equal to Gilbert and Sullivan's Savoy operas. The resulting *Of Thee I Sing* (1931) became the first musical to win the Pulitzer Prize, but its subversive satire prevented it from being filmed.

Gershwin's classical stock was also rising, courtesy of the *Concerto In F* (1925), the tone poem *An American In Paris* (1928) and his *Second Rhapsody* (1930). He wanted to achieve an artistic unity from the nation's cultural diversity, and the folk opera, *Porgy And Bess* (1935), with its integrated song and drama, proved to be a major influence on the American musical.

Anxious not to be seen solely as a "serious" composer, Gershwin went West to collaborate with **Fred Astaire** on *Shall We Dance* (1937, see Canon) and *A Damsel In Distress* (1937). However, he resented RKO's cavalier attitude to his music and signed up with independent producer **Samuel Goldwyn** for *The Goldwyn Follies* (1938), which, sadly, he didn't live to complete.

Upon his death the studios seized upon Gershwin's songbook. Posthumous pictures like *Strike Up The Band* (1940), *Lady Be Good* (1941), *Girl Crazy* (1943) and *The Shocking Miss Pilgrim* (1947) took liberties with their scores, while the biopic *Rhapsody In Blue* (1945) was an historical travesty. And Otto Preminger's 1959 adaptation of *Porgy And Bess* was little better. But MGM and Paramount respectively made better jobs of *An American In Paris* (1951, see Canon) and *Funny Face* (1957, see Canon), and Gershwin's music (whose intricate harmonics frequently reflected his restless character) has since graced such modern classics as Woody Allen's *Manhattan* (1979).

### Rhapsody In Blue

**dir Irving Rapper, 1945, 139m, b/w**

Forget the fanciful factuality involving Robert Alda, Joan Leslie and Alexis Smith and revel instead in the glorious Gershwin music that courses through this Warner Bros biopic. Oscar Levant reverentially performs the title classic and *Concerto In F*, while Al Jolson's "Swanee" and Anne Brown's "Summertime" are the songbook standouts. Ray Heindorf and Max Steiner's Oscar-nominated orchestrations and Sol Polito's photography also merit mention.

### Porgy And Bess
**dir Otto Preminger, 1959, 138m**

Al Jolson had tried to acquire the rights to George Gershwin's 1935 Catfish Row folk opera in 1950. But, instead, the Estate did a deal with Samuel Goldwyn, which it so regretted that it repossessed the rights and now forbids public screenings of this deeply flawed, but still fascinating adaptation. Things would undoubtedly have been different had Rouben Mamoulian not walked, as Otto Preminger compounded the errors made on *Carmen Jones* (1954) by trading in African-American stereotypes and dubbing the entire cast, apart from Pearl Bailey and Sammy Davis, Jr. However, songs of the calibre of "Summertime", "I Got Plenty Of Nothin'" and "It Ain't Necessarily So" remain classics of their kind.

## Betty Grable

Actor, 1916–73

Thirteen-year-old Betty Grable broke into movies in blackface in *Let's Go Places* (1929). Fox cancelled her contract when they discovered her real age, but **Samuel Goldwyn** was less fastidious and, as Frances Dean, she joined **Busby Berkeley**'s chorus for the Eddie Cantor vehicles *Whoopee!* (1930), *Palmy Days* (1931) and *The Kid From Spain* (1932).

Grable spent the early talkie period in mostly negligible light entertainments. She was better served with spots in the Fred'n'Ginger vehicle, *The Gay Divorcee* (1934) – duetting with **Edward Everett Horton** on "Let's K-nock K-nees" – and Fox's *Pigskin Parade* (1936). Then Paramount pushed her up the bill in *Thrill Of A Lifetime* and *This Way Please* (both 1937) before giving her the lead in *Million Dollar Legs* (1939).

Yet fame still eluded her, so she went to Broadway for *DuBarry Was A Lady*, only for Fox to summon her as a replacement for the indisposed **Alice Faye** in *Down Argentine Way* (1940). **Darryl F. Zanuck** next boosted the pair's supposed rivalry in *Tin Pan Alley* (1940). But Grable eventually supplanted Faye, as, while she was a less elegant singer, she was a better dancer and more ideally suited to Fox's Technicolored blend of brash optimism and cosy nostalgia.

She was soon keeping the studio afloat. Backstagers like *Coney Island* (1943) and *Pin-Up Girl* (1944) were shamelessly commercial propositions, while her principal directors, Irving Cummings, Walter Lang and George Seaton, were essentially journeymen. But, with her fresh complexion and legs insured for $250,000, Grable could be both the girl next door and the forces' sweetheart. Her non-threatening sensuality ensured that she became America's highest-paid star and featured prominently in Hollywood's box-office top ten from 1942 to 1951.

Grable attempted occasional non-musical items like *I Wake Up Screaming* (1941) and the comedies *That Lady In Ermine* (1948) and *The Beautiful Blonde From Bashful Bend* (1949). But she knew both her limitations and what her fans wanted. Consequently, her pictures (whether in period or contemporary settings) offered undemanding escapism, in which the songs were usually speciality fillers rather than integral to the plot. Moreover, she frequently romanced non-singers like Don Ameche (*Moon Over Miami*, 1941), Victor Mature (*Footlight Serenade*, 1941; *Song of the Islands*, 1942; *Wabash Avenue*, 1950), John Payne (*Springtime In The Rockies*, 1942; *The Dolly Sisters*, 1945) and Robert Young (*Sweet Rosie O'Grady*, 1943) – although she did get more tuneful support from Dick Haymes (*Billy Rose's Diamond Horseshoe*, 1945; *The Shocking Miss*

*Pilgrim*, 1947) and Dan Dailey (*Mother Wore Tights*, 1947; *When My Baby Smiles At Me*, 1948; *My Blue Heaven*, 1950; *Call Me Mister*, 1951).

Having handed the Fox blonde baton to **Marilyn Monroe** in *How To Marry A Millionaire* (1953), Grable misfired in *The Farmer Takes A Wife* (1954) and retired from the screen after *How To Be Very, Very Popular* (1955). Divorced from ex-child star Jackie Coogan, she married bandleader Harry James and they played cabaret gigs before divorcing in 1965. At the end of her long career she scored on stage in *Hello, Dolly!* (1965–67), but flopped resoundingly in *Belle Starr* (1969).

### Down Argentine Way
**dir Irving Cummings, 1940, 90m**

Bette Grable finally became a star in this horse-breeding variation on *Romeo And Juliet*, though her tepid romance with Don Ameche is a mere sideshow to Charlotte Greenwood's spirited high-kicking rendition of "Sing To Your Senorita" and the Nicholas Brothers' acrobatic tap routines. But no one can compete with the debuting Carmen Miranda, who follows her Broadway hit "South American Way" with the equally exhilarating "Mama Yo Quiero" and "Bambu".

### Coney Island
**dir Walter Lang, 1943, 96m**

Betty Grable liked this Technicolored Americana romp so much that she remade it in 1950 as *Wabash Avenue*, with Victor Mature and Phil Harris replacing George Montgomery and Cesar Romero as the carnival bosses competing for her services and favours. The respective scores were built around Ralph Rainger/Leo Robin and Josef Myrow/Mack Gordon scores, but in each case Grable also socked over oldies like "Cuddle Up A Little Closer" and "I Wish I Could Shimmy Like My Sister Kate".

### Mother Wore Tights
**dir Walter Lang, 1947, 107m**

Josef Myrow and Mack Gordon's score – which included the Oscar-nominated "You Do" – was bolstered by a raft of period standards in this typical slice of Fox feel-good, which sees finishing school snob Mona Freeman develop an aversion to parents Betty Grable and Dan Dailey's vaudeville fame. Glossy photography, chic costumes and a ventriloquist turn by Señor Wences all helped this become Grable's biggest commercial success.

## Oscar Hammerstein

Lyricist, 1895–1960

Born into a theatrical family, Oscar Hammerstein II defied his father's wishes upon graduating Columbia University (where classmates had included Lorenz Hart and Howard Dietz) by entering show business in 1917. Mentored by composer Herbert Stothart, he initially teamed with **Otto Harbach** on Rudolf Friml's *Rose-Marie* (1924/1936 and 1954) and on Sigmund Romberg's *The Desert Song* (1926/1929 and 1953). However, his most significant collaborator in this period was **Jerome Kern** (see p.215), with whom he worked on the stage hits *Sunny* (1925), *Show Boat* (1927/1936 and 1951, see Canon) and *Sweet Adeline* (1929/1935) and the films *Music In The Air* (1932), *The Cat And The Fiddle* (1934), *Roberta* (1935), *High, Wide And Handsome* (1937, see Canon) and *Lady Be Good* (1941), into which they interpolated the Oscar-winning, "The Last Time I Saw Paris".

Had his career ended here, Hammerstein would still have had a major impact on both the stage and screen musical. **Irving Berlin** claimed that he was the form's only true poet. Yet Hammerstein's lyrics also contained colloquialisms and contemporary references that made them both more relevant to the characters and immediate to the audience. He was one of the first songwriters to approach book shows from a conceptual angle, in which song was used for narrative exposition and psychological revelation. Thus, by forging a link between operetta and musical comedy, Hammerstein pioneered a uniquely American form of musical theatre that was to reach its maturity during his partnership with **Richard Rodgers** (see p.225) between 1942 and 1960.

Many considered that Hammerstein was past his best by the early 1940s – especially after the disappointment of his reunions with Romberg on *Viennese Nights* (1930), *New Moon* (1930 and 1940) and *The Night Is Young* (1935), and his struggle to turn Bizet's 1875 opera into *Carmen Jones* (1943/1954). But *Oklahoma!* (1943/1955, see Canon), Rodgers and Hammerstein's first collaboration, triumphed on Broadway and they repeated their success with *Carousel* (1945/1956, see Canon), *South Pacific* (1949/1958, see Canon), *The King And I* (1951/1956, see Canon), *The Sound Of Music* (1959/1965, see Canon) and *Flower Drum Song* (1958/1961). They also produced *State Fair* (1945) for the cinema (winning an Oscar for "It Might As Well Be Spring") and *Cinderella* (1957) for television. Occasionally, they misfired with less traditional stage shows like *Allegro* (1947), which ambitiously sought to meld dialogue and song with patterns of continuous movement. *Me And Juliet* (1953) and *Pipe Dream* (1955) also underperformed and, consequently, Hollywood overlooked them.

Rodgers and Hammerstein transformed musical theatre into an art form (although not all of their film adaptations were wholly successful). By exploring such contentious themes as race and clashing cultures, Hammerstein sought to examine the USA's place in the Cold War world, as well as its self-image and sense of responsibility to its more repressed peoples. In highlighting the prejudice, sexual prudery and naive patriotism within American society, he also stressed that the Dream was better than any illusion promised by authoritarianism. This folksy optimism now seems quaintly old-fashioned beside the wittier, more worldly wise work of Lorenz Hart, Cole Porter and George Gershwin and, consequently, in spite of his towering achievement, Hammerstein's critical reputation is currently mixed.

## Lorenz Hart

Lyricist, 1895–1943

When Lorenz Hart met **Richard Rodgers** (see p.225) in 1918, he was already suffering from the physical complexes, homosexual frustrations and alcoholic depressions that would ultimately curtail their partnership. **Lew Fields** bought their first copyrighted song, "Any Old Place With You", for *A Lonely Romeo* in 1919, but they had to wait until "Manhattan" became the pick of *The Garrick Gaieties* (1925) before finding their niche.

Steering a path between operetta and the Princess Theatre style, Rodgers and Hart explored contemporary issues, literature and history in *Dearest Enemy* (1925), *Peggy-Ann* (1926) and *A Connecticut Yankee* (1927). Touched by his blend of vernacular acuity and witty cynicism, even lesser hits like *Hands Up!* (1929/1930), *Simple Simon* and *Ever Green* (both 1930) reveal the way Hart helped redefine the lyrical style of the American song.

Hart delighted in intricate triple rhymes that sugar-coated the ills of modern life. And while his lyrics packed in the jokes and sly observations, they also contained a confessional element stemming from his troubled personal life. His parodies of traditional romantic ballads reduced passion to a physical ailment and lamented the impossibility of finding lasting love.

Having appeared briefly in Paramount's 1929 two-reeler, *Makers Of Melody,* Rodgers and Hart seemed ideally suited to Hollywood. But they were dismayed by the studios' blithe attitude to their songs in *Spring Is Here* and *Leathernecking* (both 1930) and when their entire contribution was cut from *Follow Thru* (1930) they returned East. It wasn't too long before they were lured back by a Warner Bros deal offering them $50,000 each for three musicals. But the collapse of the genre's popularity saw the contract cancelled after only one, *The Hot Heiress* (1931).

Hart remained highly cinematic in his approach to musicals and eschewed Hollywood's insistence on Broadway structures. He experimented with ways in which song and dance could progress the narrative with "Isn't It Romantic?" in *Love Me Tonight* (1932, see Canon) and used rhythmic dialogue to segue from dramatic reality to musical fantasy. But when audiences rejected *Hallelujah, I'm A Bum* (1933) – as much for its depiction of the Depression as its rhyming cues – Rodgers and Hart eased away from redefining film song and followed more standard practices in *Mississippi* (1935), *Too Many Girls* (1940) and *They Met In Argentina* (1941).

Hollywood habitually mistreated the duo's Broadway transfers (11 of their 26 shows were filmed) and classic songs were cut from the screen versions of *On Your Toes* (1935/1939), *Babes In Arms* (1937/1939), *I Married An Angel* (1938/1942), *The Boys From Syracuse* (1938/1940) and *Too Many Girls* (1939/1940), as they were, eventually, from the long-delayed adaptations of *Jumbo* (1935/1962) and *Pal Joey* (1940/1957) – even though the latter's uncompromising approach to the seedier side of life and its titular anti-hero made it a landmark show.

Rodgers had hoped to persuade the increasingly unreliable Hart to work on what would become *Oklahoma!* But he disliked the material and died shortly afterwards, although not in the melodramatic manner suggested by the shamlessly romanticized 1948 biopic, *Words And Music*.

## Lena Horne

Actor, b. 1917

Singing at the Cotton Club from 16, Lena Horne learned her craft from such celebrated musicians as Duke Ellington, Count Basie, Cab Calloway and Noble Sissle. Yet she was more comfortable with popular songs than jazz and, having debuted in the short *The Duke Is Tops* (1938), her silky smooth tones caught the ear of **Roger Edens**, who made her the first African-American to be signed to a long-term Hollywood contract.

However, Horne refused to cooperate with MGM's plan to use Egyptian Blend No. 5 make-up to pass her off as Hispanic and her principles hindered her screen career. Beside such shorts as *Boogie Woogie Dream* (1942) and the all-black musicals *Cabin In The Sky* and *Stormy Weather* (both 1943), she saw out her unhappy Hollywood sojourn in excisable guest slots in the likes of *Panama Hattie* (1942), *Thousands Cheer* (1943), *Broadway Rhythm* (1944), *Ziegfeld Follies*, *Till The Clouds Roll By* (both 1946) and *Words And Music* (1948).

Blacklisted for much of the 1950s, for her friendship with **Paul Robeson** and avowal of the Civil Rights cause, Horne continued to record and appear in cabaret before returning to film as Glinda in son-in-law Sidney Lumet's *The Wiz* (1978).

## Al Jolson

Actor, 1886–1950

Charlie Chaplin once described Al Jolson as "a great instinctive artist with magic and vitality … He personified the poetry of Broadway, its vitality and vulgarity, its aims and dreams." Yet for all his experience in burlesque, minstrelsy and on the

Shuberts' Winter Garden stage, Jolson couldn't recapture on film the intimate magnetism that transfixed live audiences. His misgivings about cinema had prompted him to abandon D.W. Griffith's silent, *Mammy's Boy*, in 1923. But the Vitaphone short, *April Showers* (1926), convinced Jolson and Warner Bros to launch the talkie era with *The Jazz Singer* (1927, see Canon) and he scored an even bigger hit with the follow-up, *The Singing Fool* (1928).

While his naturalistic acting broke with silent convention, the egotistical and ever-contradictory Jolson remained a consummate showman, selling songs in a booming, melodramatic voice. His declamatory style quickly became old-fashioned and movie audiences tired of his sentimentality and showboating in *Say It With Songs* (1929), *Mammy* and *Big Boy* (both 1930). Even his attempt to do something new, with the rhyming couplets of *Hallelujah, I'm A Bum* (1933), misfired and all efforts in *Wonder Bar* (1934), *Go Into Your Dance* (1935) and *The Singing Kid* (1936) to recapture his self-proclaimed title as "the world's greatest entertainer" fell flat.

Jolson took cameos in *Rose Of Washington Square* (1939) and *Swanee River* (1940) and later filled a handful of guest slots. But his flagging career revived unexpectedly after he dubbed **Larry Parks**' vocals in the fanciful biopics, *The Jolson Story* (1946) and *Jolson Sings Again* (1949).

**Hallelujah, I'm A Bum**
**dir Lewis Milestone, 1933, 82m, b/w**

Al Jolson's best picture was the only 1930s musical to deal directly with the Depression. Thus, this tale of New York's hobo mayor flopped with audiences demanding escapism. Still, Rodgers and Hart's score, complete with passages of "musical dialogue" that complement the couplets in S.N. Behrman's screenplay, make this a fascinating curio, made all the more enjoyable by silent clown Harry Langdon's supporting turn.

**Rose Of Washington Square**
**dir Gregory Ratoff, 1939, 86m, b/w**

Fanny Brice sued Fox for invasion of privacy on the release of this brash *film à clef* inspired by the Ziegfeld star's romance with gambler Nick Arnstein – re-created in 1968 by Barbra Streisand and Omar Shariff in *Funny Girl*. Reunited with Tyrone Power, Alice Faye counters her miscasting with a soulful rendition of "My Man", but Al Jolson (in his penultimate picture) steals the show with a clutch of golden oldies.

**The Jolson Story**
**dir Alfred E. Green, 1946, 128m**

It didn't seem to matter that Columbia's fictionalization of Al Jolson's life bore more resemblance to *The Jazz Singer* (1927, see Canon) than the facts. Audiences lapped up the chance to see Larry Parks miming to Jolson's re-recordings of his greatest hits and they even made the less reliable *Jolson Sings Again* the box-office topper of 1949. Wallowing in post-war nostalgia, the pictures rarely made for great cinema, but they more than atoned in old-fashioned, barnstorming entertainment.

## Ruby Keeler

Actor, 1909–93

In 1928, one-time speakeasy hoofer and Broadway starlet Ruby Keeler fronted an eponymous short designed to test Movietone's response to tap dancing. While in Tinseltown, she met **Al Jolson**, who followed her to New York and infamously stole her limelight during her stage breakthrough, *Show Girl* (1929), by rising from the audience to sing. Nevertheless, Keeler married Jolson and accompanied him to Hollywood. But she was rescued from his envious shadow by Darryl F. Zanuck, who signed her to Warner Bros, where she made seven of her nine features opposite **Dick Powell**, the first four of which – *42nd Street*, *Gold Diggers Of 1933*, *Footlight Parade* (all 1933, see Canon) and *Dames* (1934) – were choreographed by **Busby Berkeley**.

The studio removed her from Berkeley's influence in *Flirtation Walk* (1934), whose dance director, Bobby Connolly, also worked on *Go Into Your Dance* (1935), her sole film with Jolson, and *Shipmates Forever* (both 1935), which reunited her with Powell. They teamed again on *Colleen* (1936), but the film flopped and their partnership was terminated. Keeler left Warner Bros after having danced memorably with **Lee Dixon** on a giant typewriter keyboard in *Ready, Willing And Able* (1937).

Either side of her acrimonious divorce from Jolson, Keeler made *Mother Carey's Chickens* (1938) and *Sweetheart Of The Campus* (1940) before readily retreating into retirement. She once said of herself, "I was all personality and no talent. I couldn't act. I had a terrible voice, and now I see that I wasn't the greatest tap dancer in the world either." But while her talent was limited, her innocent optimism charmed Depression audiences and encouraged every screen-struck wannabe that they too could become a star.

## Gene Kelly

Actor, Choreographer, Director, 1912–96

Born in Pittsburgh, Gene Kelly performed in university productions and worked in his mother's dance studio before his Broadway break in *Leave It To Me* (1938). Stage fame came with *Pal Joey* (1940) and he played another everyman with everyday foibles and a supercilious, cynical streak in his MGM debut, *For Me And My Gal* (1942).

The tempering of ego was to become a key theme of Kelly's films. Though handsome, lithe, charming and ambitious, he often came across as a childlike clown seeking to prolong his carefree existence. He was more comfortable dancing with kids or his buddies than with female partners and his duets with **Rita Hayworth**, Vera-Ellen, **Cyd Charisse** and Leslie Caron lacked genuine intimacy.

If anything, Kelly was happiest dancing with props – a soda fountain and a mop in *Thousands Cheer* (1943); his own reflection in *Cover Girl* (1944); cartoon characters in *Anchors Aweigh* (1945) and *Invitation To The Dance* (1956); a dog, a statue and an unfinished building in *Living In A Big Way* (1947); a ship in a Caribbean port in *The Pirate* (1948, see Canon); museum exhibits in *On The Town* (1949, see Canon); a squeaky floorboard and a newspaper in *Summer Stock* (1950); his bedsit in *An American In Paris* (1951, see Canon); an umbrella and a streetful of puddles in *Singin' In The Rain* (1952, see Canon); and a bin lid and some rollerskates in *It's Always Fair Weather* (1955).

He also danced with **Fred Astaire** in "The Babbit And The Bromide" in *Ziegfeld Follies* (1946). But their styles could not have been more different. Whereas Astaire was influenced by the ballroom tradition, Kelly exuded both a buck-and-winging burlesque swagger and an athleticism that first emerged as an ice hockey player. "I have a lot of Cohan in me," Kelly once revealed "It's an Irish quality, a jaw-jutting, up-on-your toes cockiness – which is a good quality for a dancer to have." They even sang and dressed differently, with Kelly being casual where Astaire was precise.

Kelly's choreography was always linked to character and plot, although it also had a balletic affirmation and cinematic awareness that made it so unique. He realized that the lens flattens dance on the screen and sought innovative ways of using camera movement, visual effects, stylized sets and authentic locations to re-create the kinetic ener-

Despite a predilection for soulful sentimentality and balletic exuberance, as demonstrated in *An American In Paris* (1951), sports fan Gene Kelly always stressed the athleticism of his choreography and even made the 1958 TV show, *Dancing: A Man's Game*, to prove his case.

flawed characters chimed in with the Cold War's doubting shamus, psychological cowboy and reluctant war hero. Moreover, he was prone to showboating and occasionally overbalanced the scenario with his exuberant egotism and hankering to create dream balletic art.

Although he continued to contribute to songbook pictures like *Words And Music* (1948) and *Deep In My Heart* (1954) and headline musical originals (*Take Me Out To The Ball Game*, 1949) and adaptations (*Brigadoon*, 1954), Kelly was also keen to flex his non-musical muscles in legit roles and pseudo-balletic swashbucklers like *The Three Musketeers* (1948). He had established himself as a decent director, in collaboration with **Stanley Donen**. So, with audiences now preferring rebels to rascals, Kelly left MGM after *Les Girls* (1957) and contented himself with guest appearances in the likes of *Let's Make Love* (1960), *What A Way To Go!* (1964), *Les demoiselles de Rochefort* (*The Young Girls of Rochefort,* 1967), *40 Carats* (1973) and *Xanadu* (1980) while concentrating on directing such musicals as *Flower Drum Song* (1962) and *Hello, Dolly!* (1969).

gy and three-dimensionality of a performance. His style embodied the vigour and confidence of post-war America particularly when he burst out on to the streets in sheer *joie de vivre*.

Yet Kelly also possessed a noirish spirit, and his

### Anchors Aweigh

**dir George Sidney, 1945, 140m**

Gene Kelly landed an Oscar nomination for this lively entertainment about sailors on Hollywood shore leave, which only gets bogged down when the focus falls on

Kathryn Grayson and José Iturbi. Frank Sinatra croons Sammy Cahn and Jule Styne's "I Fall In Love Too Easily" with considerable charm, but Kelly steals the show, whether flitting around a film studio to "La Cumparsita", doing a Mexican hat dance with young Sharon McManus or duetting with Jerry Mouse in the pioneering live-action/ cartoon segment, "The King Who Couldn't Dance".

### Living In A Big Way
**dir Gregory La Cava, 1947, 103m**

Gene Kelly's least appreciated musical flopped badly on its release, as it contained only three songs and fumbled its class themes. Yet Kelly's returning GI glides through "It Had To Be You" with wealthy bride Marie McDonald and revels in partnering a dog and a statue on "Fido And Me". He outdid himself in careering around a half-completed apartment house to a medley of children's rhymes, as this joyous routine was a breathtaking combination of athleticism, slapstick, swashbuckling and stunt work that recalled Chaplin, Keaton, Lloyd and Fairbanks and fully corroborated Kelly's contention that dancing was "a man's game".

### Invitation To The Dance
**dir Gene Kelly, 1956, 93m**

Dismissed as a vanity project (as it took a mere $615,000 on its $1,419,105 budget), this long-shelved dance portmanteau was much amended before MGM finally released it. Scored by Jacques Ibert, "Circus" limned a Pierrot's tragic passion for a bareback rider, while music by André Previn and Rimsky-Korsakov respectively was used for the La Ronde-inspired "Ring Around the Rosy" and "Sinbad The Sailor", which required 57,000 frames to matte Kelly and Carol Haney with various cartoon characters. Occasionally pretentious, but still a laudable attempt to make dance accessible.

## Jerome Kern

Composer, 1885–1945

Taking piano lessons at 5, Jerome Kern was a regular theatregoer by 10 and wrote his first songs (under the influence of Franz Léhar and Victor Herbert) as a schoolboy. While working as a rehearsal pianist, he placed a couple of tunes in the Weberfields show, *An English Daisy* (1904), before studying in Heidelberg and London. This continental experience put him in New York demand for adapting European shows and, in addition to rewriting numerous songs, he interpolated over a hundred of his own into some thirty productions between 1904 and 1914, including his first hit, "They Didn't Believe Me", in *The Girl From Utah* (1914).

Kern quickly established his place in musical theatre history. Princess Theatre shows like *Very Good Eddie* (1915) and *Oh, Boy!* (1917) brought a new intimacy to the Broadway musical, although he was still capable of producing such Ziegfeld smashes as *Sally* (1920) and *Sunny* (1925), for **Marilyn Miller**. However, Kern's finest stage achievement was *Show Boat* (1927), co-written with **Oscar Hammerstein**, its blend of operettic romanticism, thematic realism, energetic musical comedy and vaudeville diversity introduced a new maturity and depth to the genre, while its mix of black and white performing styles encapsulated fifty years of American show business.

But while Kern's thirty-plus stage credits earned him the title "the father of American musical theatre", he also worked on nine movie musicals and a further eleven adapted from his Broadway shows between 1929 and 1952. He received six Oscar nominations and won twice, for "The Way You Look Tonight" from the Astaire'n'Rogers classic *Swing Time* (1936, see Canon) and "The Last Time I Saw Paris" from *Lady Be Good* (1941). Collaborating with lyricists of the calibre of Oscar Hammerstein, **Dorothy Fields**, Yip Harburg, Otto Harbach and **Ira Gershwin**, Kern proved a complex, but pure and fluent composer. Refusing to write for specific performers and resenting the manner in which jazz musicians and Hollywood producers took liberties with his songs, he preferred to work with the likes of **Irene Dunne**, who acted her renditions according to his exact interpretation.

Kern may have changed the nature of the musical, but he never set out to achieve an American vernacular. Indeed, he never surpassed the conceptual integrity of *Show Boat* and his later films harked back nostalgically to the operetta style that he originally helped to invalidate. In addition, his resistance to swing meant that he shunned contemporary American subjects and opted for stories set in Europe and Latin America – *Music in the Air*, *The Cat And The Fiddle* (both 1934), *Roberta* (1935), *One Night In The Tropics* (1940), *You Were Never Lovelier* (1942) – or in the nineteenth century: *High, Wide And Handsome* (1937, see Canon), *Can't Help Singing* (1944) and *Centennial Summer* (1946). Even the more modern *Cover Girl* (1944) had its flashbacks to the Gay Nineties.

Jerome Kern was a snob with a fierce temper and an impish wit. Far from the character portrayed by Robert Walker in the biopic *Till The Clouds Roll By* (1946), he was a perfectionist who forged the link between the musical's melodies and its narrative themes. He died from a cerebral haemorrhage in 1945.

### Roberta

**dir William A. Seiter, 1935, 85m, b/w**

Although much of Jerome Kern and Otto Harbach's Broadway score was dropped, "Smoke Gets In Your Eyes" was retained for Irene Dunne, as an exiled Russian princess who falls for American footballer Randolph Scott, after he inherits a Parisian fashion house. Highlights include "I'll Be Hard To Handle", "Lovely To Look At" and "I Won't Dance", which showcased Fred'n'Ginger's genius for acting their numbers in character – in this case, as a stranded bandleader and a showgirl posing as a Polish countess.

### Can't Help Singing

**dir Frank Ryan, 1944, 89m**

Universal cashed-in on the stage success of *Oklahoma!* with this Deanna Durbin vehicle, which earned Jerome Kern and Yip Harburg an Oscar nomination for "More And More". But there was much else to enjoy about this story of an 1847 waggon-train trek, most notably Woody Bredel and W. Howard Greene's expansive vistas and the irresistible buoyancy of the 22-year-old star, who even makes cornball numbers like "Cal-i-for-n-iay" sound good.

## Jeanette MacDonald

Actor, 1903–65

Florenz Ziegfeld claimed that Jeanette MacDonald "typified the American beauty". However her early experiences were far from glamorous, as she endured the seedier side of show business after debuting as a chorine in *The Demi-Tasse Revue* (1919). Yet no sooner had she achieved Broadway celebrity in *Yes, Yes Yvette* (1928) and *Boom Boom* (1929) than she was cast by **Ernst Lubitsch** in *The Love Parade* (1929, see Canon).

MacDonald excelled opposite **Maurice Chevalier** (see p.195) in this Ruritanian delight and scored a huge hit with "Beyond The Blue Horizon" in Lubitsch's *Monte Carlo* (1930). But she was unable to rescue such mediocrities as *The Vagabond King* and *Let's Go Native* (both 1930) and Paramount released her. *The Lottery Bride* (1930) at United Artists proved no better. Nor did the trio of comedies MacDonald made at Fox: *Oh For A Man!* (1930); *Don't Bet On Women* and *Annabelle's Affairs* (both 1931).

Paramount rescued her for reunions with Chevalier on George Cukor's *One Hour With You* (1932) and **Rouben Mamoulian**'s *Love Me Tonight* (1932, see Canon), which not only showcased her authentic soprano voice, but also allowed her to reveal an ironic eagerness to subvert operettic convention. Invariably dressed in negligées and low-cut gowns, she was both desirable and vulnerable. And her underused gift for comedy gave these battles of the sexes an acerbic frisson that was also evident in her final teaming with Lubitsch and Chevalier (*The Merry Widow*, 1934, see Canon). Unfortunately, such spirit would largely be absent from her on-screen partnership with **Nelson Eddy**.

Studio chief **Louis B. Mayer** took a lecherous interest in MacDonald, billing her as "the Girl with the Gold-Red Hair and the Sea-Green Eyes" in *The Cat And The Fiddle* (1934). Then he insisted she star with Eddy on *Naughty Marietta* (1935), a project she detested. However, the controlling move backfired, as the "Beauty and the Baritone" fell in love.

But their relationship was to be an unhappy one, with MacDonald rejecting Eddy's countless marriage proposals, as he insisted on her sacrificing her career. Over the next fifteen years, they endured numerous breakups, pregnancies and empty marriages (to Gene Raymond and Ann Franklin) while Mayer (who detested Eddy's stilted acting style and on-set mood swings) threatened to ruin them by exposing their adulterous affair unless they continued making profitable pictures like *Rose Marie* (1935). Inevitably, the tensions between them began to undermine the tentative chemistry that only truly ignited during their sung duets.

Unsurprisingly, MacDonald delivered two of her best performances away from Eddy's demoralizing influence, opposite **Clark Gable** and Allan Jones respectively in *San Francisco* (1936) and *The Firefly* (1937). But the public wanted "America's Sweethearts" together, and Mayer begrudgingly reunited them in *Maytime* (1937), *The Girl Of The Golden West* and *Sweethearts* (both 1938), on the ignored proviso that they terminated their romance.

Ultimately, it was changing taste that intervened, and following the unhappy experience of *New Moon*, their next venture, *Bitter Sweet* (both 1940) lost money and the pair worked together for the last time on *I Married An Angel* (1942). MacDonald starred unconvincingly in *Smilin' Through* (1941) and *Cairo* (1943) and cameo'd in *Follow The Boys* (1944) before winding up her screen career in Joe Pasternak's *Three Daring Daughters* (1948) and *The Sun Comes Up* (1949), which co-starred Lassie.

### Monte Carlo
**dir Ernst Lubitsch, 1930, 90m, b/w**

Wealthy playboy Jack Buchanan poses as a barber to romance Jeanette MacDonald's impoverished countess in this glorious Lubitsch concoction. The saucy wit is delicious. But it's Richard A. Whiting, W. Franke Harling and Leo Robin's integrated score that lingers longest, most notably the *Monsieur Beaucaire* opera segment and "Beyond The Blue Horizon", which combines a chugging rhythm, pulsing pistons and clacking wheels to pass MacDonald's trainboard song on to peasants in the nearby fields.

### Naughty Marietta
**dir W.S. Van Dyke, 1935, 106m, b/w**

Allan Jones's stage commitments prevented him from playing a New World mercenary opposite Jeanette MacDonald's runaway French princess in MGM's lavish adaptation of Victor Herbert's 1910 operetta. Instead, she began her enduringly popular partnership with Nelson Eddy, whose stiff performance leaves much to be desired. But her effervescence illuminates this classic fairy-tale musical (see p.257), particularly while duetting on "Ah, Sweet Mystery Of Life".

### Maytime
**dir Robert Z. Leonard, 1937, 132m, b/w**

Beauty and the Baritone were reunited for this sumptuous MGM revision of Sigmund Romberg's 1917 operetta, which ditched the entire score bar the much-reprised "Will You

Remember (Sweetheart)?" to accommodate a selection of operatic arias and a specially commissioned Robert Wright and George Forrest piece, "Czaritza", which was shaped around Tchaikovsky's *Fifth Symphony* to confirm married diva Jeanette MacDonald's passion for Nelson Eddy's penniless Parisian tenor.

### Sweethearts
**dir W.S. Van Dyke, 1938, 114m**

MGM's first three-colour Technicolor feature proved Jeanette MacDonald and Nelson Eddy's liveliest outing. But this owed more to Dorothy Parker and Alan Campbell's acerbic study of a bickering Broadway couple, whose marriage deteriorates when they're lured to Tinseltown, than Victor Herbert's 1913 operetta. Four songs were retained, (albeit with new Robert Wright and George Forrest lyrics), with Albertina Rasch's adroit show-within-a show title routine being the pick.

## Ann Miller

Actor, 1923–2004

Of Irish, French and Cherokee descent, Ann Miller began attending the same Los Angeles dance school as Judy Garland and Rita Hayworth to strengthen her legs against rickets. But it took an impromptu backstage lesson from **Bill Robinson** to inspire her and she was soon faking her age to get nightclub gigs.

Miller made her screen debut in *New Faces Of 1937* (1937), and RKO kept her in minor supports until she lit up **Frank Capra**'s Oscar-winning *You Can't Take It With You* (1938), forcing MGM to buy out her contract so she wouldn't compete with Eleanor Powell. She wowed Broadway with "The Mexiconga" in George White's 1939 *Scandals*, but stage success failed to bring better movie material. Still, Miller was always the pick of her mediocre Columbia assignments, with her ability to do five hundred taps per minute bringing pace and pizzazz to the likes of *Reveille With Beverly* (1943), *Jam Session* and *Hey, Rookie* (both 1944).

Eventually, **Arthur Freed** brought her to MGM, where she excelled in *Easter Parade* (1948, see Canon). But such gems as *On The Town* (1949, see Canon) and *Kiss Me Kate* (1953, see Canon) were outnumbered by more moderate outings like *The Kissing Bandit* (1948), *Texas Carnival*, *Two Tickets To Broadway* (both 1951), *Lovely To Look At* (1952) and *Small Town Girl* (1953), even though choreography by **Hermes Pan** and **Busby Berkeley** invariably meant that she stole the show. With the genre declining, Miller left Hollywood following *Hit The Deck* (1955) and *The Opposite Sex* (1956), but remained active on stage into the mid-1980s.

### Small Town Girl
**dir Leslie Kardos, 1953, 93m**

This would have been as transiently pleasurable as other MGM minors like *Two Girls And A Sailor* (1944) and *Three Little Girls In Blue* (1946) were it not for Busby Berkeley's choreography. Bobby Van hopping along to "Take Me To Broadway" is a genuine oddity, but Ann Miller's tap routine to "I've Gotta Hear That Beat" on a floor punctuated by the arms and instruments of 86 hidden musicians is deleriously surreal.

## Vincente Minnelli

Director, 1903–86

The critic Thomas Elsaesser called Vincente Minnelli "the virtual father of the modern musical". Born into a theatrical family (he made his stage debut at three in *East Lynne*), Minnelli's early years seemed to predestine him for the epithet. A self-taught sketch artist, he designed signs for the Minnelli Bros Dramatic Tent Show before studying at the The Art Institute of Chicago. Spells as a photographer's assistant and a window dresser followed before he joined the Balaban and Katz movie chain as a costume and set designer for their cine-variety shows.

In 1931, Minnelli went to New York to design stage shows for the Paramount Theatre, but found himself working on the *Earl Carroll Vanities* and Grace Moore's *The DuBarry* (1932), instead. He transferred to Radio City Music Hall in 1933 and spent three years designing (and eventually producing) such monthly shows as the ballet *El Amor Brujo* and the musical extravaganza, *Sheherazade*, before becoming a Broadway director with Beatrice Lillie's *At Home Abroad* (1935).

Two years later, Minnelli signed to Paramount and choreographed "Public Melody No.1" in *Artists And Models*. But his frustration at having ideas rejected for some Marlene Dietrich vehicles prompted him to buy out his contract after just six months. He returned to Broadway to direct and design *Hooray For What!* (1938) and *Very Warm For May* (1939) before **Arthur Freed** invited him to MGM, where he attached himself to various creative departments to learn his new craft.

Having helped stage "Our Love Affair" in *Strike Up the Band* (1940), Minnelli designed **Judy Garland**'s "Ghost Train" number in *Babes On Broadway* (1941). He then directed Lena Horne's segments in *Panama Hattie* (1942) to prepare for his feature debut with the sepia-tinted *Cabin In The Sky*, which was quickly followed by *I Dood It* (both 1943).

Inspired by Rouben Mamoulian, Jacques Feyder and Max Ophüls, Minnelli introduced the integrated musical to Hollywood with *Meet Me In St Louis* (1944, see Canon), which demonstrated how fully he had acquired a painter's appreciation of perspective and composition, a photographer's sensitivity to light and shade, a window dresser's feeling for colour and form, and a showman's sense of energy, polish and spectacle. Subsequently, every frame of Minnelli's films became notable for their lighting, depth of field, resonance and detail.

Using long, fluid takes that captured the action and placed the viewer at its centre, Minnelli matched Impressionist décor with Expressionist technique to reveal the character of individuals frequently struggling to find themselves and their purpose in life. The theme of art and artificiality also ran through his oeuvre and he brought a sense of fantasy to even the most realistic settings, as he indulged a penchant for symbolic stylization that was seemingly at odds with the escapist ethos of musical comedy.

Having made notable contributions to *Ziegfeld Follies* and *Till The Clouds Roll By* (both 1946), Minnelli teamed memorably with **Fred Astaire** on *Yolanda And The Thief* (1945, see Canon) and *The Band Wagon* (1953, see Canon) and with **Gene Kelly** on *The Pirate* (1948, see Canon), the Oscar-winning *An American In Paris* (1951, see Canon) and *Brigadoon* (1954). He was less inspired by the Broadway transfers *Kismet* (1955) and *Bells Are Ringing* (1960), but he gave the Freed Unit its last musical smash with the multi-Oscar-winning *Gigi* in 1958 (see Canon).

Minnelli's achievements as a stylist have counted against his reputation as an auteur and he has been accused by some critics of being more interested in beauty than art. He was certainly a romantic and was prone to populism in films like *Lust For Life* (1956) and *The Four Horsemen Of The Apocalypse* (1962). But he also handled problem pictures like *The Cobweb* (1955), *Some Came Running* (1958) and *Home From The Hill* (1960) without undue melodramatics, and cast an acerbic eye over Hollywood itself in *The Bad And The Beautiful* (1952) and *Two Weeks In Another Town* (1962). He returned to the musical for *On*

*A Clear Day You Can See Forever* in 1970 before ending his career with *A Matter Of Time* (1976), which starred his daughter with Judy Garland, **Liza Minnelli**.

### Cabin In The Sky
**dir Vincente Minnelli, 1943, 100m, b/w**

Vincente Minnelli made his directorial debut with MGM's adaptation of Vernon Duke and John Latouche's 1940 show, in which womanizing gambler Eddie "Rochester" Anderson is given a celestial last chance following the intercession of his grieving widow, Ethel Waters. Louis Armstrong and Duke Ellington elevate a spirited, if patronizing all-black morality tale, whose high spots include John William Sublett's slick dance to "Shine", Lena Horne's brisk "Honey In The Honeycomb" and Waters' sublime versions of "Taking A Chance On Love" and "Happiness Is A Thing Called Joe", the latter of which was written by Harold Arlen and Yip Harburg.

### Brigadoon
**dir Vincente Minnelli, 1954, 108m**

Minnelli disliked Lerner and Loewe's 1947 Broadway hit about a Scottish village that only materializes once a century and sulked after being denied the chance to shoot on location. Consequently, he swathed Cedric Gibbons and Preston Ames' vast Highland backdrop in phony fogs and garish Ansco Color magic hours, while the Breen Office set about the script and score. Meanwhile, Gene Kelly stubbornly attempted to turn a pseudo-operetta into a dance picture (while cutting the famous sword dance). His performance was as hammy as Cyd Charisse's was flat, but their duet on "The Heather On The Hill" is achingly romantic.

### On A Clear Day You Can See Forever
**dir Vincente Minnelli, 1970, 129m**

Minnelli had too little say in the conduct of his final musical, as his star dominated proceedings both on and off the set. Replacing Barbara Harris in Alan Jay Lerner's muddled revision of his own 1965 stage show (which he had written with Burton Lane after things hadn't worked out with Richard Rodgers), Barbra Streisand overacted throughout, as the ESP kook haunted by her past life as an eighteenth-century feminist. Paramount cut the picture to ribbons, but Yves Montand managed to salvage "Come Back To Me" and "On A Clear Day" from the much-truncated score.

## Cole Porter

Songwriter, 1892–1964

Alan Jay Lerner once opined that Cole Porter had been "born with a platinum spoon encrusted with diamonds in his mouth". The Yale graduate's affluent lifestyle dissuaded many from taking his songwriting seriously, especially after the failure of his first Broadway show, *See America First* (1916), and his struggle to make an impact following a prolonged European sabbatical. However, the success of "Let's Do It" in *Paris* (1928) established Porter's Broadway reputation for continental sophistication and colloquial wit.

He got off to an equally bad start in Hollywood, with one critic dubbing his debut, *The Battle Of Paris* (1929), a "floperetta". *Fifty Thousand Frenchmen* (1931) fared little better. But a string of Broadway triumphs was followed by "Night And Day" illuminating the **Astaire'n'Rogers** vehicle *The Gay Divorcee* (1934) and "You're The Top" and "I Get A Kick Out Of You" surviving the less than reverential transfer of the stage smash, *Anything Goes* (1936).

Adept at juxtaposing major and minor modes and fond of Latin rhythms and the beguine, Porter had a gift for innuendo and insinuation, which led to a number of his famous list songs having to be toned down for the screen. He finally got to complete his first solo film musical with *Born To Dance* (1936) and returned to MGM for *Rosalie* (1937), in which he explored the impossibility of love with some of his most autobiographical songs (he was sexually ambivalent, though married to socialite Linda Thomas).

After losing the use of both legs in a riding accident, Porter proved he could also conquer physical pain by writing "My Heart Belongs To Daddy" for Mary Martin (which she performed in *Love Thy Neighbour,* 1940) and "Begin The Beguine" – the highlight of Fred Astaire and Eleanor Powell's pairing in *Broadway Melody Of 1940* (1940).

Porter teamed with Astaire again for *You'll Never Get Rich* (1941). But few of his songs survived stage to screen adaptations of *Panama Hattie* (1941), *DuBarry Was A Lady* and *Something To Shout About* (both 1943). Moreover, he had to endure Warner Bros' blithely inaccurate biopic, *Night And Day* (1946), in which **Cary Grant** at least captured the urbanity that made Porter's gliding melodies something to be enjoyed rather than discerned.

*The Pirate* (1948, see Canon) and *Kiss Me Kate* (1953, see Canon) saw Porter reverse the trend of being more renowned for individual songs than entire scores. Yet he still produced lone gems, like "The Laziest Gal In Town" for **Marlene Dietrich** in Alfred Hitchcock's *Stage Fright* (1950).

Demoralized by the deaths of his mother and wife in the early 1950s, Porter nevertheless scored Broadway hits with *Can-Can* (1953) and *Silk Stockings* (1955, see Canon) – which were respectively filmed in 1960 and 1957 – and enjoyed mixed Hollywood fortunes with the 1956 remake of *Anything Goes* and the screen originals, *High Society* (1956, see Canon) and *Les Girls* (1957). Following the amputation of his right leg in 1958 he became prone to bouts of drinking and depression and he remained in retirement to his death in 1964.

### You'll Never Get Rich

**dir Sidney Lanfield, 1941, 88m, b/w**

Fred Astaire teamed with Rita Hayworth for this underrated Cole Porter curio about a discontented draftee who gets the girl while staging a troop show. Hayworth struts her stuff to "Boogie Barcarolle" and Astaire fizzes through "Since I Kissed My Baby Goodbye". Robert Alton's choreography for "So Near And Yet So Far" was delightful, but he got a bit carried away on the "Wedding Cake Walk", which culminated in a tank sitting atop a king-sized confection.

### Les Girls

**dir George Cukor, 1957, 114m**

The musical toyed with *Rashomon* in this flashbacking Cole Porter satire about Gene Kelly's relationships with dancers Mitzi Gaynor, Kay Kendall and Taina Elg. Kendall amuses with a tipsy "La Habanera", while she outshines Kelly on "You're Just Too, Too". While he revives for the Brando parody, "Why Am I So Gone About That Girl", this was a lacklustre way for Kelly to end his fifteen-year association with MGM.

## Dick Powell

Actor, 1904–63

A talented singer and instrumentalist from childhood, Dick Powell was emceeing when he signed to Warner Bros for *Blessed Event* in 1932. But thanks to his easy charm and casual crooning style, he quickly became the studios's top male musical lead, starring alongside **Ruby Keeler** in *42nd Street*, *Gold Diggers Of 1933*, *Footlight Parade* (all 1933, see Canon), *Dames*, *Flirtation Walk* (both 1934), *Shipmates Forever* (1935) and *Colleen* (1936), and with second wife **Joan Blondell** in *Broadway Gondolier* (1935), *Gold Diggers Of 1937* and *Stage Struck* (both 1936).

But this was the **Busby Berkeley** era and though Powell's performances were overshadowed by the flamboyant choreography in *Wonder Bar* (1934), *Gold Diggers Of 1935* (1935), *The Singing Marine*, *Varsity Show* and *Hollywood Hotel* (all 1937), even non-Berkeley musicals like *Twenty Million Sweethearts* (1934), *The Cowboy*

*From Brooklyn*, *Going Places* (both 1938) and *Naughty But Nice* (1939) have largely been forgotten. Indeed, Powell had to go on loan to Fox to land two of his better vehicles, *Thanks A Million* (1936) and *On The Avenue* (1937).

Powell's pleasing tenor also made him a major radio star and several of his film songs (usually composed by Harry Warren and Al Dubin) became hits. But he was so tired of playing affable swains that as soon as his Warner contract elapsed, he decamped to Paramount for the comedies *Christmas In July* (1940) and *It Happened Tomorrow* (1944), and thence to RKO for more noirish fare following his turn as Philip Marlowe in *Murder, My Sweet* (1944). Following a couple of outings with third wife, **June Allyson**, and a standout performance in **Vincente Minnelli**'s *The Bad And The Beautiful* (1952), Powell became one of television's first actor-producers, and also tried his hand at directing.

## Eleanor Powell

Actor, Choreographer, 1912–82

Trained in ballet and tap, Eleanor Powell made such an impact in her screen debut, *George White's Scandals* (1935), that MGM signed her to a seven-year deal. Following an extensive makeover, her healthy athleticism was unleashed in *Broadway Melody Of 1936* (1935) and the taps, back arches, high kicks, pirouettes and splits in the "Broadway Rhythm" finale made her a star.

Powell never danced in character, but always played characters who danced. Despite her limited acting abilities, she was usually cast as intelligent, self-assured women, who weren't obsessed with romance – which is just as well, as she was better suited to solos than duets and went through seven leading men in nine MGM outings.

Paired with **James Stewart** in *Born To Dance* (1936), Powell dazzled with her battleship routine to "Swingin' The Jinx Away" and the big production number became her trademark. She danced against the Manhattan skyline to "Your Broadway And My Broadway" in *Broadway Melody Of 1938* (1937), tapped up and down a percussive staircase and burst through a series of hoops for "Drum Dance" in *Rosalie* (1937), and paid tribute to **Bill "Bojangles" Robinson** during "A Pair Of New Shoes" in *Honolulu* (1939), which MGM delayed to prevent her from being overexposed.

Having teamed unconvincingly with Fred Astaire for "Begin The Beguine" in *Broadway Melody Of 1940* (1940), Powell danced with Buttons the Dog in *Lady Be Good* (1942), which also included Busby Berkeley's "Fascinatin' Rhythm" extravaganza, which required eight grand pianos, a hundred cane-carrying male dancers and a giant zigzagging curtain. This proved to be her last showstopper, as MGM sought to cut its wartime budgets and Powell was reduced to tapping out Morse messages to "On Moonlight Bay" in *Ship Ahoy* (1942), while her second outing with Red Skelton, *I Dood It* (1943), resorted to reusing footage of old routines to pad the action.

Following her sole Technicolor venture, *Thousands Cheer* (1943), Powell left MGM and retired from the screen after *Sensations Of 1945* (1945), in which she danced with a horse and atop a giant pinball table. She later cameo'd in *The Duchess Of Idaho* (1950).

### Born To Dance

**dir Roy Del Ruth, 1936, 105m, b/w**

Cole Porter personally chose James Stewart to introduce "Easy To Love" in this genial hybrid of *42nd Street* (1933, see Canon) and *Follow The Fleet* (1936). Virginia Bruce made an even better job of "I've Got You Under My Skin" before Eleanor Powell, in her first starring role, stole the show with her dazzling dancing to "Rap-Tap-Tap On Wood" and "Swingin' The Jinx Away", which was staged with superabundant panache by Dave Gould on the deck of a stylized battleship.

### Broadway Melody Of 1940

**dir Norman Taurog, 1940, 102m, b/w**

A comedy of errors saw George Murphy break into the big time in this Cole Porter original. Hollywood's finest dancers, Eleanor Powell and Fred Astaire, eventually got to duet on "I Concentrate On You" and the sublime "Begin The Beguine", after Fred had glided solo through "I've Got Me Eyes On You". Yet for all their individual expertise, they

Billed as "the world's greatest female tap dancer", Eleanor Powell could hit five taps per second, and this "machine-gun rapidity" proved perfect for the battleship finale of *Born To Dance* (1936).

proved something of a mismatch and Powell later missed the chance to dance with Gene Kelly when *Broadway Melody Of 1943* was abandoned.

### Lady Be Good
**dir Norman Z. McLeod, 1941, 111m**

The Gershwins were upstaged by Jerome Kern and Oscar Hammerstein's Oscar-winning "The Last Time I Saw Paris" in this shameless bowdlerization of their 1924 show, which interpolated a slender storyline about squabbling songwriters Ann Sothern and Robert Young. The title song and "Hang On To Me" survived, along with "Fascinatin' Rhythm", which inspired Busby Berkeley's intoxicating finale, featuring a fast-tapping, top-hatted Eleanor Powell, and one of the most spectacular sets that MGM ever devised.

## Elvis Presley

Actor, 1935–77

Memphis truck driver Elvis Presley became rock'n'roll's first superstar by blending rhythm'n' blues, country and gospel with his own unique energy, sensuality and vulnerability. His recordings for Sun and RCA were cultural landmarks and Hollywood seized upon him to revitalize a flagging genre.

But, for all his looks and country charm, Elvis couldn't act. Moreover, the studios didn't understand the music that had made him famous, while the Production Code prevented him from gyrating his notorious pelvis. As a result, Presley found himself slotted into 31 formulaic scenarios that offered little musical novelty and, ultimately, even less polish. Until the mid-1960s, his pictures did decent box-office, but they increasingly came to rely on glamorous locations to disguise the docility of the songs and the lack of chemistry between the bored King and his identikit leading ladies.

Debuting in *Love Me Tender* (1956), Elvis soon settled into playing misunderstood outsiders and fun-loving everymen, whether they were wannabe rockers (*Loving You*, 1957), convicts (*Jailhouse Rock*, 1957), genial delinquents (*Wild In The Country*, 1961), boxers (*Kid Galahad*, 1962), twins (*Kissin' Cousins*, 1964), water-skiing instructors (*Clambake*, 1967) or doctors (*Change Of Habit*, 1969).

But the Elvis that went into the Army was very different from the one that emerged in *G.I. Blues* (1960). The rock rebel had become an all-round entertainer and his films grew cosier and less credible. He was invariably assigned slipshod screenplays and journeymen directors and rarely appeared opposite stars of his own magnitude. Only Stella Stevens (*Girls, Girls, Girls*, 1962), **Ursula Andress** (*Fun in Acapulco*, 1963) and Ann-Margret (*Viva Las Vegas*, 1964) provided anything approaching vibrant love interest, although Barbara Stanwyck and Joan Blondell respectively lent some faded class to *Roustabout* (1964) and *Stay Away, Joe* (1968). It was as though producers like **Hal Wallis** knew they only had to have Presley show up and sing to satisfy his legion of loyal fans, who ensured that nine of his soundtrack albums went gold.

The songs in *Blue Hawaii* (1961) were better than most and *Flaming Star* (1960) offered a sterner acting challenge. But Presley was reportedly embarrassed by *Harum Scarum* (1965), although *Tickle Me* (1965), *Frankie And Johnny* (1966) and *Live A Little, Love A Little* (1968) were scarcely better.

Presley was insulated from the changes reshaping the pop scene in the wake of **The Beatles** and his musical reputation declined steeply. Yet no sooner had his career revived with a 1968 comeback telecast, than he became ensconced in the even more stultifying Vegas cabaret circus and his 1970s disappeared in a blur of jumpsuits, pills and fast food. In 1976, **Colonel Tom Parker** priced Presley out of Barbra Streisand's remake of

*A Star Is Born* (1976). Within a year, the musical's last great hope had passed into legend.

### Jailhouse Rock
**dir Richard Thorpe, 1957, 96m, b/w**

Elvis Presley demonstrated a choreographic ingenuity in his third MGM vehicle, as his Berkleyesque routine for the title track captured the raw physicality of his pre-Army image. He also gave a splendidly surly display, as the manslaughtering con who becomes a rock idol on his release from the pen. Jerry Lieber and Mike Stoller's score provided a string of hits, including "Treat Me Nice", "Baby, I Don't Care" and "Young And Beautiful", with the latter suggesting the tamer pop image the studio would soon foist upon The King.

### Viva Las Vegas
**dir George Sidney, 1964, 86m**

Few of Elvis' outings matched the formulaic fun of this story of a racing driver who falls for a swimming teacher. The songs may not be up to the standard of "Blue Suede Shoes" (*G.I. Blues*, 1960), "Can't Help Falling In Love" (*Blue Hawaii*, 1961) or "Return To Sender" (*Girls, Girls, Girls*, 1962), but Ann-Margret proves a redoubtable co-star, particularly on "The Lady Loves Me".

## Richard Rodgers

Composer, 1902–79

A decade after learning to play the piano by ear and firmly under the influence of Jerome Kern, 16-year-old Richard Rodgers first teamed with **Lorenz Hart**. By the mid-1920s, the duo were renowned for literate, sophisticated songs, whose simple, lilting melodies perfectly complemented the ribald, often risqué lyrics. But their relationship was often uncomfortable, as Rodgers increasingly criticized the innuendo and self-pity that informed much of Hart's later work.

Rodgers was always a man of the musical theatre rather than a hit-penning tunesmith. He preferred composing entire scores to the individual pieces he produced for *Dancing Lady* and *Nana* (both 1933). He was also deeply resentful of Hollywood's habit of cutting stage songs, especially when a landmark work like *On Your Toes* (1935/1939) was stripped of everything bar choreographer **George Balanchine**'s interpretation of "Slaughter On Tenth Avenue".

Consequently, Rodgers was infinitely more protective of the integrated scores he produced with **Oscar Hammerstein** (see p.209). Whereas he had presented Hart with melodies to lyricize, he now set Hammerstein's words to music after extensive discussion about the song's diegetic purpose. Whether ascending or descending the simple scale, his strains were always sweet and nostalgic (although some complained that his style calcified after the failure of *Allegro*, 1947).

Surviving Hammerstein (despite losing his left jawbone to cancer), Rodgers wrote five songs for the 1962 remake of *State Fair*. Sadly, they proved as undistinguished as later stage shows like *Do I Hear A Waltz?* (1965), on which he collaborated with **Stephen Sondheim**.

## Ginger Rogers

Actor, 1911–95

Starting out in vaudeville, Ginger Rogers played Broadway in *Top Speed* (1929) and *Girl Crazy* (1930) before committing to movies. Few could have anticipated that the spirited, self-sufficient blonde in Paramount's *Young Man Of Manhattan* (1930) and Pathé's *Carnival Boat* (1932) would soon be on her way to musical immortality. Her scene-stealing presence in *42nd Street* and *Gold Diggers Of 1933* (both 1933, see Canon) persuaded RKO to team her with **Fred Astaire** (see p.189) in *Flying Down To Rio* (1933). Yet it took six more pictures – one of which saw her loaned to Warner Bros for Dick Powell's *Twenty Million Sweethearts* (1934) – before Rogers was reunited with Astaire on *The Gay Divorcee* (1934) and seven more musical gems followed until 1939.

Reliant on choreographer **Hermes Pan** to teach her the routines, Rogers was an underestimated dancer. She might have lacked Eleanor Powell's technique, Cyd Charisse's elegance, Rita Hayworth's beauty and Ann Miller's energy, but she was unquestionably Astaire's best partner. They were physically, stylistically and intellectually mismatched, yet they exuded empathy and elegance in idiosyncratic romantic comedies that were illuminated by their incomparable dance duets. Katharine Hepburn had it right when she averred that "she gives him sex, and he gives her class".

Rogers continued to appear in dramas and comedies throughout the Golden Age and

With Fred wooing to win Ginger, *The Gay Divorcee* established the screwball romantic formula that prompted Katharine Hepburn to declare that "she gives him sex and he gives her class".

returned for each musical with diminishing enthusiasm. Nevertheless, it took considerable courage to split from Astaire and she was ultimately vindicated by her best actress Oscar playing a working-class girl in *Kitty Foyle* (1941).

At the encouragement of her manager mother, Rogers effectively avoided musicals from then on, starring only in *Lady In The Dark* (1944) before partnering Astaire again in *The Barkleys Of Broadway* (1949). However, she later appeared in the BBC's *Clarissima* (1964) and stage versions of *Hello, Dolly* (1965) and *Mame* (1969).

### Flying Down To Rio
**dir Thornton Freeland, 1933, 89m, b/w**

History was made in this madcap entertainment, as Fred Astaire and Ginger Rogers' debut duet atop seven white grand pianos during "The Carioca" renders Brazilian blueblood Dolores Del Rio's romance with bandleader Gene Raymond an instant irrelevance. Not even Dave Gould's slickly excessive aerial routine, positioning scantily clad chorines on biplane wings to Vincent Youmans, Edward Eliscu and Gus Kahn's breezy title track, could compare.

### The Gay Divorcee
**dir Mark Sandrich, 1934, 107m, b/w**

Fred'n'Ginger's first starring vehicle established the "loathe at first sight" formula that would sustain the series, as she mistakes his song-and-dance man for the co-respondent who will help secure her divorce. They only dance together for around ten minutes, but their seductive duet on "Night And Day" (the only song retained from Cole Porter's Broadway score) and the Art Deco extravagance of the Oscar-winning showstopper "The Continental" transformed them into musical icons.

## Frank Sinatra

Actor, 1915–98

Although he possessed one of the twentieth century's most distinctive voices, Frank Sinatra didn't show well in musicals. The majority of his starring vehicles were negligible and when he did land better projects he was overshadowed by **Gene Kelly** in *Anchors Aweigh* (1945), *Take Me Out To The Ball Game* (1949) and *On The Town* (1949, see Canon), and by **Marlon Brando** and **Bing Crosby** respectively in *Guys And Dolls* (1955, see Canon) and *High Society* (1956, see Canon). He certainly wasn't short of talent, as he danced adequately and oozed emaciated charm. But the egomaniacal Sinatra simply didn't have the temperament for musical cinema, as he disliked both the rehearsing and retakes required to achieve its easy-looking perfection.

Sinatra sang with the Hoboken Four before joining Harry James and **Tommy Dorsey**'s bands. His screen debut came unbilled in *Las Vegas Nights* (1941), and he hit the top after press agent George Evans conjured up the bobby-soxer phenomenon and dubbed him "The Voice".

RKO signed him for *Higher And Higher* (1943) and *Step Lively* (1944), but it was Sinatra's partnership with Kelly at MGM that established him as a film star. However, solo ventures like *It Happened In Brooklyn* (1947) and *The Kissing Bandit* (1948) proved disappointing and his rendition of "Ol' Man River" in *Till The Clouds Roll By* (1946) was a lamentable miscalculation.

In the early 1950s, Sinatra's romance with **Ava Gardner** did much to tarnish his reputation, while a submucosal haemorrhage curtailed his singing – although fans hadn't taken to his more relaxed phrasing in *Meet Danny Wilson* (1952) and the film had tanked.

Consequently, once Sinatra had established a new audience with **Nelson Riddle**-produced albums like *Songs For Swinging Lovers* (1956), he refused to do formulaic musicals and went after dramatic roles like Maggio in *From Here To Eternity* (1953), for which he won the best supporting actor Oscar. He occasionally returned to the genre for *Pal Joey* (1957), *Can-Can* (1960) and *Robin And The 7 Hoods* (1964), and delivered Oscar-winning songs in *Three Coins In The Fountain* (1954), *The Joker Is Wild* (1957) and *A Hole In The Head* (1959). But Ol' Blue Eyes now saved his best for record, TV specials and cabaret.

### Pal Joey

**dir George Sidney, 1957, 111m**

Oh, that this had been made in 1944, when Gene Kelly could have reprised the stage role that had made him a star. But MGM refused the loan him to Columbia and seventeen years elapsed before Kim Novak pushed Rita Hayworth into the supporting role of the older woman opposite a suitably cynical, but typically uninvolved Frank Sinatra. "Zip", "Bewitched, Bothered, And Bewildered" and "I Could Write A Book" were retained from Rodgers and Hart's 1940 score, while "My Funny Valentine" and "The Lady Is A Tramp" were interpolated by George Duning and Nelson Riddle. Perhaps the genre's greatest lost opportunity.

## Barbra Streisand

Actor, Songwriter, b. 1942

Having won a Greenwich Village talent contest at 18, Barbra Streisand established a nightclub reputation before making her first Broadway bow with a minor role in *I Can Get It For You Wholesale* (1962). Stardom soon followed, as her strong, controlled voice (as capable of comic numbers as torch songs) shoed her into the role of Fanny Brice in *Funny Girl* (1964), which she reprised on film four years later, winning an Oscar (in a tie with Katharine Hepburn for *The Lion In Winter*) on her debut.

Critical of herself and others, her perfectionism didn't please everybody on the set of **Gene Kelly**'s *Hello, Dolly!* (1969), with Walter Matthau later conceding that "I had no disagreements with Barbra Streisand. I was merely exasperated at her tendency to be a complete megalomaniac."

Streisand has since continued to rake in the Emmys and Grammys for her TV specials and hit albums, while her concerts command ever-more-astronomical fees. But, since Vincente Minnelli's *On A Clear Day You Can See Forever* (1970) and the misfiring Brice sequel, *Funny Lady* (1975), she has concentrated on comedies and dramas.

Indeed, she has made only two further musicals, winning a best song Oscar for "Evergreen" in the 1976 rock remake of *A Star Is Born* (which one critic dubbed "A Bore Is Starred") and co-writing, directing and headlining *Yentl* (1983), which brought her direction a Golden Globe. But Streisand's voice very much remains her trademark and she top-charted with the Oscar-winning theme to *The Way We Were* (1973).

### Funny Girl

**dir William Wyler, 1968, 155m**

After taking Broadway by storm, Barbra Streisand won an Oscar for her bravura display as Fanny Brice in this lavish re-creation of her relationships with showman Florenz Ziegfeld (Walter Pidgeon) and gambler, Nick Arnstein (Omar Sharif). She's in fine voice on Jule Styne and Bob Merrill's "People" and such Brice themes as "My Man" and "Second Hand Rose". But she also acquits herself well in Herbert Ross production numbers like "Don't Rain On My Parade" and the parodic "His Love Makes Me Beautiful" and "The Swan". However, Ross's sequel, *Funny Lady* (1975), disappointed, despite its Kander and Ebb score, Streisand's enthusiasm and James Caan's supporting turn as impresario Billy Rose.

### Hello, Dolly!

**dir Gene Kelly, 1969, 146m**

Carol Channing, Ginger Rogers, Martha Raye, Pearl Bailey and Ethel Merman had all taken the title role in Jerry Herman's long-running Broadway smash, based on

Barbra Streisand takes a break with William Wyler on the set of *Funny Girl*. Choreographer Herbert Ross reportedly assisted the veteran director in staging some of the film's standout set pieces, including "Don't Rain On My Parade".

Thornton Wilder's play, *The Matchmaker.* But Fox miscast Barbra Streisand opposite a less-than-impressed Walter Matthau and then watched in horror as Gene Kelly lost control of both her performance and the picture, which ended up losing around $9 million despite contributions from a who's who of MGM stalwarts. "Before The Parade Passes By" and the title song make splendid use of the 1890s New York settings, but this is consistently hamstrung by its own grandiosity.

### Yentl
**dir Barbra Streisand, 1983, 134m**

There's much to admire about Barbra Streisand's long-cherished adaptation of Isaac Bashevis Singer's short story, "Yentl, The Yeshiva Boy". Streisand is admirably restrained as the Torah-loving, turn-of-the-century Polish girl, whose impersonation of a man is jeopardized by her growing affection for fellow student, Mandy Patinkin, while David Watkin's photography is evocatively poetic. But the pacing is overly reverential and Michel Legrand and Alan and Marilyn Bergman's Oscar-winning songs are an unpersuasive mix of arch psychobabble and showbiz kitsch.

## Shirley Temple

Actor, b. 1928

Between 1934 and 1940, Shirley Temple made 26 features. She held her own against stars like Gary Cooper, Carole Lombard and Alice Faye, while **John Ford** directed her in *Wee Willie Winkie* (1937). Her pictures earned Fox millions and mothers everywhere modelled their daughters on her. Yet, while Temple's achievement was remarkable for one so young, she had more confidence and charisma than talent. Her musicals did little to advance the genre and have dated badly.

She was just 6 when she stole the show with "Baby Take A Bow" in *Stand Up And Cheer* (1934) and by year's end, she had radiated geniality and enjoyment in *Little Miss Marker* and sung "On The Good Ship Lollipop" in *Bright Eyes*. She was a phenomenon, whose miniature Oscar lauded her for "bringing more happiness to millions of children and millions of grown-ups than any child of her age in the history of the world".

Her innocence and optimism epitomized the nation's self-image, as she made light of being orphaned in nine films, and peace- or match-made in a further six. Moreover, she was classless and could dance without prejudice with **Bill "Bojangles" Robinson** in *The Little Colonel*, *The Littlest Rebel* (both 1935), *Rebecca Of Sunnybrook Farm* and *Just Around The Corner* (both 1938).

However, the guileless Miss Fixity of *Curly Top* (1935), *Dimples*, *Captain January* (both 1936) and *Heidi* (1937) felt forced by the time of *The Blue Bird* (1940) and, having failed to make the transition to adult roles, Temple fittingly became a diplomat.

### Curly Top
**dir Irving Cummings, 1935, 75m, b/w**

Previously filmed in 1919 and 1931, Jean Webster's *Daddy Long Legs* gave Shirley Temple the chance to sing "Animal Crackers In My Soup" and perform both a hula dance and some taps atop a grand piano, in between matchmaking sister Rochelle Hudson and handsome benefactor, John Boles. The story resurfaced with Fred Astaire and Lesley Caron in 1955.

### Stowaway
**dir William A. Seiter, 1936, 86m, b/w**

Shirley Temple really showed her mettle in 1936. She sang Donizetti in *Captain January*, tapped to Bill Robinson's choreography in *Dimples* and held her own against Fox songbird Alice Faye in both *Poor Little Rich Girl* and this formulaic confection, which the amazing 8-year-old enlivened by speaking Chinese and doing impressions of Eddie Cantor, Al Jolson and Ginger Rogers (complete with her own Fred Astaire doll)!

## Harry Warren

Composer, 1893–1981

Harry Warren scored 92 entries on radio's *Your Hit Parade* chart between 1935 and 1950. Only Irving Berlin's 33 comes remotely close to his record. But the snobbery of critics who rank Broadway over Hollywood has derogated Warren's place in songwriting history.

A former chorister and drummer boy, with a love of Puccini, Warren worked behind the scenes at Vitagraph's Brooklyn studios before he began plugging and composing songs after World War I. With several hits already to his credit, he debuted on screen with five songs interpolated into Rodgers and Hart's *Song Of The Flame* (1930). However, he couldn't settle in California and only the Depression persuaded him to accept a pairing with **Al Dubin** on Warner Bros' *42nd Street* (1933, see Canon).

The picture helped revive the flagging musical and the pair became **Busby Berkeley**'s most dependable collaborators. Warren's ability to switch between waltz, march and slow blues kept Berkeley's ever-more elaborate routines relevant and fresh, whether in classic backstagers like *Gold Diggers Of 1933*, *Footlight Parade* (both 1933, see Canon) and *Dames* (1934) or in star vehicles for the likes of Eddie Cantor (*Roman Scandals*, 1933), Al Jolson (*Wonder Bar*, 1934, and *Go Into Your Dance*, 1935) and Dick Powell (*Twenty Million Sweethearts*, 1934, and *Hard To Get*, 1938).

In all, Warren and Dubin wrote some twenty pictures together, winning an Academy Award for "Lullaby Of Broadway" from *Gold Diggers Of 1935* (1935). But the strain of lightening the Depression with catchy, optimistic tunes took its toll on Dubin, who finally succumbed to his morphine addiction in 1945.

Having shared an Oscar nomination with **Johnny Mercer** for Louis Armstrong's "Jeepers Creepers" in *Going Places* (1938), Warren decamped to Fox, where he relieved the gloom of the war with a string of hits for the studio's major stars, Alice Faye, Betty Grable and Carmen Miranda. With **Mack Gordon**, he scored *Down Argentine Way*, *Tin Pan Alley* (both 1940), *That Night In Rio*, *Weekend In Havana* (both 1941), the Glenn Miller duo of *Sun Valley Serenade* (1941) and *Orchestra Wives* (1942), *Springtime In The Rockies* (1942), *Sweet Rosie O'Grady* and *Hello, Frisco, Hello* (both 1943).

Warren concluded his Fox stint with *The Gang's All Here* (1943) and *Billy Rose's Diamond Horseshoe* (1944) before moving on to MGM, where he reunited with Mercer for *The Harvey Girls* (1946), which included the Oscar-winning "On The Atchison, Topeka And The Santa Fe". He also enjoyed four collaborations with **Fred Astaire** – *Yolanda And The Thief* (1945, see Canon), *Ziegfeld Follies* (1946), *The Barkleys Of Broadway* (1949) and *The Belle Of New York* (1952). But he disliked the liberties the studio took with *Summer Holiday* (1948, see Canon) and *Summer Stock* (1950) and largely freelanced for the remainder of his career, racking up eleven Oscar nominations in total, thanks to songs like **Dean Martin**'s "That's Amore" from *The Caddy* (1953). In semi-retirement from the mid-1950s, Warren may never have been a critics' favourite. But this most prolific and durable of composers was respected by show people for his melodic accessibility and easy expertise.

## Esther Williams

Actor, b. 1923

The epitome of glamorous Hollywood escapism, Esther Williams' musicals were ludicrously beautiful trifles, in which water, smoke, fire, costumes, colour and chorines were ingeniously fashioned into spectacles of geometric precision, athletic prowess and pure fantasy that often recalled the diving sequences in **Leni Riefenstahl**'s *Olympia* (1938).

Williams herself had been due to compete in the 1940 Helsinki Games when they were postponed because of the war and, instead, swam alongside Johnny Weissmuller in **Billy Rose**'s 1939 *Aquacade*. She was spotted by MGM and made her screen debut in *Andy Hardy's Double Life* (1942). Her first starring role came in *Bathing Beauty* (1944) and for the remainder of the decade she was the studio's most reliable box-office star.

No one featured on the cover of more fanzines, and over the next eleven years Williams earned MGM somewhere upward of $80 million. Unsurprisingly, it built a pool for her and developed special waterproof make-up and pioneering underwater photography techniques. It even found a way to team her with the cartoon favourites Tom and Jerry in *Dangerous When Wet* (1953).

Despite the commercial success of *Fiesta*, *This Time For Keeps* (both 1947), *On An Island With You* (1948) and *Neptune's Daughter* (1949), the critics were not impressed and even the washed-up Fanny Brice could snipe, "Wet she's a star. Dry she ain't." Audiences rebelled when she spurned her one-piece costumes for the likes of *Take Me Out To The Ball Game* (1949), which was directed by **Busby Berkeley**, who later designed her extravagant routines in *Easy To Love* and the Annette Kellerman biopic, *Million Dollar Mermaid* (both 1953).

Subsequently, Williams was confined to formulaic diversions, in which her spirited independence was eventually tamed by such masterful men as **Van Johnson** (*Thrill Of A Romance*, 1945; *Easy To Wed*, 1946; *Duchess Of Idaho*, 1950) and **Howard Keel** (*Pagan Love Song*, 1950; *Texas Carnival*, 1951; *Jupiter's Darling*, 1955). But her screen career collapsed after MGM ceased making musicals in the mid-1950s.

### Take Me Out To The Ball Game
**dir Busby Berkeley, 1949, 93m**

Gene Kelly and Stanley Donen provided the story idea and handled many of the musical segments in this boisterous, if routine period saga, in which Kelly and Frank Sinatra's baseball-playing showmen compete for the attention of team boss Esther Williams. The score, by Roger Edens and Comden and Green, was pretty undistinguished. But Sinatra and Betty Garrett have fun with "It's Fate, Baby, It's Fate", while Kelly performs within himself until he unleashes a series of barrel-rolls in "The Hat My Father Wore On St Patrick's Day". Busby Berkeley never directed again.

### Million Dollar Mermaid
**dir Mervyn LeRoy, 1952, 115m**

Esther Williams is perfectly cast in this biopic of swimming sensation Annette Kellerman. But the picture belongs to Busby Berkeley, whose re-creation of the Australian star's New York Hippodrome aquacades is truly stunning. Returning to his trusty top shots and variations on line and curve, he raised Williams on a geyser above a 30ft canopy waterfall for a graceful swan dive and then had her drop 50ft from a swing into a wheel of chorines before elevating her on a platform lit by 500 sparklers. George Folsey captured the multi-coloured water and scarlet and gold smoke more tastefully than such gloriously gaudy tat deserved.

### Dangerous When Wet
**dir Charles Walters, 1953, 95m**

Esther Williams swims the English Channel to buy her Arkansas farming parents Charlotte Greenwood and William Demarest a Jersey bull in what would have been a routine vehicle, had not the "bathing beauty" joined Tom and Jerry in a composited underwater dream sequence.

### Easy To Love
**dir Charles Walters, 1953, 95m**

No one remembers Tony Martin crooning in this MGM splashfest. But who can forget the Busby Berkeley finale on

Busby Berkeley, the "Million Dollar Dance Director", used four hundred electrically controlled pots to shoot red and yellow smoke fifty feet into the air for this Esther Williams extravaganza in *Million Dollar Mermaid* (1952).

Florida's Lake Eloise, in which eighty waterskiiers carrying giant flags speed along a route flanked by geysers shooting 60ft into the air. And then there's Esther Williams being hoisted by a helicopter for an 80ft plunge into a V formation of skiers moving at 35mph – from which she emerges to shoot through a pool, wherein a hundred girls form the outline of Florida, before leaping over the heads of the orchestra into a beaming close-up. Brilliant, breathtaking madness.

# Songwriters in a minor key

Hundreds of lyricists and composers flocked to Hollywood during the Golden Age of the movie musical. Some were marquee names. But several less familiar talents also scored classic films and shows with enviable consistency.

## Frank Loesser

Songwriter, 1910–69

A lyricist turned all-round composer, the self-trained Frank Loesser wrote memorable songs for dozens of mediocre films either side of his breakthrough with "Two Sleepy People" in *Thanks For The Memory* (1938). Broadway success with *Where's Charley?* (1948/1952) and an Oscar for "Baby It's Cold Outside" from *Neptune's Daughter* (1948) punctuated a trio of **Betty Hutton** vehicles – *Perils Of Pauline* (1947), *Red, Hot And Blue* (1949) and *Let's Dance* (1950). But he closed his career more impressively, with *Hans Christian Anderson* (1952), *Guys And Dolls* (1955, see Canon) and the Pulitzer-winning *How To Succeed In Business Without Really Trying* (1961/1966).

### Hans Christian Andersen
**dir Charles Vidor, 1952, 120m**

Audiences adored this reverie about the fabled Danish storyteller (Danny Kaye) as much as the critics detested it. Samuel Goldwyn commissioned sixteen screenplays over fifteen years before settling on this fact-free excuse for such enticing Frank Loesser fairy-tale palimpsests as "The Ugly Duckling", "Thumbelina", "Inchworm" and "The King's New Clothes" and the rousing story songs, "Wonderful Copenhagen", "I'm Hans Christian Andersen" and "No Two People". Roland Petit's lengthy ballet for wife Zizi Jeanmaire is less winning, however.

### How To Succeed In Business Without Really Trying
**dir David Swift, 1967, 121m**

Robert Morse and Rudy Vallee re-created their Broadway roles in this overlooked adaptation of Frank Loesser's Pulitzer-winning satire about a window cleaner who becomes a kingpin in the World Wide Wicket Company. The occasionally staid staging of the material and the absence of several stage hits lessened its value. But "The Company Way", "Grand Old Ivy" and "Brotherhood Of Man" prove as rousing as "I Believe In You" is poignant.

## Alan Jay Lerner and Frederick Loewe

Songwriters, Lerner 1918–86, Loewe 1904–88

The Berlin-born son of the male lead in the 1905 production of *The Merry Widow*, classically trained Frederick Loewe survived by cowpoking and prizefighting before teaming with Harvard and Juilliard graduate Alan Jay Lerner in 1942. Their initial stage collaborations were unexceptional, but **Agnes De Mille**'s choreography ensured that *Brigadoon* (1947/1954) became a hit. Following Lerner's MGM moonlighting on *An American In Paris* (1951, see Canon) and *Royal Wedding* (1951), the pair came to rival **Rodgers and Hammerstein** with the integrated Broadway successes *Paint Your Wagon* (1951/1969), *My Fair Lady* (1956/1964, see Canon) and *Camelot* (1960/1966), as well as the Oscar-winning screen original, *Gigi* (1958, see Canon).

### Camelot
**dir Joshua Logan, 1967, 178m**

After years of complaining about dubbed musicals, the critics savaged this $15 million adaptation of Lerner and Loewe's 1960 Broadway sensation because neither Richard Harris (King Arthur) nor Vanessa Redgrave (Guinevere) could sing. Harris's performance was unfavourably compared to Richard Burton's, especially in his delivery of "How To Handle A Woman" and "If Ever I Should Leave You". But Joshua Logan's typically bombastic direction scarcely helped.

## Jule Styne

Composer, 1905–94

A child piano prodigy, Jule Styne entered films as a vocal coach before he began composing for B-musicals and Westerns. He earned the first of his eight Oscar nominations with *Hit Parade Of 1941* (1941), but it was his collaboration with **Sammy Cahn** on vehicles for Frank Sinatra (*Step Lively*, 1944; *Anchors Aweigh*, 1945; *It Happened In Brooklyn*, 1947) and Doris Day (*Romance On The High Seas*, 1948; *It's A Great Feeling*, 1949; *West Point Story*, 1950) that established him as a major composer. He divided his time between Hollywood and Broadway after debuting on stage with *High Button Shoes* (1947), and teaming with Leo Robin, **Comden and Green**, and Stephen Sondheim on hits like *Gentlemen Prefer Blondes* (1949/1953), *Bells Are Ringing* (1956/1960) and *Gypsy* (1959/1962). Having won an Oscar nomination with the theme tune to *Three Coins In The Fountain* (1954), he helped launch Barbra Streisand with *Funny Girl* (1968).

### Gentlemen Prefer Blondes
**dir Howard Hawks, 1953, 91m**

Jane Russell and Marilyn Monroe have a ball as Dorothy Shaw and Lorelei Lee, the gold-digging showgirls from Little Rock, in this lively take on Anita Loos' saucy classic. Teasingly choreographed by Jack Cole, Monroe's "Diamonds Are A Girl's Best Friend" is the pick of Jule Styne and Leo Robin's score, but Russell is touchingly coquettish cruising a ship gym to Hoagy Carmichael and Harold Adamson's "Ain't There Anyone Here For Love?" Russell's partnership with Jeanne Crain on *Gentlemen Marry Brunettes* (1955) proved much less amusing.

### Gypsy
**dir Mervyn LeRoy, 1962, 149m**

Once again Ethel Merman saw a Broadway *tour de force* dismissed by Hollywood, as Rosalind Russell was hired to give this game but overarching display, as the 1920s stage mother driving the careers of the young Gypsy Rose Lee and June Havoc. Natalie Wood was even more miscast in the title role. But Robert Tucker's choreography has a cheeky charm and Jule Styne and Stephen Sondheim's score contains such durable hits as "Let Me Entertain You", "Small World" and "Everything's Coming Up Roses". Bette Midler headlined Emile Ardolino's bouyant 1993 TV movie remake, which re-created Jerome Robbins' original dance routines.

## James Van Heusen

Composer, 1913–90

Best known for optimistic uptempo tunes, but equally capable of elegant romantic ballads, Jimmy Van Heusen followed the familiar path along Tin Pan Alley and the Great White Way to Hollywood. Following six **Bing Crosby** musicals with James V. Monaco, he forged a partnership with **Johnny Burke** that produced songs for six of the seven *Road To...* movies and the Oscar-winning "Swinging On A Star" from *Going My Way* (1944). In all, Van Heusen worked on 23 Crosby pictures between 1943 and 1964, by which time he and **Sammy Cahn** had begun collaborating with Frank Sinatra. In addition to some seminal album tracks, they also penned Academy winners for *The Joker Is Wild* (1957) and *A Hole In The Head* (1959).

# A touch of classical

Hollywood regularly tried to instil a little culture into its patrons. But, whether their tenors and sopranos were singing opera, operetta or sophisticated show songs, the studios were always careful to ensure that they were as easy on the eye as they were on the ear.

## Mario Lanza

Actor, 1921–59

Dubbed "the voice of the century" by Arturo Toscanini, Mario Lanza joined MGM after war service disrupted his stage career. He debuted imposingly in *That Midnight Kiss* (1949) and was re-teamed with **Kathryn Grayson** for *The Toast Of New Orleans* (1950). Lanza reached his peak in *The Great Caruso* (1951), but following *Because You're Mine* (1952), he quit *The Student Prince* (1954) – although his replacement, Edmund Purdom, was dubbed with his majestic tenor. Increasingly ill-disciplined and prone to obesity and addictions to pills and alcohol, Lanza struggled on in the unworthy vehicles *Serenade* (1956), *Seven Hills Of Rome* (1958) and *For The Last Time* (1959) before dying at 38.

### The Great Caruso

**dir Richard Thorpe, 1951, 109m**

Countless liberties were taken with the life of the Neopolitan tenor who took the New York Met by storm. But Mario Lanza was seemingly born to play legendary singer Enrico Caruso and he handles the Verdi, Donizetti and Gounod as well as "The Loveliest Night Of The Year", which was arranged for the film by Irving Aaronson and Paul Francis Webster and became Lanza's biggest hit after "Be My Love" from *The Toast Of New Orleans* (1950).

## Kathryn Grayson

Actor, b. 1922

Hired by MGM as the new Deanna Durbin, coloratura soprano Kathryn Grayson debuted in *Andy Hardy's Private Secretary* (1941). But her lead in *Seven Sweethearts* (1942) suggested that she couldn't carry a picture and she was paired with **Gene Kelly** in *Thousands Cheer* (1943) and *Anchors Aweigh* (1945) and **Frank Sinatra** in *It Happened In Brooklyn* (1947) and *The Kissing Bandit* (1948). Following *Two Sisters From Boston* (1946), producer **Joe Pasternak** twice teamed with her Mario Lanza and three times with Howard Keel, on *Show Boat* (1951), *Lovely To Look At* (1952) and *Kiss Me Kate* (1953, see Canon). She showed well in the Grace Moore biopic, *So This Is Love* (1953), but the rise of Ann Blyth limited her opportunities and she ended her career on loan for the operettas *The Desert Song* (1953) and *The Vagabond King* (1956).

## Howard Keel

Actor, 1917–2004

MGM's successor to **Nelson Eddy**, Howard Keel gained stage experience in London and New York before making an immediate screen impact with his unique brand of swaggering charm in *Annie Get Your Gun* (1950, see Canon). His rendition of "Anything You Can Do" with **Betty Hutton** became a classic and further hits followed *Show Boat* (1951). Despite the success of *Calamity Jane* (1953), *Kiss Me Kate* (1953, see Canon) and *Seven Brides For Seven Brothers* (1954, see Canon), the musical's Golden Age was waning and Keel took his swan song in *Kismet* (1955). Although he remained a stage favourite, features like *The Day Of The Triffids* (1962) and *The War Wagon* (1967) were few and far between. However, he did return to the limelight in the TV soap, *Dallas* (1981–91).

## Jane Powell

Actor, b. 1929

Signed by MGM from radio at 15, Jane Powell embarked upon a series of adolescent frivolities for the **Pasternak Unit**, including *Holiday In Mexico* (1946), *Three Daring Daughters*, *A Date With Judy* (both 1948), *Nancy Goes To Rio* and *Two Weeks With Love* (both 1951). She stepped up in class for *Royal Wedding* (1951) with **Fred Astaire**, but was soon back breezing her way through *Rich, Young And Pretty* (1951), *Small Town Girl* and *Three Girls And A Sailor* (both 1953). Her stunning Durbanesque soprano and winsome personality were best employed in *Seven Brides For Seven Brothers* (1954, see Canon), but she left MGM following *Hit The Deck* (1955) and bowed out of screen musicals with the *The Girl Most Likely* (1957).

### Royal Wedding

**dir Stanley Donen, 1951, 93m**

Stanley Donen went solo on this story inspired by Adele Astaire's marriage to Lord Charles Cavendish. Jane Powell and Peter Lawford make a handsome couple. But, while she charms with Burton Lane and Alan Jay Lerner's "Too Late Now" and keeps pace with Fred Astaire on "How Could You Believe Me When I Said I Loved You When You Know I've Been A Liar All My Life", this is all about Nick Castle's ingenuity and Astaire's peerless grace, as he waltzes with a hat-stand to "Sunday Jumps" and dances on the walls and ceiling of a revolving room to "You're All The World To Me".

# The uniques

**Although singers, dancers and comics were its bedrock, vaudeville was also home to a bewildering array of speciality acts, whose diversity defied easy categorization. The film musical also delighted in showcasing these unique talents, who often acquired cult followings that still persist.**

## Sonja Henie

Actor, 1912–69

Having won Olympic gold in three consecutive Winter Games from 1928, Norwegian skater Sonja Henie arrived in Hollywood off the back of a sell-out icecapade. She made eight of her thirteen features at Fox, starting with *One In A Million* (1936), which made so much money that the studio built her own outdoor rink. Pert and peppy, Henie was aware of her limitations and short shelf-life and insisted on $75,000 plus percentage points for every film after *Thin Ice* (1936). *Happy Landing*, *My Lucky Star* (both 1938), *Second Fiddle* and *Everything Happens At Night* (both 1939) put her in the box-office Top 10. But while *Sun Valley Serenade* (1941), *Iceland* (1942) and *Wintertime* (1943) were just as enjoyable, her moment had passed and she returned to her ever-popular ice shows.

### Sun Valley Serenade
**dir H. Bruce Humberstone, 1941, 86m, b/w**

Sonja Henie's seventh Fox outing saw her Norwegian war refugee beat bitchy Lynn Bari to John Payne's heart. But, apart from Hermes Pan's extraordinary "black ice" finale, Henie had to play second fiddle to both the wisecracking Milton Berle and Joan Davis and the debuting Glenn Miller, whose rendition of Harry Warren and Mack Gordon's "Chattanooga Choo-Choo" is elevated to classic status by the fabulous footwork of the Nicholas Brothers and Dorothy Dandridge.

## Jimmy Durante

Actor, 1893–1980

Nicknamed "Schnozzola" on account of his bulbous nose, the enduringly popular Jimmy Durante worked as a ragtime pianist and vaudevillian before Broadway success in **Florenz Ziegfeld**'s *Show Girl* (1929) took him to Hollywood. Although MGM signed him for five years, it didn't really know how best to exploit his rasping voice and self-mocking, malapropping clowning and alternated him between musicals and comedies. Rarely rising above second banana, he had showy song spots in *Speak Easily*, *The Phantom President* (both 1932), *Palooka* (1934), *Little Miss Broadway*, *Start Cheering* (both 1938) and *Music For Millions* (1944). He later enlivened vehicles for emerging stars like June Allyson (*Two Girls And A Sailor*, 1944, and *Two Sisters From Boston*, 1946), Frank Sinatra (*It Happened In Brooklyn*, 1947) and Esther Williams (*This Time For Keeps*, 1947, and *On An Island With You*, 1948) before concentrating on stage and television work. He returned to the screen in 1962 to reprise his role in the 1935 Broadway show, *Jumbo* (1962).

## Carmen Miranda

Actor, 1909–55

Carmen Miranda had five films and three hundred recordings to her credit before brief Broadway success brought her to Hollywood for *Down Argentine Way* (1940). Mangling the language and sporting the colourful costumes, gigantic heels and floral- or fruit-trimmed bahiana headresses that had made her a Latin hit, she lit up Fox's Good Neighbour musicals *That Night In Rio* and *Weekend In Havana* (1941) before being assimilated into all-American vehicles like *Springtime In The Rockies* (1942), *Greenwich Village* and *Something For The Boys* (both 1944). The popularity of "The Brazilian Bombshell" declined following "The Lady With the Tutti-Frutti Hat" routine in *The Gang's All Here* (1943), although she was permitted a rare romantic lead in *Copacabana* (1947).

### That Night In Rio
**dir Irving Cummings, 1941, 90m**

The musical standouts of this Alice Faye and Don Ameche remake of *Folies Bergère* were Harry Warren and Mack Gordon's "I Yi Yi Yi Yi (I Like You Very Much)" and "Chica Chica Boom Chic", which Hermes Pan choreographed to bolster Carmen Miranda's reputation for scene-stealing support. Leon Shamroy and Ray Rennehan's Technicolor lensing of Richard Day and Joseph C. Wright's wondrously excessive décor makes this a kitsch treat.

# The underused

Hollywood treated African-American performers disgracefully throughout the studio era. Inevitably reduced to stereotypes, black musical stars also suffered the indignity of having their numbers shot in isolation so that they could be cut from prints destined for the Deep South. Consequently, some of the genre's most dazzling talents were scandalously marginalized.

## Bill "Bojangles" Robinson

Actor, 1878–1949

Bill Robinson began dancing at 8, although he spent a decade waiting tables before making it on the black and white vaudeville circuits. Emphasizing the feet and legs, he used personality and technique to transform tap, and his highly influential style brought black dance into the mainstream. Following Broadway success in *Blackbirds Of 1928*, Bojangles entered films with *Dixiana* (1930), and his famous "stair dance" was the highlight of *The Little Colonel* (1935), the first of four teamings with **Shirley Temple**. But Hollywood's blinkered approach to African-American performers limited his opportunities to shorts like *Harlem In Heaven* (1938) and the loosely autobiographical feature, *Stormy Weather* (1943).

### Stormy Weather

**dir Andrew L. Stone, 1943, 77m, b/w**

An African-American who's who, including Cab Calloway, Katherine Dunham and the Nicholas Brothers, was assembled for this Bill Robinson *film à clef*. But it's old Bojangles and Lena Horne who dominate proceedings, as Harlem entertainers who fall out in Memphis, only to patch up years later at a troop show. Horne's take on Harold Arlen and Ted Koehler's "Stormy Weather" is exceptional, while Fats Waller swansongs with "Ain't Misbehavin'", as he died en route to New York after the shoot.

## Ethel Waters

Actor, 1896–1977

Raised in abject poverty and first married at 12, Ethel Waters started in vaudeville at 17 as Sweet Mama Stringbean. Recording from 1921, she played the Cotton Club and Carnegie Hall and secured her Broadway reputation with shows like *Plantation Revue* (1925), *Blackbirds Of 1930* and *Stormy Weather* (1933). She also became radio's first black star and scored a huge hit with "Am I Blue?" from *On With The Show* (1929).

Colour-bound Hollywood confined her to shorts like *Rufus Jones For President* (1933) and *Bubbling Over* (1934) and guest slots in *Gift Of Gab* (1934), *Tales Of Manhattan* (1942) and *Stage Door Canteen* (1943). She even played **Jeanette MacDonald**'s maid in *Cairo* (1942). Only *Cabin In The Sky* (1943) showcased her lilting and hugely influential blend of gospel, blues and jazz to advantage, although she received an Oscar nomination for *Pinky* (1949) and further acclaim for *The Member Of The Wedding* (1952).

## The Nicholas Brothers

Actors, Fayard 1914–2006, Harold 1921–2000

The sons of musicians, Fayard and Harold Nicholas began dancing as vaudeville juveniles before becoming fixtures at the Cotton Club.

They followed the shorts *Black Network* and *Pie, Pie Blackbird* (both 1932) with a string of dazzling speciality routines, mostly choreographed by **Nick Castle**, at Fox. While they invariably stole the show in *Down Argentine Way*, *Tin Pan Alley* (both 1940), *Sun Valley Serenade*, *The Great American Broadcast* (both 1941), *Orchestra Wives* (1942) and *Stormy Weather* (1943), their contributions were usually cut for southern audiences. **Gene Kelly**, however, insisted on performing alongside them with **Judy Garland** for "Be A Clown" in *The Pirate* (1948, see Canon), but they tired of American showbiz segregation and spent much of the 1950s in Europe.

# The dependables

While many performers are indelibly linked to the musical, only a handful of directors specialized in the genre. Yet Hollywood could call on the services of a select group of filmmakers, who, for all their versatility, always seemed to be most inspired by musical subjects.

## Walter Lang

Director, Producer, 1898–1972

After a varied directorial career dating back to 1925, Walter Lang unexpectedly found his métier with the bright, brash Fox musical. Starting with *Tin Pan Alley* (1940), he directed **Betty Grable** in eight undemanding and hugely enjoyable slices of Technicolored Americana. He also guided Ethel Merman through *Call Me Madam* (1953) and the CinemaScope spectacle, *There's No Business Like Show Business* (1954), and followed **Rodgers and Hammerstein**'s screen original, *State Fair* (1945), with *The King And I* (1956, see Canon), for which he received an Oscar nomination. Ever versatile, Lang ended his association with the genre with Danny Kaye's *On The Riviera* (1951), the Jane Froman biopic, *With A Song In My Heart* (1952), and Cole Porter's *Can-Can* (1960).

**Moon Over Miami**
**dir Walter Lang, 1941, 91m, b/w**

This musicalization of *Three Blind Mice* (1938) would resurface as *Three Little Girls In Blue* (1946) and *How To Marry A Millionaire* (1953). There was nothing particularly memorable about Ralph Rainger and Leo Robin's agreeable score, but the gloriously gaudy Technicolor and Hermes Pan's choreography enlivened Betty Grable, Carole Landis and Charlotte Greenwood's attempts to snare Don Ameche, Robert Cummings and Jack Haley.

**With A Song In My Heart**
**dir Walter Lang, 1952, 117m**

One of Hollywood's better biopics, this life of Jane Froman – who continued her career despite sustaining terrible injuries in a plane crash while on a 1943 troop tour – benefits from Susan Hayward's knowing performance and Froman's full-throated dubbing of such signatures as Rodgers and Hart's title tune and the Gershwins' "Embraceable You". Hayward would draw another Oscar nomination playing Lillian Roth in *I'll Cry Tomorrow* (1955).

## Charles Walters

Director, Choreographer, 1911–82

A dancer from the mid-1930s, Charles Walters was choreographing on Broadway when he was hired by MGM. Following *Seven Days' Leave* (1942), he designed dances for such prestige pictures as *Girl Crazy* (1943), *Meet Me In St Louis* (1944, see Canon) and *Summer Holiday* (1948, see Canon) before making his full directorial bow with *Good News* (1947). His use of bold colours, unexpected angles, fluid camera movements and imaginative cutting gave his routines intuitive rhythm, spirit and style, while his sensitivity to performance endeared him to the studio's biggest stars (particularly **Judy Garland**, with whom he danced in *Presenting Lily Mars*, 1943).

Walters collaborated with Gene Kelly on *DuBarry Was A Lady* (1943) and *Summer Stock* (1950), Fred Astaire on *Easter Parade* (1948, see Canon), *The Barkleys Of Broadway* (1949) and *The Belle Of New York* (1952), Esther Williams on *Texas Carnival* (1951), *Easy To Love* and *Dangerous When Wet* (both 1953) and Leslie Caron on *Lili* (1953), for which he was Oscar nominated, and *The Glass Slipper* (1955). Following *High Society* (1956, see Canon), he subsisted on comedies, although he returned to musicals for **Billy Rose**'s *Jumbo* (1962) and *The Unsinkable Molly Brown* (1964).

### Good News

**dir Charles Walters, 1947, 95m**

Previously filmed in 1930 and once slated for Mickey Rooney and Judy Garland, DeSylva, Brown and Henderson's 1927 stage hit was revived with considerable élan by the debuting team of Charles Walters and screenwriters Betty Comden and Adolph Green. Six of the original songs were retained for this campus caper about a jock and a swot, including the spirited ensemble pieces "Lucky In Love" and "The Varsity Drag". Joan McCracken led the choreographic highlight, "Pass That Peace Pipe", which had originally been devised for Garland and Gene Kelly in *Ziegfeld Follies*.

### Lili

**dir Charles Walters, 1953, 81m**

Leslie Caron is enchanting in this Paul Gallico tale of an orphan who is wooed by the adorable marionettes controlled by crippled puppeteer Mel Ferrer. Charles Walters created her a stylized ballet with Dorothy Jarnac, but it's less memorable than Bronislau Kaper and Helen Deutsch's infectious "Hi-Lili, Hi Lo". More significantly, this became the first movie to be adapted into a Broadway show, when *Carnival* opened in 1961.

## George Sidney

Director, 1916–2002

Starting as an MGM messenger, George Sidney rose steadily through the production ranks and, after winning consecutive Oscars for best live-action short, he proved himself a steady director of both Pasternak and Freed musicals with *Thousands Cheer* (1943), *Anchors Aweigh* (1945), *The Harvey Girls* (1946), *Annie Get Your Gun* (1950, see Canon), *Show Boat* (1951) and *Kiss Me Kate* (1953, see Canon), as well as the **Esther Williams** vehicles, *Bathing Beauty* (1944) and *Jupiter's Darling* (1955). However, he struggled at Columbia with *The Eddy Duchin Story* (1956) and *Pal Joey* (1957) and with the all-star misfire, *Pepe* (1960). He bounced back with the pop duo *Bye Bye Birdie* (1963) and *Viva Las Vegas* (1964) before closing his career with *Half A Sixpence* (1968). There was little art in Sidney's musicals, but he packed song'n'dance numbers with emotional, visual and diegetic energy, which enabled performer and viewer alike to immerse themselves in the routine.

### Bye Bye Birdie

**dir George Sidney, 1963, 112m**

A debuting Dick Van Dyke re-created his 1960 Broadway role in this peppy rock parody, inspired by Elvis's induction into the army. However, his henpecked press agent is blown off the screen by Ann-Margret, as Conrad Birdie's biggest fan. "Put On A Happy Face", "Kids" and "A Lotta Livin' To Do" are the pick of Charles Strouse and Lee Adams' score, although Onna White's staging of "The Telephone Hour" and the "Sultan's Ballet" catch the eye.

## Stanley Donen

Director, Choreographer, Producer, b. 1924

Stanley Donen was a chorus boy when he met **Gene Kelly** during the Broadway run of *Pal Joey* (1940). Having choreographed *Best Foot Forward* (1941) together, Donen came to Hollywood to assist Kelly on *Cover Girl* (1944) and they subsequently shared the story credit on *Take Me Out To The Ball Game* (1949) and the directing chores on *On The Town* (1949, see Canon), *Singin' In The Rain* (1952, see Canon) and *It's Always Fair Weather* (1955). The success of his solo venture, *Royal Wedding* (1951), led to *Give A Girl A Break* (1953) and the **Sigmund Romberg** biopic, *Deep In My Heart* (1954). But Donen enjoyed his greatest success with *Seven Brides For Seven Brothers* (1954, see Canon), which epitomized his gift for using the camera to capture the energy of a performance and the essence and emotion of a number. However, such was the state of the genre that he managed only four more solo musicals – *Funny Face*, *The Pajama Game* (both 1957, see Canon), *Damn Yankees* (1958) and *The Little Prince* (1974) – although he acclimatized quickly and successfully to other genres.

### Damn Yankees

**dir George Abbott, Stanley Donen, 1958, 110m**

Gwen Verdon, Ray Walston and Jean Stapleton reprised their Broadway roles for this lively adaptation of Richard Adler and Jerry Ross' 1955 smash, while Tab Hunter was drafted to play the Washington Senators' baseball fan transmogrified into star player via Faustian pact with Walston's Mr Applegate. The score suits the storyline admirably, but hits were at a premium beside Verdon's showstopper "Whatever Lola Wants", the "Two Lost Souls" ballet, and her duet with choreographer Bob Fosse on "Who's Got The Pain"

# The bright sparks

Youthful exuberance was always a key component of the movie musical. Indeed, a little genial eagerness could even compensate for any deficiencies in the acting, singing or dancing departments.

## June Allyson

Actor, 1917–2006

The husky-voiced June Allyson arrived in Hollywood to reprise her Broadway role in *Best Foot Forward* (1943). Initially seen as MGM's answer to Betty Hutton, she was frequently teamed with **Van Johnson** and became the studio's girl-next-door in musicals like *Girl Crazy* (1943), *Two Girls And A Sailor*, *Music For Millions* (both 1944), *Two Sisters From Boston* (1946) and *Good News* (1947). She delivered a standout rendition of "Thou Swell" in *Words And Music* (1948), but spent the 1950s as the perfect wife, most notably in *The Glenn Miller Story* (1954). Later musicals, *The Opposite Sex* and *You Can't Run Away From It* (both 1956), proved lacklustre.

### The Glenn Miller Story

**dir Anthony Mann, 1954, 116m**

Joe Yukl dubs James Stewart's trombone playing in this formulaic, but sincere biopic about a musician searching for his distinctive swing sound. The real musical hot spot was Louis Armstrong and Gene Krupa's jam on "Basin Street Blues", although there won't be a dry eye as June Allyson listens to "Little Brown Jug" over the radio at the anachronistic denouement.

## Betty Hutton

Actor, 1921–2007

Band singer and Broadway starlet Betty Hutton made an immediate impact in Paramount's *The Fleet's In* (1942). Nicknamed the "Blonde Bombshell", she was considered effervescent or overbearing according to taste. But she boosted wartime morale in such musicals as *Star Spangled Rhythm* (1942), *Here Come The Waves* (as twins), *And The Angels Sing* (both 1944), *The Stork Club* (1945) and the **Preston Sturges** comedy, *The Miracle Of Morgan's Creek* (1944). In between the biopics *Incendiary Blonde* (1945), *The Perils Of Pauline* (1947) and *Somebody Loves Me* (1952), Hutton enthusiastically headlined *Red, Hot And Blue* (1949) and *Annie Get Your Gun* (1950, see Canon) and teamed with Fred Astaire on *Let's Dance* (1950). But her career collapsed amidst contractual wrangles following *The Greatest Show On Earth* (1952).

## Donald O'Connor

Actor, 1925–2003

In vaudeville as an infant and established in films after *Sing, You Sinners* (1938), Donald O'Connor was the embodiment of the song'n'dance man. Yet he spent most of his career in B-musicals, as Universal sought to turn him and **Peggy Ryan** into a budget Judy Garland and Mickey Rooney team in the likes of *Chip Off The Old Block* and *The Merry Monahans* (both 1944). Despite a scene-stealing turn in Deanna Durbin's *Something In The Wind* (1947), he was best known as the sidekick of *Francis The Talking Mule* when he was cast in *Singin' In The Rain* (1952, see Canon). High-profile parts in *I Love Melvin, Call Me Madam* (both 1953), *There's No Business Like Show Business* (1954) and *Anything Goes* (1956) followed, but he never topped the extraordinary comic athleticism of his sublime "Make 'Em Laugh" routine.

## Debbie Reynolds

Actor, b. 1932

Ex-beauty queen Debbie Reynolds had a million seller to her credit – "Aba Daba Honeymoon" from *Two Weeks With Love* (1950) – when she landed the role of a lifetime in *Singin' In The Rain* (1952, see Canon). She exuded the same ebullient charm in *I Love Melvin* and *The Affairs Of Dobie Gillis* (both 1953). But Reynolds always possessed more comic timing than musical ability and the harder she tried in *Give A Girl A Break* (1953), *Athena* (1954), *Hit The Deck* (1955) and *Bundle Of Joy* (1956, opposite singer-husband **Eddie Fisher**), the better suited she seemed to vehicles like *Susan Slept Here* (1954) and *Tammy And The Bachelor* (1957). She drew an Oscar nomination for *The Unsinkable Molly Brown* (1964), but her screen musical career ended ignominiously with *The Singing Nun* (1966).

### The Unsinkable Molly Brown

**dir Charles Walters, 1964, 128m**

Debbie Reynolds acts up a storm in this MGM adaptation of Meredith Willson's 1960 show about a Colorado foundling struggling for acceptance in Denver society, after husband Herve Presnell uncovers a gold mine. It's old-fashioned and self-conscious stuff. But Peter Gennaro's choreography on "Belly Up To The Bar, Boys" and "He's My Friend" adds zest to a fact-based tale, whose title comes from an episode aboard the *Titanic*.

# The dancing queens

**Hollywood mostly viewed its female dancing stars as potential partners for Fred Astaire and Gene Kelly. Consequently, their athleticism, elegance and versatility hasn't always been fully appreciated.**

## Rita Hayworth

Actor, 1918–87

Rita Hayworth was **Ginger Rogers**' cousin. She began dancing at six and, under her own name, Margarita Cansino, partnered her famous father, Eduardo, before becoming a Latin typecast in some 25 B-pictures. Her luck changed at Columbia, where the non-musicals *Only Angels Have Wings* (1939) and *Blood And Sand* (1941) persuaded mogul **Harry Cohn** that he had a star on his hands. He hired **Fred Astaire** to partner Hayworth in *You'll Never Get Rich* (1941) and *You Were Never Lovelier* (1942) and **Gene Kelly** for *Cover Girl* (1944). But while she exuded elegance and grace opposite such peerless performers, she was less effective in *My Gal Sal* (1942) and *Tonight And Every Night* (1945). She was memorably dubbed for "Put The Blame On Mame" in *Gilda* (1946) and "The Heat Is On" in *Miss Sadie Thompson* (1953), and Jo Ann Garner's polite phrasing jarred with Hayworth's sizzling routines to "Bewitched, Bothered And Bewildered" and the "Zip" striptease in *Pal Joey* (1957).

### You Were Never Lovelier

**dir William A. Seiter, 1942, 97m, b/w**

Fred Astaire reteamed with Rita Hayworth for this gossamer story about a gambling dancer wooing the choosy oldest daughter of Buenos Aires hotelier Adolphe Menjou. He waited 45 minutes to dance, but Jerome Kern and Johnny Mercer's score eventually afforded several opportunities for charming duets ("Dearly Beloved", "I'm Old Fashioned" and the title song), as well as the rousing foot-tapper, "The Shorty George".

### Cover Girl

**dir Charles Vidor, 1944, 107m**

Rita Hayworth was the nominal star of this flashbacking story of a Brooklyn club dancer who emulates her grandmother's rejection of the high life for love. But, while she holds her own on such Jerome Kern and Ira Gershwin numbers as "Make Way For Tomorrow" and "Long Ago And Far Away", this plush Columbia bibelot was more significant for the emergence of Gene Kelly as a dancer-choreographer, most notably in the "Alter Ego" number, in which he challenge dances with his reflection in a shop window.

## Lucille Bremer

Actor, 1917–96

Having danced with the Philadelphia Opera Company and as a Rockette at Radio City Music Hall, the redheaded Lucille Bremer had only minor Broadway roles in *Panama Hattie* (1940) and *Lady In The Dark* (1941) to her credit when **Arthur Freed** decided to groom her for stardom. She started well, as Judy Garland's older sister in *Meet Me In St Louis* (1944, see Canon), and then excelled as **Fred Astaire**'s partner in "This Heart Of Mine" and "Limehouse Blues" in *Ziegfeld Follies* (1946). But her second teaming with Astaire, *Yolanda And The Thief* (1945, see Canon), proved a critical and commercial disappointment (although it has since been significantly reappraised). Following *Till The Clouds Roll By* (1946), Freed let Bremer go and she retired on her marriage to a Mexican millionaire after three poor pictures at Eagle-Lion.

Rita Hayworth was sufficiently light on her feet twice to keep pace with Fred Astaire, but her singing was always dubbed by such unsung vocalists as Anita Ellis, Jo Ann Greer and Nan Wynn.

## Vera-Ellen

Actor, 1926–81

Fresh from The Rockettes, Vera-Ellen figured in a clutch of Broadway shows before **Samuel Goldwyn** brought her to Hollywood for **Danny Kaye**'s *Wonder Man* (1945) and *The Kid From Brooklyn* (1946). The studio made few musicals and, so, Fox borrowed her for *Three Little Girls In Blue* (1946) and *Carnival In Costa Rica* (1947). Fortunately, MGM had bigger plans for her and she shone opposite Gene Kelly in "Slaughter On Tenth Avenue" in *Words And Music* (1948) and as Miss Turnstiles in *On The Town* (1949, see Canon). She then co-starred with Fred Astaire in *Three Little Words* (1950) and *The Belle Of New York* (1952). *Call Me Madam* (1953) and the Kaye reunion, *White Christmas* (1954), were made on loan to Fox and Paramount respectively, and Vera-Ellen made her last musical, *Let's Be Happy* (1957) – as she had *Happy Go Lovely* (1951) – in Britain.

### Wonder Man
**dir H. Bruce Humberstone, 1945, 98m**

Danny Kaye is an acquired taste, but his distinctive knack for musical farce was perfectly suited to this story of a murdered showman whose mischievously vengeful spirit possesses his bookish brother. Virginia Mayo and a debuting Vera-Ellen just about keep pace, as Kaye hurtles through such Sylvia Fine set pieces as a sneezing version of "Otchi Tchorniya" and the brilliantly parodic "Opera Number", which also manages to be germane to the plot.

### The Belle Of New York
**dir Charles Walters, 1952, 82m**

Swapping Hugh Morton/Gustaf Kerker's score for nine songs by Harry Warren and Johnny Mercer, Arthur Freed and Charles Walters made a decent fist of this story of a marriage-shy playboy who falls for a Salvation Army belle. Fred Astaire and Vera-Ellen dance delightfully with the changing seasons on "Thank You Mr Currer, Thank You Mr Ives" and the city's rooftops on "Seeing's Believing". But, ever the perfectionist, Astaire had to repeat his sand shuffle to "I'm A Dancin' Man" because he disliked his costume and the contrasting takes are included in *That's Entertainment III* (1994).

## The ladies of the chorus

The chorus is the unsung star of the Hollywood musical. Whether singing or dancing, **chrous girls** added vigour and spectacle to routines in every period of the genre's history. In the early days, the chorus line provided risqué glamour in the grand Ziegfeldian manner and **Busby Berkeley** cinematized these tableaux for Depression-era audiences. But the rise of the integrated musical, with its public performance and dream ballets, meant that the chorines had to be more than merely statuesque décor. They had to be able to dance rather than pose, and so **specialized dance troupes** replaced the showgirls, who drifted off into extra work, modelling and burlesque.

Betty Grable, Virginia Bruce, Lucille Ball, Lynn Bari and Paulette Goddard all started out in the chorus, but they had their sights set on stardom. Berkeley, however, could count on what amounted to his own *corps de chorus*, which included such **Hollywood pin-ups** as Dottie Coonan, Mary Dees, Sheila Ray, Adele Lacy, Lynn Bailey and Mary Cassidy, as well as his **close-up favourites** Melba Marshall, Eleanor Bailey, Lois Lindsay, Ethelreda Leopold, Gwen Seeger and Vicki Benton.

Competition for spots in Berkeley's ensemble was intense, with 723 women auditioning for just three parts in one *Gold Diggers* picture. Chorus chores were also hard work, with **exhausting rehearsals** being followed by prolonged shoots, which frequently entailed lots of late nights and early mornings. When they weren't on set, the chorines spent hours in dance studios and gyms in the hope of catching a casting director's eye. And many often had to resort to less lucrative stints at Central Casting or to **escorting bachelor stars** to premieres and nightclubs. Some chorines married well within the industry, but the majority had to settle for a more mundane existence and some **marvellous memories**.

# Puttin' On The Ritz: how musicals work

Arthur Freed and Nacio Herb Brown with Anita Page and Bessie Love, who played "Harmony Babies" Queenie and "Hank" Mahoney in MGM's first talkie, *The Broadway Melody* (1929).

# Puttin' On The Ritz: how musicals work

Musicals may appear to be effortless and accessible entertainments, but the classical Hollywood style is based on fixed rules developed for, and unique to, the genre. They apply to masterpieces and second features alike, and viewing pleasure can only be enhanced by knowing something more about the conventions bracing the escapist façade.

## Musical duality

Musicals are often criticized for having flimsy and formulaic plotlines, but narrative flow is not the genre's primary concern. The musical is not subject to the single-hero focus or the causal-chronological progression essential to other genres. Instead, **everything revolves around lovers**. The lure of the musical derives from the oppositional aspects of the sweethearts, and the way these are resolved by the song-and-dance routines establishes the structure and meaning of the film.

**Romance** is the musical's stock situation, but psychology, motivation and suspense are less important than the contrasting behaviour of the male and female leads. Consequently, shots are composed and arranged not in a linear sequence, but in parallel pairs that draw attention to the similarities and differences of the characters who will eventually become the **pivotal lovers**.

Indeed, such is the bond between the twosome that they're often linked in the audience's mind by similar or oppositional actions (such as a song, an event, an attitude, a prop, a location or a camera angle) even before they meet, and this **duality** is infinitely more crucial than linearity in understanding musical mechanics.

The interest lies, therefore, not in whether the stars will get together (because it's inevitable that they will), but in how love will find its way. The protagonists invariably come from different class or cultural backgrounds, and upon first meeting, discrepancies of age, morality, ambition, attitude to life, or approach to love/sex conspire to keep them apart. However, they're sufficiently intrigued by each other to make **tentative compromises**. He, frequently the lower-born of the two, gradually confounds her first impressions by displaying unexpected gentility, while she reveals a passion that is initially suppressed beneath her demure exterior. There were gender reversals, including *Living In A Big Way* (1947) and *Gentlemen Prefer Blondes* (1953), but they were rare.

The song and dance routines spring from these sociopsychological tensions. They establish the couple's personality traits and highlight areas of disparity and similitude. Moreover, as there was no pre-marital canoodling for much of the musical's heyday, solos and duets became **courtship rituals** that persuaded the hero and heroine that they were made for each other. Thus, it's character rather than narrative contrivance that drives the story, which usually involves a common enterprise that can only come to fruition if **true love prevails**.

As it seeks to show how seemingly irreconcilable characteristics and themes – freedom/order, tradition/progress, work/entertainment, passion/romance – can be harmonized, the musical depends primarily on duality. It suggests a very **conservative world-view** in sociopolitical terms (which posits that marriage is the only suitable reward for men and women seeking either beauty, riches or security), but where structure and meaning are concerned, it's pretty radical in comparison with other genres. Of course, not every musical operates along quite the same lines. But, as Rick Altman identified in his pioneering and masterly work of genre theory, *The American Film Musical*, the majority have sufficient shared characteristics in their structure and style to identify certain core procedures.

## Plot

Where the structure of a Hollywood musical is concerned, simultaneity and similarity matter more than psychological motivation and temporal flow. Contrasting and paralleling of the key signifiers (see box on p.252) was done rather blatantly in the operettas of **Jeanette MacDonald** and **Nelson Eddy**, and not much more subtly in the musical comedies of **Fred Astaire** and **Ginger Rogers**. But Vincente Minnelli, for example, disguised the links in *An American In Paris* (1951, see Canon), so that it wasn't quite so obvious at the outset that **Gene Kelly** and **Leslie Caron** were better suited together than with Nina Foch and Georges Guétary, respectively. However, where all these films coincide is in their foregrounding of couples. Indeed, where the American musical is concerned, **the couple is the plot**.

Such was the centrality of twosomes that many musicals included **secondary pairings**. Some provided comic relief from the main romance, such as Lupino Lane and Lillian Roth in *The Love Parade* (1929, see Canon), and Edward Everett Horton and Helen Broderick in *Top Hat* (1935, see

Canon). Others took the form of **romantic rivalries**, like those between Marilyn Monroe and Jane Russell in *Gentlemen Prefer Blondes*, and Bing Crosby and Frank Sinatra in *High Society* (1956, see Canon). Three couples contrasted in *Meet Me In St Louis* (1944, see Canon), *On The Town* (1948, see Canon) and *Bye Bye Birdie* (1963), while *Seven Brides For Seven Brothers* (1954, see Canon) speaks for itself.

In the case of **child stars** like Shirley Temple, Deanna Durbin and Judy Garland, when romance couldn't be an issue, they were teamed with mentor figures who became confidants or co-conspirators in their bids to conquer adversity or find new paramours for their widowed parents or older siblings. Such cupidic tactics also worked for **comedy partnerships** like the Marx Brothers, Laurel and Hardy, and Abbott and Costello, who rarely had love interests of their own, yet were frequently instrumental in matchmaking their singing co-stars.

Although she's just as keen to snag a millionaire as Marilyn Monroe, Jane Russell asks "Ain't There Anyone Here For Love?" in the gym of a luxury liner in *Gentlemen Prefer Blondes* (1953).

Lovers also frequently found themselves in opposition because of the film's thematic preoccupations. These almost inevitably revolved around the clash between either the work ethic and the pleasure principle or between high art and popular entertainment. In films as different as *Yolanda And The Thief* (1945, see Canon), *The Music Man* (1962), *My Fair Lady* (1962, see Canon) and *The Sound Of Music* (1965, see Canon) the central attraction is forged between a staid character and a free spirit, with the first's

# Musical matchmaking

It's popularly believed that musicals don't have any profound meaning – they're simply slices of escapist entertainment. But because of the deft use of **repetition**, even viewers who don't want to delve too deeply for significance will be exposed to the message. While the stars and their contexts may have changed from film to film, the basic format of dual focus and the triumph of love (complete with the implied promise of marital bliss) remained consistent. This was achieved by reflecting the **male–female duality** in the five principal aspects of the film:

**Setting** Art directors consciously paralleled or contrasted the rooms that lovers inhabited, either individually or together. Domiciles and dressing rooms, fashions and furnishings **echoed and clashed** with each other, as the sets and locations were employed to reinforce the couple's competing or complementary characteristics (with the emphasis usually being on his virility and her domesticity).

**Shot selection** Lovers were most easily paired off in a **two-shot**, in which our hero and heroine form one of many couples within the frame (as in "The Carioca" in *Flying Down To Rio*, 1933), though solo or group solo shots were just as useful when similarly balanced. Consequently, the most effective sequences in musicals were those that intercut between solo and duet shots to provide visual balance.

**Song** As the Hollywood formula dictated that the lovers spent more time circling each other than courting, the sung solo carried much of the genre's musical and **emotional burden**. But solos were rarely left in isolation. A song started by one lover, for example, would often be continued by the other or reprised later in the action. Similarly, a melody associated with one devotee would crop up as background music in a scene featuring their partner. Another recurrent tactic was to provide the lovers with **balancing songs**, such as Gene Kelly's "Nina" and Judy Garland's "Mack The Black" in *The Pirate* (1948, see Canon).

The **duet** implied a romantic culmination and was reserved for momentous encounters and the finale. There were two basic styles of duet. In the first, the lovers sang alternate verses, as in "If I Loved You" from *Carousel* (1956, see Canon), while another **echo technique** saw them responding line by line, as in "Anything You Can Do" in *Annie Get Your Gun* (1950, see Canon). By the 1950s, the studios resorted to more gimmicky compositions, such as splitting the screen into quarters for the tandem rehearsal number featuring Bing Crosby, Donald O'Connor, Mitzi Gaynor and Zizi Jeanmaire in *Anything Goes* (1956).

**Dance** Something of an exception to the duality rule, individual dance routines weren't always matched. Fred Astaire and Gene Kelly's **solos**, for example, were as much designed to showcase their agility and artistry as provide character insight (although they sometimes did both). But their female co-stars were rarely accorded their own dance spots to maintain the dual focus. Yet dance still served a strong psychological and physical purpose, as passion inspires the lovers to become **perfect partners** who would rather join together than dance alone.

**Personality** Mutually irreducible throughout, musicals also relied on the personality of the stars or the characters they play to sustain the **sexual tension** between lovers. Jeanette MacDonald's sophisticated soprano contrasted with Maurice Chevalier's *chansonnier* insouciance, while Mickey Rooney's energetic enthusiasm was tempered by Judy Garland's vulnerable reticence. Among dancers, Gene Kelly's athletic bravura was offset by Leslie Caron's balletic fragility, while Fred Astaire's ballroom polish was complemented by Cyd Charisse's vampish elegance.

sense of responsibility juxtaposed with the last's more reckless charm. Alternatively, in *Little Miss Broadway* (1938) and *The Band Wagon* (1953, see Canon), show people respectively win out over the Establishment and theatrical pomposity.

Such **thematic oppositions** added complexity to the plot of the musical. Yet they also enhanced the audience's sense of satisfaction, as viewers saw barriers familiar from their own daily or filmic experience being broken down. Moreover, by setting itself against work and highbrow culture, the Hollywood musical was consistently justifying its own existence, demonstrating that while labour is laudable and art admirable, it's **entertainment** that's the key to life.

Whatever the setting or theme, compositional or choreographical style, the musical demonstrates time and again that **opposites attract**, and that the best partnerships are forged through mutual individuality. Such liaisons proved so

"The Carioca" in *Flying Down To Rio* (1933) was choreographed by Dave Gould, who won the first Oscar in the short-lived category for best dance direction.

central to the Hollywood variety because they typified the twin American tenets of freedom and order: just as the musical's romantic couples find a way to unite, so do their disparate worlds meld together for mutual benefit. The denouement of a musical is a symbol of the **American Dream**, as it showed how everyone could rub along regardless of race, creed, age or class (although there were some notable exceptions). Yet, while all the story's surface problems appear to have been smoothed out by the sealing kiss, the audience rarely got to see the supposed happy ever after. This is because the film had striven so hard to establish marriage as the ideal that it would tarnish the illusion if post-nuptial ennui (let alone infidelity or problem children) was allowed to intrude. The musical might have been permitted a measure of counter-cultural latitude, but it had its **conservative civic duties**, too.

## Style

All films actually work because of a duality – ie people sitting in the dark are prepared to lose themselves in the lives of figures on an illuminated screen. But, while there is a divide between the auditorium and the *mise-en-scène*, it is uniquely bridged in musicals by the fact that both the audience and the characters dwell in their own recognizable realities, from which they can find mutual release in a song or dance routine that reflects their **shared aspirations** and dreams. The musical, more than any other genre, trades on the contrasts between life and art, reality and the imagined, and the experienced and the idealized in order to lead the viewer away from the daily grind into a world of stylization, beauty and rhythm.

In early **backstage stories**, the showstopping production numbers provided both the hard-working artistes and the Depression-struck audience with an **escape** from drudgery. But from the 1940s, dreams provided similar breaks from reality and allowed both characters and viewers to indulge in a shared sense of fantasy. Fantastical sets offered another way to evade the humdrum, such as the Art Deco interiors that epitomized the elegance of the Astaire-Rogers vehicles. However, as film assumed a greater **authenticity** (born of wartime experience), more plausible reasons had to be found to transcend reality, including hypnotism (*The Pirate*, 1948, see Canon), intoxication (*Summer Holiday*, 1948, see Canon), psychoanalysis (*Lady In The Dark*, 1944) and reincarnation (*On A Clear Day You Can See Forever*, 1970).

But while it was important for musicals to achieve credible visual transits from the real to the ideal, it was even more crucial to ensure a smooth passage between words and music, sound and song. In order to accomplish this, the film musical had to abandon its trademark duality during musical passages to realize a **unified soundtrack**.

In an ordinary film, sounds made within the world of the story (eg ambient sound, dialogue, prop noises, etc) are recorded on one track, while the score is confined to another. But in a musical, the music is part of the film's reality and it takes precedence over any background noises in order to heighten the sense of fantasy it creates. Sometimes, however, the song and sound tracks are merged – most notably when environmental noise augments the lyrics – as the fusion strengthens the link between the idyllic and the everyday. This admixure is reinforced by what Rick Altman calls an **audio dissolve**, which enables a smooth transition from conversation to the first lines of the lyric and thence to the full orchestral accompaniment. Such transitions take us to the **magical place** in musicals where anything is possible and reality becomes the ideal.

The easiest way to present a song was to stage it in a performance setting, like a theatre, nightclub, radio station or movie studio. However, it proved trickier to introduce off-screen orchestral and/or choral accompaniment in a supposedly "real life" situation. The most frequently used tactic was to have the singer accompanied by a visible source of sound – like an instrument – before the off-screen musicians joined in. But others employed more delicate means to blur the line between reality and fantasy. **Fred Astaire**, for example, frequently slipped from narrative to song by either increasing the musicality of his speech or emphasizing the rhythm of his gait. Others crossed the divide by humming or whistling the opening bars of the melody, among them **Gene Kelly** in *Singin' In The Rain* (1952, see Canon), whose puddle-jumping routine to the title track even proceeded to reverse the audio dissolve gambit by allowing normality to resume as the orchestration tailed off.

Even the film's language and spatial organization are affected by this transformation. The everyday dialogue is replaced by rhyming, rhythmical lyrics, while the seemingly casual placement of people and props within the frame takes on a new formal order that responds solely to the prompting of the music.

Just as the musical relies on rhythm to provide a link between the realistic and the romantic through the audio dissolve, it also requires a visual equivalent. Altman calls this a **video dissolve**, as it uses the established filmic segue of superimposing images to condense, coincide or recapture past events either to reinforce those in the present or to anticipate those still to come. The video dissolve had a technical and a thematic function. It was often used to link an image in the opening credits with the film's setting, as in *Meet Me In St Louis*, when a monochrome tintype transforms into the first Technicolor view of the Smith family residence. Similar **transitions** were employed to summon up reminiscences (*Maytime*, 1937, and *Cover Girl*, 1944) or introduce idealized memories (*Till The Clouds Roll By*, 1946) or shared memories (*Paint Your Wagon*, 1969). They could also compress time – such as that between the discarding of Jack Buchanan's Faustian drama and the triumph of Fred Astaire's revue in *The Band Wagon* – or separate an anticipatory climactic coda from the remainder of the action, as in *The Harvey Girls* (1946) and *Singin' In The Rain*.

The audio and the visual dissolve are crucial to the musical, as they preserve the conceptual separation between such categories as soundtracks, shots and levels of reality, while also establishing conceptual continuation between the ideal and the real. But unless the romantic leads undergo what Altman calls a **personality dissolve**, then the audiovisual ingenuity will count for nothing. The personality dissolve occurs because the repressed nature of one lover's personality proves compatible with a complementary characteristic in the beloved. In *High, Wide And Handsome* (1937, see Canon), for example, this meant that **Irene Dunne**'s nomadic resourcefulness echoed **Randolph Scott**'s love of the land, while in *Funny Face* (1957, see Canon) Fred Astaire's pragmatic photographer found a Paris match with Audrey Hepburn's idealistic intellectual. This **attraction of opposites** occurs because somewhere along the way, one character gets the inkling that the other completes them – either during a song, a dance, a dream or a

## Gotta sing, gotta dance

It's one of the paradoxes of the movie musical that so contrived, controlled and wholly artificial a format as the song should be used to express spontaneous and **intimate emotions**, as well as long-suppressed aspirations. It's a wonder that audiences ever bought into such audiovisual sleight of hand, especially as the on-screen performer was invariably**lip-synching** to a pre-recorded track (which had frequently been dubbed by a professional singer). What's more, characters were always note perfect; they never got out of breath when they sang and danced simultaneously; and they sounded equally loud and clear whether they were depicted in long shot or close-up.

No one appeared to question where the **ambient sound** disappeared to for the duration of the routine. Indeed, viewers seemed happy to accept that not only could bystanders in the majority of musical sequences hear the same accompaniment as the singer – even though they were supposed to be inhabiting a real world and there was no sign of an orchestra – but that they also instinctively knew the melody and frequently joined in the chorus. There were rare exceptions, however – in *Singin' In The Rain* (1952, see Canon) neither the cop watching **Gene Kelly** splashing along the street nor the soaked soul to whom he gives his umbrella seem aware of the fact that they're participants in a glorious song-and-dance number.

This disregard for aural, spatial and narrative logic was worthy of the *nouvelle vague* – at its most subversive. No wonder Anna Karina and Jean-Paul Belmondo declare their desire to be in "a musical by Gene Kelly" in **Jean-Luc Godard**'s *Une femme est une femme* (*A Woman Is A Woman*, 1961). Yet such seeming anomalies were all part of the musical's grand design to impart the ideal into the real. Consequently, no one batted an eyelid when total strangers burst into song in the unlikeliest settings. In no other genre were the imagery and characterization so led by the soundtrack, and it's the musical's ability to persuade viewers to accept such **filmic ethereality** that remains its most unsung achievement.

seduction sequence (that invariably ends with the seducee returning to their senses and, thus, postponing the clinch until the finale).

Another means of gauging emotions was for the lovers to create a piece of make-believe in which they could assess the other's suitability without making a formal declaration, as in **Fred'n'Ginger**'s "Let's Call The Whole Thing Off" banter in *Shall We Dance* (1937, see Canon). Indeed, dance was another means of sounding out feelings (although we know love is almost inevitably in the air from the moment the female lead duets with either Kelly or Astaire). The sweethearts could also discover that they share an ideal place, such as a cottage, a ranch or farm, a castle or palace, an exotic utopia, a fantasy realm or even a stage or film set. Yet a compromise always has to be made before they can meet as soul mates in this **wonderland** and fulfil their dreams – just as the viewer has to surrender the preconceptions and preoccupations of daily life for the musical to fully weave its spell.

# Musical sub-genres

The musical plays on our fixation with other people, places and periods. It recognizes that we're suckers for **glamour**, illusion, romance and **nostalgia** and, so, its main sub-genres give us lashings of each. The perspicacious Rick Altman has designated the main three divisions as the fairy-tale musical, the show musical and the folk musical. Many of the films from the genre's early years (before it had fully established its credentials) and also from its fifty-year slide into near-torpor (when it seemed bent on deconstructing itself out of existence) don't fit easily (if at all) into these categories. But the majority of Hollywood musicals produced between 1933 and 1957 most certainly qualify.

## The fairy-tale musical

The first musicals were largely aimed at a female audience and sought to trade on the success of silent melodramas featuring the likes of **Rudolph Valentino** and Roman Novarro, which linked imperilled innocents with **exotic lovers**. Law breaking and rebellion symbolized masculine sexual potency, and heroines seemingly longed to be mastered by such manly men (who often masked their machismo with weak alter egos).

Such **Beauty and the Beast storylines** suggested that while the male was driven by his lusts, the female was only waiting for the moment to surrender to her own. Hence, many early musicals (most of which owed much to operetta, see p.7) centred on flawed fellows (*The Desert Song* and *The Vagabond Lover*, both 1929), military men (*Bride Of The Regiment*, 1930, and *Kiss Me Again*, 1931), Latin lotharios (*Rio Rita*, 1929, and *Cuban Love Song*, 1931) and historical heroes (*The Rogue Song* and *Song Of The Flame*, both 1930).

The emphasis shifted on to more universally accessible and infinitely more sophisticated romantic comedies in the wake of **Ernst Lubitsch**'s *The Love Parade* and **Rouben Mamoulian**'s *Love Me Tonight* (1932, see Canon). These **Ruritanian fantasies** started out by allowing spectators in on jokes made at the expense of characters unable to see past their own prejudices. But once the audience had grasped both the basic situation and the traits of the divided lovers, the reliance on such detaching devices as irony, parody and innuendo was replaced by a combination of illusionism, emotionalism and the story's primary themes in order to win us over to the stars' cause.

*Love Me Tonight* also established the convention by which a character leaves an everyday existence to find fulfilment in a **fantasy world**. Numerous variations were wrought on this theme over the years. The town-and-country gambit recurred in, among others, *A Damsel In Distress* (1937), *Holiday Inn* (1942) and *White Christmas* (1954). An exotic resort was concocted for *The Gay Divorcee* (1934), *Monte Carlo* (1930) and *Moon Over Miami* (1941). A European destination served in *Gold Diggers In Paris* (1938), *Royal Wedding* (1951) and *Call Me Madam* (1953) and a **Latin American locale** in *Flying Down To Rio* (1933), *Weekend In Havana* (1941) and *Yolanda And The Thief*. An historical setting was summoned up for *New Moon* (1940), *A Connecticut Yankee In King Arthur's Court* (1949) and *Where Do We Go From Here?* (1945), while imaginary lands were devised for *The Wizard*

With her extravagant costumes and effervescent personality, Carmen Miranda personified the Latin spirit in such 1940s Hollywood musicals as *Weekend In Havana* (1941).

*Of Oz* (1939, see Canon), *Brigadoon* (1954) and *Alice In Wonderland* (1951). Even the Hollywood of recent memory was reinvented as a **nostalgic neverland** in *Singin' In The Rain*.

Hollywood continued to indulge its passion for faraway settings into the 1950s, with Paris enhancing its reputation for romance in *An American In Paris*, *Silk Stockings* (1957, see Canon), *Les Girls* (1957), *Funny Face* and *Gigi* (1958, see Canon). But, as modernity hit the 1960s, the fairy-tale musical could only find refuge in tenement buildings (*Bells Are Ringing*, 1960) and skyscrapers (*How To Succeed In Business Without Really Trying*, 1967), as well as on campus (*On A Clear Day You Can See Forever*). Even as the traditional communities broke down, there was a spate of musicals about **misfits** and outsiders that included *My Fair Lady*, *The Sound Of Music*, *Hair* (1979) and *Godspell* (1973).

Yet, while its settings and themes were constantly shifting, the sub-genre's **romantic core** remained largely unchanged. The leading male continued to be seen as the "real" character and the female as the "ideal", in order to bring about a combination of body/soul and lust/love that could meet in mutual passion/affection. And in the majority of cases, the woman didn't recognize the man's potential charm until he forgot his inhibitions and began to sing or dance. This **resistance element** not only drove the narrative, but it also put the viewer (who would have seen their hero perform earlier in the action) firmly on the side of the pursuer. Once the object of his affection realized that he was mate material, the audience could begin to will them both into conquering adversity and finding true love.

# Hollywood ballet

Some of the earliest American films featured dancers like Ameta, Chrissie Sheridan and Annabella (whose Butterfly Dance was particularly popular with Kinetoscope viewers). Yet, while it embraced the "**dream ballet**" in the 1940s, Hollywood has rather fought shy of classical dance.

**Cecil B. De Mille** staged an elaborate electrical ballet aboard a Zeppelin in *Madam Satan* (1930). But, while the corps de ballet was occasionally included as a sophisticated alternative to a chorus line, screen ballet has invariably tended towards the **parodic**, whether it was Buster Keaton in *Easy Go*, Bert Wheeler and Robert Woolsey in *Half Shot At Sunrise* (both 1930), Fred Astaire in *Shall We Dance* (1937, see Canon) and *The Band Wagon* (1953, see Canon), or Gregory Morton in *Bye Bye Birdie* (1963).

However, concerted efforts to legitimize Hollywood ballet were made by the great choreographer, **George Balanchine**. Having devised "Romeo And Juliet" and "Water Nymph" for his wife **Vera Zorina** in *The Goldwyn Follies* (1938), he created "Slaughter On Tenth Avenue" for her in Ray Enright's bowdlerization of Rodgers and Hart's Broadway hit, *On Your Toes* (1939). But even Balanchine was forced to dumb down with Zorina's seven-minute *Swan Lake* lampoon in *I Was An Adventuress* (1940) and her rendition of "That Old Black Magic" in *Star-Spangled Rhythm* (1942).

Balanchine's rival, **Leonide Massine**, was confined to such Technicolored Warner Bros shorts as *Gay Parisian* and *Spanish Fiesta* (both 1941), the last of which featured the **Ballet Russe de Monte Carlo** and Tamara Toumanova, who was as often seen in exotic dramatic roles (she narrowly missed out on *Casablanca*, 1942) as she was dancing in such biopics as *Tonight We Sing* (1953; as Anna Pavlova) and *Deep In My Heart* (1954; as Gaby Deslys).

Toumanova also figured in Gene Kelly's *Invitation To The Dance* (1956). Dismissed as a vanity project (as it took a mere $615,000 on its $1,419,105 budget), this long-shelved **dance portmanteau** required 57,000 frames to matte Kelly and Carol Haney with various cartoon characters.

But such speciality pictures were exceptions, despite ballet featuring prominently in the likes of Dorothy Arzner's *Dance, Girl, Dance* (1940) and Ben Hecht's *Spectre Of The Rose* (1946). Even such pivotal artists as **Katherine Dunham** (who had founded the anthropological dance movement and introduced African and Caribbean rituals into American choreography) were restricted to shorts like *Carnival Of Rhythm* (1941) and guest segments in *Stormy Weather* (1943), *Casbah* (1948) and *Mambo* (1954).

The classically trained **Cyd Charisse** had a higher Hollywood profile, but she was only rarely allowed to exhibit her ballet skills in such MGM vehicles as *The Unfinished Dance* (1947) and *Meet Me In Las Vegas* (1956), and in Roland Petit's *Black Tights* (1960) – a portmanteau offering comprising "The Diamond Cruncher", "Cyrano", "A Merry Mourning" and "Carmen" – which was narrated by Maurice Chevalier and co-starred Petit's wife, Zizi Jeanmaire, and Moira Shearer.

Subsequently, Balanchine directed Mendelssohn's *A Midsummer Night's Dream* (1967) and **Rudolph Nureyev** and Robert Helpmann collaborated on Marius Petipa's *Don Quixote* (1973). But, *Nutcracker: The Motion Picture* (1986) and *George Balanchine's The Nutcracker* (1993) have since stood in isolation, alongside such **ballet dramas** as *The Turning Point* (1977), *Slow Dancing In The Big City* (1978), *The Company* (2003) and the Mikhail Baryshnikov duo, *White Nights* (1985) and *Dancers* (1987).

## Hollywood opera

In 1893, **Thomas Edison** declared that he was pursuing moving pictures "to have such a happy combination of photography and electricity that a man can sit in his own parlor and see depicted upon a curtain the forms of the players in opera upon a distant stage and hear the voices of the singers". Five years later, American Mutoscope released a two-minute version of Donizetti's *The Daughter Of The Regiment*. But, ironically, America produced more opera films during the **silent era** than it has done since the coming of talkies.

While such stage stars as Enrico Caruso and Geraldine Farrar mummed in features, George Webb began producing **Webb's Singing Pictures** (1914–17), using a primitive sound-on-disc system. Vitaphone followed suit a decade later and many of the 64 **opera shorts** made between 1926 and 1930 still survive. Howard Higgins and Lew Seller also began making highlights packages called **Operalogues** for Educational Films in 1932. However, it was the little-known Joe W. Coffman who produced America's first complete sound opera, when he used the Vi-T-Phone sound process to record the San Carlo Grand Opera Company of Long Island in a version of Leoncavallo's *Pagliacci* in 1931.

Some of the leading singers of the 1930s starred in opera-themed vehicles. The baritone **Lawrence Tibbett** became the first operatic movie star in *The Rogue Song* and *New Moon* (both 1930), while **James Melton** displayed a pleasing populism in *Stars Over Broadway* (1935) and *Sing Me A Song* (1936) that was emulated by Everett Marshall (*I Live For Love, 1935*), George Houston (*The Melody Lingers On*, 1935) and Michael Bartlett (*Follow Your Heart*, 1936). The leading divas were **Lily Pons**, who exuded Gallic charm in *I Dream Too Much* (1935), *That Girl From Paris* (1936) and *Hitting A New High* (1937), and the glamorous soprano **Grace Moore**, who earned an Oscar nomination with her performance in *One Night Of Love* (1934).

Audiences proved resistant, but Hollywood hankered after **cultural respectability**, and numerous faux operas were commissioned for mainstream musicals. In 1936 alone, Erich Wolfgang Korngold devised "Romeo And Juliet" for Jan Kiepura and Gladys Swarthout in *Give Us This Night*, Gerard Carbonara created "Isabelle" and "Bal Masque" for Mary Ellis in *Fatal Lady*, while **Oscar Levant** cobbled "Carnival" for *Charlie Chan At The Opera*. **Nelson Eddy** tackled fictitious libretti in *Maytime* (1937), *Balalaika* (1939) and *The Phantom Of The Opera* (1943), while "Arlesiana" and "The Loves Of Fatima" were respectively composed for *Wife, Husband And Friend* (1939) and *Everybody Does It* (1949), which were both adapted from James M. Cain's short story, "Career In C Major".

Opera was also used for **comic effect** in such mock backstagers as *The Great Lover* (1932) and *A Night At The Opera* (1935), while works by Auber and Balfe served as backdrops for **Laurel and Hardy** in *Fra Diavolo* (1933) and *The Bohemian Girl* (1936). It occasionally cropped up in the least likely places, with Marion Talley guesting in the Gene Autry oater, *Follow Your Heart* (1936), while arias from *Rigoletto* and *Carmen* were reworked into cowboy songs for Tex Ritter in *Ridin' The Cherokee Trail* (1941).

But, while excerpts abounded in **concert pictures** like *Carnegie Hall* (1947), Mitchell Leisen's biopic of impresario Sol Hurok, *Tonight We Sing* (1953), and the films of **Mario Lanza**, complete operas, like Gian Carlo Menotti's *The Medium* (1951), were very rare. Teresa Stratas headlined *Salome* in 1974, but even **Luciano Pavarotti** had to be content with singing greatest hits like "Nessun Dorma" in the strained vanity project, *Yes, Giorgio* (1982).

Subsequently, the leading light in American screen opera has been **Peter Sellars**. However, his revisionist renditions of Mozart's *Cosi Fan Tutti* (1989), *Don Giovanni* and *The Marriage Of Figaro* (both 1990) were mostly seen by scandalized aficionados.

## The show musical

The show musical focuses squarely on the successful realization of a creative, often **all-American enterprise**, whether it was a stage work, a Hollywood movie, a radio broadcast or a fashion shoot. Thus, while the fairy-tale style owed much to its European antecedents, the show variety's inspiration was primarily indigenous, with **vaudeville** being a major influence from *The Jazz Singer* (1927, see Canon) onwards.

Many early **backstagers**, like the *Broadway Melody* series and countless Al Jolson vehicles, were sentimental affairs, with the stories fawning on cute kids, or performers making romantic sacrifices for the good of the show. But Warners Bros' take on the subject was more upbeat and emphasized the **communal aspects of show business** alongside the artistic, fiscal and personal incentives of success. Another of the backstager's secrets was its pandering to the public's fascination with celebrity. By allowing the audience behind the scenes, the show musical gave viewers the vicarious thrill of receiving information that was denied to the in-film patrons. In addition, the division between the wings and the boards reinforced the generic fixation with the real and the ideal, with the spatial liberties taken during the finale routines serving to enhance the **authenticity** of the preambling melodrama.

Behind the scenes of *The Broadway Melody* (1929), the first musical to win the Academy Award for best picture and the template for the backstagers that dominated the genre in the early sound era.

The backstager was, therefore, built upon three tenets: the romantic nature of creation precipitating love (either between the producer/ writer and his star or between two of the principals), the **success of the show** depending upon the state of the couple's relationship, and love finding true expression in music (as the hero's ingenuity and devotion brought out the heroine's latent musicality and passion).

The implication that women were to be seen and men were to be heard, that he was the artist and she was his muse, was crucial to the majority of 1930s backstagers, particularly the **Busby Berkeley** quartet of *42nd Street* (1933, see Canon), *Gold Diggers Of 1933* (see Canon), *Footlight Parade* (1933, see Canon) and *Dames* (1934). Yet, while it conformed to the standard Hollywood practice of privileging male creativity, such a tactic was also rather forced upon the studios by virtue of the fact that the available stars were male singers (Al Jolson, Dick Powell, Bing Crosby) and female dancers (Ruby Keeler, Eleanor Powell, Joan Caulfield). There were exceptions, of course, with **Jeanette MacDonald** the lone female star singer (although she was always teamed with a marquee name), while Fred Astaire both sang and danced, but with Ginger Rogers.

Backstagers were, initially, very much an urban form, with the action essentially confined to **rehearsal halls**, dressing rooms, cheap apartments and eateries before it was allowed to take centre stage on opening night. However, variations were soon found to keep the format fresh, involving parades (*Flirtation Walk*, 1934), sporting events (*Pigskin Parade*, 1936), **barnyard amdrams** (*Babes In Arms*, 1939) and rodeos (*Girl Crazy*, 1943). Eventually, troop shows (*Thank Your Lucky Stars* and *This Is The Army*, both 1943), classical-contemporary hybrids (*Three Smart Girls*, 1936, and *Thousands Cheer*, 1943) and fashion shoots (*Cover Girl* and *Funny Face*) were added to the mix. Even **biopics** of popular composers and showbiz icons like *The Great Waltz* (1938) and *Yankee Doodle Dandy* (1942, see Canon) counted, as they chronicled the evolution of an artistic talent.

Although it strove to achieve a balance, the show musical frequently placed greater emphasis on the ideal than the real. Hence, even a daringly deglamorized film like *Ziegfeld Girl* (1941) still ended with a **showstopper**. But with post-war audiences expecting increased authenticity, it became harder to peddle the cornball and kitsch on which the backstager relied. Following the likes of *Easter Parade* (1948, see Canon), *The Barkleys Of Broadway* (1949), *Jolson Sings Again* (1949) and *A Star Is Born* (1954, see Canon), a significant number of musicals began to explore how the **pressures of performing** impacted on showbiz relationships, particularly marriage. Moreover, romance and communitarianism no longer guaranteed the success of a creative enterprise, as carnality increasingly came to replace courtship and the **business** came to matter more than the show.

Consequently, the musical's twin myths of the pain/pleasure of putting on a show and the purity of young love were banished from musical realism, and the genre struggled to survive the loss. Less than forty years after it was first launched, it became apparent to everyone in Hollywood that the musical was now primarily about the bottom line and that no amount of spooning and Juning could disguise the fact. The sub-genre had **lost its innocence**, and with it went much of its appeal.

## The folk musical

The folk musical aimed to persuade people to forget the present by enticing them with a mythicized version of America's sociocultural past. These **Americana musicals** relocated the operetta's romanticized Ruritanian settings to the States, enabling films like *The Little Colonel* (1935), *Mississippi* (1935), *The Girl Of The Golden West* (1938) and *In Old Chicago* (1937) to gloss over contemporary political or economic problems and produce picturesque, anecdotal **period pieces** that bore little resemblance to historical fact.

The majority of folk musicals had a rural, small-town or farm setting and centred around rituals that brought the **community** together. However, some folk musicals, like *San Francisco* (1936), *Little Nellie Kelly* (1940), *Centennial Summer* (1946) and *In The Good Old Summertime* (1949), had inner-city settings. But these usually took place at a time when communities were still tightly knit and were more akin to urban villages than ghettoized neighbourhoods. Indeed, even the odd New York musical had a folk feel to it, including *Hallelujah, I'm A Bum* (1933), *It Happened In Brooklyn* (1947), *The Belle Of New York* (1952) and *Flower Drum Song* (1961). But the pre-eminent social grouping was the **family**. From *Meet Me In St Louis* onwards, the thickness of multi-generational bloodlines became central to the folk musical milieu, with eccentric grandparents, fondly fussing parents, marriageable daughters and spirited younger siblings forming the typical unit.

So snug was the folk scenario that the beloved frequently lived next door, as in *Meet Me In St Louis*, *Summer Holiday* and *One Sunday Afternoon* (1948). The **juvenile crush** was reflected in the contentment of the parental relationship, which not only implied that true love never died, but which also reinforced the social validity of marriage and a stable home. Even the wiser, older heads played their part in the romance, as the lovers turned to them for advice, as they did in several Rogers and Hammerstein musicals, as well as in the likes of *West Side Story* (1961, see Canon) and *Finian's Rainbow* (1968).

Given the folkloric nature of the sub-genre's setting, it would be reasonable to assume that traditional song and dance played a significant part in the folk musical's rubric. **Spirituals** and **folk songs** both seemed ideally suited to the Americana style. Indeed, all but two of the songs in King Vidor's *Hallelujah!* (1929, see Canon) were gospel-inspired, and spirituals were also heard in the likes of *The Little Colonel*, *Mississippi* and *Cabin In The Sky* (1963). But traditional folk songs proved difficult to integrate into the standard plotline without seeming contrived. So,

## Americana chic

Pitched somewhere between heritage and myth, the folk musical's traditionalism extended to the visual sources chosen to convey the sense of an idealized past. The work of **regional artists** like Thomas Eakins, Thomas Benton, John Curry, Grant Wood, and Currer and Ives were key to achieving the required blend of period authenticity and **nostalgic pictorialism**. But, while the studios sought to create a remembered reality, what actually emerged was an infinitely more potent romanticism that relied on prints, paintings, photographs, postcards, calendars, maps and engravings to reinforce their cod-communal vision of a united nation.

Even when Hollywood began making greater use of actual locations from the 1950s, such **outdoor authenticity** was invariably tempered by a mythological vision that derived from the movies rather than from fact. This is most readily apparent in folk musicals with **Western** settings, like *Oklahoma!* (1955, see Canon), *The Unsinkable Molly Brown* (1964) and *Paint Your Wagon* (1969) which owed more to the iconography of John Ford than frontier reality.

following Broadway's lead, Hollywood commissioned folk pastiches that exploited the rhythms, rituals and customs of folklore. **Jerome Kern** and **Oscar Hammerstein** were particularly skilled in this regard and their *Show Boat* stylings were much imitated.

As the songs became more easily integrated into the narrative, distinctive kinds began to reoccur. There were paeans to individual states ("California Here I Come" and "All I Owe To I-o-way"), neighbourhoods ("Manhattan" and "Chinatown, My Chinatown"), modes of transport ("On The Atchison, Topeka And The Santa Fe" and "The Surrey With The Fringe On Top") and community revels ("Our State Fair" and "It Was A Real Nice Clambake"), while other tunes celebrated seasons, holidays, ethnic groupings, historical eras and the full panoply of past and present rhythms, melodies and harmonies – from barbershop and minstrelsy to ragtime, country and rock.

This emphasis on **recurring cycles** and familiar happenings enabled the audience to become more closely bound into the story than had been the case with the more formal set pieces in the fairy-tale and show musicals (which were, in any case, more about aspiration than experience). Indeed, there was a greater interchangeability between the performer and the spectator in the folk musical. Figures were invariably positioned in circular formations within the frame, so that anyone (from a secondary character to an onlooker) could chip in with a lyric or a dance step.

The quality of the performance mattered less than the simple joy of expression, and as a consequence of this inclusivity, the songs in folk musicals became noted for their **natural delivery style**. Indeed, trained voices were rarely heard in folk settings, although there were exceptions, most notably Jeanette MacDonald and Nelson Eddy in *Rose Marie* (1936) and Howard Keel and Jane Powell in *Seven Brides For Seven Brothers*. Much more suited to the folk style were easy listening talents like **Judy Garland**, Gene Kelly and **Frank Sinatra**, whose ability to act as they sang made their melodies seem more organic. However, while traditional-style songs fitted relatively easily into the sub-generic format, **folk dances** did not. Square dances, hoedowns and barn socials were group activities that were usually associated with specific festivals. And though they provided some mass spectacle and plenty of folksy nostalgia, their calendar specificity proved narratively restrictive. Moreover, they lacked intimacy.

So, once again, Hollywood followed the Broadway lead and introduced routines inspired by **New American Ballet pioneer**s like Martha Graham, Eugene Loring and Agnes De Mille. Such innovative choreography reduced the distance between dancing and acting and enabled dance to become an indicator of plot development and character psychology rather than just an exhibition of the performer's skill. Moreover, the likes of *Oklahoma!* (1955, see Canon) helped make the **dream ballet** become part of the musical tradition and, by giving dance a narrative function, it became easier to integrate it into the storyline (although many folk musicals still left room for speciality numbers).

The notion that nature inspires the creation of music (often serving as a model for the melody itself) and that the rhythm of life is tantamount to dance is one of the folk musical's key recurring ploys. The remainder revolve around the couple's relationship. One of the lovers tends to represent the **stability of the soil**, while the other possesses energy and ambition. In *High, Wide And Handsome*, **Randolph Scott** personified this dependability, while **Irene Dunne** epitomized the free spirit. However, this situation was reversed in *Oklahoma!* and set a trend in which the man embodied wanderlust, ambition and individualism, while the woman had the interests of the community at heart, whether as a home-maker, rancher, teacher or librarian. But these traits often led to conflict, for while the man was prepared to travel to fulfil his destiny, this was seen as infidelity by a woman intent on **putting down roots**.

Such dissonance jeopardized the outcome of a **communal enterprise** – whether it was the formation of a state (*Oklahoma!*), the foundation of a town (*The Harvey Girls*), the sustaining of a household (*Meet Me In St Louis*) or the survival of a company (*Summer Stock*, 1950) – which depended primarily on the momentum provided by the lovers' passion. In the folk style, the hero and the heroine were **equals and opposites**, with

Americana chic in *Oklahoma!* (1955): Ado Annie (Gloria Grahame) and Ali Hakim (Eddie Albert) dressed in their Sunday best look on as Curly McLain (Gordon MacRae) kisses Gertie Cummings (Barbara Lawrence), his date at the box social.

the man representing the sky and the woman the earth, and together they created **new life**. The community's prosperity, therefore, hung on the permanence provided by matrimony, as it fostered the procreation and colonization that alone could guarantee the triumph of order over chaos, particularly in such frontier musicals as *Calamity Jane* (1953).

But it was not all sweetness and light in the folk musical. Sexual energy often resulted in **macho rivalry** – as between Randolph Scott and Charles Bickford in *High, Wide And Handsome* and Gordon MacRae and Rod Steiger in *Oklahoma!* – and **female cattiness** – as between Judy Garland and Angela Lansbury in *The Harvey Girls*. Much importance was laid on the **oppositional characters** in folk musicals, as they not only threatened the happiness of the lovers, but also their romanticized environment. Loose women, out of towners, nasty neighbours, bad influences and mean-spirited villains all menaced the small-town consensus (and, in times of war and national emergency, Hollywood played up the threat of such malevolents to encourage civic vigilance). But in the main, the folk musical advocated that the best way to preserve the fabric of society was to give everyone a stake in its success. Yet such blatant American Dreaming ignored past problems and present prejudices, falsely perpetuating the USA's reputation as the **Land of the Free**.

Where, for example, are the non-white performers in these idyllic folksy fantasies? The majority of them were reduced to playing faithful servants and scaredy-cat sidekicks, who were rarely entrusted with songs (and when they were, the spots were invariably cut before screenings in the Deep South). When the studios deigned to make **all-African-American musicals**, they proved to be a mixture of the folk and fairy-tale styles, with Dixie being romanticized into a neverland where **plantation workers** sang all day and were so in tune with the land that they embodied its rhythms. Considering the size of the black audience, it's surprising that Hollywood didn't make more pictures as patronizing as *The Green Pastures* (1936) and *Cabin In The Sky*. But whether the moguls deemed such pictures too expensive for their market or recognized the offensiveness of the material, well-meaning, but ill-judged offerings like *Carmen Jones* (1954) and *Porgy And Bess* (1959) were few and far between.

Throughout its history, the folk musical trod a fine line between revealing Hollywood's complicity with a modern society that has abandoned folk values (apart from exploiting them for profit) and disguising its intention by making **traditional ideals** seem permanent in an ever-changing world. Occasionally, the studios threatened to expose folk kitsch in films like *Red Garters* (1954) and *It's Always Fair Weather* (1955), with the latter having the media seeking to exploit the tensions between a trio of war buddies. However, by having Gene Kelly, Dan Dailey and Michael Kidd reunite as musketeers against some mobsters, MGM managed simultaneously to scuff the folk sheen and leave it alluringly intact.

With the genre as a whole already in danger of becoming a cultural backwater, *Nashville* (1975, see Canon) finally **shattered the myth** of the folk musical and did so by taking the same 1776 commemoration as *Centennial Summer*. Otto Preminger's film had been as much a celebration of victory in World War II as the 1876 World Fair. But by lamenting the impact of Vietnam and Watergate on the American psyche, **Robert Altman** succeeded in showing that the spirit of 1946, let alone 1776 and 1876, had gone forever – and with it the folk musical's very reason to exist.

# A World Of Entertainment: the international musical

Catherine Deneuve in *Les parapluies de Cherbourg* (*The Umbrellas Of Cherbourg*, 1964). With five nominations, Jacques Demy's sublime masterpiece is still the most cited foreign-language musical in Oscar history.

# A World Of Entertainment: the international musical

Despite the recent vogue for World Music, musical taste, like a sense of humour, is something of a localized phenomenon. Consequently, film industries across the globe have devised their own forms of musical entertainment to showcase performers whose appeal rarely traverses borders. In some countries, the genre has become a cinematic staple, yet it has been largely overlooked by film scholars and is only fleetingly discussed in specialist histories. This whistle-stop tour seeks to provide a tempting introduction.

# Africa

North Africa dominated the continent's musical production until the 1970s, when the newly independent sub-Saharan nations began celebrating their **diverse cultures** in song and dance.

Over a third of the features produced in **Egypt** between 1931 and 1961 were musicals. Singer-composer Muhammad 'Abd al-Wahhab and Layla Murad were among the biggest names in the early Arabic phase. But Murad's actor-director husband, **Anwar Wagdi**, introduced foreign influences to "Hollywood on the Nile" and a new exuberance characterized the musicals of directors like Ahmad Badrakhan and Henri Barakat, as well as such stars as Farid al-Atrash and Samia Gamal, who was a renowned belly dancer.

Singer 'Abd al-Halim Hafiz came to epitomize the new national spirit under President Nasser, and he was superbly played by Ahmed Zaki in **Sherif 'Arafa**'s biopic, *Halim* (2006). But the musical declined rapidly after his best-loved success, *My Father Is Up A Tree* (1969). Subsequently, pop pin-ups like 'Amr Diab and Muhammad Fu'ad have prevailed in such brash entertainments as *Ice Cream In Glim* (1992) and *Abracadabra America* (1993), although 'Arafa and **Youssef Chahine** respectively cast a satirical eye towards the heydays of vaudeville and cinema in *Silence, Listen!* (1990) and *Silence, We're Rolling* (2001).

Egyptian movies largely dictated the style of the North African musicals that began emerging in the late 1960s, but few made much international impact before **Moufida Tlatli's** exquisitely contentious *Silences Of The Palace* (1994) and Raja Amar's equally subversive *Satin Rouge* (2002). The first significant **sub-Saharan musical** was Med Hondo's *West Indies* (1975), but the presence of celebrated musician **Papa Wemba** ensured a wider audience for *La vie est belle* (*Life Is Rosy*, 1987), which could be described as the African *42nd Street*. The **Hollywood influence** was also strong on Darrell James Roodt's *Sarafina!* (1992), as Whoopi Goldberg starred as an ANC-supporting teacher, while the dance numbers recalled *West Side Story* (1961, see Canon). But the most impressive African musicals were both inspired by **Georges Bizet**. Mark Dornford-May's *U-Carmen e-Khayelitsha* (2005) won the Golden Bear at the Berlin Film Festival, but it lacked the style and spontaneity of Joseph Gaï Ramaka's *Karmen Geï* (2001), in which the music cascades irresistibly from an everyday reality that throbs with life, thanks to the vibrant design and mottled cinematography.

## Belly dance

Although the emphasis in Egyptian musicals is usually on song, belly dancing has been a popular facet since **Bad'ia Masabni** performed in Mario Volpi's *Queen Of Theatres* (1936). Most musicals contained at least one dance, although they were usually restricted to nightclub sequences and parties. Masabni's protégées, Tahiyya Carioca and Samia Gamal, illuminated dozens of pictures, including Henri Barakat's *The Love Of My Life* (1947) and Niazi Mostafa's *A Cigarette And A Glass* (1955). However, the child star Fayruz and one-time circus performer Na'ima 'Akif were also popular. More recently, **traditional dancers** like Nelly and Sharihan have been supplanted by Fifi 'Abdu and Lucy, who incurred the wrath of religious groups with their more blatantly **erotic style**.

### Silence, We're Rolling (Skoot hansawwar)

**dir Youssef Chahine, 2001, Egypt, 102m**

This fond lampoon of the *masala* melodrama and the screwball comedy passes occasional asides on class, age and gender prejudice. But, while the plotlines involving Tunisian movie star Latifa, gold-digging wannabe Ahmed Wafik and her daughter Rubi and chauffeur's son Mostapha Chaaban are just a tad too formulaic, the musical numbers have a pastiched pizzazz that recalls Merchant-Ivory's *Bombay Talkie* (1970).

### U-Carmen e-Khayelitsha

**dir Mark Dornford-May, 2005, SA, 126m**

This Xhosa version of Bizet's opera, *Carmen*, never quite escapes its stage roots and several of the glorious score's highlights remain stubbornly static. Yet there's no denying the ingenuity of relocating the story to a South African township nor the power of Pauline Malefane's performance, as the cigarette factory siren who so inflames religious cop Andile Tshoni that her fixation with visiting singing star Zweilungile Sidloyi can only end in tragedy.

## Asia

Just as Egypt shaped screen trends in North Africa, so India (see p.285) has exerted a prodigious influence over musical cinema across vast swathes of Asia. Yet even where the **Bollywood effect** was most keenly felt, the highly diverse national industries have always produced their own stars who have proudly upheld indigenous musical traditions.

Singers Najah Salam and Samira Toufic and the belly dancer Nadia Gamal became icons in the Lebanon, while George Ovadiah was renowned in Israel for escapist entertainments known as "**bourekas**". P. Ramlee exerted a major influence on the genre in Singapore and Malaysia, while Rhoma Irama came to prominence in Indonesia, and the Philippine scene in the 1960s was dominated by such glamorous actresses as Amalia Fuentes, Gloria Romero, Rosemarie Sonora, Nora Aunor and Vilma Santos.

The **Thai musical** continues to flourish, thanks largely to stylized pastiches of bygone styles like Wisit Sasanatieng's *Tears Of The Black Tiger* (2000), Pen-Ek Ratanaruang's *Mon-Rak transistor* (*Transistor Love Story*, 2001) and Apichatpong Weerasethakul and Michael Shaowanasai's *The Adventure Of Iron Pussy* (2003). Tsai Ming-liang has similarly sustained the **Taiwanese musical** by inserting mischievous song sequences into *The Hole* (1998) and *The Wayward Cloud* (2005), which lampoon both imported Hong Kong musicals and the "healthy variety" and "three room" pictures produced in the 1960s and 70s.

Although features like Fang Peilin's *The Singer* (1946) and Wu Can's *Orioles Among Willow Leaves* (1948) were full of popular songs, the musical never really caught on in **China**. The Communists preferred spectacular revues like Wang Ping's *The East Is Red* (1965). But the success of Sang Hu and Huang Sha's *Liang Shanbo And Zhu Yingtai* (1954) – which Charlie Chaplin hailed as "a Chinese Romeo and Juliet" – alerted them to the greater propaganda potential of opera. Between 1970 and 1972, Beijing sanctioned several **Revolutionary Model Operas**, including *Taking Tiger Mountain By Strategy* and *Legend Of The Red Lantern*, as well as the ballets *The Red Detachment Of Women* and *The White-Haired Girl*.

Fifth Generation filmmaker, **Chen Kaige**, recalled the sounds outlawed during this Cultural Revolution in *King Of The Children* (1984) and *Life On A String* (1991), before returning to the **Peking Opera** of the 1920s and 30s for *Farewell, My Concubine* (1993). But Tian Zhuangzhuang's *Rock'n'Roll Kids* (1988) sparked a musical revolution and **rock** has since featured heavily on the soundtracks of such Sixth Generation pictures as

Joe Odagiri and Zhang Ziyi in *Princess Raccoon* (2005). The Chinese actress spent six months studying dance for this stylized musical, while also mastering the unique mix of Mandarin and phonetic Japanese used for her dialogue and lyrics.

Zhuang Yuan's *Beijing Bastards* (1993).

Japan's militarist rulers had little time for musicals like Masahiro Makino's **samurai burlesque**, *Duelling Ballads Of The Mandarin Ducks* (1939). But they exploited the popularity of **Ri Koran** (aka Li Xianglan) with Manchurian audiences to spread pro-occupation propaganda in films like *Song Of The White Orchid* (1939), *Vow In The Desert* and *China Nights* (both 1940), which earned her the nickname, "the Judy Garland of Japan". Hideko Takamine and Hibari Misora were also popular child stars. Misora later formed part of The Three Girls – with Chiemi Eri and Izumi Yukimura – in **teen musicals** like *So Young, So Bright* (1955), while Takamine starred as a socially conscious stripper in Keisuke Kinoshita's *Carmen Comes Home* (1951) and *Carmen's Pure Love* (1952), which owed much to the early style of René Clair.

The *tanuki goten* musical also grew in popularity in the 1950s and **Seijun Suzuki** fondly recalled its blend of folk fantasy and costume romance in *Princess Raccoon* (2005). But the following decade saw **pop bands** like The Drifters, The Spiders and The Tigers dominate the genre, which has only occasionally been revived with such contrasting pictures as **Takashi Miike's** gleeful horror pastiche, *The Happiness Of The Katakuris* (2001), and **Tetsuya Nakashima's** *Memories Of Matsuko* (2006), which parodied *Citizen Kane* (1941) *Amélie* (2001) and *Moulin Rouge!* (2001).

### Princess Raccoon
**dir Seijun Suzuki, 2005, Jap, 111m**

Combining stylized studio settings and pastiche CGI effects, this fairy-tale operetta stars Joe Odagiri as a prince evading his enviously narcissistic father, Mikijiro Hira, while striving to impress the eponymous Zhang Ziyi. But while the visuals are suitably eye-catching, the score veers unpersuasively between rap and aria, samba and Oriental folk song. Consequently, this is something of a multi-cultural musical muddle.

## Australia

Australia produced a clutch of musicals in the early sound era, with music-hall veteran George Wallace starring in the "burlesque operetta", *His Royal Highness* (1933), and the rags-to-riches romp, *Let George Do It* (1938). But the film industry all but collapsed between 1940 and 1970 and the genre went into abeyance.

Eventually, in 1965, star Ian Turpie and a debuting **Olivia Newton-John** co-starred with a multi-coloured sheep in Joe McCormick's *Funny Things Happen Down Under* (1965), while **Jim Sharman** warmed up for *The Rocky Horror Picture Show* (1975, see Canon) with *Shirley Thompson Versus The Aliens* (1972), which he described as "a psychological thriller cum 1950s rock musical/science fiction/fantasy movie". Such revisionism also informed Gillian Armstrong's **punk "putting on a show" saga**, *Star Struck* (1982), Ken Annakin's Gilbert and Sullivan update, *The Pirate Movie* (1982), and Yahoo Serious's rock lampoon, *Young Einstein* (1988). However, the prime parody of the period was New Zealander **Peter Jackson**'s gloriously tasteless *Meet The Feebles* (1982).

In 1994, Terence Stamp, Hugo Weaving and Guy Pearce dragged up to lip-sync to a selection of camp classics in **Stephan Elliott**'s *The Adventures Of Priscilla, Queen Of The Desert*. But the most innovative Australian musicals of recent times bookended **Baz Luhrmann**'s "Red Curtain" trilogy. Impeccably designed by Catherine Martin, *Strictly Ballroom* (1992) and *Moulin Rouge!* (2001) restored an exuberance and integrity to musical performance that had long been absent from more self-conscious American movies.

## Moulin Rouge!

Orpheus meets MGM in Belle Époque Paris in this dazzling entertainment, which turns on bohemian poet **Ewan McGregor**'s bid to keep courtesan **Nicole Kidman** out of the clutches of Richard Roxburgh's lascivious duke, while also ensuring the success of Jim Broadbent's show, *Spectacular-Spectacular*. Director **Baz Luhrmann**'s set pieces, like "Diamonds Are A Girl's Best Friend" and "Like A Virgin", are pitched somewhere between Busby Berkeley, Vincente Minnelli and Bollywood. But the "Elephant Love Medley" is the crowning achievement of this wildly romantic and genre savvy treasure that took $340 million worldwide and became the first musical in 22 years to be nominated for a best picture Oscar.

All they need is love: Satine (Nicole Kidman) and Christian (Ewan McGregor).

### Meet The Feebles

**dir Peter Jackson, 1989, Aus, 98m**

There really is something to offend everyone in this gleefully outrageous "spluppet creature feature". Drug abuse, projectile vomiting, ejaculation, copraphilia and urination all occur backstage on what's supposed to be a family show, whose cast bears a non-too-subtle resemblance to The Muppets. And that's before Sebastian, the fox director, lets rip with a showstopper extolling the joys of sodomy.

### Strictly Ballroom

**dir Baz Luhrmann, 1992, Aus, 94m**

A decade after it was first performed as an amateur production, the story of a moody dancer who defies the worthies at his local ballroom society became an instant feel-good favourite. Paul Mercurio and Tara Morice's nocturnal *pasa doble* to "Time After Time" provides the sensual highlight, but the stylized flashback to Barry Otto's ruinous attempt to introduce his own steps at the Pan-Pacific championships is a gem.

## The Caribbean

Rita Montaner launched the **Cuban musical** with *Sucedió en la Habana* (*It Happened In Havana*, 1937). But besides the spirited Blanquita Amaro, the best talent was invariably lured to Hollywood or the various Hispanic film industries.

The genre continued to decline under Castro, although **documentaries** like *Cuba baila* (*Cuba Dances,* 1960) established the tradition continued by Wim Wenders in *The Buena Vista Social Club* (1999). In 1981, **Manuel Octavio Gómez** attempted a revival with *Patakín*, an ambitious hybrid of the Beach Blanket and Soviet tractor musicals. Since then, Enrique Pineda Barnet crafted the 1920s backstager *The Belle Of The Alhambra* (1989) and Benito Zambrano followed a couple of maverick musicians in *Habana Blues* (2005).

The Caribbean's only other significant musicals have come from **Jamaica**. Perry Henzell's *The Harder They Come* (1972) introduced **reggae** to the wider world, but Theodoros Bafaloukos brought an edgier realism to his variation on Vittorio De Sica's *Bicycle Thieves* (1938), with *Rockers* (1979). Subsequently, Rick Elgood and Don Letts have teamed twice on *Dancehall Queen* (1997), whose soundtrack mixed reggae, rap and techno, and *One Love* (2003), which combined the plotlines of William Shakespeare's *Romeo And Juliet* and *Footloose* (1984).

**The Harder They Come**
**dir Perry Henzell, 1972, Jam, 98m**

While it's remembered for such songs as "You Can Get It If You Really Want", "Many Rivers to Cross", "Pressure Drop" and the title track, this was a combustible blend of blaxploitation and Third Cinema, in which Henzell used the crime spree that transforms Jimmy Cliff from a country wannabe into a chart-topping outlaw to expose the corruption, greed and hypocrisy of Kingston society.

## O'Disney

Former Disney animator, **Don Bluth**, was based in Ireland for a decade. His first production, *All Dogs Go To Heaven* (1989), featured a Cajun alligator in an Esther Williams pastiche, while Glen Campbell played an Elvis-like rooster in *Rock-A-Doodle* (1992), which riffed on *The Wizard Of Oz* (1939, see Canon). Barry Manilow wrote the songs for the Hans Christian Andersen adaptation, *Thumbelina* (1994), but the **Irish venture** ended, later the same year, with the misfiring fairy tale, *A Troll In Central Park* (1994).

# Europe

Europe provides plentiful evidence for those convinced that musicals don't travel. Occasional pictures from France (see p.277), Germany (see p.281), Spain (see p.288) and the United Kingdom (see p.289) have reached wider arthouse audiences. But the vast majority of Euro musicals – from the *fado* dramas of the Portuguese diva Amália Rodrigues to the arabesques of Turkish saz icon Orhan Gencebay – have been produced for local consumption.

The musical dominated **Austrian cinema** until the 1960s. Stars flocked to appear in **Viennese operettas** during the 1930s, among them Jarmila Novotna, Marta Eggerth, Jan Kiepura and Franziska Gaal. **Willi Forst** was the genre's leading director and he was succeeded by the prolific Franz Anton, whose long career ended with *Johann Strauss: The King Without A Crown* (1987).

Despite its rich musical heritage, **Italy** has little reputation for musical movies besides filmed operas, starring such tenors as Beniamino Gigli (*I pagliacci*, 1943/1947) and Tito Gobbi (*Rigoletto*, 1946). The 1950s saw studios in Naples churn out over four hundred *filone napoletano*, but these low-budget combinations of classical and popular song never had the nationwide appeal of the *musicarello*, which flourished into the 1960s with pop stars like Adriano Celentano and Rita Pavone.

**Belgium** has exported more than its share of musicals, with **Chantal Akerman**'s *Golden Eighties* (1986) being followed by Gérard Corbiau's classically oriented *The Music Teacher* (1988) and *Farinelli* (1995). But they lacked the commercial appeal of such Irish-based outings as Peter Chelsom's *Hear My Song* (1990) and Alan Parker's *The Commitments* (1991), the cult cachet of Finn Aki Kaurismäki's *Leningrad Cowboys Go*

*America* (1989), and the sheer edginess of **Lars von Trier**'s *Dancer In The Dark* (2000) and fellow Dane Stefan Fjeldmark's CGI romp, *Terkel In Trouble* (2004).

Even fewer musicals made it past Checkpoint Charlie. According to Dana Ranga's documentary, *East Side Story* (1997), only forty musicals were made in the **Eastern Bloc** before the collapse of Communism. Cineastes detested their triviality, studio heads considered them a waste of precious resources and politicians regarded them as dangerously pro-capitalist. Even the film-makers who produced them saw them merely as opportunities to subvert the tenets of **Socialist Realism**. Yet they struck a chord with audiences behind the Iron Curtain and many of their songs are now nostalgic standards.

## Yiddish musicals

Fanny Brice performed the Yiddish dialect number, "It's Gorgeous To Be Graceful", in Thornton Freeland's Hollywood musical, *Be Yourself* (1930). But it was another New Yorker, **Molly Picon**, who became the Yiddish musical's biggest star in the Polish pictures *Yiddle With His Fiddle* (1937) and *Little Mother* (1938). Back in the States, Moishe Oysher took the **Al Jolson** role in *The Cantor's Son* (1937), Llya Motyleff's reworking of *The Jazz Singer* (1927, see Canon) before playing the fast living lead in *The Singing Blacksmith* (1938). This was directed by the versatile **Edgar G. Ulmer**, who also guided "the Yiddish Fred Astaire", Leo Fuchs, through *American Matchmaker* (1940). However, production ceased following Joseph Berne's revue, *Catskill Honeymoon* (1949).

16-year-old Andrew Strong was cast in *The Commitments* (1991) after his father lost his voice during rehearsals.

Contrary to popular belief, **Warsaw Pact musicals** weren't populated solely by prancing Stakhanovites or crooning collective farmers. **Czech classics** like Oldrich Lipský's jazz Western, *Lemonade Joe* (1964), and Vladimir Svitáček and Jan Roháč's pacifist revue *If A Thousand Clarinets* (1964), were mischievously subversive. Moreover, references to The Beatles in Bulgarian Ludmil Kirkov's *A Nameless Band* (1981) and Pole Radoslaw Piwowarski's *Yesterday* (1985) revealed the influence of decadent Western music. Indeed, by the 1960s, **East German musicals** were reflecting the demands of the public and not the Party. Karin Schröder emerged as the "socialist Doris Day" in Gottfried Kolditz's *Geliebte weiße Maus* (*The Small White Mouse*, 1964), while Frank Schöbel became "the Elvis of the East" in Joachim Hasler's *Heisser Sommer* (*Hot Summer*, 1968) and *Nicht schummeln, Liebling* (*No Cheating, Darling*, 1972). Hungarian Péter Tímár recalled these heady days in *Dolly Birds* (1997), but Kornél Mundruczó's *Johanna* (2005) owed more to the **operatic tradition**.

### Dancer In The Dark
**dir Lars von Trier, 2000, Den, 140m**

This Dogme95 variation on the musical combined improvised dramatic scenes with interiorized song-and-dance sequences that were filmed live with a hundred hand-held cameras meticulously positioned around the set. Tensions between Von Trier and Björk earned the picture considerable notoriety before it took best actress and the Palme d'Or at Cannes. However, critics were divided by the anti-American sentiments and excessive melodramatics, as a Czech emigré with a rare sight disorder goes to the gallows for killing the cop who stole the savings she was hiding for an operation to prevent her son from contracting the same condition.

### Terkel In Trouble (Terkel i knibe)
**dir Stefan Fjeldmark, Kresten Vestbjerg Andersen, Thorbjorn Christofferson, 2004, Den, 78m**

A galaxy of British talent (including a scene-stealing Johnny Vegas, as the alcoholic, motor-biking Uncle Stewart) was assembled for the dubbed version of this Danish musical, which is packed with kid-friendly tunes sporting gloriously rude English lyrics written by Willie Dowling. Pitched somewhere between *Jimmy Neutron* and *South Park*, the story centres on the hapless Terkel (Adrian Edmondson), who causes an obese, lovesick classmate to plunge to her death, before alienating his best mate Jason (Ben Bishop) and then falling foul of the new botany teacher (Toby Stephens) on a field trip. With something to offend everyone, this has become a cult gem.

### Leningrad Cowboys Go America
**dir Aki Kaurismäki, 1989, Fin/Swe, 80m**

With their parodic winkle-pickers and sharply slicked quiffs, Finland's most eccentric combo sets out to take the US by storm, with their frozen bass player's coffin in tow. However, the best gig that manager Matti Pellonpää can get them is a wedding in Mexico and they acquire a secondhand Cadillac (from a cameoing Jim Jarmusch) for the trip – which includes several one-night stands en route. It's a bit like *The Blues Brothers* (1980) on quaaludes.

### The Commitments
**dir Alan Parker, 1991, Ire, 117m**

The audition sequences, in which Robert Arkins searches for musicians who share his love of soul, set the tone for this rousing slice of North Dublin life, which culminates in the band imploding after Wilson Pickett fails to show up for the jam session that might have secured them a recording contract. Andrew Strong delivered a powerhouse performance as the gutsy front man, while backing vocalists Bronagh Gallagher, Maria Doyle and Angeline Ball made slinky contributions to a soundtrack that spawned two bestselling albums.

### Johanna
**dir Kornél Mundruczó, 2005, Hun, 109m**

Drug addict Orsi Tóth emerges from a coma with the power of sexual healing in this hospital opera, whose fluid, stylized visuals (meticulously created by a trio of steadicamming cinematographers) bear the distinctive imprint of co-producer Béla Tarr – especially in their sinister evocation of the nocturnal corridors and wards. But it's the avowedly modern score by Zsòfia Tallér that gives this striking picture the eccentric audacity and disarming power to transcend its narrative inconsistencies and conceptual implausibilities.

## France

Despite pioneering several sound systems during the silent era, French cinema was rather slow to take to the talkies.

**Remakes** of Maurice Chevalier's Hollywood hits and French versions of **German operettas** (with Henri Garat and Lilian Harvey) dominated production until **René Clair** made imaginative use of song, music and contrapuntal sound in *Sous les toits de Paris* (*Under The Roofs Of Paris*, 1930), *Le million* (1931), *A nous la liberté* (*Freedom For Us*, 1931) and *Quatorze juillet* (*The Fourteenth Of July*, 1933), whose visual fluency heightened the naturalism of the soundtrack.

## Chantons sous la pluie

The Hollywood musical was already virtually moribund when **Jacques Demy** and composer **Michel Legrand** produced *Les parapluies de Cherbourg* (*The Umbrellas Of Cherbourg*, 1964), their latterday **operetta** exploring the Americanization of France. Yet despite Demy's status among the *auteurs* of the *nouvelle vague*, this bittersweet confection – in which provincial garage mechanic Nino Castelnuovo returns from Algerian War service to discover that his girlfriend, Catherine Deneuve, has married older jeweller Marc Michel on the advice of her umbrella shop-owning mother, Anne Vernon – owes more to the audiovisual schemata of MGM than the jump cuts and captions of Truffaut or Godard.

Exquisitely photographed by **Jean Rabier**, art director **Bernard Evein**'s designs are so precise (Demy had parts of the town painted specially) that not only do they correspond to the tone of Legrand's various operatic arias and jazzy *chansons*, but they also provide a symbolic commentary on both the characters and action as they switch location. The storyline is undeniably melodramatic (although it broke the MGM mould by plumping for a downbeat ending), but this was one of the few French films of the early 1960s to allude to the hugely contentious conflict in Algeria, and this unflinching attitude to **everyday reality** counters the accusations of those who dismiss this deceptively complex masterpiece of being candy-coloured whimsy.

**Catherine Deneuve** won the best actress prize at Cannes, but the vocal performances of the entire ensemble are impeccable. One of the glories of the **French New Wave**, this has lost none of its power to enchant and has even acquired additional resonance from its defence of the indigenous in our increasingly globalized world.

Despite the audiovisual influence of MGM, Jacques Demy's bittersweet musical was a lament for a nation succumbing to American cultural imperialism.

Some 1300 features were produced in France in the 1930s, and 686 contained two or more songs. Yet the musical failed to establish itself as a distinctive genre. Instead, filmmakers inserted *chansons réalistes* to strengthen the sense of communality and struggle that informed **proletarian melodramas** that were often set in the urban backstreets. The various street singers, music-hall turns and nightclub performers were usually no more than passing figures. But the likes of Fréhel, Florelle and Damia symbolized a **working-class integrity** that made their comments on the action all the more profound. **Edith Piaf** also featured as a realist singer in such downbeat dramas as *Étoiles sans lumières* (*Star Without Light*, 1945) and authenticity was even key to *Zouzou* (1934) and *Princesse Tam Tam* (1935), starring the African-American stage icon, **Josephine Baker**.

But there was also a demand for **escapism**. **Maurice Chevalier** returned to France for Julien Duvivier's *L'homme du jour* (*The Man Of The Hour*, 1937) and René Clair's *Le silence est d'or* (*Man About Town*, 1947), and Georges Milton and Fernandel headlined similar light entertainments. The 1930s also saw the flourishing of the *operette filmée*, with Henri Garat and Meg Lemonnier forming a charming partnership in romantic confections like *La chaste Suzanne* (*The Girl In The Taxi*, 1937), and Yvonne Printemps co-starring with husband Pierre Fresnay in such lavish **costume pieces** as *Les trois valses* (*The Three Waltzes*, 1938) and the Offenbach biopic, *La valse de Paris* (*Paris Waltz*, 1950).

Provincial audiences, however, preferred the rougher, readier musicals of the **Corsican balladier**, Tino Rossi (*Mariella*, 1936), and such breezy Charles Trenet vehicles as *Je chante* (*I Sing*, 1938). **Georges Guétary**, star of *Les aventures de Casanova* (*Loves Of Casanova*, 1947), was also briefly popular, but he lacked the matinée dash of the Spanish-born Luis Mariano, who was successfully paired with Carmen Sevilla in *Andalousie* (*Andalusian Dream,* 1950), *Violetas imperiales* (1952) and *La belle de Cadix* (1953).

Many musical films continued to have a **showbiz background**, among them Jean Renoir's *French Can-Can* (1954), which pitched Jean Gabin and Edith Piaf into the early days of the Moulin Rouge. But song had been reduced to an incidental aspect of French cinema by the time such *yé-yé* idols as Johnny Hallyday and Sylvie Vartan paired in *D'où viens-tu, Johnny?* (*Run, Johnny, Run,* 1964). However, the *nouvelle vague* did as much as pop to revive screen song, with Anna Karina, Claude Brasseur and Sami Frey dancing the Madison in the iconic café sequence in **Jean-Luc Godard**'s *Bande à part* (*Band Of Outsiders*, 1964).

The maestro of the **New Wave musical** was **Jacques Demy**. Seduced by its references to *On The Town* (1949), critic Georges Sadoul described *Lola* (1960), as "a kind of musical without songs and dances", and the influence of Stanley Donen, Vincente Minnelli and René Clair was also evident in the "pop-opera", *Les parapluies de Cherbourg* (*The Umbrellas Of Cherbourg,* 1964). Demy and composer **Michel Legrand** tried to repeat the formula with *Les desmoiselles de Rochefort* (*The Young Girls Of Rochefort*, 1967), for which they imported Gene Kelly and George Chakiris to partner **Catherine Deneuve** and Françoise Dorléac. But while the numbers were staged with aplomb, they didn't always emerge smoothly from the gossamer storyline. Consequently, the film disappointed at the box office, as did Demy's subsequent outings, *Peau d'âne* (*Donkey Skin*, 1970), *The Pied Piper* (1971), *Une chambre en ville* (*A Room In Town*, 1982), *Parking* (1985) and *Trois places pour le 26* (1988).

**Alain Resnais**, Demy's contemporary on the fringes of the *nouvelle vague*, has also acquired a reputation for musicals. He typically made past, present and imagined incidents collide in *La vie est un roman* (*Life Is A Bed Of Roses*, 1983), but he returned to more traditional musical territory for *On connaît le chanson* (*The Same Old Song*, 1997) and *Pas sur la bouche* (*Not On The Lips*, 2003). François Ozon attempted a similar conceit with *8 Femmes* (*8 Women*, 2002), while Olivier Ducastel and Jacques Martineau also demontrated a partiality to **throwback musicals** in *Jeanne And The Perfect Guy* (1998) and *Cockles And Muscles* (2005).

**Occasional songs** rather than full-scale scores have continued to be the norm, in films as different as Jean-Jacques Beineix's *Diva* (1982), **Luc Besson**'s *Subway* (1985), Christophe Barratier's *Les choristes* (*The Choir*, 2004) and Xavier Giannoli's *The Singer* (2006). A growing number of soundtracks have incorporated such imported styles as reggae (*La haine*, 1994), rap (*Bye-Bye*, 1995) and Algerian Raï (*100% Arabica*, 1997), while **Tony Gatliff** has used Romany rhythms in *Latcho drom* (*Safe Journey*, 1993), *Gadjo dilo* (*The Crazy Stranger*, 1997), *Vengo* (*I Come*, 2000), *Swing* (2002), *Exils* (2004) and *Transylvania* (2006). Yet all of these diverse pictures uphold the French musical's **unique tradition** of making song and dance an integral part of everyday life.

### À nous la liberté (Freedom For Us)

**dir René Clair, 1931, Fr, 97m, b/w**

Song was used to cynical effect in this scathing parable about the dehumanizing nature of industry, which reunites two escaped jailbirds, with Henri Marchand now a tramp and Raymond Cordy an industrialist, who has modelled his phonograph factory on their prison. Although Georges Auric's score is superb, Clair later regretted using operetta to make political points. But the film, which influenced Chaplin's *Modern Times* (1936), has lost none of its wit, ingenuity or social insight.

### Zouzou

**dir Marc Allégret, 1934, Fr, 92m, b/w**

Josephine Baker's Martinique-born laundress moves to Paris with her adoptive brother, Jean Gabin, and gets a job at the music hall where he's an electrician to pay for his defence after he's falsely accused of murder. The *42nd Street* twist is a touch trite, but the musical interludes are superb, whether it's Baker impudently impersonating the star of the show, or the Haiti number, in which she swings inside a birdcage that's as outsize as the other stylized props.

### Princesse Tam Tam

**dir Edmond T. Gréville, 1935, Fr, 77m, b/w**

Packed with exotic colonial clichés, this Pygmalion story opens with novelist Albert Préjean wondering whether he could pass off Tunisian shepherdess Josephine Baker as a princess, in order to exact revenge on his wife's infatuation with a maharajah. However, the ruse is exposed at a swish *soirée*, as the drunken Baker gyratingly joins the Arabian Nights floor show. The twist ending is a bit tatty, but the stop-motion animation and miniature sets in the big set-piece are mesmerizing.

### On connaît le chanson (The Same Old Song)

**dir Alain Resnais, 1997, Fr, 120m**

Scripted by Agnès Jaoui and Jean-Pierre Bacri, this satisfyingly knotted romantic comedy riffs on the Dennis Potter style of musical by having the characters sing key lines rather than entire songs to reveal their thoughts and feelings. With classics by Maurice Chevalier, Edith Piaf, Charles Aznavour, Jacques Dutronc, Johnny Hallyday, France Gall and Jane Birkin in the mix, this is chic, slick and hugely entertaining.

### Pas sur la bouche (Not On The Lips)

**dir Alain Resnais, 2003, Fr, 115m**

Enacted on Jacques Saulnier's classily stylized period set by a cast singing all the songs live, this mischievous social, cultural and psychological satire manages to be both entirely theatrical and wholly cinematic. Harking back to the patter classics of Ernst Lubitsch and René Clair, it also pokes fun at both French and American types and, thus, manages to be simultaneously nostalgic and modern.

### 8 femmes (8 Women)

**dir François Ozon, 2002, Fr, 103m**

Stuffed with allusions to French and American movies, this dazzling ensemble gem works as both an intriguing whodunnit and an intoxicating cine-puzzle for film buffs. With the cast elegantly attired by Pascaline Chavanne revelling in both the acidic one-liners and the pop pastiches, this is impossible to dislike – all the more so because of the sinister sadness simmering beneath the pristine surface.

## Germany

Although talkies arrived in Germany with Hanns Schwarz's *Melodie des Herzens* (*Melody Of The Heart*, 1929), the popular image of the nascent German sound film is **Marlene Dietrich** singing "Falling In Love Again" in **Josef von Sternberg**'s *Der blaue Engel* (*The Blue Angel*,1930). However, Dietrich was snapped up by Paramount. So, it was **Willy Fritsch** and **Lilian Harvey** who truly launched the genre with such classic *Tonfilmoperetten* as Wilhelm Thiele's *Liebeswalzer* (*Waltz Of Love*, 1930) and Erik Charell's *Der Kongress tanzt* (*The Congress Dances*, 1931), and

### Musical mädchen

**Lilian Harvey** Born in London, but raised in Berlin, Lilian Harvey is best known for the eight UFA musicals she made with **Willy Fritsch**, including *Einbrecher* (*Burglars*, 1930) and *Glückskinder* (*Lucky Kids*, 1936). A lively dancer and excellent singer, she misfired in Hollywood with *My Weakness* and *I Am Suzanne* (both 1933) and returned to team with director-lover Paul Martin on such acclaimed vehicles as *Fanny Elssler* (1937) and *Capriccio* (1938). Hounded by the **Gestapo** after war broke out, she concluded her screen career in France with *Serenade* and *Miquette* (both 1940).

**Renate Müller** Director **Reinhold Schünzel** captured Renate Müller's sassy, stylish vibrancy in eight musical comedies, including *Saison in Kairo* (*Season In Cairo*,1933), with Willy Fritsch. However, a combination of ill health and a resistance to **Nazi film policy** stalled her career and she proved less effective in such sanitized offerings as *Eskapade* (1936) and *Togger* (1937). Müller died in 1937, having possibly been pushed from a hospital window. She was played by Ruth Leuwerik in the 1960 biopic, *Liebling der Götter* (*Sweetheart Of The Gods*).

**Marika Rökk** Marika Rökk was born in Cairo, but raised in Hungary. She had danced in Paris and New York before making her first films, *Why Sailors Leave Home* (1930) and *Kiss Me Sergeant* (1932), in Britain. But under the tutelage of future husband, **Georg Jacoby**, she emerged as Germany's answer to Eleanor Powell in such chic pictures as *Und Du, mein Schatz, führst mit* (*And You My Darling Will Go Along*, 1937) and *Frauen sind doch bessere Diplomaten* (*Women Really Do Make Better Diplomats*, 1941). Yet while hits like *Hallo, Janine!* (1939) and *Es war eine rauschende Ballnacht* (*One Enchanted Evening*,1939) kept coming, she never really learned to tone down her full-on exuberance, and while her dancing was athletic and powerful it lacked emotion and sensuality. She kept busy after the war, but Jacoby's *Sensation In San Remo* (1951) and *Die Geschiedene Frau* (*The Divorcée*, 1953) were somewhat passé.

**Zarah Leander** Although she was known as the **Nazi Garbo**, the contralto Zarah Leander was actually lured to Germany as a replacement for Marlene Dietrich. She had made films in her native Sweden and Austria, but fame came in Detlef Sierck's *Zu neuen Urfen* (*To New Shores*, 1937) and *La Habanera* (1937). Carl Froelich's *Heimat* (1938) and *Das Herz der Königin* (*The Heart Of A Queen*,1940) also proved popular, but her biggest wartime hits were **Rolf Hansen**'s *Die grosse Liebe* (*The Great Love*, 1942) and *Damals* (1943). She fled to Sweden in 1943 – much to the fury of **Propaganda Minister Joseph Goebbels**, who had always considered her an "Enemy of Germany". She returned in such post-war showcases as *Gabriela* (1950), *Cuba Cabena* (1952) and *Ave Maria* (1953), and continued to perform into her seventies – becoming a **gay icon** and drag queen favourite in the process.

the musical comedies *Die Drei von der Tankstelle* (*The Three From The Gas Station*, 1930) and *Ein blonder Traum* (*A Blonde Dream*, 1932).

Acerbic dialogue, saucy innuendo and cheerful ditties characterized many Weimar musicals, including the **Renate Müller** duo, *Die Privatsekretärin* (*The Private Secretary*, 1931) and *Viktor und Viktoria* (1933), which were both directed by Reinhold Schünzel. Yet the most distinctive musical of the period was **G.W. Pabst's**

Lilian Harvey as glover Christel Weinzinger in *Der Kongress tanzt* (1931). The press dubbed Harvey "the sweetest girl in the world", while her partnership with Willy Fritsch made them "the dream pair of German movies".

*The Threepenny Opera* (1931), in which Lotte Lenya repeated her stage triumph as Pirate Jenny in Kurt Weill and Bertolt Brecht's revision of *The Beggar's Opera*. The Nazis suppressed the film. But **Propaganda Minister Joseph Goebbels** recognized the value of escapist entertainment and musicals and comedies accounted for over half of Germany's screen output between 1933 and 1945.

While Lilian Harvey, Marta Eggerth and Jenny Jugo sustained the **traditional operetta**, Schünzel and Fritsch brought a touch of **Hollywood panache** to *Amphitryon* (1935), a sparkling renovation of Plautus, whose **populism** delighted Goebbels. However, he was more partial to the semi-naked eroticism of La Jana's dances in *Es leuchten die Sterne* (*The Stars Are Shining*,1938), which he passed off as paeans to classical sculpture and the body beautiful.

La Jana and Renate Müller both died young, leaving Hungarian **Marika Rökk** to become a major star in husband Georg Jacoby's *Gasparone* (1937). Rökk's heroines invariably had to choose between a career and domesticity before finding love and fulfilment. But no one suffered or sacrificed more melodically than the Swede **Zarah Leander**, who invariably passed through temptation, transgression, remorse and redemption in hugely popular films like Detlef Sierck's *Zu neuen Ufern* (*To New Shores*, 1937) and *La Habanera* (1937), and Rolf Hansen's *Die gross Liebe* (*The Great Love*, 1943) and *Damals* (*Back Then*, 1943).

In **West Germany**, operetta was gradually supplanted by **Heimat musicals** like Hans Deppe's *Schwarzaldmädel* (*Black Forest Girl*, 1950) and Geza von Bolvary's *Schwarzwaldmelodie* (*Black Forest Melody*, 1958), which made copious use of folk songs, arias and rustic instruments to celebrate the spirit and tradition of the nation, while also providing some **nostalgic reassurance** in an uncertain Cold War world. The most famous of these *Heimatfilme* were Wolfgang Liebeneiner's *Die Trapp-Familie* (1956) and *Die Trapp-Familie in Amerika* (1958), which predated **Rodgers and Hammerstein**'s *The Sound Of Music* (1965, see Canon).

Audiences eventually came to prefer *Schlagerfilme* like *Ich hab mein Herz in Heidelberg verlore* (*I Lost My Heart In Heidelberg*, 1952), which were inspired by chart hits. **Pop acts** like Conny Froboess and Peter Kraus also scored in *Wenn die Conny mit dem Peter* (*When Conny Met Peter*, 1958). But the musical all but disappeared during the **New German Cinema** phase, although music was used innovatively in Werner Schroeter's study of gay aesthetics, *Der Tod der Maria Malibran* (*The Death Of Maria Malibran*, 1971), Hans-Jürgen Syberburg's epic take on Wagner's *Parsifal* (1982), and Edgar Reitz's exceptional *Heimat* trilogy (1984, 1992 and 2004). Subsequently, in *Die Comedien Harmonists* (1998), Joseph Vilsmaier recalled the anti-Semitic pressures that led to the break up of the eponymous *a capella* group that had appeared so memorably in the famous 1931 "gunboat operetta", *Bomben auf Monte Carlo* (*Monte Carlo Madness*).

## Der Kongress tanzt (The Congress Dances)

**dir Erik Charell, 1931, Ger, 92m, b/w**

Ufa took a considerable risk in entrusting its biggest-ever budget (1,639,950 Reichsmarks) to debuting director Erik Charell. But the stage specialist produced a picture whose lightness, elegance and musical ingenuity rivalled anything produced by Lubitsch, Clair and Mamoulian. Fifty-four minutes were devoted to music, with the highlights being a ballet for musical chairs and Lilian Harvey's epic coach ride to "This Happens Only Once And Never Again". However, Goebbels banned the film in 1937, as Charell, producer Erich Pommer and composer Werner Richard Heymann were all Jewish.

### The Threepenny Opera (Die Dreigroschoper)

**dir G.W. Pabst, 1931, Ger, 112m, b/w**

Bertolt Brecht sued the producers for toning down the anti-capitalist content in this adaptation of his landmark stage collaboration with composer Kurt Weill. Furthermore, many of their original songs were cut. But Andre Andreiev's evocative décor and Fritz Arno Wagner's superb photography created a stylized visual setting for Rudolf Forster's roguish turn as lowlife Mackie Messer and Lotte Lenya's mesmerizing performance as Pirate Jenny.

### Viktor und Viktoria

**dir Reinhold Schünzel, 1933, Ger, 100m, b/w**

Renate Müller is a delight in this musical comedy classic, as the struggling singer who poses as a female impersonator at the suggestion of buddy, Hermann Thimig. However, complications set in when she falls for the suave Adolf Wohlbrück (Anton Wahlbrook), who can't understand why he feels so strongly about another chap. A fascinating memoir of the Berlin cabaret scene, this easily surpasses the remakes starring Jessie Matthews (1935), Anna Cordy (1957) and Julie Andrews (1982).

### Gasparone

**dir Georg Jacoby, 1937, Ger, 80m, b/w**

Goebbels attempted to block Marika Rökk's casting in this Graustarkian fantasy. But she responded with a typically bravura performance as the niece of bistro-owner Oskar Sima, who has invented a daring bandit to deflect attention from his coffee-smuggling activities. However, local prefect Leo Slezak is as determined to get his man as he is to secure son Heinz Schorlemmer an aristocratic wife. With its mischievous masquerades and tangled romantic alliances, this lavish showcase for the effervescent Rökk makes for lively escapist entertainment.

### La Habanera

**dir Detlef Sierck, 1937, Ger, 98m, b/w**

Partially filmed in Tenerife at the height of the Spanish Civil War, this musical melodrama was designed to confirm Zarah Leander's reputation as the new Swedish Nightingale. But director Detlef Sierck used the tale of Leander's rebellion against tyrannical Puerto Rican landowner Ferdinand Marian and the renewal of her passion for old flame Karl Martell to subvert Nazi notions of racial supremacy and colonial adventure. Moreover, Leander's ardent performance contrasted strikingly with the portrayals of dutiful Aryan womanhood given by her compatriot, Kristina Söderbaum. A noble and courageous act of cinematic resistance.

### Die Trapp-Familie

**dir Wolfgang Liebeneiner, 1956, Ger, 106m**

Loosely based on the memoirs of Maria von Trapp, this is more of a melodrama than *The Sound Of Music* (1965). But the sentimental singing is suitably appealing and Ruth Leuwerik is much less saccharine than Julie Andrews. Composer Franz Gothe returned for the 1958 genial, but less engrossing sequel, *Die Trapp-Familie in Amerika*.

### Comedian Harmonists

**dir Joseph Vilsmaier, 1997, Ger, 124m**

Staged with Hollywood panache, this formulaic, but fascinating biopic chronicles the career of the eponymous multipart-harmony sextet – from its formation in 1920s Berlin, through its triumphs across Europe and the US, to its brush with the Nazis for refusing to jettison three Jewish members. Ably played, handsomely photographed and musically charming.

## Hong Kong

Such was the popularity of **Chinese opera** that a quarter of Hong Kong's entire screen output to 1939 was devoted to these *xiqu* pictures. However, the film industry collapsed during World War II and its revival owed much to the **Mandarin musicals** of Shanghai exile **Zhou Xuan** in the late 1940s.

"The Golden Voice" made such an impact in films like *Orioles Banished From The Flowers* (1948) that a succession of *xiansheng* or "sing-song" girls followed, including **Bai Guang**, "the Magnetic Low Voice" who emerged as the best-known of these "sour beauties" in such *noir*ish offerings as *Blood-Stained Begonia* (1949). But the growing **influence of American music** and Hollywood movies prompted such urban musicals as Yi Wen's *Mambo Girl* (1957), which starred Ge Lan (aka Grace Chang), whose trendy heroines in *Air Hostess* (1959) and *The Wild Wild Rose* (1960) inspired copycat ventures for Zhang Zhongwen, Li Mei, Le Di and Lily Ho.

Before Cantonese became the dominant cinema language in the mid-1960s, its speciality had been low-budget operas nicknamed **"seven day wonders"**, which included on-screen lyrics to encourage audiences to **sing along**. The popular pairing of Yam Kim-fai and Pak Suet-sin brought a new sophistication, however, and **John Woo** remade their 1959 hit, *Tragedy Of The Emperor's Daughter*, as *Princess Cheung Ping* in 1976. But the queens of the **Cantonese musical** were **Chan Po-chu** (aka Connie Chan) and **Josephine Siao**. Having teamed in Lee Tit's *Eternal Love* (1966) – in which Chan played a male academic who falls for Siao after she nurses "him" back to health – Chan headlined youth movies like *Girls Are Flowers* (1966), while Siao followed musical comedies like *Romance Of A Teenage Girl* (1966) by playing an "Ah Fei" delinquent in the classic "A-Go-Go" picture, *Teddy Girls* (1969). The genre faded in the 1970s, but many **Canto-Pop stars** have since found movie fame, including Anita Mui, Leslie Cheung, Andy Lau, Jacky Cheung, Karen Mok and Faye Wong.

## India

The **world's biggest film industry** is synonymous with song and dance. It's been estimated that some 250,000 screen songs (*filmi*) were written between 1931 and 1990. But the musical isn't a genre, either in **Bollywood** or in any other of India's diverse regional traditions – it's a template that's followed by pictures as different as historicals and mythologicals, romances and melodramas, comedies and horrors, thrillers and actioners. It would require a survey of the whole of sub-continental cinema to explain its methodologies and identify its finest achievements, so for now we'll concentrate on some of the unsung figures behind the scenes.

The **All-India singing style** was established by **K.L. Saigal** in such films as P.C. Barua's *Devdas* (1935). But few could match "the Golden Voice of the Silver Screen", among them Noor Jehan, Suraiya and Kishore Kumar. Consequently, the studios introduced the practice of performers **lip synching** to recordings made by playback singers like Mukesh, Shamshad Begum, Kumar Sanu, Mohammed Rafi, Lata Mangeshkar and her sister, Asha Bhosle, who were in great demand for their ability to modulate their delivery to suit both the tone of the song and the personality of the on-screen star.

Equally crucial to the success of this conceit were the **music directors** who wrote and pro-

### Pakistan

The **Urdu film industry** was based in Lahore before Partition in 1947. The relocation of such key Bollywood figures as Ghulam Haider and Noor Jehan ensured that **Lollywood** continued to use song and dance in the traditional Indian manner. Over the years, Inayat Hussain Bhatti, Salim Raza, Mehdi Hassan, Masood Rana, Naseem Begum, Mala, Naheed Akhtar, Runa Laila and Humaira Channa have ranked among the finest **playback singers**, while the top music directors have included G.A. Chishti, Feroze Nizami, Abdul Hameed and Nazir Ali.

duced the *filmi*.Their lyrics were almost always germane to the plot, even though the accompanying dance routines became increasingly **fantastical** after the introduction of colour in the 1960s, (a result of audiences' craving for escapism and spectacle). Among the **key pioneers** were Ghulam Haider and Naushad Ali, who were succeeded by S.D. and R.D. Burman. In the 1950s the father-son duo introduced the **Western influences** that have been further modified more recently by brothers Jatin-Lalit and the "King of Indian Pop", **A.R. Rahman**.

## Latin America

Such is the widespread popularity of the **diverse musical styles** of Central and South America that singers have always ranked among the major stars of the Argentinian, Brazilian and Mexican film industries.

Music has always been at the heart of **Argentinian cinema**, with many theatres having an *orquestra típica* to accompany silent features. Several band leaders went into the talkies, but the first musical star was tango singer **Carlos Gardel**, who enchanted audiences in *Las luces de Buenos Aires* (1931) and *Melodía de arrabal* (*Suburban Melody*, 1933). Following his death in a plane crash in 1936, the mantle passed to **Libertad Lamarque**, the "Queen of Tango", who also proved herself to be a fine dramatic actress in *Besos brujos* (*Bewitching Kisses,* 1937) and *Madreselva* (*Honeysuckle,* 1938).

However, the musical had a low critical reputation and it often had to subsist on **shoestring budgets**. Yet singers like Niní Marshall and Tito Lusiardo remained popular with working-class audiences, while Lolita Torres's musical comedies acquired a **cult following** in the Soviet Union in the 1950s. The musical was finally accorded some overdue legitimacy in 1985, when Fernando E. Solanas paid handsome tribute to pioneering director **José A. Ferreyra** in *Tangos, el exilio de Gardel* (*Tangos, The Exile Of Gardel*).

The **Brazilian musical** is synonymous with the *chanchada*. Rooted in **carnival**, the Rio music hall and radio variety, it was popularized by such early musicals as *Alô, Alô Brasil* (1935), which starred **Carmen Miranda** and established both the backstager tradition and the trend for lampooning Hollywood cliché. Such pictures mostly appealed to the **lower classes** and were packed with sambas, *marchas*, *baiãos* and boleros that owed little to the flimsy plotlines. The Atlântida Cinematográfica company brought a new **satirical sophistication** to musical comedies like *Carnaval no fogo* (*Carnival On Fire*, 1949), which starred the popular duo of Grande Otelo and Oscarito. However, the *chanchada* declined in the 1960s, although its influence was still evident in the musical knockabout, *Os Trapalhôes And The King Of Football* (1986), which teamed the band Os Trapalhôes and Pelé.

The **Mexican musical** was more diverse. Arcady Boytler's *La mujer del puerto* (*Woman Of The Port*, 1933) launched the *cabaretera* melodrama, in which wronged women fought fate and weak men succumbed to scheming vamps in society's lower depths. The **Cuban rumbera**, Ninón Sevilla, continued the tradition in Alberto Gout's *Aventurera* (1949) and *Sensualidad* (1950), which paved the way for the likes of Marga López, and Meche Barba, whose bad girls danced to the imported rhythms of the rumba, conga, mambo and cha-cha.

Such **gritty realism** was the complete antithesis of the mythologized nostalgia peddled in the *ranchera*, whose *mariachi* style was established in

Fernando de Fuentes's *Allá en el Rancho Grande* (*Over On The Big Ranch*, 1936), with René Cardona and Tito Guízar. The most idolized singing *charro* was **Jorge Negrete**, who exuded macho decency in pictures like *¡Ay Jalisco, no te rajes!* (*Oh Jalisco, Don't Quit Now!*, 1941). His Everyman persona was assumed by Pedro Infante in such *arrabal* outings as *Nosotros los pobres* (*We, The Poor*, 1947), which sentimentalized the squalor of the inner-city slums.

Tin Tan and Resortes – the alter egos of comics Germán Valdes and Adalberto Martínez – brought a **surreal wit** to the genre as it declined during the 1950s. And new stars like Lola Beltrán, Luis Aguilar and Angélica María were unable to stem the tide of the *fichera* (a raunchier version of *cabaretera*) and the *sexycomedia*, which prevailed into the 1980s. However, a **touch of class** has since been restored by Maria Novaro in *Danzón* (1991) and by Paul Leduc in *Barroco* (1988), *Latino Bar* (1990) and *Dollar Mambo* (1993).

## Soviet Union

As with the vast majority of Soviet cinema in the 1930s, the musical was encouraged for its **propagandist potential**. However, even the notoriously humourless film chief **Boris Shumyatsky** recognized the morale-boosting value of escapist entertainment and allowed the musical more satirical latitude than most other genres.

Although Igor Savchenko launched the Soviet musical with *Accordion* (1934), its finest practitioners were **Grigori Alexandrov** and **Ivan Pyriev**, who had studied together at Moscow's Proletkult Theatre. Full of eccentric characters, camera tricks, animated interludes and slapstick sequences, Alexandrov's *Jolly Fellows* (1934) starred his wife, **Lyubov Orlova**, who went on to headline the box-office hits, *The Circus* (1936), *Volga-Volga* (1938) and *The Shining Path* (1940), which all poked gentle fun at the Kremlin's imposed style of **Socialist Realism**.

Pyriev's pictures were less subtle and owed much to the Stakhanovite cult and the hyberbolic spirit of **folk art**. Everything was larger than life in films like *The Rich Bride* (1938), *Tractor Drivers* (1939) and *The Swineherd And The Shepherd* (1941), which testified to the prosperity of the countryside and the health of its residents. They starred **Marina Ladynina**, a diminutive blonde who lacked Orlova's sophistication, but more than atoned in pluck and typicality. However, *At Six O'Clock In The Evening After The War* (1944) was criticized for trivializing the struggle against the Nazis, and Pyriev and Ladynina only made one further musical, *Cossacks Of The Kuban* (1950).

A greater emphasis was placed on opera, ballet and classical music in the 1950s, although Eldar Ryazanov enjoyed considerable success with the **revue**, *Carnival Night* (1956), and Dmitri Shostakovich included some rock'n'roll in Gerbert Rappaport's *Cheryomushki* (1963). Subsequently, Karen Shakhnazarov attempted to revive the musical comedy with *We Are Jazzmen* (1983) and *Winter Evening In Gagry* (1985). But **rock music** has since dominated the soundtracks of Russian features like Svetlana Stasenko's *Shantytown Blues* (2004).

### Volga-Volga

**dir Grigori Alexandrov, 1938, 104m**

Alexandrov refined his heroic pastiche approach in this breezy steamboat comedy, in which Lyubov Orlova's provincial letter carrier triumphs over the bureaucrat in charge of the Moscow Musical Olympiad. The songs sound jaunty enough, but their lyrics occasionally pack a political punch.

## Spain

Spanish silent cinema had drawn heavily on the popular style of **stage operetta** known as *zarzuela* and it remained a key influence on the musicals directed by *padrinos* **Florián Rey** and **Benito Perojo** in the early 1930s. Rey is best known for thirteen collaborations with his tempestuous wife, **Imperio Argentina**, the most enduring of which are *La Hermana San Sulpicio* (*Sister San Sulpicio*, 1934), *Nobleza baturra* (*Rustic Gallantry*, 1935) and *Morena Clara* (*The Fair-Skinned Gypsy*, 1936). However, they divorced after she reportedly had an affair with Hitler, while they were in Berlin making *Carmen de la Triana* (*Carmen*, 1938) and *La canción de Aixa* (*Aixa's Song*, 1939).

Following the success of *La verbena de la Paloma* (*Paloma Fair*, 1935), Perojo forged his own profitable partnership with **Estrellita Castro** on *Mariquilla terremoto* (*Mariquilla The Bombshell*, 1938) and *Suspiros de España* (*Sighs Of Spain*, 1938). Despite the **Catholic Church**'s objection to their flagrant displays of **female independence**, Franco's censors tolerated these *folklórista* musicals, which made huge stars of Juanita Reina (*La blanca Paloma*, 1942), Concha Piquer (*Filigrana*, 1949), Carmen Sevilla (*La Hermana San Sulpicio*, 1952), Lola Flores (*Morena Clara*, 1954), Paquita Rico (*Curra veleta*, 1955) and Sara Montiel, whose **showbiz melodrama**, *El último cuplé* (*The Last Song*, 1957), remains a Spanish classic.

Male singers like Luis Mariano and Juanito Valderrama simply couldn't compete. And the 1950s **child stars** Pablito Calvo and Joselito were similarly eclipsed by **Marisol**, who charmed audiences as a spirited orphan in **Luis Lucia's** *Un rayo de luz* (*A Ray Of Light*, 1960) and *Ha llegando un ángel* (*An Angel Has Arrived*, 1961) before maturing into a sassy teenager in Lucia's *Las cuatro bodas de Marisol* (*Marisol's Four Weddings*, 1967). Rocío Dúrcal and the identical twins, Pili y Mili, followed in her wake, while Mario Camus' *Cuando tú no estás* (*When You're Not Here*, 1966) established Raphael as their male counterpart. But, while **pop music** was beginning to overrun the genre, the ultra-chic Concha Velasco opted for a colour remake of *La verbena de la Paloma* (1963), which she followed with a string of hit romantic comedies, like *¿Pero … en qué país vivimos?* (*What A Country!*, 1967), opposite "the Voice of Spain", **Manolo Escobar**.

By contrast, Franciso Rovira Beleta earned Oscar nominations for his **flamenco ballets** *Los Tarantos* (1963) and *El amor brujo* (*A Love Bewitched*, 1967), which dancer Antonio Gades remade with director **Carlos Saura** in 1986, as the concluding part of a trilogy that had begun with *Bodas de sangre* (*Blood Wedding*, 1981) and *Carmen* (1983). Saura has since explored other Spanish styles of song and dance in *Sevillanas* (1992), *Flamenco* (1995), *Tango* (1998), *Salomé* (2002) and *Iberia* (2005), while also recalling the lot of the **wartime vaudevillian** in *¡Ay, Carmela!* (1990). But their arthouse success has only occasionally been matched by the likes of Jaime Chávarri's *The Things Of Love* (1989), Emilio Martínez Lázaro's *The Other Side Of The Bed* (2002) – each of which spawned lesser sequels – and Ramón Salazar's Almodóvarian transsexual saga, *20 centímetros* (2005), which jovially referenced everything from MGM to MTV.

### ¡Ay, Carmela!

**dir Carlos Saura, 1990, Sp, 95m**

Although strewn with coarse comedy, this is a deeply moving memoir of the Spanish Civil War, in which small-time vaudevillians Carmen Maura and Andres Pajares exhibit true artistic integrity when asked to perform before Fascist troops and condemned prisoners of war. The entire ensemble excels, but Maura particularly impresses as the blowsy dame who comes to embody the spirit of resistance in her heroic swan song.

### El otro lado de la cama (The Other Side Of The Bed)

**dir Emilio Martinez-Lazaro, 2002, Sp, 104m**

With Ernesto Alterio cheating on Paz Vega with buddy Guillermo Toledo's girlfriend Natalia Verbeke, this musical rom-com couldn't be more formulaic. But the familiar round of deceptions, suspicions, accusations and excuses is enlivened by some slick shifts in tone and pace. And while the song-and-dance routines occasionally smack of gimmickry, they're boldly executed and highly entertaining.

## United Kingdom

Noël Coward once lamented, "the only trouble with the British is that they have never taken light music seriously enough … We just don't have the choreographers, the orchestrators, the dancers, the technicians to cope with the complexities of a big musical." Unfortunately, where the cinema was concerned, Britain didn't really have the directors, the composers or the performers, either.

Some 220 musical films were produced in the UK in the 1930s. Many were **third-rate quota quickies** that have long been forgotten. But even once-acclaimed musicals featuring such major stars as Anna Neagle (*Bitter Sweet*, 1933), Jessie Matthews (*Evergreen*, 1934), Jack Buchanan (*Brewster's Millions*, 1935) and Lupino Lane (*The Lambeth Walk*, 1939), and **music-hall favourites** like Jack Hulbert (*Jack Ahoy!*, 1933), Gracie Fields (*Sing As We Go*, 1934), Cicely Courtneidge (*Things Are Looking Up*, 1935) and George Formby (*Come On George*, 1939) are becoming increasingly obscure. British television channels still screen musicals made in Hollywood during the 1930s and 40s. But homegrown talents like The Crazy Gang (*O-Kay For Sound*, 1937), Tommy Handley (*It's That Man Again*, 1943), Arthur Askey (*Band Waggon*, 1940) and Tommy Trinder (*Champagne Charlie*, 1944) are now largely spurned.

The failure of such **prestige pictures** as *Gaiety George* and *London Town* (both 1946) – both of which were made with American assistance – clearly tarnished the British musical's reputation. But films of enduring quality were produced, including the **Powell and Pressburger** trio of *The Red Shoes* (1948), *Tales Of Hoffman* (1951) and *Oh, Rosalinda!!* (1955), and Peter

The "Peter Pan of Pop", Cliff Richard, is now known as a family entertainer, but he adopted a surlier, Elvis-like persona in early films like *Expresso Bongo* (1959).

Brook's adaptation of John Gay's *The Beggar's Opera* (1953), in which **Laurence Olivier** did all his own singing, as MacHeath.

It wasn't until tastes changed that British musicals began to make an **international impact**. Coffee bar pictures like *The Golden Disc* (1958) and *Expresso Bongo* (1959) were copied on the continent. But while **Tommy Steele** could graduate from such sub-Elvis vehicles as *The Tommy Steele Story* (1957) and *The Duke Wore Jeans* (1958) into Hollywood entertainments like *Half A Sixpence* (1967) and *Finian's Rainbow* (1969), **Cliff Richard** failed to crack America, despite the domestic popularity of *The Young Ones* (1961), *Summer Holiday* (1963) and *Wonderful Life* (1964). Bands seeking to emulate **The Beatles**' success in *A Hard Day's Night* (1964), *Help!* (1965) and *Yellow Submarine* (1968) were similarly frustrated, although John Boorman's Dave Clark Five outing, *Catch Us If You Can* (1965), has since acquired cult status.

Indeed, Britain was better known towards the end of the **swinging sixties** for more traditional musicals like Carol Reed's Oscar-winning *Oliver!* (1968), **Richard Attenborough**'s *Oh! What A Lovely War* (1969), Ronald Neame's *Scrooge* (1970) and Ken Russell's *The Boy Friend* (1971). However, the iconoclastic Russell was soon challenging the conventions of the genre with **Pete Townshend**'s rock opera, *Tommy* (1975), and the composer biopics, *The Music Lovers* (1971), *Mahler* (1974) and *Lisztomania* (1975), which couldn't have contrasted more with the **scuffed nostalgia** of the David Essex duo, *That'll Be The Day* (1974) and *Stardust* (1975), Richard Loncraine's Slade drama, *Flame* (1974), and Franc Roddam's Who-inspired **mods and rockers** saga, *Quadrophenia* (1979).

Subsequently, a number of directors have revisited the musical, including Alan Parker (*Bugsy Malone*, 1976, and *Pink Floyd – The Wall*, 1982), Julian Temple (*The Great Rock'n'Roll Swindle*, 1980, *Absolute Beginners*, 1986, and *Joe Strummer: The Future Is Unwritten*, 2007), and Kenneth Branagh (*Love's Labours Lost*, 1999, and *The Magic Flute*, 2007). But the sheer **diversity** of pictures like Alex Cox's punk biopic *Sid And Nancy* (1986), the operatic portmanteau *Aria* (1987), Iain Softley's Fab Four memoir *Backbeat* (1993), Bob Spiers's *Spice World* (1997), Mark Herman's *Little Voice* (1998), Gurinder Chadha's **Bollywoodized** *Bride & Prejudice* (2004), Stephen Frears' *Mrs Henderson Presents* (2005), and Keith Fulton and Louis Pepe's *Brothers Of The Head* (2006) suggests that the British musical is currently more of a rattlebag than a genre.

### Evergreen

**dir Victor Saville, 1934, UK, 91m, b/w**

Jessie Matthews lived up to her reputation as "The Dancing Divinity" in this transfer of her 1930 stage hit, *Ever Green*. As the daughter who masquerades as her music-hall star mother, Matthews revelled in African-American Buddy Bradley's choreography, especially to "Dancing On The Ceiling" and the production number atop a wedding cake.

### Sing As We Go

**dir Basil Dean, 1934, UK, 80m, b/w**

Scripted by J.B. Priestley, this was the epitome of the British Depression musical, as mill worker Gracie Fields gets on her bike to Blackpool and accepts a variety of jobs before helping John Loder reopen the mill. It may be brashly comical and rousingly optimistic, but this also anticipates the social realist style of the Kitchen Sink era.

### Come On George

**dir Anthony Kimmins, 1939, UK, 88m, b/w**

Songs like "I'm Making Headway Now" may not be among George Formby's most memorable, but this horse-racing comedy best showcases his winning blend of gormless geniality and accidental pluck, as he's duped into riding a bucking nag named Maneater under the impression it's a docile creature called The Lamb.

## A Hard Day's Night

Sharing the **day-in-the-life** strategy that the Maysles brothers had planned for their *Yeah Yeah Yeah* documentary, this is the most important **rock musical** ever made. Its director, **Richard Lester**, was something of a movie magpie and, just as John Lennon and Paul McCartney drew on rhythm'n'blues, rock'n'roll and showtune ballads for their inspiration, so Lester borrowed liberally from Buster Keaton, Direct Cinema, Free Cinema, Federico Fellini and the *nouvelle vague* for his unconventional approach to narrative and image-making. In the process, he accidentally became the **godfather of MTV**, as he sought ways of breaking from the lip sync and strum approach to filming pop. But even when he had no option, as in **The Beatles**' climactic TV appearance, he used angle, lighting and rapid editing to fashion an anti-performance style that was later slavishly followed by such shows as *Top Of The Pops*.

### The Red Shoes
**dir Michael Powell, Emeric Pressburger, 1948, UK, 133m**

Perhaps the classiest backstager ever produced, the story of ballerina Moira Shearer's conflicted relationships with impresario Anton Walbrook and composer Marius Goring is sublimely mirrored by the Hans Christian Andersen ballet she dances with Leonide Massine. Majestically choreographed by Robert Helpmann and photographed by Jack Cardiff, this occasionally precious picture earned Oscars for Brian Easdale's score and Hein Heckroth and Arthur Lawson's décor.

### Expresso Bongo
**dir Val Guest, 1959, UK, 108m**

Adapted by Wolf Mankowitz from his own stage show, the *Pal Joey* of the British pop musical splendidly captures the atmosphere of the Soho coffee bar scene, while also subverting wannabe rocker Cliff Richard's naive optimism with lashings of cynicism, supplied by Laurence Harvey's opportunistic talent agent. A neglected social realist classic.

### Help!
**dir Richard Lester, 1965, UK, 90m**

The Beatles's second feature turns around a religious cult's determination to recover a sacred ring from drummer Ringo Starr's finger. It proved less influential than *A Hard Day's Night* (1964) but the band dynamic remains strong and edgy, while the widescreen colour staging of superior songs like "Help!" and "Ticket To Ride" was as innovative as the Bond chic pastiche was subversively cool.

Reprising his stage role as Fagin in *Oliver!* (1968), Ron Moody was nominated for best actor at the Academy Awards.

### Catch Us If You Can

**dir John Boorman, 1965, UK, 91m**

Challenging the myths of celebrity and *la dolce vita*, this antidote to the Swinging Sixties feels like a pop take on Ingmar Bergman's *Wild Strawberries*, especially when bickering marrieds Yootha Joyce and Robin Bailey join stuntman Dave Clark and model Barbara Ferris in their search for something more meaningful than mod cons, convenience foods and disposable culture. But it's ultimately more *vague* than *nouvelle*.

### Half A Sixpence

**dir George Sidney, 1967, UK, 148m**

Lavishly filmed in Britain by Paramount, Beverley Cross and David Heneker's musicalization of H.G. Wells's novel *Kipps* is both made and marred by Tommy Steele's over-exuberant turn as the draper's assistant whose crush on socialite Penelope Horner alienates sweetheart Julia Foster. Gillian Lynne's choreography is equally prone to excess. But there's something infectious about songs like "Flash, Bang Wallop" and "If The Rain's Got To Fall".

### Yellow Submarine

**dir George Dunning, 1968, UK, 85m**

The Beatles only contributed a live-action coda and a handful of new songs to this psychedelic cartoon, in which the dubbed Fabs deliver Pepperland from the music-hating Blue Meanies. But the back catalogue inspired sequences of considerable charm and surreality, which invaluably captured the graphic ingenuity of Flower Power.

### Oliver!

**dir Carol Reed, 1968, UK, 153m**

Winning five Oscars from its eleven nominations, plus an honorary statuette for choreographer Onna White, this is Britain's best shot at a Hollywood musical. Lionel Bart's cornball score is much loved. But it's the excellence of the cast and Carol Reed's appreciation of Dickens's art and humanity that makes this stage transfer such affecting cinema.

### Oh! What A Lovely War

**dir Richard Attenborough, 1969, UK, 139m**

The debuting Richard Attenborough made a solid job of filming Joan Littlewood's stage satire on the follies and calamities of the Great War by keeping the all-star cast connected to the music-hall conceit. But some turns stand out, most notably Laurence Olivier's game of leapfrog and Maggie Smith's chilling recruitment drive, along with the terrifying final aerial shot of the vast cemetery.

### The Boy Friend

**dir Ken Russell, 1971, UK, 135m**

MGM bankrolled this lampoon of Warner Bros' *42nd Street*. But it lacks the finesse of the studio's greatest works, as egotistical iconoclast Ken Russell is more concerned with the smug vulgarity of his Busby Berkeley pastiches than the Jazz Age subtleties of Sandy Wilson's 1954 stage show. Nevertheless, Twiggy and Tommy Tune are delightful, and guilty pleasures abound amidst the excess.

### Tommy

**dir Ken Russell, 1975, UK 111m**

The trademark Ken Russell overkill works to perfection in this adaptation of Pete Townshend's rock opera, which uses the rise to pinball stardom of a deaf, dumb and blind kid (Roger Daltrey) to expose the hypocrisy of organized religion. Elton John, Tina Turner, Eric Clapton and Ann-Margret best capture the spirit of the score's cynicism and the film's baroque superfluity.

### Bugsy Malone

**dir Alan Parker, 1976, UK, 93m**

There are many moments in this tweenage pastiche of 1930s gangster movies when the kiddie cute becomes squeamishly disconcerting. But the splurge guns and gung-ho conviction of a cast slickly led by Jodie Foster and Scott Baio allay the majority of these *Mini Pops* fears and almost atone for the brazen mediocrity of Paul Williams's score.

### Spice World

**dir Bob Spiers, 1997, UK, 93m**

Snootily dismissed on its release by a celebrity-obsessed media that created the cultural vacuum which made manufactured acts like The Spice Girls possible, this is the *Hard Day's Night* of the Girl Power and Britpop era, with Ginger, Scary, Sporty, Baby and Posh being expertly packaged in a picture stuffed with pastiched pop iconography and stellar walk-ons. Now a kitsch classic.

# **Over the rainbow:** the wider picture

Arthur Freed, Judy Garland and Fred Astaire on the set of *Easter Parade* (1948). Garland had never met Astaire before he replaced Gene Kelly (who had broken his ankle playing touch football) and she was too nervous to speak to him until they had been formally introduced.

# Over the rainbow: the wider picture

So you've read the history of the movie musical and can't wait to get watching. But where can you find old favourites and new discoveries on video and DVD? Moreover, how can you get hold of soundtracks and the stars' greatest hits for your various music systems? What about books, sheet music and memorabilia? Maybe this will help...

## Audiovisual

### Video and DVD

Until recently, the afternoon schedules on British terrestrial television (particularly at weekends) could always be relied upon to provide a ready supply of film musicals. Now they're something of a small-screen rarity, and subscriptions are required to gain access to nostalgia channels like **Sky Cinema 1 and 2** and **TCM**. Yet, even then, musicals are still nowhere near as prevalent on UK cable and satellite as they are in the US.

The good news is that an increasing number of musicals are becoming available on **DVD**, many boasting such extras as commentaries, deleted scenes and/or production numbers, original trailers and star biographies. However, the supply is still a trickle and only the most celebrated titles have so far been released in the UK, with the unfortunate consequence that

## That's Entertainment!

Released with the tagline "Boy! Do we need it now", *That's Entertainment!* (1974) contained **clips** from over sixty **MGM movies** made between 1929 and 1958. With guest hosts including Fred Astaire, Gene Kelly, Bing Crosby, Frank Sinatra and James Stewart, it was less a greatest hits compilation than a **celebration** of the studio's artistry and a lament for the passing of the Hollywood musical. The highlights were shrewdly selected to combine **nostalgia** and an enticement to a new generation of musicals fans, and the film quickly became the highest grossing musical picture in MGM history.

Rather than simply repeating the formula for *That's Entertainment, Part Two* (1976), director **Gene Kelly** introduced a more self-deprecatory tone that allowed for the inclusion of the **cornball**, as well as the classic. However, an air of slick smugness pervaded the proceedings, and MGM had to resort to reuniting with **Fred Astaire** for the first time since their rendition of the Gershwins' "The Babbitt And The Bromide" in *Ziegfeld Follies* (1946) to disguise the quotidian quality of some of the clips.

Recognizing that it had even fewer genuine showstoppers to draw on, *That's Entertainment! III* (1994) featured a number of fascinating **outtakes**, including Fred Astaire performing "I Wanna Be A Dancin' Man" from *The Belle Of New York* (1952) in contrasting costumes, **Cyd Charisse** miming to the same "Two Faced Woman" recording that Joan Crawford used in *Torch Song* (1953) and Charisse and Gene Kelly swooning through a duet cut from *Brigadoon* (1954). However, **Judy Garland** provided the genuine gems, with snippets from "March Of The Doagies" (*The Harvey Girls*, 1946) and "Mr Monotony" (*Easter Parade*, 1948, see Canon) showing alongside hints at what *Annie Get Your Gun* (1950, see Canon) might have looked like had she not been replaced by Betty Hutton. Yet the most arresting moment came when **Lena Horne** denounced the racial bigotry that had so restricted her screen career.

**video cassette** stock of otherwise unavailable titles hasn't been maintained.

You may already have your own preferred online stores, but the most reliable source of new and **secondhand movie musicals** is **Amazon**. You're likely to find a wider choice on the US-based amazon.com than on amazon.co.uk, but you'll need an NTSC VCR, or a Region 1 or multi-region DVD player to play North American products. The prices are often more competitive on **eBay**, which also has a happy knack of turning up rarer items. But beware, lurking on eBay are some unscrupulous traders, who will advertise a film with its original VHS or DVD artwork and then dispatch a pirated copy.

If you have access to the 8-track of the digital age – the **laser disc player** – there are some enticing collections available secondhand, although it's a shame that gems like **The Dawn of Sound** series (which contains selections of Vitaphone shorts, as well as full-length early talkies) and such compilations as *The Busby Berkeley Collection* have not been transferred to more user-friendly formats.

## LPs, CDs and MP3s

Weighty tomes have been devoted to the discographies of America's leading popular song composers and performers, and it would be pointless here trying to pick a path through the decades of vinyl that have been issued since the 1920s. Besides, **CDs** are more readily available and the sound quality is often infinitely superior to crackling collectors' items.

**Soundtrack albums** of the individual titles mentioned in the Canon and elsewhere in this text have been released in various formats over the last fifty years. However, only the classics are readily available on CD, and you might have to scout around in **secondhand record shops** and online for less-vaunted titles on LP. Greatest hits collections by the major movie stars are more easily obtainable on places like Amazon and through download services like **iTunes** and **mp3.com**, although they don't always restrict themselves to screen songs. It's even more frustrating trying to find **compilations of film songs** by the great songwriters – particularly featuring the original artists.

Original cast recordings, like this *High Society* (1956) soundtrack featuring Louis Armstrong, Bing Crosby, Grace Kelly and Frank Sinatra, are always more treasurable on vinyl.

## Sheet music

Sheet music for popular songs has been published in the United States since the early nineteenth century. Those interested in its history would be advised to browse **D.W. Krummel's** essay "Publishing And Printing Of Music" in the *New Grove Dictionary Of American Music* (Macmillan, 1986) or such websites as the **Music Library Association** (www.musiclibraryassoc.org), Parlor Songs (parlorsongs.com), Levy Sheet Music (levysheetmusic.mse.jhu.edu) and the Duke University Library (library.duke.edu/music/sheetmusic/collections.html).

Printed collections of songs by the major songwriters and performers should be available from music shops and Internet booksellers. However, there are several online sites offering **downloadable instrumental scores** (primarily for piano), including Sheet Music Plus (www.sheetmusicplus.com), Music Notes (www.musicnotes.com/sheetmusic), Sheet Music UK (www.sheetmusicuk.com), Music Room (www.musicroom.co.uk) and the Free Sheet Music Guide (www.freesheetmusicguide.com).

# Books

As far as academics, musicologists and theatre snobs are concerned, the film musical is very much the poor relation of its illustrious stage forebear. Consequently, while there are hundreds of comprehensive and authoritative studies of **American musical theatre** and popular song, the equivalent canon on Hollywood is numbered only in tens. As for movie musicals from around the world, they're rarely afforded a mention even in the most scholarly national histories.

All the books mentioned below should be available from good **bookshops** (especially those online). But if you're having trouble tracking anything down, try one of the most useful resources on the entire Internet, **AbeBooks** (www.abebooks.com), which corrals international secondhand and antiquarian booksellers on to a single site.

## Origins

### Operetta: A Theatrical History
Richard Traubner (Doubleday, 1983)

An enthusiastic and accessibly scholarly history of stage operetta, although Gerald Bordman's *American Operetta* (OUP, 1981) provides useful analysis of the US evolution. Lower brow entertainments are admirably covered in Bernard Sobel's *A Pictorial History Of Burlesque* (Bonanza Books, 1956) and *A Pictorial History Of Vaudeville* (Citadel Press, 1961) and Anthony Slide's *The Encyclopedia Of Vaudeville* (Greenwood Press, 1994) and *The Vaudevillians* (Arlington House, 1981).

### Black Musical Theater: From Coontown To Dreamgirls
Allen L. Woll (Lousiana State University Press, 1989)

The political, social and showbiz aspects of this neglected area of study are covered with insight and authority in this pioneering text. Those particularly interested in minstrelsy should consult Robert Toll's *Blacking Up* (OUP, 1974).

## Stage musicals

### The Broadway Musical
Ethan Morden (OUP 1998–2001, St Martin's Press, 2003)

This hugely impressive history comes in five peerless volumes: *Make Believe* (1920s); *Beautiful Morning* (1940s); *Coming Up Roses* (1950s); *Open A New Window* (1960s); *One More Kiss* (1970s). Those requiring more of a whistle-stop approach should go for coffee-table tomes like Laurence Maslon and Michael Kantor's *Broadway: The American Musical* (Little Brown), and Ken Bloom and Frank Vlastnik's *Broadway Musicals: The 101 Greatest Shows Of All Time* (Black Dog and Leventhal, both 2004).

### Encyclopedia Of The Musical
Stanley Green (Cassell & Company, 1976)

Stanley Green is a reliable musicals scholar and this solid companion is complemented by *The World Of Musical Comedy* (Barnes, 1960) and *Broadway Musicals Show By Show* (Hal Leonard Books, 1985). For simple facts and figures, however, try Gerald Bordman's *American Musical Theatre: A Chronicle* (OUP, 1978) and Richard C. Norton's three-volume *A Chronology Of American Musical Theater* (OUP, 2002).

# Songs

### The American Musical Film Song Encyclopedia
Thomas S. Hischak (Greenwood, 1999)

This is the most compact reference to screen song. Stephen Suskin's *Show Tunes 1905–1991: The Songs, Shows And Careers Of Broadway's Major Composers* (Limelight Editions, 1992) is the stage equivalent, while anyone trying to build up a collection will need Jack Raymond's *Show Music On Record: From The 1890s To The 1980s* (Ungar, 1982) and *Movie Musicals On Record: A Directory Of Recordings Of Motion Picture Musicals, 1927–87* (Greenwood Press, 1989), which was edited by Richard Chigley Lynch.

# History

### The First Hollywood Musicals
Edwin M. Bradley (McFarland, 1996)

A wonderful film-by-film assessment that revives the long-forgotten musicals of the early sound era and makes you wish that more of them were still available – even though the majority seem to have been amateurish in the extreme. If you prefer more detailed narrative accounts of the talkie boom, look no further than Richard Barrios's *A Song In The Dark: The Birth Of The Musical Film* (OUP, 1995), Scott Eyman's *The Speed Of Sound: Hollywood And The Talkie Revolution 1926–1930* (Simon & Schuster, 1997) and Rick Altman and Richard Abel's *The Sounds Of Early Cinema* (Indiana University Press, 2001).

### Can't Help Singing: The American Musical On Stage And Screen
Gerald Mast (Overlook Press, 1987)

This is probably the most considered general history of the film musical. Even so, Mast is occasionally prone to over-analysis and tends more towards Broadway than Hollywood.

### Gotta Sing, Gotta Dance: A Pictorial History Of Film Musicals
John Kobal (Hamlyn, 2nd edition, 1983)

Dismissed by some for being more enthusiastic than scholarly, this is a knowledgeable, accessible and superbly illustrated account of the screen musical that even devotes chapters to its evolution in Europe. The sections based on personal interviews are particularly intriguing.

### The Hollywood Musical
Ethan Mordden (St Martin's, 1981)

This is a solid account by a doyen of musical studies and is more reliable than Denny Martin Flinn's *Musical!: A Grand Tour* (Schirmer Books, 1997), more thorough than coffee-table tomes like *The Best, The Worst, & Most Unusual: Hollywood Musicals* (Beekman House, 1983), more comprehensive than Ted Sennett's *Hollywood Musicals* (H. N. Abrams, 1981) and John Russell Taylor and Arthur Jackson's blend of brief narrative and selective compendium, *The Hollywood Musical* (Secker & Warburg, 1971).

Arthur Freed worked on musicals at MGM from 1929 to 1960. His genius lay in giving stars like Judy Garland and Fred Astaire the creative freedom to work their magic.

### MGM's Greatest Musicals: The Arthur Freed Unit

Hugh Fordin (Da Capo Press, 1996)

Based on unique access to Arthur Freed's archive and his former collaborators, this is simply one of the best books on the musical ever written. Impeccably researched, hugely readable and casting new light on everything from *The Wizard Of Oz* to *Bells Are Ringing*, this is essential for anyone intruiged by MGM and its Golden Age.

### The Movie Musical From Vitaphone To 42nd Street, As Reprinted In A Great Fan Magazine

Ed. Miles Kreuger (Dover, 1975)

A lovingly compiled memory lane compendium that traces the genre's early history through the pages of *Photoplay* (1926-33). In addition to countless production still and glamour shots, the anthology also includes reviews, biographies, features, advertisements and titbits of choice gossip.

### The Melody Lingers On: The Great Songwriters And Their Movie Musicals

Roy Hemming (Newmarket Press, 1986)

An excellent introduction to the masters responsible for the great American songbook. A necessary companion volume is Alec Wilder's *American Popular Song: The Great Innovators 1900–1950* (OUP, 1972).

### Through The Screen Door

Thomas S. Hischak (McFarland, 2004)

Countless movie musicals began life on stage and this sensible survey is far less censorious about the process than, say, Robert Matthew-Walker's *Broadway To Hollywood* (Sanctuary, 1996). Hischak is also the author of the encyclopedic and eminently useful *American Plays And Musicals On Screen* (McFarland, 2005).

### Opera On Screen

Ken Wlaschin (Beachwood Press, 1997)

Not every musical depends on songs in the AABA format. This comprehensive compendium covers pretty much what it says on the jacket, as does Scott Yanov's *Jazz On Film* (Backbeat, 2001).

### Rock Films

Linda J. Sandahl (Facts on File, 1987)

There are more books on rock and pop musicals than is perhaps merited. But while this and Marshall Crenshaw's *Hollywood Rock* (HarperCollins, 1994) offer a no-fuss film-by-film approach, *Celluloid Jukebox: Popular Music And The Movies From The 50s*, edited by Jonathan Romney and Adrian Wootton (BFI, 1996), and K.J. Donnelly's *Pop Music In British Cinema* (BFI, 2001) are a touch more cerebral. The best of the more specialized items are Eric Braun's *Elvis Film Encyclopedia* (Batsford, 1997), Roy Carr's *The Beatles At The Movies* (UFO Music, 1991) and Bob Neaverson's *The Beatles Movies* (Cassell, 1999).

## Reference

### The Hollywood Musical

Clive Hirschhorn (Crown, 1981)

Treating minor musicals with the same enthusiasm and expertise as the classics, this is an invaluable, but increasingly hard-to-find volume that belies its coffee-table format by packing in plotlines and insights between the copious illustrations. A must.

### The Great Hollywood Musical Pictures

James Robert Parish and Michael K. Pitts (McFarland, 1992)

Covering some 350 features, this is more selective than Hirschhorn, but it's much more detailed. Unfortunately, this mine of fact, opinion and anecdote is usually only available secondhand and, consequently, it's become somewhat expensive.

### The Virgin Encyclopedia Of Stage And Film Musicals

Ed. Colin Larkin (Virgin Books, 1999)

Admirable on both the artists and their films, this may be more comprehensive than Green's *Encyclopedia Of The Musical Film*, but it's not always as authoritative and there are some surprising omissions. Nevertheless, it offers superior coverage of British musicals and the diverse efforts of the post-studio era.

### Encyclopedia Of The Musical Film
Stanley Green (OUP, 1981)

Stanley Green is one of the greats of musical literature and this A-Z provides dependable coverage of the most important screen musicals and the people who made them. A second edition of the invaluable companion volume, *Hollywood Musicals Year By Year*, was published by Hal Leonard in 1999.

### Film Choreographers And Dance Directors
Larry Billman (McFarland, 1997)

A peerless dictionary of the dance directors whose role in the movie musical has always been overshadowed by that of the performers and songwriters. If only someone would do something similar for the art directors, cinematographers and costume designers.

### Television Musicals
Joan Baxter (McFarland, 1997)

As you'd expect of McFarland, this is an invaluable volume providing plots, casts, credits and critiques for 222 small-screen shows transmitted between 1944 and 1996. Also useful, although less specifically about musicals, is William Torbert Leonard's two-volume *Theatre: Stage To Screen To Television* (Scarecrow, 1981).

## Theory

### The American Film Musical
Rick Altman (Indiana University Press, 1987)

Genres studies is the cornerstone of cinematic academe. Yet the musical has largely been neglected, as it lacks the kudos or currency of horror, sci-fi, noir or crime. Rick Altman is by far the musical's most passionate and accessible academic champion and this is a splendidly lucid and cogent textbook that illustrates its points with major movies rather than trawling in B-unit backwaters. It's also much less pompous than Jane Feuer's highly regarded, but occasionally factually shaky *The Hollywood Musical* (Indiana University Press, 1982).

### The Cambridge Companion To The Musical
Edited by William A. Everett and Paul R. Laird (CUP, 2002)

Judiciously combining musical history and theory, this multi-authored survey provides a decent introduction to the genre, although its emphasis is primarily on the stage show. Once you've mastered the basics, you can move on to the more imposing essays contained in *Genre: The Musical* (Routledge, 1981) and *The Hollywood Musicals Reader* (Routledge, 2001), which were edited by Rick Altman and Steven Cohan respectively.

## Biographies

Popular biographies are a notoriously unreliable source of information about film stars. Their authors either have an axe to grind or a reputation to restore, or they fail to strike the right balance between anecdote and analysis. **Autobiographies** are even less valuable, especially as musicals folk have a habit of being unusually generous to their co-workers and rarely provide rigorous insight, let alone dish any dirt. However, the majority of the titles listed here avoid such pitfalls and offer serviceable evaluations of the genre's key personnel.

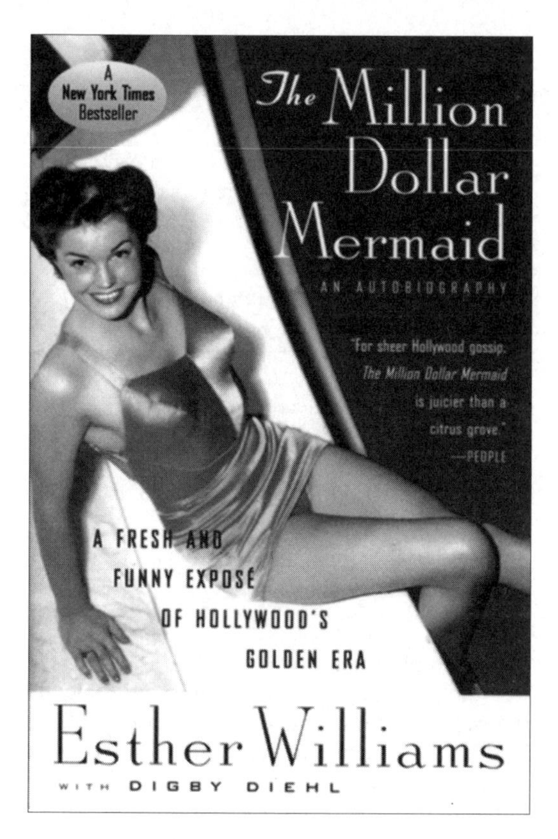


Anyone seeking illustrated introductions to their favourite stars should check out **Citadel Press's** "The Films Of…" series, while those needing greater detail should try **Greenwood's collection** of biobibliographies. Particularly worthy of mention are Tony Thomas's gloriously illustrated *The Busby Berkeley Book* (Thames and Hudson, 1973) and *Sweethearts* (Dutton, 1994), Sharon Rich and Jon Eddy's compelling account of Jeanette MacDonald and Nelson Eddy's private and professional relationship. Of the many autobiographies available, the most showbizzy is Ginger Rogers's *Ginger: My Story* (HarperCollins, 1991), the most engagingly unreliable is Vincente Minnelli's *I Remember It Well* (Doubleday, 1974) and the most refreshingly candid are Shirley Temple's *Child Star: An Autobiography* (Warner, 1989) and Esther Williams's *The Million Dollar Mermaid* (Pocket Books, 1999).

### Starring Fred Astaire
Stanley Green and Burt Goldblatt (Dodd, Mead, 1973)

A comprehensive career overview that's packed with anecdotes, insights and illustrations. But nothing surpasses Arlene Croce's examination of the RKO era in *The Fred Astaire And Ginger Rogers Book* (Galahad Books, 1972).

### Judy
Gerold Frank (Da Capo, 1999)

Refusing to wallow in the myths and miseries, this sensible study is as much interested in the artist as the tragic icon. Anne Edwards's more concise *Judy Garland: A Biography* (Simon & Schuster, 1974) is similarly sympathetic, while Edward Epstein and Joe Morella's *Judy: The Films And Career Of Judy Garland* (1969) sticks to the pictures.

### Gene Kelly: A Biography
Clive Hirschhorn (Regnery, 1974)

This model of screen biography is getting hard to find, so you may have to make do with Tony Thomas's trusty *The Films Of Gene Kelly: Song And Dance Man* (2/e, Citadel, 1991) and picture-led volumes like Sheridan Morley and Ruth Leon's *Gene Kelly: A Celebration* (Pavilion, 1997) and Alvin Yudoff's *Gene Kelly: A Life Of Dance And Dreams* (Watson-Guptill Publications, 2001).

# Websites

## Screen

Unlike other film genres (with the possible exception of the Western), the musical is hardly prolific nowadays. Consequently, there is a distinct lack of either **fanzines** devoted to movie musicals or dedicated festivals and conventions similar to those attendant on Horror and Sci-Fi. DeAgostini did produce a **collector's series of magazines** in 2006, complete with a free DVD, but they contained a lot of glossy padding. Fortunately, there are numerous websites celebrating the musical film.

### Class Act

www.classicmoviemusicals.com

With A-Z listings of films, actors, music and composers, this is an invaluable "who's who" and "who's in what" guide to 80 years of Hollywood musicals. Each entry is stuffed with facts and figures and it also advises on VHS and DVD availability. A decent companion is the Dance History Archive (www.streetswing.com/histmain.htm), which covers stage and screen gems.

### Musicals 101: The Cyber Encyclopedia Of Musicals

www.musicals101.com

Compiled by the estimable John Kenrick, this ambitious and accomplished site is a treasure trove of histories, chronologies, essays, reviews, photo galleries and diverse reference materials. Covering every aspect of the stage and screen musical from lyrics and dance to performance rights and putting on a show, the crisply written features approach opera, operetta, vaudeville, Broadway, Hollywood, radio, television and audio with unassuming expertise.

### MusicWeb Encyclopedia of Popular Music

www.musicweb-international.com/encyclopaedia

Based on *The Penguin Encyclopaedia Of Popular Music* (1989), this collection of over 4000 entries ranges from Abba to ZZ Top. But it also offers extensive coverage of the key songwriters and singers from the golden ages of the stage and screen musical.

### Internet Movie Database

www.imdb.com

If you simply require details of the cast, characters and crew of a particular musical, the IMDB is invaluable. However, it is far from infallible. Its external reviews are very much a mixed bag, the trivia is often unsubstantiated and information on dates, distributors and running times is generally more accurate in annuals like *The Radio Times Guide To Films* and *Halliwell's Guide To Films And Video*.

### Reel Jewels

www.reeljewels.com

A good catch-all site, where steady performers like Dick Powell, Irene Dunne, George Murphy, Don Ameche, John Payne, Jack Haley, Jane Powell, Rosemary Lane, Shirley Jones, Rita Hayworth and Rosemary Clooney are included alongside the genre's bigger names.

## Performers online

Although there are a handful of official pages online, the vast majority of websites devoted to musical performers are compiled by fans. This means they are enthusiastic, reasonably maintained and hugely well meaning. However, as they are invariably amateur shrines, the standard of writing and information varies greatly and you would always be better advised to consult a book than plough through pages of uncritical and often unreliable hagiography. Official sites are, naturally, even more protective of their subjects.

**June Allyson** www.juneallyson.com

**Julie Andrews** www.julieandrews.co.uk/intro.htm

**Louis Armstrong** www.satchmo.net

**Fred Astaire** www.fredastaire.net

**The Beatles** www.beatles.com

**Eddie Cantor** www.eddiecantor.com

**Cyd Charisse** cydcharisse.net

**Maurice Chevalier** members.tripod.com/~compmast/chevalie/chevalie.html

**Doris Day** www.dorisday.net

**Deanna Durbin** www.hovers.nl/museum.htm

**Alice Faye** www.alicefaye.com

**Judy Garland** www.jgdb.com and www.thejudyroom.com

**Betty Grable** grableonline.tripod.com

**Kathryn Grayson** www.kathryngrayson.com

**Rita Hayworth** members.tripod.com/~claudia79

**Bob Hope** www.bobhope.com

**Al Jolson** www.jolson.org

**Danny Kaye** www.angelfire.com/film/dannykaye

**Gene Kelly** members.aol.com/humorone/gene.htm

**Mario Lanza** www.rense.com/excursions/lanza

**Jeanette MacDonald** members.aol.com/jmacfan

**Gordon MacRae** www.patfullerton.com/gordonmacrae.html

**Ethel Merman** www.mrlucky.com/ethel

**Ann Miller** www.wic.org/bio/amiller.htm

**Liza Minnelli** www.cmgworldwide.com/stars/minnelli/index.php

**Carmen Miranda** www.carmenmiranda.net

**The Nicholas Brothers** www.nicholasbrothers.com

**Eleanor Powell** classicmoviefavorites.com/powell

**Elvis Presley** www.elvis.com

**Debbie Reynolds** www.debbiereynolds.com

**Ginger Rogers** www.gingerrogers.com

**Mickey Rooney** www.mickeyrooney.com

**Frank Sinatra** www.franksinatra.com

**Barbra Streisand** www.barbrastreisand.com

**Shirley Temple** www.shirleytemplefans.com/main.htm

**John Travolta** www.travolta.com

**Vera-Ellen** www.geocities.com/SoHo/4439/vera_ellen.html

**Esther Williams** www.esther-williams.com

### Red Hot Jazz
www.redhotjazz.com

Such shamefully neglected African-American icons as Ethel Waters, Bessie Smith, Duke Ellington and Eubie Blake rub shoulders with jazz giants and bandleaders like Paul Whiteman, the Dorsey brothers, Benny Goodman and Artie Shaw.

### All-Movie Guide
www.allmovie.com

The place to go for accurate and enjoyable film synopses. Its sister-site All-Music Guide (www.allmusic.com) also offers decent pen portraits and discographies.

## Stage

Considerably more online attention has been devoted to Broadway, where the musical continues to thrive. However, as there is rarely much overlap between the songs in a **Broadway show** and its Hollywood adaptation, let alone cast continuity, such websites are of more use to aficionados of the genre as a whole than merely movie fans.

### Internet Broadway Database
www.ibdb.com

The official database for Broadway theatre information is the stage equivalent of IMDB. The musical is well represented, with details of casts, scores, dates and venues enabling you to compare the original show with the movie adaptation. Less authoritative, but occasionally useful are Musical Heaven (www.musicalheaven.com), **Musicals. Net** (musicals.net) and the Musical Cast Album Database (www.castalbumdb.com), which provides details of 17,687 artists and 28,346 song titles.

# Memorabilia

## Posters

In the days when cinema programmes changed twice a week and the Hollywood studios distributed their films and publicity materials through big-city exchanges, **movie posters** and **lobby cards** were dispatched with the release print and exhibitors were honour-bound to pass them on intact to the next venue. Consequently, original posters from the musical's first decade are pretty hard to come by. However, the system was centralized with the establishment in 1940 of the **National Screen Service**, which leased and later sold posters to exhibitors and enthusiasts until 1979.

Numerous **collections of film posters** have been published, the most cohesive being those compiled by Tony Nourmand. However, more pertinent to this genre is *Musical Movie Posters* (Bruce Hershenson, 1999), edited by Richard Allen and Bruce Hershenson. For the Broadway perspective, see Tom Tumbusch's *Broadway Musicals: A History In Posters* (Tomart Publications, 2004) and Steven Suskin's *A Must See!: Brilliant Broadway Artwork* (Chronicle Books, 2004).

Original copies and **reproductions** of individual posters are available from countless websites, including eBay. The following sites deal specifically with posters, and are reportedly among the most reputable, but it's a good idea to do your own research into any **online outlet** before making a substantial purchase: Art.com (www.art.com), Films on Disc (www.filmsondisc.com/movieposterarchives.htm), Reel Classics (www.reelclassics.com/Musicals), Art Posters (www.art-posters.net) and Movie Market (www.moviemarket.co.uk).

## Lobby cards

Lobby cards were first printed in the 1910s and remained on view in **cinema foyers** until the majority of Hollywood studios ceased producing them during the multiplex boom of the mid-1980s. They were usually issued in sets of eight (although some sets comprised two, ten, twelve or sixteen cards) and came in standard (11in x 14in), mini (8in x 10in) or jumbo (14in x 17in) sizes. A typical set would contain a **title card**, a series of **scene cards** – depicting the headline stars and key supporting players in posed stills – and some **scenery cards** (or "dead" cards), featuring shots of the backdrops and the extras.

Fewer books have been published on this more specialized area, but John Kobal's *Foyer Pleasure: The Golden Age Of Cinema Lobby Cards* (Aurum Press, 1982) and Kathryn Leigh Scott's duo, *Lobby Cards: The Classic Films* (Pomegranate Press, 1987) and *Lobby Cards: The Classic Comedies* (Pomegranate Press, 1988), are splendid introductions for those starting their own collections. You can usually find a decent selection to buy on the likes of Movie Market (www.moviemarket.co.uk), Archival Photography (www.arch-photo.com/musicals.html), and, of course, eBay.

## Cigarette cards

Cigarette cards first appeared in 1879. The first **film star cards** were issued in the 1910s and the heyday lasted until 1940. Given free inside cigarette packets, the cards were popular in dozens of countries around the world, but the majority of sets were produced by **British companies** like Carreras, Gallaher and Godfrey Phillips. Sets comprising photographic or **hand-drawn portraits** were by far the most common, although there were also many collections of production stills, graphic reproductions of famous scenes, and caricatures. Paper shortages during the World War II signalled the decline of the cigarette card. However, stars would continue to grace cards given away with chocolate, biscuits, tea and bubble gum until the trading card boom began in the 1980s.

Although several **valuation guides** are available, there is no single volume dedicated to movie cigarette cards. However, Troy Kirk's **The Movie Card Site** (www.moviecard.com) is an exceptional resource that provides details of sets from Germany, Chile, Australia and the US, as well as the umpteen UK collections. The site also has occasional sets for sale or auction, as do Murray Cards (www.murraycards.com), Franklyn Cards (www.franklyncards.com) and Cigarette Cards Plus (www.cigarettecardsplus.co.uk).

The most aesthetically pleasing cigarette cards were designed in Germany and featured international stars, as well as local icons.

# Picture credits

The publishers have made every effort to identify correctly the rights holders and/or production companies in respect of film stills featured in this book. If despite these efforts any attribution is incorrect, the publishers will correct this error once it has been brought to their attention on a subsequent reprint.

## Cover Credits

Fred Astaire, courtesy of the Kobal Collection.

## Illustrations

Corbis: (6) © Bettman/Corbis Kobal Collection: (129) MGM Warner Bros (258) 20th Century Fox (261) MGM United Artists Library of Congress: (4) Primrose & West's Big Minstrels, c.1856 (9) Historic American sheet music, "Look For The Silver Lining", Music A-5699, Duke University Rare Book, Manuscript and Special Collections Library, (13) Weber & Fields, c.1920 Moviestore Collection: (16) MGM Warner Bros (23) Warner Bros (32) Warner Bros (34) Warner Bros (36) Warner Bros (40) MGM (45) MGM Warner Bros (49) MGM (53) Paramount Pictures (58) MGM (62) Columbia Pictures Rhino (66) 20th Century Fox (72) Dreamworks Paramount Pictures Laurence Mark Productions (78) MGM Warner Bros (85) American Broadcasting Company Warner Bros (91) MGM Warner Bros (93) Cinergi Pictures Entertainment Inc Dirty Hands Productions Hollywood Pictures Summit Entertainment Buena Vista (99) Paramount Pictures (104) Paramount Pictures United International (114) MGM Warner Bros (118) MGM Warner Bros (123) Paramount Pictures Kino (138) Magna Corporation Rogers & Hammerstein Productions 20th Century Fox CBS/Fox Samuel Goldwyn Company (146) 20th Century Fox CBS/Fox Fox Video Image Entertainment (151) Warner Bros (163) 20th Century Fox CBS/Fox Magnetic Video (172) RKO Radio Pictures Warner Criterion Collection Turner Home Video (179) MGM Warner Criterion Collection CBS (181) MGM Warner United Artists CBS/Fox (188) Universal (193) (195) Paramount Pictures Kino Video (202) 20th Century Fox Columbia Pictures (205) MGM United Artists (214) MGM Warner Bros (223) MGM (226) RKO Radio Pictures Warner Bros (229) Columbia Pictures Rastar Pictures (233) Loew's MGM United Artists (245) Columbia Pictures (251) 20th Century Fox (253) RKO Radio Pictures Warner Turner Home Video (265) Magna Corporation Rogers & Hammerstein Productions 20th Century Fox CBS/Fox Samuel Goldwyn Company (272) Nippon Herald Films Yume Pictures (274) Bazmark Films 20th Century Fox (276) Beacon Communications Dirty Hands Productions First Film Company 20th Century Fox United Artists (278) Parc Film Madeleine Films Beta Film GmbH Criterion Collection Koch Lorber Films (282) Universum Film United Artists (289) Val Guest Productions Kino Video (291) Romulus Films Warwick Film Productions Columbia TriStar Ronald Grant Archive: (96) Warner Bros (110) MGM Warner Bros (133) Warner Bros Paramount Pictures 20th Century Fox (153) MGM Universal Pictures Criterion Collection (158) MGM Warner Criterion Collection (297) MGM Warner Bros.

# Index

Page references to films discussed in the Canon chapter and people described in the Icons chapter are indicated in **bold**.

## A

# B

# C

## D

# E

# F

# G

# H

## I



## J



## K

## L

# M

## N



## O

# P



# Q

# R

# S

# T

# U



# V



# W

## X



## Y



## Z

Jessica Winter
THE ROUGH GUIDE TO
British Cult Comedy
Julian Hall
THE ROUGH GUIDE TO
comedy movies
THE ROUGH GUIDE TO
Cult Movies
THE ROUGH GUIDE TO
westerns
Paul Simpson
THE BOOK
THE MOVIE
THE TRUTH
THE ROUGH GUIDE TO
gangster movies
THE ROUGH GUIDE TO
horror movies
ALAN JONES
kids' movies
PAUL SIMPSON
THE ROUGH GUIDE TO
sci-fi movies
JOHN SCALZI
THE ROUGH GUIDE TO

ROUGH
GUIDES

ROUGH GUIDES

# Listen Up!

"You may be used to the Rough Guide series being comprehensive, but nothing will prepare you for the exhaustive Rough Guide to World Music . . . one of our books of the year."

**Sunday Times, London**

## ROUGH GUIDE MUSIC TITLES

Bob Dylan • The Beatles • Blues • Classical Music • Elvis • Frank Sinatra
Heavy Metal • Hip-Hop • iPods, iTunes & music online • Jazz • Book of Playlists
Led Zeppelin • Opera • Pink Floyd • Punk • Reggae • Rock • The Rolling Stones
Soul and R&B • Velvet Underground • World Music Vol 1 & 2

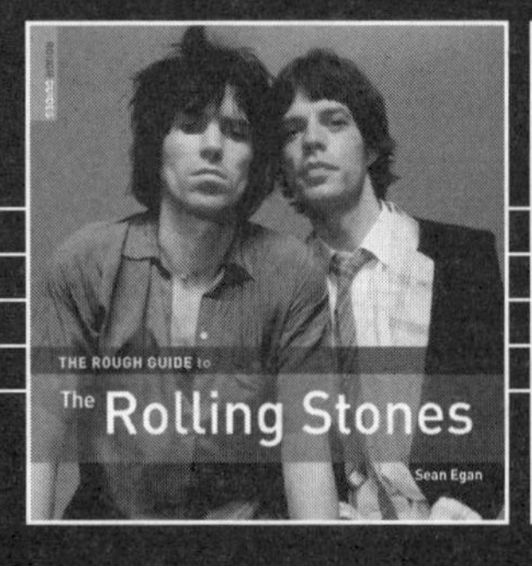


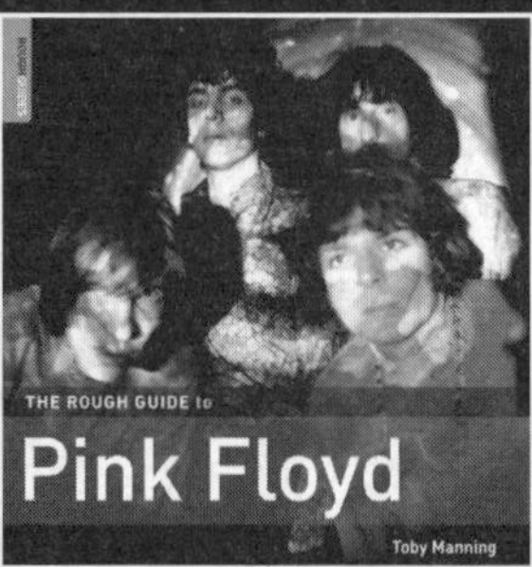


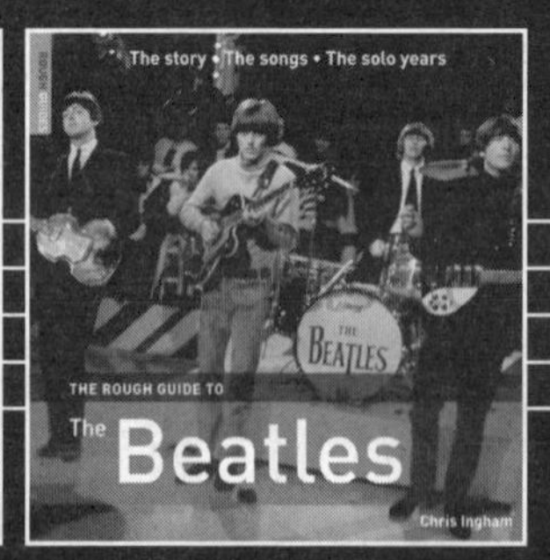

BROADEN YOUR HORIZONS